Prologue to a Farce

THE HISTORY OF COMMUNICATION

Robert W. McChesney and
John C. Nerone, editors

*A list of books in the series appears
at the end of this book.*

Prologue
to a Farce

Communication
and Democracy
in America

MARK LLOYD

UNIVERSITY OF ILLINOIS PRESS

Urbana and Chicago

Library of Congress Cataloging-in-Publication Data

Lloyd, Mark.
Prologue to a farce : communication and democracy in America / Mark Lloyd.
p.   cm.—(The history of communication)
Includes bibliographical references and index.
ISBN-13: 978-0-252-03104-5 (cloth : alk. paper)
ISBN-10: 0-252-03104-0 (cloth : alk. paper)
ISBN-13: 978-0-252-07342-7 (pbk. : alk. paper)
ISBN-10: 0-252-07342-8 (pbk. : alk. paper)
1. Communication policy—United States—History.   2. Democracy—United
States.   I. Title.
P95.82.U6L58   2006
302.240973—dc22   2006020912

To Kelly
who gives me hope

Contents

Part III. Reclaiming Our Republic

Acknowledgments

This book is a product of many years of experience and study. I can hardly name all of the influences, much less thank all of the librarians in Boston, Cambridge, and Washington who were so patient with me, the students who inspired me, the colleagues and teachers who challenged me to clarify my thoughts, and the friends who encouraged me to put them on these pages. I am especially indebted to Richard John, Kay Mills, and Bob McChesney, true historians who provided thoughtful comments and saved me from too many errors to mention. I would like to acknowledge a special debt to Ceasar McDowell, who helped me form the Civil Rights Forum on Communications Policy and brought me into the fold at the Massachusetts Institute of Technology. Many of the ideas presented here were developed at the Forum and honed at MIT. Thanks as well to Ike Colbert and David Thorburn, who provided support, constructive criticism, and guidance while I was there. I would also like to thank Woody Wickham, formerly of the MacArthur Foundation; Jon Funabiki, Alan Jenkins, Becky Lentz, and Alison Bernstein at the Ford Foundation; and Helen Brunner and the "sisters" at the Alfred P. List Foundation for all their support over the years. A special thanks to Gara LaMarche at the Open Society Institute, a true servant of democracy, and to my good friend Jack Willis, who provided both financial support and wise counsel. Thanks as well to Larry Grossman, who through the Digital Promise project continues to prod our elected representatives to support what Madison calls "popular knowledge." Many of the ideas in this book were first articulated in an essay Larry commissioned me to write with funding from and published by the Century Foundation.

Thanks also to Susan Kretchmer; the Computers Professionals for Social Responsibilities, and Sage Publications. Many of the ideas presented here about the impact of advanced communications technologies on our democracy were first presented at a CPSR conference and were published by Sage. Thank you to Kerry Callahan, who has shepherded this project with patience and good humor. And finally, thank you to my first teachers, my parents. What is written in these pages does not suggest agreement by those who have guided or supported me, and while I take full responsibility, this book would not be possible without their help.

Introduction

On October 5, 2000, I sat in a private room at the Museum of Television and Radio in New York listening to Bill Kennard, the chairman of the Federal Communications Commission (FCC), practice a speech about the public interest obligations of broadcasters. At the time I was leading a national coalition called People for Better TV, and aside from helping to rustle up an audience and pay for coffee, my role was to introduce Bill. Listening to him prepare, I was excited about the strength and breadth of his embrace of our work. He would tell the nation:

> I want to cut the Gordian knot of public interest vs. financial interests, and outline clear, tangible public interest obligations that broadcasters can commit to. I want to ensure that the American people are suitably compensated for the use of their valuable spectrum, and that underutilized portions of this precious resource are returned to them as soon as possible. And I want to see that the awesome power and remarkable ubiquity of television is put to the service of our democracy, rather than at the expense of it. We are the strongest, most vibrant democracy this world has ever seen. But we owe it to ourselves and to the nations who view us as a role model of democratic governance to realize the enormous promise of communications technologies old and new in serving and enhancing democracy.[1]

It had taken us a couple of years to secure this commitment from the chairman of the FCC. Over the course of that time, I introduced Bill to a few dozen of our coalition members at his boardroom in Washington and at a community center in San Francisco. We also met with other commissioners at locations across the country, collected thousands of signatures, monitored television stations and inspected the public files of stations in a dozen communities, and submitted several formal petitions and comments to the FCC.

About three weeks earlier, on September 14, 2000, the FCC proposed a set of public interest rules, quoting heavily from our submitted comments. The core of those rules focused on making the local broadcaster more accountable to the local community, "to replace the issues/programs list with a standardized form and to enhance the public's ability to access information on a station's public interest obligations by requiring broadcasters to make their public inspection files available on the Internet."[2] This was the lynchpin, the first step toward bringing the public back into a civic conversation dominated and limited by local television broadcasters. While it was just the first step, it was a step forward. We were not struggling to save established rights under attack, we were advancing.

In many ways, this moment at the Museum of Television and Radio would also be the culmination of a personal journey. Inspired by the civil rights movement of the 1960s and the youth and Black Power protests of the 1970s, I became a broadcast journalist. I produced public affairs programs and news reports and documentaries at a time when the industry was just opening up to community voices and young black journalists. The years between 1972 and 1984 were a sort of golden era of public interest broadcasting in the United States. I did not know this, of course, until they were over. By 1985 I was producing newscasts at CNN in Washington, D.C., and was soon convinced that the only way to reverse the trend of superficial happy talk and the obsession with celebrity was to push for change from the outside.

After graduating from Georgetown Law School, I worked for a few years at a law firm in Washington specializing in representing the communications industry. But soon I helped to found an organization to bring the concept of equal rights for citizens into the debate over communications policy—the Civil Rights Forum on Communications Policy. Through this organization, and with the help of many others, I was able to draw together a diverse coalition that included the American Academy of Pediatrics, the Consumer Federation of America, the League of United Latin American Citizens, the National Association of the Deaf, the National Organization for Women, the National Urban League, Mark Crispin Miller's Project on Media Ownership at NYU, the U.S. Catholic Conference, and over a hundred other organizations in over a dozen communities across the country.[3] As Mark would write in one of our early proposals to our main funder, the Open

Society Institute, we believed that "by making TV better, we would make America better." On that early morning in October in New York, I was convinced that the chairman of the FCC was with us all the way. He would say:

> We call ourselves the greatest democracy in the history of the world, and we undoubtedly are. But, frankly, the disarray and disinterest of our mass media towards fulfilling its crucial democratic commitments give me serious pause.
>
> For fifty years, the solemn public interest commitment of broadcasters, borne of their role as public trustees of the airwaves, has deteriorated in the face of financial pressures and an increasingly competitive marketplace.
>
> Indeed, we reached a new low last week, when two of the four major networks—NBC and Fox—chose to preempt the first debate of the most hotly contested Presidential election in four decades for sports and entertainment programming.[4]

I was convinced that Bill's conviction to do something about the sad state of television was genuine. I had known him for several years, having served with him on a board for a teen shelter in Washington before I was a lawyer and before he was at the FCC. I had watched him vilified as he challenged Congress to do something about the cost of airtime for political speech. I understood that he did not take lightly the task of battling the National Association of Broadcasters, a group he once worked for. We hoped that our setting at the Museum of Television and Radio would help the industry understand that we were only calling them to their most honored past and their most cherished ideals of service to a democracy. But we both knew, as we stood only blocks away from the world headquarters of the major television networks, that Bill was issuing a challenge that would be ignored.

The People for Better TV coalition formed in response to a little-known provision in the 1996 Telecommunications Act that gave existing broadcasters additional access to the electromagnetic spectrum for free. Why was this important?

By 1996 very little of the electromagnetic spectrum allocated by the federal government was free. Prior to 1981, when a broadcast license expired competing applicants could engage in a comparative hearing and challenge the existing broadcaster. Increasingly, inventive engineers would find parts of the spectrum they could use that the broadcasters could not. Licenses for this spectrum were also open to competition. The comparative hearing process was eliminated during the Reagan years, and for a time the FCC would issue licenses based on a "powerball"-type lottery. In 1994, at the direction of Congress, the FCC stopped lotteries and started auctioning licenses. Those auctions raised billions of dollars in only a couple of years.

Then a method was found to broadcast digital television signals. Instead of sending out a regular television broadcast, this signal sent out information in the digital language of computers. But if broadcasters were going to make a transition to digital they would need additional spectrum. Even though others were paying for access to the spectrum, broadcasters did not want to have to pay for licenses they had historically received for free. Despite spending the 1980s attacking the public trustee model, a model that required them to act on behalf of the local public in exchange for their free license, the broadcasters argued they were indeed public servants, and would continue to be as they broadcast digital television signals. Consequently, in the 1996 Telecommunications Act Congress gave existing broadcasters the exclusive use of an additional 6 megahertz of the public airwaves, a gift worth billions of dollars.[5] But when Congress authorized the commission to "issue additional licenses for advanced television services,"[6] it made clear that "nothing in this section shall be construed as relieving a television broadcasting station from its obligation to serve the public interest, convenience, and necessity. In the Commission's review of any application for renewal of a broadcast license for a television station that provides ancillary or supplementary services, the television licensee shall establish that *all of its program services* on the existing or advanced television spectrum are in the public interest" (emphasis added).[7]

People for Better TV argued that the FCC could not issue licenses to existing broadcasters to operate digital signals without first determining the public interest obligation of the digital licensee, and that the public interest obligation of the digital licensee could not be determined without a public proceeding.[8] So, in 1999 the FCC initiated an inquiry on the public interest obligations of TV broadcasters, prominently citing the People for Better TV petition.[9]

When our coalition began most Americans knew very little about a transition to Digital TV.[10] The stories about DTV, or High-Definition TV (HDTV), tended to focus on how expensive the television sets would be and how wonderful the digital pictures would be. By November 1998, television stations in the nation's largest cities began to transmit a second signal. We wanted to use this transition to revisit the issue of the broadcasters' public interest obligations. But we also thought this new technology offered both potential and perils for democracy.

The transition to DTV is sometimes compared to other technological leaps, such as the introduction of motion pictures in a world once dominated by photographs and paintings, or the switch from black-and-white to color television. But the transition to DTV is more like the transforming appearance of television into a world that knew only radio. As television combined radio and film, DTV combines the compelling power of television with the potential interactivity and information access of personal computers.[11] For this very reason, DTV represents not only the single biggest technological leap television viewers have experienced in decades, but a change with vast social and economic consequences.

DTV's most famous promise is the sharper, motion-picture-quality image it offers. But there is another, perhaps more important benefit of DTV. Because DTV will communicate in the digital language of computers, television stations will be able to transmit far more information than traditional television. This means broadcasters can use the same amount of public spectrum to transmit five or more channels. They can also send additional information along with the picture (such as stock quotes, or closed captioning, or the price of products shown on the screen). In addition, when combined with a two-way telephone or cable service, DTV will be interactive like computers. This marriage of the television set and personal computer into a single home appliance will result in potentially powerful educational opportunities, inspiring entertainments, and improvements to community life and democratic engagement.

Like most possibilities, DTV will also have its perils. It could bring even more of the things most of us don't like about television and the Internet. It could create another opportunity for an invasion of privacy. It could bombard us with even more commercials. It could be used to limit the amount of good television programming available for free.

Through digital technology, marketers will be able to collect information about individuals. Indeed, they will have an incentive to collect that information because they can sell it to others and use it to target commercial advertisements to family members. Marketers currently track web site use and purchases over the Internet. Thanks to the convergence of Internet and television technologies, marketers will track not only this activity, but which programs viewers watch, when they watch, and how often they watch. Commercials will be targeted not only to individual viewers and households, but to individual television sets within a household.

Enhanced information about viewer preferences will also allow DTV broadcasters to learn which programs viewers value most, and which programs they might be able to put on pay-per-view. Unless the rules change, the FCC will be unable to limit the sort of program broadcasters put on pay-per-view (perhaps the Superbowl or a political convention), or what broadcasters can charge for a program. Finally, while most Americans are now concerned about the level of violence and the amount of sexual activity on television, imagine how concerned they will become when violent, hyper-real computer games and the personal sex services of the Internet combine with HDTV.[12]

With the help of polls and focus group sessions conducted by Celinda Lake, People for Better TV was able to put together a compelling set of recommendations and a simple message—"What do we get back for the giveaway?" It was a message that resonated with a strong majority of voters across party lines, regions, and almost any other division one could imagine.

These were days of great optimism. Still, we understood we faced great obstacles. The most difficult aspect of organizing the work of the People for Better TV coalition was finding a way to communicate to the American public about reforming the medium that dominated communications in America. We were able to get bits and pieces of our message out in local newspapers, on radio and cable programs, and, of course, on a substantial Internet web site, but we had little access to television. Our organizing relied upon a healthy old-fashioned outreach to churches and associations, but if anything clarified our determination that we had picked the correct target it was the clear power of private commercial television to limit our access to the place most Americans turned to for information.

We were also concerned about the extraordinary lobbying power of the National Association of Broadcasters (NAB). We were concerned that even if we got our rules passed at the FCC, we would be thwarted in Congress. So we asked Ralph Neas to join us. Ralph helped lead an effort to prevent the Senate confirmation of right-wing jurist Robert Bork, who was nominated to the Supreme Court by President Reagan. Working with Ralph we instigated a letter from a bipartisan group of lawmakers, Republican Senators Sam Brownback and John McCain, and Democratic Senators Joe Lieberman and Robert Byrd. Chairman Kennard's response to the senators borrowed heavily from the People for Better TV coalition.[13] But by the time of the response it was all too late.

As the world looked on in astonishment, by a 5–4 vote the U.S. Supreme Court reversed the Supreme Court of Florida and stopped a count of votes that would have confirmed that Vice-President Al Gore won Florida and the 2000 presidential election. Within a matter of weeks, all of our supporters at the FCC were gone, and our most consistent detractor at the FCC, Michael Powell, would be named FCC chairman.

Powell had no patience for talk of the public interest. I was present at the breakfast meeting during the NAB Convention in Las Vegas in 1998, when Powell said, "The night after I was sworn in, I waited for a visit from the angel of the public interest, I waited all night but she did not come. And, in fact, five months into this job, I still have had no divine awakening."[14] Powell would not even allow a vote on the rulemaking regarding the public interest obligations of broadcasters.

The relationship between politics and communications policy could not have been clearer. All of our legal reasoning and economic analysis and grassroots organizing were for nothing. A new political regime meant not only the loss of an opportunity to advance democratic debate, it meant a loss of funding and a loss of the coalition it had taken us two years to put together. The battle would revert to protecting old rules that frankly had not proven to be very effective at securing democratic speech.

This book is the result of my efforts to understand what had happened to the ideal of democratic deliberation. I wanted to get under the skin of present policy debates to see if I could find a deeper reasoning, beyond the platitudes about a free market, beyond even the notion that the public owns the airwaves. There was something in the ebb and flow of politics determining the structure of our public conversation, and it was something deeper than the complaints of liberal or conservative media bias. Why was the debate over public policy in the United States so dominated by private corporations? When did this begin? Why was there an opening during the raucous years of the 1960s and 1970s when I was entering the field of journalism? Why were the economic apologists for the ruthless capitalists given such credence? Why does there seem to be a general agreement about the importance of competition, while concentration of ownership increases? What did any of this have to do with the founders and our structure of governance? Could anything really be done to allow a broader public deliberation about the issues that confront us, in the face of the distractions of celebrity and sensationalism?

As I began to read beyond my usual load of FCC notices and trade press and court decisions, I became more aware of the work of recent historians attempting to capture a better sense of the history of communications in the United States. The historians Richard John, Menahem Blondheim, Amy Friedlander, Kenneth Lipartito, Milton Mueller, Susan Douglas, Robert McChesney, Kay Mills, Megan Mullen, Janet Abbate, and so many others were extending and deepening the work of Harold Innis and Erik Barnouw. I was relearning old lessons on the impact of the early Post Office, the growth of the telegraph, yellow journalism, and the Associated Press wire service, the struggles between AT&T and the early independent telephone systems, the rise and fall of the muckrakers, the relationship between the military and the broadcast and satellite and computer industries, the early hopes for cable television, and much more.

Joyce Appleby, Lynn Hunt, and Margaret Jacob write: "Having a history enables groups to get power, whether they use a past reality to affirm their rights or wrest recognition from those powerful groups that monopolize public debate. History doesn't just reflect; it provides a forum for readjudicating power and interests."[15]

I am not a historian. I am a journalist with some training in legal analysis and argument, and political science and theory. I embarked on this project to reveal at first for myself and then for the reader the political struggle for both freedom and equality in the United States and the relationship between that struggle and communications policy. I hope to reclaim a previously disconnected history clouded in myth and prejudice, and to assert a connection between the goals of James Madison and the goals of Martin Luther King Jr.

Even as I was conducting my inquiry, the ground was shifting. By the fall of 2003, Michael Powell was pushing through rules advancing the agenda of the old Reagan-FCC. The Powell rules would eliminate antitrust rules put in place in the earliest days of television. The new rules increase the television national ownership cap, allow a broadcaster to own more than one television station in a single market, and allow television stations to combine with a newspaper in the same market. This rule making was adopted by the vote of three (Republicans) to two (Democrats), despite overwhelming public opposition.[16]

The noble goal of a communications policy that reflects our democratic values rather than the selfish values of a commercial market seems hardly within reach, but not because the public is in opposition. The opposition is a very small elite who happen to dominate our public arena, and their control is tightening. This elite continues to consolidate its power, not because this is what the public wants, or because this is the "natural" outcome of market forces, but because they have political power. This is not where the republic began. But the problems are not new, they began over 150 years ago.

This book is a small contribution to the work of thousands of citizens who act every day as if this is a republic in which their independent and informed judgment matters.

PART I

Communications and Democracy in America

1

The Challenge of American Democracy

A popular Government, without popular information,
or the means of acquiring it, is but a Prologue to a Farce
or a Tragedy; or, perhaps both. Knowledge will forever
govern ignorance: and a people who mean to be their
own Governors, must arm themselves with
the power which knowledge gives.

—James Madison

The ongoing American experiment in democracy is failing.[1] And it is failing because we have allowed our public sphere to be dominated by the interest Madison called merchants.

The ideals of political equality and a government that operates in response to the informed consent of the governed are for most Americans only romantic notions. Our republic, the unique American mechanism for realizing the will of the people, is something warm and fuzzy to salute or sing about at best. At worst it is viewed as a dysfunctional and unreliable interference. But, in the main, it is regarded as merely another service provider, an odd cousin to the market.

A variety of modern lamentations seem to focus not on the hard disappointing facts of civic ignorance and political inequality, but on whether the left or the right of the governing class can ever just get along and steer the ship of state consistently.[2] This focus does not look quite deep enough.

The small portion of the U.S. academy concerned about communications and governance seems to have developed a preoccupation with the German political theorist Jürgen Habermas and his disagreements with Kant and Marx.[3] There is also a lingering enchantment in the academy with Michel Foucault's relativism and his focus on the power of discourse.[4] These examinations are largely too academic and tend toward abstraction. Furthermore, I remain unconvinced that the Europeans Foucault and

Habermas are preferable to William James or Walter Lippmann. I refer in these pages, however, to a certain key concept associated with Habermas: the public sphere. So let me explain what I mean by that.

A public sphere is the place or places where people are engaged in creating, sharing, and gathering information they use to make decisions about the public good. The key point I am drawing attention to is not only the place (a town hall or in front of a computer screen) but whether the discussion is generally more about a public decision rather than a private one. People sitting in a bar reacting to each other while they watch the president's State of the Union address are within the public sphere I have in mind. People sitting in a bar ordering drinks for themselves are not.[5]

My focus here is on information created to inform public deliberation rather than entertainment. This is not to say that entertainment does not often have a profound impact on our culture, including our politics. Indeed, entertainment from minstrel shows to pornography has resonated strongly in the political arena, and oftentimes the more subtle and less deliberate the intent, the more dangerous the impact on society. James Carey has written with great insight about these effects.[6] But this is not my focus here, so the circus and movies and video games will not play a part in this discussion.

My focus on information about the action of elected representatives, indeed the definition of the public sphere I offer, borrow strongly from Cass Sunstein's Madisonian goals of "government by discussion."[7] Sunstein argues that Madison understood the American republic to put a premium on broad, reasoned discussion among political equals, and he relies largely upon Madison's arguments against the Sedition Act to support this conception.

"The right of electing the members of the Government constitutes . . . the essence of a free and responsible government," and "the value and efficiency of this right depends on the knowledge of the comparative merits and demerits of the candidates for the public trust." Indeed, the power represented by a Sedition Act ought, "more than any other, to produce universal alarm; because it is leveled against that right of freely examining public characters and measures, and of free communication among the people thereon, which has ever been justly deemed the only effectual guardian of every other right."[8] Unlike Sunstein, however, my focus is not on the First Amendment prohibition of federal abridgement of citizen speech, but on the role Madison would advance for federal promotion of citizen speech.

I would also like to distinguish here between citizen speech and what we think of now as the media. After I had completed the first draft of this book,

Paul Starr's book, *The Creation of the Media,* was published.[9] Starr's book is a very good study of a wide variety of media and how they developed through World War II. While he takes some note of politics, his focus is, as his title suggests, on the beginnings of modern media. This emphasis is very different than mine. I place communications policy at the center of the structure of the U.S. republic. My focus is less on the development of media than on the relationship between our unique republic and how the abandonment of the founders' citizen-focused communications policy has hurt the operation of that republic.

I do owe a large debt to Michael Sandel, who argues in his book *Democracy's Discontent* that our common, our public, discontent is the triumph of our lived philosophy of amoral individual rights (which he calls liberalism or procedural democracy) over community.[10] Despite my appreciation for his analysis, it is still difficult to see that a battle waged and won by intellectuals, whether they are Lippmann and Dewey or Foucault and Habermas, would solve the American problems with communications and democracy. With all due respect to Sandel, our lived democracy is not the result of philosophical triumphs. Our lived democracy, our discontent results from the misoperation of governing structures, structures we the living create and tolerate.

Nor do I find any hope in the fading fad of the "civility" crusaders,[11] or the dubious calls to morality by public bullies such as William Bennett.[12] Even accepting the claims that we are less civil and less moral than those at some other time, this does not lead to an improvement of our access to the information necessary to govern our community.

Putting aside the relatively recent decline in more strenuous local political activity documented by Robert Putnam,[13] the citizens of the United States barely turn out to vote. In his book, *The Good Citizen,* Michael Schudson rightly warns us against romanticizing either the 1950s, Putnam's age of bowling leagues and civic associations, or any other supposedly golden age of civic engagement.[14] The ideals embodied in our republic have too often been little more than ideals. But as Schudson suggests, "Progress or decline is not the real question."[15] The real question is: What is the governing structure that will allow us to address the serious public injustices in our present?

But are we equipped to answer that question? Forty years of studies confirm that the average U.S. citizen remains stubbornly, shockingly ignorant about our republic.[16] And, as William Greider asked, Who will tell the people?[17]

The news media in America most people rely upon, whether newspaper or television, is first and foremost a space for advertisements. After every war and every election the barons of mass media express a befuddled guilt about the superficiality of their reporting and they promise to do better. But they fail to tell the public about their increased profits. The fire of cannon in the night sky, the loss of human lives, the campaign rally, and the final vote count are simply spectacles to bring audiences in the tent to hear the latest pitch for a rejuvenating shampoo.

Some suggest that the problem is not that we have too little popular information but that we have too much. We are bombarded with more data than we can process, with twenty-four-hour news shows blasting at us in our homes, in our cars, on street corners and electronic billboards, even in some elevators. But, surely, the latest car chase or celebrity marriage cannot be what Madison meant by the popular information needed to arm ourselves for self-governance. Despite the expansion of the news wherever we look, there is little if any reporting or discussion about the legislation being drawn up at City Hall, the State House, or Capitol Hill.

In his description of how the American public was kept in the dark about the multibillion-dollar savings and loan disaster, William Greider describes a problem that extends beyond an obsession with trivia. The so-called media watchdogs simply fail to report adequately on what the people's representatives are doing. One reason for this, according to Greider, is that "to cover the full range of complex regulatory battles with any depth would require a substantial number of reasonably sophisticated reporters and lots of patience—an investment of resources that very few news organizations are able or willing to make."[18]

In other words, private corporations determine whether the people acquire information needed to govern themselves based in large part on whether the investment in resources is profitable. We are provided information about pop stars or car crashes because corporations deem that information less costly (financially and politically) to produce than a report on what our representatives are doing at the local, state, or federal levels. Thus, the claim of news corporations that they only give the public what it is interested in rings hollow. How can the public become bored and apathetic about events we do not even know are happening?

Some argue that "the government" is the problem with our nation and so the less of it we have the better off we will be. Garry Wills devoted a book, *A Necessary Evil,* to countering Thomas Jefferson's outdated canard that that government is best which governs least.[19] I will not repeat his answer to this ahistorical proposition. I would simply counter that even in wanting different things, Americans clearly want many things that only government can provide: a clean environment, affordable health care, safe streets, and so on. The answer to the problems of achieving our ideals of political equality and democratic deliberation is not to be found in limiting the only mechanism that can help us improve our society.

Despite the ahistorical contempt expressed toward government, in the end, we the people are responsible for the state of our democracy. No alien power imposed our government upon us. Whether through action or inaction we determine what we govern and whether our government is bad. If Lincoln was right, we are the government.

Governing structures are not limited to voting districts. Governance is not simply eliminating butterfly ballots or properly counting dimpled chads. Governance in a democracy involves the operation of mechanisms to encourage informing citizens of their interests and creating the means for them to both effectively express their interests and see that these interests are manifest. The challenge we face in our republic is maintaining a structure of governance that is able to advance our goals of political equality and the finding of consensus about the public good. More than markets, more than a system of education, or health care, or transportation, the ability of a government to facilitate political communication among its citizens determines the success of the democratic experiment.

What follows is not an argument about campaign finance reform; our democracy's problems are deeper and more intrinsic than the current popular debate over soft money and issue ads would suggest. Nor is this an argument about standards in journalism; our communication problems will not be corrected by a return of Edward R. Murrow. While the challenge of democratic statecraft and the problem of communications are universal, what I wrestle with here is particular to America. It is unique to our mechanism of governance, the republic in other words, constructed by the founders and modified in the give and take of politics over the course of two centuries.[20] Consequently, very little of this book will take up the very different course of communications policy traveled by other nations.

The founder most recognized as the father of our Constitution, James Madison, thought that political communication was such an essential instrument of our unique republican democracy that more than merely allowing freedom of speech was required to protect it. Madison helped to *enable* all Americans to communicate. He did this by supporting legislation that simultaneously subsidized the spread of popular information and advanced what would become the largest part of our early federal govern-ment—the Post Office.

Of all the founders, Benjamin Franklin is most often associated with the post. But, as with so many other aspects of our unique state, the founder who seemed to most appreciate the role of the post within the mechanism of our republic was James Madison. Madison's advocacy of the Postal Act of 1792 put communication service and a subsidy for political discourse at the center of our republic. A fortified postal service provided the equal ability of a diverse group of Americans, even noncitizens, to receive and express the popular information Madison deemed a necessary condition for public consent of government action.

The equal ability of Americans to communicate has been undermined not by the advance of technology or some alien power. Citizen access to popular information has been undermined by bad political decisions. These decisions date back to the Jacksonian Democrats' refusal to allow the Post Office Department to continue to operate telegraph service. The most powerful communications tool was deliberately placed in the hands of one faction in our republic: commercial industry. This faction has had many names over the course of our history. Madison called them the mercantile faction; Lincoln called them capital; Theodore Roosevelt called them Trusts; today we call them Corporate America. Neither Progressive era reforms nor new communications technologies have been able to correct the problems resulting from government abdication of a responsibility to advance the equal capability of citizen discourse. The failure of market-driven journalism and the failure of democratic politics are both related to the structural fault created by this and subsequent political decisions—decisions buried deep in the American system, asleep under the rubble of history.

Liberty, Equality, and Diversity

To see the fault it is necessary to understand the American system, particu-larly the shifting plates that intersect at the fault. Hidden deep below our Americanness lie the ever-shifting bedrock goals of liberty and equality. There is a popular and wrong-headed notion that liberty and equality are necessarily at odds. The fact that the goals of liberty and equality shift is one of our strengths—this shifting allows us to progress. In many ways our democratic project is about taking seriously what Habermas would call bourgeois clichés and turning them into public reality. There is undeniable progress from a nation that protected slavery to a nation that abhors it. The shifting of these subterranean plates is also one of our weaknesses in that in our growth we lose sight of important certainties.

One of those lost certainties was a view of liberty as strenuous self-governance. No king, no lord would govern us; we would be free to govern our own community. This civic liberty to participate fully in the deliberation of the common good has warped to a focus on what the founders called "luxury"—we call it "consumer comfort." The founders' view of equality focused on the political equality of citizens. The founders' notion of a strenuous participating liberty is not necessarily incompatible with their view of political equality.

The current dominant view of liberty, as in the liberty to be let alone or freedom from economic constraints, however, does not fit comfortably with our current dominant notion of equality, which is focused more on social standing than political power. This shifting of ideas about liberty and equality and the expansion and contraction of these ideals are constant and never far beneath even the calmest surface. Sandel is right to alert us to this shift, this confusion of focus. What Sandel fails to explain is that the exercise of political power, not philosophical argument, is behind the change.

Let me be clear. This work is not really about the problems with modern mass media. It is about democracy. It is about the relationship between politics and governance, particularly *the governance problem* of a communications policy to support a republic.

Our common failure, through our government, to promote democratic communications has nearly destroyed the bedrock requirements of republican participation and consent so necessary to our form of democracy. The abdication of a government duty to provide for the diverse political communications between citizens has allowed our democracy, our republican mechanisms of deliberation, to wither under the dominance of one faction.

Many readers will undoubtedly argue that modern private communications services are much better suited to providing popular information than government. This is a popular and not unreasonable proposition, and I argue later that there should be a place for private communications services in a republic. To allow large corporations, one faction of our nation, to dominate the creation and dissemination of what we call news, however, destroys the careful balance struck by the founders between a variety of competing factions. Because contested information is so important to our republic, we should never have allowed one faction to dominate our public sphere. Corporate liberty has overwhelmed citizen equality.

To retrieve our republic does not require us to divorce liberty from equality. The goal is not to put an end to the shifting tensions, but to manage these ideals properly. Our work is not to stop redefining our ideals of liberty and equality; it is to make certain that the sovereign people are engaged as participants in that work.

Allow me to complicate this assertion. The challenges we face are far more complex than our persistent Platonic-like tendency toward dualism (liberty or equality, black or white, big government or small, republican or democrat) would suggest. This habit of thinking is not always helpful in our richly diverse democracy. Even when occasionally illuminating, splitting every problem into two sides (as if there were not four or more, or as if the two sides did not substantially and importantly overlap) crowds out true diversity of opinion and with it an ability to see and wrestle with the complexity of our democracy. It is this very diversity, as Whitman thought, that is our greatest gift.

Madison understood our Constitution to be alive, ever under debate, ratification, and alteration through legislation and amendment. He understood that our republican democracy, our unique governing structure, was designed to manage a constant debate between an ever-shifting set of interests represented by many factions. Those interests derive not only from the different peoples who make up the American quilt, but the many ideas contained in the broad notions of liberty and equality. Madison and Hamilton and many other members of the committee that wrote our Constitution and helped form the early republic understood that "a more perfect union" would require much more than the simple balancing of two or three sides. The founders themselves represented more than two or three sides. Our challenge is not only how to balance and hold fast to the notions of a participating liberty and political equality, it is also how to best take advantage of the diverse contributions of all our citizens.[21] So, how and whether truly different factions participate in the balancing, in the decision-making process that is democracy, is also our subject.

The American republic requires the active deliberation of a diverse citizenry, and this, I argue, can be *ensured* only by our government—by the only social institution established to operate for the general welfare. Put another way, providing for the equal capability of citizens to participate effectively in democratic deliberation is our collective responsibility. We do not satisfy that responsibility by leaving it up to even a perfectly free market.

Ensuring democratic debate and decision making is at least as vital as the defense of our republic. If we do not manage our democratic deliberation, if we do not take care of it, what republic indeed is there to defend? We would not put the defense of our democracy in the hands of one faction of our country. A politician proposing that we leave our national defense to one faction, perhaps international corporations, would be laughed out of office. We should not put the management of our democratic deliberation in the hands of that faction—but this is what we have done. In handing over the reins of political communication to global business interests, we have turned our backs on our republic.

New Means of Communication

A common assumption is that because our circumstances have changed dramatically since the time of the founders, the founders' notions of what a democracy requires are no longer relevant. As Richard Reeves pointed out in 1982, 150 years after Tocqueville's tour of America, "the miracles that were invented after Tocqueville—in communications there was the telegraph, the rotary press, radio and then television—inevitably changed the techniques of the political process he observed."[22]

What Reeves misses is that the major change was not the fact of new means of communication, but the shifting of control over the means of communication. With this shifting of control, from public to private, came the first serious crack in the structure of American governance. The move away from enabling citizen communication altered the fundamental system of governance Tocqueville found so remarkable. With this change the meliorating power of communicating associations would soon be dwarfed by business and government. Again, what I mean to emphasize is not the fact of new technology, but the fact that policies have not been advanced to protect the ability of citizens to participate effectively and equally in a democracy.

As Reeves writes: "Information is power; control over the flow of information in a democracy is essential to the exercise of political power. What we know, and when we know it inevitably determines our actions as individuals, citizens, officials—as a nation." Reeves' main concern is television (and for good reason, as I discuss later); however, the problem is not simply the mesmerizing effects of television, it is the shift to a drastically altered and unequal communications environment. The way citizens become informed has changed dramatically, but not just because of technology.

For example, in the early days of the nation people depended upon newspapers and pamphlets and public notices, and, most important, public meetings (in lecture halls and taverns) to learn and to deliberate over events in their community.[23] The face-to-face, neighbor-to-neighbor nature of communication helped to steer this focus. Print publication helped to inform local action so that it could work in concert with national concerns, but it was not so powerful as to overwhelm what Harold Innis calls "the oral tradition."[24]

It should be clear that I do not mean to suggest that the introduction of new technologies did not have an impact. New technologies, even the pony express, had an impact on communication. Moreover, I consider scientific and technological advances potential benefits to a republic. While this book looks at what James Carey and John Quirk call the "rhetoric of the technological sublime,"[25] what I mean to emphasize is the impact of political structure on technology and the failure of U.S. policy to protect our democracy.

Not even two decades has passed since Richard Reeves retraced Tocqueville's journey, and his concerns about media now seem quaint. Besides radio and television we now have cable, the Internet, satellite and digital television. Modern communication is not only faster and more engaging, it is dominated by national concerns. People learn from their local radio and television more about the president's arguments with Congress and the pregnancy of a movie star than about what the mayor and city council are arguing over in their community. They tend not to get their information face to face, but face to machine, isolated in their homes, away from any possibility of a neighbor shouting, "Well what are we going to do about it?"[26]

The altered impact of new communications technologies does not argue for government abandonment of enabling citizen communication. Indeed, as communications technologies become even more important to democratic participation, the government's inherent responsibility to protect and advance democratic engagement is increased.

The Altar of the First Amendment

As Newton Minow has observed, all too often Americans use the First Amendment to end discussions of communications policy.[27] It should be clear by now that my focus here is not freedom of speech or the press. This freedom is all too often an exaggeration. Harold Innis may have been only slightly exaggerating when he wrote, "Freedom of the press . . . has become the great bulwark of monopolies of the press."[28] At the very least, blind references to freedom of speech or the press serve as a distraction from the critical examination of other communications policies.

Ithiel de Sola Pool's *Technologies of Freedom* is a good example of the idealization of freedom of speech in America.[29] Although it is one of the best books on the history of communications, its premise, that technology frees while government policy constricts speech, is far too simple an understanding of either the First Amendment or democratic deliberation. Perhaps if his editor had suggested the title *Technologies of Equality* he might have provided us a broader view of the history of communications policy in the United States. Howard Zinn's *A People's History of the U.S.* is a good antidote to Pool's romantic view of the First Amendment.[30]

Michael Sandel traces what happened to the political debate about the communications requirements of an engaged citizenry, but like most other commentators who write about communication issues, Sandel overlooks the importance of postal service, of government support for citizen speech. Sandel jumps immediately to a discussion about the limits of government censorship. But the shift Sandel traces is useful. Drawing from Alexander Meiklejohn, Sandel notes that the first purpose of the First Amendment was to provide citizens with the "fullest possible participation in the understanding of the problems" a self-governing citizenry must decide. But now, he notes, while "the courts continue to acknowledge the importance of free speech to the exercise of self-government, courts and constitutional commentators alike increasingly defend free speech in the name of individual self-expression."[31] Thus, the purpose of free speech is warped to protect global corporations and block rules that would promote democratic governance.[32]

As Sandel points out, our current policy debates and the actions that result from them suggest we have traveled off course on a long dark road. Starting as a nation that defined liberty as the ability to join in governing ourselves, we have become a disconnected people who define liberty as the ability to purchase consumer goods. What Sandel misses is that the problem is not only the warp to our public philosophy of free speech, but that the government has abandoned its role of advancing the communications capabilities of real people. The First Amendment limits on government interference with speech, the press, assembly, and petitions are of great importance. The First Amendment deserves Pool's, Sandel's, and our attention. This book certainly does not ignore the First Amendment. I only seek to place it in a context with other communications policies.

*   *   *

Our democracy was founded as a complex balance of competing factions and based on the twin ideals of liberty and equality. This balance involved checks within the federal government, a division of powers between the federal government and state governments, and the work of individual citizens and associations acting outside of government. The founders assumed that divisive factions would be engaged in an ongoing debate about the ever-shifting challenges facing local and national communities. A key element in managing this balance and these divisive interests was the federal embrace of a responsibility to ensure the communications capability of all. This key element has been lost and so has the balance. Much of what follows is the story of how the government abandoned its responsibility to enable citizen communication and to maintain a balance of power between competing factions in our republic, and how alternative policies have failed to correct this key problem.

The political argument of this book is an attempt at statecraft. I hope the reader will find the argument supported by my *construction* of a political history of communications policy. As I indicated earlier, I am not a historian and I will rely upon a wide variety of current historians engaged in an ongoing and contentious project to get history straight. In other words, even though I have reviewed a great deal of primary source material, I am largely indebted to secondary sources. I emphasize the word *construction* because I would like to acknowledge that I am not providing just the facts. My focus on political equality, my preoccupation with race, my emphasis on the ideas of political leaders, indeed even my certainty that the telegraph was at least as important as the railroad are all lenses through which to extract meaning from murky past complexities. In advancing this construction, I want to be clear that I am not recommending we return to the communications policies of the founders in addressing the complex interaction of global economic interests and democratic governance today. The point is not that there was some ideal period in our history. The point is only that we have much to learn from going back to our beginnings and looking at the impact past policies have had on democratic engagement.

With history as a backdrop, I then attempt to lay out where we stand today, including a description of several local successes and struggles to establish communications policies that improve democratic engagement. Finally, I propose how we can begin putting a new Humpty Dumpty back on the wall.

2

The Role of Communications
in the Democratic Experiment

It has been frequently remarked that it seems to
have been reserved to the people of this country, by
their conduct and example, to decide the important
question, whether societies of men are really capable or
not of establishing good government from reflection and
choice, or whether they are forever destined to depend for
their political constitutions on accident and force.

—Alexander Hamilton

Constructing a Republic

The problem of democracy taken up by the men who gathered in Philadelphia in 1787 was borrowed from the Greeks and Romans and informed by a small collection of European political philosophers.[1] I do not mean to suggest that what is loosely referred to as "Western civilization" is the only place we may look to understand how to create a republic. I only suggest that this is where the founders looked.[2]

Unlike the true (and failed) revolutionaries in France and Russia, American colonists did not seek to establish a wholly new system of governance, but to reform the so-called mixed constitution of England and to operate it independently. The founders were generally wealthy men who had prospered under British rule, but wanted a say in how the colonies should be run. The first attempt, the first experiment to operate a republic under the Articles of Confederation, failed miserably. In this twin sense the writers of our Constitution were less revolutionaries than they were reformers. While they looked to the small, walled republics of ancient homogeneous city-states, they understood that their challenge was unique. They wanted to create a republic, but this second attempt would be to bind together a diverse and fractious citizenry spread out across a wide geographic area. This effort at a "more perfect union" by consent had never been done before. To accomplish it they would ultimately establish a set of communications policies unique in the history of the world.

One place to begin to understand the role of communications in solving the problem of democracy is 1644. This is when John Milton argued against prepublication censorship of religious views, in the classic *Areopagitica:* "And though all the winds of doctrine were let loose to play upon the earth, so Truth be in the field, we do injuriously, by licensing and prohibiting, to misdoubt her strength. Let her and Falsehood grapple; who ever knew Truth put to the worse, in a free and open encounter?"[3]

Milton's argument that Truth and Falsehood should be allowed to grapple in a free and open encounter served as a basis for the ideas of John Locke. Locke argued in his *Second Treatise of Civil Government* that the protection of an individual's right to speak also protects the social good of a public debate of ideas.[4] The founders were steeped in the writings of Milton and Locke.

Moreover, the ability to speak uncensored by government and to speak with power in their local community was a strong normative value in colonial America, afforded to some degree by the great distance between the colonists and the English government. However, the problem of democratic communication in America is still unresolved when the federal state promises not to "abridge" the speech of the people.[5] The notions of Milton and Locke take us only part of the way, they do not tell us how to *protect the field* where Truth and Falsehood may grapple. In some respects, this is because Milton and Locke are concerned with the problem of liberty, not equality.

Communicating political views freely, that is, without government interference, does not mean that citizens will be able to communicate equally. To some extent, the problem is nicely caught in A. J. Liebling's famous remark, "freedom of the press is guaranteed only to those who own one."[6] Here we meet another tension inherent in our democracy, the goal of achieving some measure of political equality along with liberty. The ability to convey and receive information is a form of political power. Policies that privilege one group's ability to communicate over another establish political inequality. Unlike the Greeks and the Romans, or their very class-minded counterparts in Britain, the founders were acutely aware of the problem of inequality. This was, after all, the source of their troubles with England.

Many of the British subjects in America were in this country because of the harsh treatment they had received by the upper classes in England. While some adventurers undoubtedly sought financial opportunity not easily found in a rigid feudal economy, others sought refuge from discrimination resulting from their family status or their religious beliefs. Once they were in America, colonials were not treated as equals before the law of the British Crown. The cry "no taxation without representation" was a call for the right to representation in the British Parliament, or at least a call for equal treatment as subjects of the British king. It was, however the colonists split those hairs, a call for political equality with their British counterparts. This call for equality was in fact the first goal. Only after equality was clearly out of reach, only after the petition for representation was rejected, did the founders seek liberty.

Moreover, as Roger Wilkins has written, the founders well understood the pain and degradation of inequality because the practice of slavery was so prevalent. Because they were, many of them, slaveholders, they knew what it was to be a slave, and they would risk their lives and their fortunes to not be slaves.[7]

Still, much of the founders' political thinking about inequality was not homegrown, but was borrowed from very radical eighteenth-century challenges to the idea that monarchs were partly divine, a necessary link between god and mortal. It was Jean-Jacques Rousseau who most powerfully advanced the notion that "all men are created equal," a political idea and practice not at all self-evident. The founders were steeped in the intellectual debates circulating in Europe in the mid-1700s, and prominent in that debate were the ideas of Rousseau.[8] In his *Discourse on the Origins and Foundations of Inequality Amoung Mankind,* Rousseau boldly suggested that man was inherently (that is, in a state of nature) free and equal. He also argued that inequality was the result of relatively newborn passions of ambition and greed, which led to the "usurpations of the rich, the pillagings of the poor."[9] Rousseau dared to argue that the wealthy monarchs were not enthroned by God, as they and the church claimed, but by force. "Force alone upheld him, force alone overturns him."[10]

If the bold Massachusetts advocate James Otis had no hesitation citing Rousseau,[11] Jefferson would be more cautious. Connor Cruise O'Brien suggests that Jefferson, ever the shrewd politician, was wary of being associated with Rousseau's agnosticism.[12] As O'Brien argues, while Jefferson never acknowledged his debt to Rousseau, the influence is striking. At the very least the library of books Jefferson sold to Congress suggests that Jefferson had read Rousseau. More important, some of Jefferson's arguments mirror Rousseau's best and worst. Jefferson's intense appreciation of pedagogy fits easily with Rousseau's; unfortunately, so does Jefferson's nonsense about forcing people to be free and the utility of revolutionary bloodshed.

After liberty and equality, the third pillar in the founders' construction of a new republic was the check and balance of faction. Balancing interest against interest was a preoccupation of those who thought about the nature of man and the basics of statecraft in the seventeenth and eighteenth centuries. Here the founders looked to Baron Charles de Montesquieu. Montesquieu's arguments about the importance of balancing interest against interest were prominently cited by both Hamilton and Madison in the *Federalist Papers.*[13]

Albert Hirschman argues convincingly in *The Passions and the Interests* that the focus on the use of countervailing powers derived from religious notions about balancing the sinful passions of avarice, ambition, and sexual lust against the virtuous passions of reverence and duty to family and home.[14] These catechisms reverberate today in the images of a devil and an angel sitting on either shoulder of a man. Hamilton was only drawing from the political thinking of the time when he argued for the reelection of the president in the *Federalist Papers,* as a balance of the office holder's avarice against his vanity.[15]

But it is Madison's analysis of counteracting faction that has drawn, deservedly, the most attention. Madison begins his contribution to the *Federalist Papers* with a caution about factions. "Among the numerous advantages promised by a well-constructed Union, none deserves to be more accurately developed than its tendency to break and control the violence of faction."[16] By faction, Madison meant both majority and minorities organized by some "passion" or interest. Madison believed, with David Hume, that factions were "sown in the nature of man." Looking around him, he saw a "landed interest, a manufacturing interest, a mercantile interest, a moneyed interest, with many lesser interests." He viewed the "principal task" of legislation "the regulation of these various and interfering interests."[17]

It is important to stop here for a moment and understand the relationship between the idea of faction and what Sunstein calls a "broad public." As stated earlier, and as will be repeated again, a core Madisonian concept is the deliberation of independent (free) and equal citizens to determine what is best for "we the people." This concept assumes that differences will arise and that compromises will be made. The "evil" arises when passions are so strong, when interests are so divided, that the only choice is separation of the community. The founders believed the colonies were better off together, despite their strong separate interests. The dominance of any one faction would destroy the fragile federal union.

Heavily influenced by Locke and Rousseau and Montesquieu, those engaged in the statecraft to improve upon the Articles of Confederation would establish a democracy where freedom of speech would be a norm, efforts would be made to ensure citizens had an equal ability to communicate, and the necessary evil of factions would be checked and balanced within the government. These three pillars would inform the communications policy of the early republic.

A Word about James Madison

The challenge the founders faced was new. Constructing a nation dedicated to the goals of political liberty and equality while accepting the contentious nature of their fellow men was difficult enough. To do this in collaborative deliberation, to overcome the all too evident factions separating them was extraordinary. Frankly, they failed in many respects. But they left room for their failures, such as the monumental and nearly catastrophic failure regarding slavery, to be corrected. This took more than the study of the ancients and more contemporary philosophers. It required the ability to apply abstract ideas to hard granular reality. It required being skeptical of certainty but hopeful of improvement. It required a willingness to experiment. James Madison should not be idealized, but of all the founders he embodied these qualities.

Madison was a southern slaveholder and our fourth president. He was a slight and reserved man, overshadowed not only by his neighbor Thomas Jefferson but by his wife Dolley. He did not have Alexander Hamilton's grasp of finance, John Marshall's facility with the law, or John Adams' experience in foreign affairs. Despite a substantial body of writing, he did not leave the sort of diaries and letters that give such life to Benjamin Franklin. There is no great monument to his honor in the nation's capital, but Madison is widely regarded as the father of our Constitution. It was Madison who introduced our Bill of Rights, though he initially opposed it.[18] He was a principal founder of the Democratic Party,[19] though he is well remembered for his warnings against political factions.[20] Most of Madison's achievements are described in scores of popular books,[21] where his complexities and contradictions are glossed over, and scholarly texts,[22] where the slightest apparent shifts in his opinion are debated heatedly. More obscure, but key to our purposes, were Madison's support and explanations of the Post Office Act of 1792. What did Madison think?

Madison scholar Lance Banning writes that "we cannot simply freeze a single frame from the extended process of his thinking and present it as the essence of his understanding." Madison himself would caution that his own understanding of the Constitution developed gradually, and that the Constitution's meaning came about "only in the course of national action and debate." Most important, "Madison did not portray himself and other framers as the givers and definers of the law, guiding and instructing a passive nation. He pictured the framers, instead, as having been involved in a communicative interchange with a superior—the body of the people—who played a very active role."[23]

Madison's view of the postal service and the role of communications in a democracy was subtle and complex. While he lauded the ability of the American communications system to bring far-flung citizens into a discussion with their representatives in federal government, he also feared the ability of this communication to bring into conflict a community made in some ways more harmonious because its members lived in relative isolation.[24] One of the reasons northern merchants could get along with southern slaveowners, and vice-versa, was their great distance from one another. Despite the inevitable disagreements made possible by communicating, Madison believed the communication of differences was fundamental to democracy and democracy was worth the risk.

When Sunstein writes about a "Madisonian conception," he means the goal of "broad communication about matters of public concern among the citizenry at large and between citizens and representatives." Madison believed that a proper course could be achieved through a diversity of expressed views, a sort of "government by discussion."[25] There are parts of Madison's writings, notably his most famous contribution (No. 10) to the *Federalist Papers*, that would seem to contradict this view. But, as Banning warns, this is too narrow, too frozen a view of Madison's thinking. In addition to Sunstein's "Madisonian conception" I would emphasize Madison's willingness to give ground, to see how events played out. This willingness can be seen in his reaction to a provision of the Constitution he opposed, the provision of equal state representation in the Senate. It was "not impossible," he wrote, that the provision might prove "more convenient in practice than it appears to many in contemplation."[26] Madison was willing to change his mind, he was able to learn.

The Communication System of the Early Republic

In Article One, Section 7 of the Constitution the founders gave Congress the power to establish "Post Office and post Roads." This was the foundation of a communications system that would come to dwarf any other communications system the world had ever seen. But just what did that clause mean?

There was no debate about providing Congress the power to establish a postal service and post roads. After all a postal service of some sort was in operation under British colonial rule beginning in 1711. While they attempted legislation spelling this out in 1788, the leaders of the early republic would not pass legislation regarding postal service until the Second Federal Congress. However, to think this failure was an indication that mail delivery was insignificant to the political leaders of the day would be a mistake. As Richard John points out, establishing a postal system in the early republic was "one of the thorniest and most intractable problems that the new regime confronted."[27]

The same year the Constitution was ratified, Dr. Benjamin Rush advocated that a postal system, the "true non-electric wire of government," be used to distribute "knowledge of every kind . . . through every part of the United States."[28] Rush's emphasis on the responsibility of the federal government for educating, indeed creating, citizens capable of self-governance challenged the revenue-generating rationale established under British policy. Rush's proposal was extraordinarily hopeful, as there was nothing about the American postal system in 1787 to suggest it could handle such a responsibility.

Between 1775 and 1792, American mail service was a pale twin of the royal postal system established in British North America. The American system operated on the assumption that it would not only support itself but contribute revenue to the Treasury; it was, as New York financier Gouverneur Morris[29] observed, "the most agreeable tax ever invented."[30] Fiscal concerns, not civic concerns, dominated postal policies in colonial America through the first Congress. Prior to the war, the heaviest users of the post were merchants. But once the war began to interfere with trade, postal revenue dropped sharply, and service declined as a result. Mail service was so bad, military commanders George Washington and Nathaniel Greene established their own couriers to maintain communication with the federal government.[31]

Ten years after the end of the war, the American postal system included sixty-nine offices, only two more than the British had established by 1765. More troubling was that these post offices were still largely located at ports along the Atlantic seaboard, while the U.S. population was now extended well into the Trans-Appalachian wilderness.[32] The pressures to do something about the post were increasing; members of the federal legislature were hearing from their constituents. Those pressures helped to spur a shift away from the British fiscal rationale of postal service.

In January 1791, Massachusetts Congressman Theodore Sedgwick heard from Samuel Henshaw, a resident of his district living in Northampton, Massachusetts. Henshaw was concerned about the relocation of the federal government from New York to Philadelphia. Northampton residents were only a short boat ride from the federal capital when it was in New York. According to Henshaw, they "seemed almost to hear" congressional debates but after the move "we scarce know you are in session. This in my mind proves the necessity of post roads through all parts of the Union—people would then have early information & be influenced by it."[33]

Dr. Rush and citizen Henshaw would be very pleased with the Post Office Act of 1792. There were three cornerstones of the Post Office Act. First, newspapers would be given preferential treatment. Second, Congress assumed control over the designation of postal routes. Third, federal officers were prohibited from surveillance. As John writes, taken together these measures made the Post Office Act of 1792 "a landmark in American communications policy and one of the most important single pieces of legislation to have been enacted by Congress in the early republic."[34]

As compared to Dr. Rush, President Washington offered a very different rationale for national postal service. No doubt influenced by his years as military commander, Washington thought preferential treatment for newspapers was a means of keeping citizens informed of the actions of their leaders. In his Fifth Annual Address, Washington argued for a repeal of postage on newspapers under the assumption that "a faithful representation of public proceedings, diffused without restraint throughout the United States," would secure "the affections of the people governed by an enlightened policy."[35] Madison, on the other hand, had other goals in mind.

While Madison expressed concern about the potential harm of public opinion in the *Federalist Papers*, and argued that the difficulty of communicating over the vast geography of the colonies would serve to limit the power of factions, in 1791 he published an essay declaring that public opinion was the "real sovereign in every free" government. As John writes, "Madison was primarily concerned with encouraging the citizenry to participate in public affairs." To accomplish this he would advance the Post Office Act of 1792 for the "*circulation of newspapers through the entire body of the people.*"[36] Madison was in favor of reduced rates but against the elimination of postage rates for newspapers. Madison argued that postage "above half a cent, amounted to a prohibition ... of the distribution of knowledge and information."[37] Madison's clear focus was not on returning funds to the Treasury, but ensuring citizens had the means to govern themselves. The 1792 act not only provided that newspapers would be charged less than letters, it also provided that any newspaper printer could send without charge a copy of his paper to every news printer in the country. These were very strong subsidies for the expression of political ideas. These subsidies were not awarded to personal or commercial correspondence.

By 1794, Madison's civic rationale for postal policy had taken a strong hold. Newspapers accounted for 70 percent of the total weight handled by mail carriers, but contributed only 3 percent of total postal revenue.[38] By 1795, even those most concerned about federal revenue to the U.S. Treasury, such as outgoing Treasury Secretary Hamilton, conceded the civic importance of mail service.[39]

Not only was the importance of communications in the early republic evidenced not only by the newspaper subsidy, but it served as a basis for the expansion of post roads, even on routes that could not financially justify service. While the postal system consisted of a mere 1,875 miles of post roads in 1792, by 1800 postal roads stretched 22,309 miles.[40] While it was rumored that President Jefferson briefly considered abolishing the Post Office,[41] the expansion of the postal service actually increased while he was in office, linking the big cities on the Atlantic coast to the independent farmers spreading out toward the Mississippi. The 903 post offices established by 1800 more than doubled to 2,300 by 1810.[42]

In an age of television and the Internet, it may be difficult to understand how important the postal system was in early America, but as Theda Skocpol writes in "The Tocqueville Problem,"[43] "the postal system was the biggest enterprise of any kind in the pre-industrial United States." Skocpol goes further to argue that while the postal system was vital to commerce, it was even more important for civil society and democratic politics. The importance of communication, particularly of government-facilitated communication, to civil society and democracy is also emphasized by Richard John in his important book *Spreading the News: The American Postal System from Franklin to Morse.* John argues that the federal postal system was not only the largest government institution, and the largest single employer, but that this government-facilitated means of communication was in and of itself an agent of change.[44]

The Impact of the Post Office Act of 1792

As Richard John writes, the Post Office Act of 1792 "transformed the role of the newspaper press in American public life."[45] In 1800 there were 241 newspapers in the United States; sixteen of them were dailies while most of the others were weekly papers. By the time Alexis de Tocqueville visited the new republic in the 1830s, there were over seven hundred newspapers and over sixty of them were dailies. In many ways the period immediately after the founding highlighted the founders' mistakes—slavery and an inability to recognize the legitimate rights of either women or Native Americans chief among them—so this period should not be romanticized. But beyond these important limitations, the three pillars of the founders' republic—the freedom of citizens to participate in government, political equality among recognized citizens, and the check and balance of factions within government—were evident, particularly in communications.

Despite the fact that Tocqueville did not remark on the First Amendment, he understood the American revulsion toward press censorship as a necessary consequence of a sovereignty of the people. "When the right of every citizen to a share in the government of society is acknowledged, everyone must be presumed to be able to choose between the various opinions of his contemporaries and to appreciate the different facts from which inferences may be drawn. The sovereignty of the people and the liberty of the press may therefore be regarded as correlative."[46]

The "liberty of the press" was a norm, but government interference was also practiced on occasion, most notably the Alien and Sedition Acts of 1798 and during the War of 1812, when postal officers regularly interfered with the transmission of newspapers. As John writes, these exceptions can be regarded as abnormal and were not tolerated for long.[47] The Alien and Sedition Acts expired after two years and postal interference with the mails was tolerated only during the roughly two-and-a-half years of the War of 1812.

Tocqueville observed communication in the United States to be connected to governance. The communication was not merely, not even predominantly, social, it was political expression conveyed in large part through politically powerful associations—facilitated by newspapers. He wrote: "In order that an association among some democratic people should have any power, it must be a numerous body. The persons of whom it is composed are therefore scattered over a wide extent, and each of them is detained in the place of his domicile by the narrowness of his income or by the small unremitting exertions by which he earns it. Means must then be found to converse every day without seeing one another, and to take steps in common without having met. Thus hardly any democratic association can do without newspapers."[48] Tocqueville draws our attention here not to newspapers as tools for commercial advertisements, but as tools necessary to associations for purposes of political power. Tocqueville's appreciation for "associations" was not centered on their charitable works, but on their power in the political realm. He understood the association as a mechanism for liberty, as a part of the U.S. system. As Benjamin Barber argues, part of the genius of the U.S. system was not only creating adversaries within the government (the much touted three-part system of government with its checks and balances) but "encouraging the growth of an unofficial representative system (of lobbyists, interest groups, voluntary associations) to challenge, balance, and complement the official representative system."[49] Empowering associations by subsidizing the distribution of newspapers was an important element of early communications policy.

For all of Tocqueville's appreciation of associations, he failed to see the federal government as an aid to them. "Nothing strikes a European traveler in the United States more than the absence of what we would call government,"[50] he wrote, yet he was astonished at the extent of the post particularly when compared to that in his native France. "The post, that great instrument of intercourse, now reaches into the backwoods. . . . In 1832, the district of Michigan, which . . . was hardly more than a wilderness, had developed 940 miles of post roads. The almost entirely unsettled territory of Arkansas was already covered by 1,938 miles of post roads. . . . There is not a province in France [where] the natives are so well known to one another as the thirteen millions of men who cover the territory of the United States."[51] By the time Tocqueville arrived in the United States, federal postal service had well eclipsed France's and Britain's. In 1829, President Andrew Jackson invited the postmaster general onto the cabinet. This elevation only reflected the fact that for many Americans, particularly those in the West, the Post Office *was* the federal government.[52] By 1832, the 8,764 federal postmasters made up over three-quarters of the entire federal civilian workforce, delivering 16 million newspapers. By contrast the federal army consisted of 6,332 men.[53]

Again, the rationale for the postal service was not government-to-citizen communication. Congressional franking privileges, which allowed free delivery of mail both from and to government officials, would probably serve Washington's ends. Subsidizing the distribution of newspapers by allowing carriage at low rates, indeed subsidizing newspapers by allowing free delivery to printers, went far beyond simple government-to-citizen communication. It was Madison's civic vision, a vision that elevated the importance of popular information and public opinion that would dominate communications policy in the early republic.

Despite the long history of the fiscal rationale to determine postal policy, indeed despite the real need for federal revenue, except for a temporary increase in postage rates during the War of 1812, Congress would not increase postage rates for newspapers until 1918.[54] The clear policy of the early republic put postal service first, even at the risk of postal deficits. Postal historians Wesley Everett Rich and Wayne E. Fuller have argued that major postal debates in the early republic centered on a choice of service versus revenue. Fuller argues that service-first won over, and quotes Representative Clyde Kelly in 1931: "there will be no change in the service-first policy of the United States Post Office."[55] As John writes, "revenue generation remained at best, but a minor refrain."[56] While the Post Office Department would return some surplus to the government on and off, "few regarded this as the major rationale for the enterprise as a whole.... During the various postal debates that took place between 1794 and 1834, the pivotal issue was never whether the postal surplus should be returned to the treasury but rather how the postal surplus ought to be spent."[57]

*   *   *

A central argument of this book is that our democratic system of checks and balances is out of kilter. One faction has come to dominate democratic deliberation. Kevin Phillips[58] and others, notably Charles Beard,[59] argue that wealthy Americans have always dominated our political discourse. I suggest here that nascent industrial/financial interests, perhaps best represented by Alexander Hamilton, were very different, and substantially offset by the agrarian/slaveholding interest perhaps best represented by Thomas Jefferson. Thus, while wealth was dominant it was divided against itself. The check of agrarian power in the South was balanced against the rise of mercantile/financial power in the North.

Madison and Jefferson clearly feared mercantile/financial interests. Despite Montesquieu's arguments that "the natural effect of commerce is to lead to peace," the founders' experience with their most important commercial partner, England, was anything but peaceful.[60] They also saw first-hand that the loyalties of wealthy traders were not necessarily with their colonial brothers but with the country that brought them profits.[61] The founders' Scottish contemporary, Adam Smith, wrote with stern conviction about the effects of a nascent capitalism on the faction of merchants: "The minds of men [merchants] are contracted, and rendered incapable of elevation. Education is despised, or at least neglected, and the heroic spirit is almost utterly extinguished."[62]

Smith was particularly distrustful of political power exercised by economic interests, and frequently insisted that legislation proposed by business "ought always to be listened to with great precaution, and ought never to be adopted till after having been long and carefully examined, not only with the most scrupulous, but with the most suspicious attention. It comes from an order of men, whose interest is never exactly the same with that of the public, who have generally an interest to deceive and even to oppress the public, and who accordingly have, upon many occasions, both deceived and oppressed it."[63] As Hirschman writes, Smith shared with Rousseau great skepticism about the *douceur* (that is, the kindly) effects of capitalism as predicted by Montesquieu, and instead saw in the emerging capitalism possibilities for corruption and decadence.

Though conservatives are fond of quoting Tocqueville's observation of a close tie and a necessary relation between freedom and industry, they ignore his advice to limit particularly the political power of financial interests: "It must be admitted that these collective beings, which are called companies, are stronger and more formidable than a private individual can ever be, and that they have less of the responsibility for their own actions; whence it seems reasonable that *they should not be allowed to retain so great an independence of the supreme government as might be conceded to a private individual*" (emphasis added).[64] While this particular dispute over the effects of capitalism and the tendencies of the mercantile faction may have been lost on Hamilton, it was certainly not lost on Jefferson, who considered Smith's *The Wealth of Nations* one of the best books on political economy[65] and whose ideal citizen was the economically independent farmer.[66]

There were private entities engaged in delivering mail in the 1830s; indeed, a U.S. monopoly on postal service would not be established until 1851.[67] Yet the Post Office Act of 1792 established a system of communication to which all could have equal access, regardless of wealth. As John notes, "Who paid for the newspaper subsidy? Not the central government . . . to reduce the cost of securing political information for citizen-farmers . . . Congress increased the cost of doing business for merchants."[68]

The founders gave lukewarm support to funding an army, debated intensely over organizing a national bank, failed to provide support for a national educational system, but spent substantial resources and established additional taxes on private commercial interests to make political communications possible throughout the territory. If Tocqueville failed to be explicit about the importance of the postal service in American life in the 1830s, Francis Lieber, another renowned political theorist of the day, would be clear. Lieber ranked the postal system, along with the mariner's compass and the printing press, as "one of the most effective elements of civilization."[69] Unlike the compass and the printing press, the U.S. postal system of the period between 1800 and 1830 was the direct result of government policy, specifically the Post Office Act of 1792.

All this is not to say that this early period in the republic was a golden age of communications in the United States. Mail was not only slow, it was too often interfered with and disrupted. The early press tended to be overtly partisan and far less interested in what we today would call objective reporting. Large groups of people—women and blacks held in slavery—were not allowed to participate equally in public debate. But Madison could reasonably argue that the improvement of the nation's communications system brought about by the Post Office Act would help prevent the "degeneracy of a free government."[70]

Our particular democratic structure puts a priority on the free and equal ability of citizens to communicate with each other. In order to maintain a wide range of checks and balances (interest against interest, association action balanced against government prerogative, state responsibility balanced against federal duty), the federal government was quite protective of its duty to convey political communication to the remotest territory. This, at least, is where we started.

PART II

A Brief History of U.S. Communications Policy

3

The Break: The Telegraph from Jackson to Hayes (1830–1876)

> In the hands of individuals or associations the telegraph may become the most potent instrument the world ever knew to effect sudden and large speculation— to rob the many of their just advantages, and concentrate them upon the few. If permitted by the government to be thus held, the public can have no security that it will not be wielded for their injury rather than their benefit.
>
> —Postmaster General Cave Johnson, 1845

How did we shift from a structure of governance that facilitated communications through the post to a set of policies that now, without amendment, has put even the postal service "in the hands of individuals"? The story begins only a few decades removed from the ratification of the Constitution.

In the early 1800s a dramatic shift was taking place in the republic. Between 1812 and 1821 six western states entered the Union with constitutions providing for universal white male suffrage or a close approximation, and between 1810 and 1821, four of the older states substantially dropped property qualifications for voters.[1] The beneficiary of this expansion of suffrage was Andrew Jackson.

While the republicanism of the time of the founders stressed the connection between property and citizenship, a new American democracy was forming that equated citizenship with the right to vote regardless of property. In debate at the convention reconsidering the constitution for the state of New York in 1821, David Buel Jr. argued that objections to universal suffrage were based on a view of society more like European kingdoms than America. The United States was not a class-based society, Buel argued, and for two principal reasons. In addition to the "common school" in many parts of the country, which provided basic civic education regardless of wealth, Buel noted that the existence of the "universal diffusion of information" preserved Americans from European vices.[2] Buel and a growing chorus of Americans pushing for expanded suffrage took up the Madisonian banner connecting popular information with self-rule. A greater democracy was possible in America because more people had access to information important to their ability to govern themselves.

As Richard John has argued, the quite unique American system of communications was by its nature revolutionary. As a result of the "universal diffusion of information" more and more Americans were prepared to participate and, indeed, to demand the freedom of self-governance. As the beneficiary of the founders' communications policies, Andrew Jackson and his followers might be expected to protect and expand the government role in communications. The Jacksonian Democrats did no such thing. The political rivalry between Jacksonian Democrats and the Whigs would set the stage for the American abdication of responsibility for citizen communication.

The Telegraph and the Battle over Federal Action

In 1838, just a few years after Tocqueville's journey to the United States, Samuel Findley Breese Morse demonstrated to President Martin Van Buren and a congressional committee an odd contraption. It consisted of a pen attached to one end of a pivoted arm, a magnet pulling at a piece of iron, and a windup clock motor that drew a paper strip under the pen. What stirred Morse, and what should have stirred the nation's executive and select legislators, was the ability of this device to create markings on the paper in response to current flowing through a wire to the magnet. This odd collection of devices was largely based on experiments conducted in Europe beginning nearly seventy-five years earlier (since the reign of that other tinkerer in electricity, Benjamin Franklin). Like many of those earlier devices Morse's contraption was an instrument that could transmit and receive information electronically over long distances.[3]

Morse, a professor of art at what would become New York University and a tinkerer in electric devices, believed that God had put him on earth to improve communication between distant people and nations. Some members of Congress expressed the view that Morse was something of a mystic, perhaps under the spell of the so-called sciences of mesmerism and Millerism (a sect predicting the Second Coming of Christ would occur in 1842). Morse was petitioning for funds to develop an experimental telegraph line.

Van Buren, a Jacksonian Democrat, and Congress, dominated by such Democrats, would disappoint Morse. Morse would have to wait another five years for another party to dominate policy making in Washington before his dream of government support would be possible.

Perhaps the most important policy decisions that veered away from the course set by the founders were those decisions involving the telegraph. Those decisions were as follows: (1) early investment in development of the technology; (2) abandonment of control of that technology to private industry, except for military purposes; (3) continuing subsidy of the industry; and (4) a weak response to the emergence of private monopoly or oligopoly control over national communications. This set of policies was a clear break from the communications framework established in the earliest days of the republic. This break would set a pattern that would come to determine U.S. communications policy. It was a pattern favoring what Madison called the mercantile faction. It was a pattern, a public philosophy, that supports a vibrant commercial market but weakens a democracy.[4] But what caused this clear break from the course set by the Post Office Act of 1792? In order to understand this break, it is necessary to understand the political debates at the time they occurred, and the leaders and ideas in contest at the time of those debates.

The Jacksonian Democrats

The great shift in the republic brought about by the ascension of the Jacksonian Democrats has been much debated by modern scholars of the era. Richard Ellis makes a strong case that it is a mistake to discount wholly the traditional view of that period as a rise of the common man and displacement of aristocracy, even while acknowledging this view as incomplete.[5] The major problem of this era was finding a way to balance factions while enlarging both the freedom to participate in governance and political equality. How would the leaders of the mid-1800s balance the various factions of the republic?

Both the telegraph and the railroad represented extraordinary technical advance in the mid-nineteenth century. A central argument of this book is that the development of technology is highly dependent upon a political framework. Perhaps the most lasting political development of the 1830s was the fruition of the political party.

Ronald Formisano argues persuasively that despite their evident electioneering in 1800, the Federalists and the Democrat-Republicans were not full-fledged political parties.[6] Under Andrew Jackson, the Democratic Party became a lasting vehicle for organizing political participation. Parties not only educated previously excluded citizens and got them to vote, they also exerted some control over party officials in government, both elected and appointed. Parties corralled competing factions under one banner, getting representatives from different parts of the nation to work together and vote alike. This last point is particularly important to emphasize.

Parties are not factions. Parties contain different factions. Within the political party one faction may dominate on issues most important to it, another faction may dominate on other issues. The Jacksonians reinvented the political party as an organization that would capture the mechanism of the government, and they wielded that mechanism toward the ends of a variety of factions within the party. All this was new with the Jacksonian Democrats. In understanding the direction of communications policy in the mid-1800s, it becomes important to understand both the Jacksonian Democrats and the Whigs who organized to oppose them. So who were the Jacksonian Democrats?

Jacksonian Democrats saw themselves as hard-scrabble populists and direct descendants of Jefferson. Andrew Jackson benefited from an odd coalition of agrarian interests and out-of-power New Englanders, and campaigned with the slogan, "Let the People Rule!" According to the introduction to the Jacksonian *United States Magazine and Democratic Review,* "A strong and active democratic government, in the common sense of the term, is an evil, differing only in degree and mode of operation, and not in nature, from a strong despotism."[7] Jacksonians fiercely opposed the idea of federal power, and turned their ire on the Second Bank of the United States.

Chartered by Congress in 1816 for twenty years, the bank was empowered to act exclusively as the federal government's fiscal agent, holding U.S. deposits, making transfers of federal funds to the states, and dealing with any payments or receipts with which the federal government would be involved. More important, the national bank also had the right to issue bank notes and lead the state banks "in all that is necessary for the restoration of credit, public and private," according to the charter. Though subject to supervision by Congress and the president, the Bank of the United States was 80 percent privately owned, and its owners, claimed the Jacksonians, represented one faction, the financial elite in Philadelphia. As far as the Jacksonians were concerned, the national bank was an example of the problem with a powerful federal government; its instruments tended to become captured by aristocratic manipulation.[8] In his attack on the Bank of the

United States, Jackson made perhaps the clearest statement of his party's philosophy:

> It is to be regretted that the rich and powerful too often bend the acts of government to their selfish purposes. Distinctions in society will always exist under every just government. Equality of talents, of education, or of wealth cannot be produced by human institutions. In the full enjoyment of the gifts of Heaven and the fruits of superior industry, economy, and virtue, every man is equally entitled to protection by the law; but when the laws undertake to add to these natural and just advantages artificial distinctions, to grant titles, gratuities, and exclusive privileges, to make the rich richer and the potent more powerful, the humble members of society—the farmers, mechanics, and laborers—who have neither the time nor the means of securing favors to themselves, have a right to complain of the injustice of their Government. There are no necessary evils in government. Its evils exist only in its abuses. If it would confine itself to equal protection, and as Heaven does its rains, shower its favors alike on the high and the low, the rich and the poor, it would be an unqualified blessing.[9]

The bank, of course, was not the only, and perhaps was not even the most lucrative, federal privilege. The Post Office Department, with its offices and routes controlled exclusively by the federal government, was a major source of political patronage and concern for the Jacksonians. In addition to the debate over the Second Bank of the United States, there was a major political debate over a proposed 1,100-mile "National Southern Post Road" to stretch between Washington and New Orleans. On the eve of Jackson's inauguration, Congressman John Bell of Tennessee, an eloquent Jacksonian, warned that such a federal investment would transform the federal government into a "great central power," more formidable than the founders had imagined.[10]

The Jacksonian Democrats were also generally opposed to the newspaper subsidy, even as pressure was gaining in Congress to further reduce or eliminate any requirement for payment. In 1832, Jacksonian Democrats blocked an effort in Congress to eliminate newspaper postage by one vote. At first glance the Jacksonians seemed to have adopted Madison's position that token newspaper postage would encourage delivery. But unlike Madison, the Jacksonians wanted to prevent the widespread circulation of city papers into the territories.[11]

Still, as opposed as they were to "internal improvements" and newspaper subsidies, the Jacksonians appreciated, perhaps too well, the benefits of political patronage that could be distributed through the Post Office. This patronage created the necessary financial incentives to reward an army of campaign workers in the newly forming political parties. The clearly partisan dismissal and appointment of thousands of postal workers after the Jackson administration took the reins was a major political scandal for Jackson.[12] But the Jacksonians did not merely replace existing postal officers; during their twelve-year reign (two terms under Jackson and one under Martin Van Buren), Jacksonians nearly doubled the number of postal officers from 8,764 in 1831 to 14,290 in 1841,[13] and post offices increased from 8,450 in 1830 to 13,468 in 1840.[14]

The Post Office Department under Jackson and Van Buren operated in fiscal and political turmoil. This was due not only to the great expansion of service, it was also the result of corrupt contracting procedures. In 1823, for example, the Post Office paid the ten largest mail contractors in the country a total of $118,000 a year. In 1833, the total had increased to $439,000. As John writes, "No improvement in level of service could possibly have justified such an enormous increase."[15] At least one postal clerk, Obadiah Brown, resigned in disgrace, unable to defend himself against the charge that he personally profited from an agreement with a mail contractor. The corruption in the Post Office led to an extensive review and reform of postal accounting policy by Congress, including reluctant Democrats, with the Post Office Act of 1836.[16]

Quoting Jacksonian journalist, Anne Royall, John writes that the postal system under Jackson had become "an irresistible and gigantic enemy, in the shape of an electioneering machine." To control the Post Office was to control national politics.[17] The Jacksonian Democrats understood the Post Office as a source of partisan political power, even while banging the drum for small government. As Sandel argues, Jacksonian Democrats opposed government subsidies (including, for some, the operation of the Post Office) to slow the advance of a capitalist economy on behalf of agrarian interests.[18]

The Whigs Take Control

In 1840, John Tyler, of the Whig Party, was elected vice-president, but soon found himself president. William Henry Harrison ("Tippecanoe") died only thirty-one days after taking office. The Tyler years were the first and last to be dominated by the Whig Party, for Whigs also controlled for the first and last time both houses of Congress. Having failed in his petition to the Jacksonian Democrat Van Buren and his fellow partisans in Congress, Morse tried the Whigs. In 1843, over Democrat Congressman Cave Johnson's objections, the Whig-dominated Congress granted Morse $30,000 (a considerable sum at the time) to build a telegraph line from Washington to Baltimore. The first prong of U.S. communications policy was put in place. With this grant of federal funds, Morse had the support he needed to resolve many of the remaining fundamental engineering problems of telegraph service. How would the wires be insulated? Would they be above or below ground? The federal government would provide the crucial support to answer these questions.

Why did this now largely forgotten early American political party fund Morse's ideas, when the Jacksonian Democrats would not? Whigs argued for a political and economic arrangement that synthesized Hamiltonian fiscal measures and Madisonian internal improvements with Jeffersonian principles emphasizing strong local self-government and an electorate of active economically independent producers. Fairly or not, the Whigs were seen by many (including Lincoln, who was a Whig before the formation of the Republican Party) as the party of old-line aristocrats. These aristocrats included both the southern slaveholders and the financial interests in the North that benefited from agricultural trade. Though the Virginian slaveholder Tyler was an early supporter of the Democrat Andrew Jackson, he broke with him on the issue of nullification and became a Whig.

A short explanation of the battle over nullification will serve to explain the Whigs and introduce one of the most important political divisions of the time. Former Vice-President John C. Calhoun argued forcefully in 1832 that a state had the right to nullify federal laws, to decide for itself which federal laws to observe or reject. This was an argument derived in some measure from Jefferson's covert battle against the Alien and Sedition Acts put in place during the administration of John Adams. Shortly after Jackson's election in November 1832, the South Carolina legislature voted to nullify federal tariff laws and to prepare to secede from the Union if efforts were made to collect federal tariffs after February 1, 1833. In December 1832, Jackson issued a Proclamation on Nullification, declaring "disunion by armed force is treason." Old Hickory, as Jackson was called, began mobilizing troops and vowed to hang Calhoun if South Carolina went through with its threat. Congress, supporting Jackson, passed a bill authorizing the use of troops to collect tariffs, but it also passed legislation gradually reducing federal tariffs. South Carolina rescinded its nullification legislation. Out of this fire, what Ellis calls the "uneasy but real alliance between Jackson's most powerful enemies"—John Calhoun and Henry Clay—was formed.[19] By 1834 the party of Calhoun and Clay would call themselves Whigs.

But a different understanding of "states' rights" was not all that separated the Whigs and the Jacksonian Democrats. While the issue of sovereignty (that is, Which entity had the ultimate authority in our governing structure, the states or the federal government?) was at the core of the debate between the Jacksonian Democrats and the Whigs, the emotionalism of the debate drew its power from earlier fears of the danger of a monarch (as the Whigs viewed Jackson) and the fears of an aristocracy (as the Jacksonians viewed the Whigs). Thus, the dispute between these two parties came to center largely on the role of the federal government in promoting economic growth.

Whigs were the party of slaveowners and wealthy northern mercantile and banking interests, and they argued for an activist federal government to guide national economic development. Whigs could appreciate the national economic benefits of government investment in a new system of communication by electronic telegraph. Moreover, Whigs believed in the power of communication in instilling republican values and loyalty to the central government. Henry Clay's "American System" is as good a description as any of the mix of Whig economic and civil policy.

Clay argued that high tariffs imposed on imports would protect American manufacturing from foreign competition, and a national bank eased commercial transactions and encouraged investment by establishing a reliable currency. So despite the trouble over nullification, the Whigs did not generally oppose tariffs or taxes, certainly not for improvements made as a result of federal distribution to state coffers. What they most opposed was any encroachment upon state power. Clay and the Whigs argued that national transportation and communication investment promoted commerce, national harmony, and moral fortitude in an expanding territory. According to one Christian Whig journal: "The sooner we have railroads and telegraphs spinning into the wilderness, and setting the remotest hamlets in connexion [sic] and close proximity with the east, the more certain it is that light, good manners, and christian refinement will become universally diffused." Moreover, taxes to fund massive internal improvements and then distributed to the states would create, according to Clay, "a new and powerful bond of affection and of interest" between the states and territories and the federal government. Such bonds of affection were evident by the frequent requests for post roads and service from the states and territories.[20] In light of these arguments, Whig support of Morse's telegraph becomes easy to understand.

Whigs were as concerned about the concentration of power as Jefferson or Jackson. They were most concerned, however, about the concentration of political power in the executive, and the imperious behavior of Jackson, and later even the Whig Tyler, would fuel their ideological fire. Like their English namesakes, Calhoun, Clay, and the American Whigs saw the greatest threat to a republican form of government to be the arbitrary power of an executive. "The Whigs of the present day are opposing executive encroachment, and a most alarming extension of executive power and prerogative," declared Clay. Whig political cartoons lampooned President Jackson as "King Andrew I," and Tippecanoe (Harrison, that is) won office on a platform of executive restraint.[21] It is perhaps not surprising that the great battles that took place during Tyler's term were between the Whig Congress and the Whig executive (President Tyler) whose office they so mistrusted.

The Whig candidate for president, Henry Clay, clearly stated his party's position regarding the telegraph in 1844: should the telegraph be put in the hands of "private individuals they will be able to monopolize intelligence and to perform the greatest operations in commerce and other departments of business. I think such an engine ought to be exclusively under the control of the government."[22]

So the Morse telegraph line between Washington and Baltimore began operation in 1844, and was under authority of the Post Office Department by the next year. During the first six months the cost of operation was $3284.17, but telegraph revenue was only $413.44. The first telegraph line was idle most of the time, operating at only 15 percent of capacity. In addition to its novelty, one of the main reasons for its underemployment was where it went to and from. In 1844, neither Washington nor Baltimore was a major urban center of the country. Moreover, the short distance between the two cities was already connected by regular rail service.[23] The Baltimore-Washington telegraph line was appropriate for technical experiments, not market experiments.

Jacksonian Democrats Take Back Control

In 1844, James K. Polk was elected president by a slim majority, defeating the Whig candidate Clay. This election also ended the Whigs' control of Congress. Democrat Polk was sometimes called "Young Hickory" in recognition of his mentor "Old Hickory" Andrew Jackson. Like Jackson, Polk opposed a national bank and "internal improvements." In 1845, Congress, again under the control of Jacksonian Democrats, declined to purchase the Morse patent. A new American course was now set, even as argument over federal control over the telegraph would continue beyond the Civil War.

Congressman Cave Johnson of Tennessee was one of the Jacksonian Democrats who laughed at Morse during the Tyler administration. Johnson introduced an amendment to the bill proposed to support Morse that suggested that if the Congress wished to promote electromagnetism it ought also to encourage Mesmerism and send half the proposed sum to the leader of that religious sect. This same Johnson was a confidential friend and advisor of Polk, and was one of the first officers to be selected to serve in the Polk cabinet—as postmaster general.[24]

Johnson is rightly credited with improving the postal service. Under his tenure postal rates were lowered, and payment by the sender was established, as was the use of stamps. Johnson also took steps to protect the federal government monopoly in the carriage of the mails. But Johnson attacked both the government franking privilege and the newspaper subsidy. "Why," he asked, should "those who buy and sell newspapers . . . have the cost of transportation paid out of the revenues of the great body of the people?"[25] Still, Johnson supported the Post Office Department's control over the telegraph service, even though he believed "revenues could not be made equal to its expenditures." Johnson contended, "an instrument so powerful for good or evil cannot with safety to the people be left in the hands of private individuals uncontrolled by law."[26] Johnson was arguing that telegraph service was too important to be put in private hands, whether or not it could be operated on a break-even basis.

Sentiment for the government to control the operations of the telegraph was also strong in the merchant community. Many feared that unscrupulous traders could monopolize information and manipulate commodity markets. A group of Baltimore merchants warned Congress in 1847 that the new technology was simply too powerful to be left under private control. "The obvious fact," the merchants declared, that control of the new technology "places into the hands of its managers to a great extent the interests of merchants, of the press, of the government itself, and indirectly of the whole people, is sufficient to show the danger of leaving it in the hands of private individuals. Its affinity to the post office, its agency in regulating commerce among the several States, and its obvious utility in directing most promptly the movements of armies and fleets, point unerringly to the government of the United States, as the authority to which this instrument ought to be entrusted."[27]

In his book, *The Creation of the Media*, Paul Starr argues that the failure of some state-financed internal improvement projects, particularly canals, made the majority of legislators wary of supporting a service that might not break even.[28] Yet pressures for improvements to support western settlement continued. Moreover, during this time, what has been called the cheap postage movement was beginning, and as Wayne Fuller writes, by the 1840s, a majority of Congress agreed that "there was no more reason for the Post Office to be self-supporting than for the army and navy to pay their own way."[29] With the Post Office Act of March 3, 1851, Congress reduced postage, allowing a letter to be carried up to 3,000 miles for 3 cents postage prepaid, 5 cents if collected on delivery. Letters beyond 3,000 miles paid double those rates.[30] Moreover, the 1851 act directed that "no post-office now in existence shall be discontinued, nor shall mail service on any mail route in any of the States or Territories be discontinued or diminished, in consequence of any diminution of the revenues that may result from this act; and it shall be the duty of the Postmaster-General to establish new post-offices, and place the mail service on any new mail routes established, or that may hereafter be established, in the same manner as though this act had not passed."[31] This defeat of the cost-basis rationale for postal service would not be revisited for over a hundred years.

But the decision to reject federal control over the telegraph was made, and there would be no turning back with the Jacksonians in power. Unlike the Post Office promoted by the founders and embraced by the citizens, control of the telegraph would be put in the hands of a few private citizens. Not only did this momentous policy determination make little sense in the context of the times, it would make even less sense in light of subsequent subsidies.

* * *

It is difficult to accept that privatizing telegraph service is what the Jacksonians intended. They were as invested as the Whigs in the notion that economic policy should be judged by its ability to cultivate the qualities of character in citizens required by self-government. While the Whigs abhorred power concentrated in the executive, Jacksonians professed hostility to nearly any form of concentrated power. As Jackson declared in railing against the Bank of the United States, this "great monopoly," if not destroyed, would have passed "from the hands of the many to the hands of the few, and this organized money power from its secret conclave would have dictated the choice of your highest officers and compelled you to make peace or war, as best suited their own wishes. The forms of your Government might for a time have remained, but its living spirit would have departed from it."[32]

So rather than inspiring enterprise and loyalty as the Whigs argued, Jacksonian Democrats believed internal investments would undermine an

economy of small independent producers, engaged in just the sort of virtuous occupations a self-governing citizenry required. "The planter, the farmer,
the mechanic, and the laborer all know that their success depends upon their
own industry and economy." Such citizens, Jackson declared, "desire nothing
but equal rights and equal laws."[33] However, "many of our rich men have not
been content with equal protection and equal benefits, but have besought us
to make them richer by act of Congress."[34]

Federal operation of a telegraph system was seen by the Jacksonians as
both another tax on those who could afford it least and as another opportunity to concentrate power in government. But at odds with their desire to
reduce the power of the federal government, the Jacksonians appreciated
the political benefits of patronage the Post Office provided, as mentioned
above. In addition, their desire for a polity comprised of independent farmers was tied to a thirst for more territory. This thirst led to a doubling in size
of the nation during the administration of Young Hickory (through initiatives military and otherwise partly begun during the prior administration).
Post roads especially were necessary to the westward march. It would soon
become clear that the telegraph would also be necessary to settling the west.

Federal Subsidy and the First Private Monopoly

Polk was a one-term president, replaced by the man he put in charge of the
Mexican War, Zachary Taylor. Taylor was nominated by the Whigs but died
after sixteen months in office. The last Whig president was Millard Fill-
more, who, as was typical of the Whigs, was not renominated by his party.
Despite several attempts, the Whigs never regained sufficient power to
return control over the telegraph to the Post Office. But their support was
essential to completing the first part of the pattern of American communications policy: (1) early development support, (2) followed by a relinquish-
ing of control to the private sector, (3) the substantial subsidization of
private interests, and (4) a weak response to monopolization.

In 1857 Congress voted to support laying a transatlantic telegraph cable,
and, more important, in 1860 Congress passed the Pacific Telegraph Act,
providing substantial subsidies to private business to construct a transcontinental telegraph line.[35] As John writes, the "transcontinental telegraph
owed its impetus less to commercial considerations than to political fiat."[36]
There is no adequate explanation for this shift. In 1857 and 1860, the
Democrats controlled not only the presidency, but enough votes in Congress to block any subsidy to the telegraph industry.

What had happened? Around 1845 Morse offered to sell all his rights to the telegraph to the United States for $100,000. Congress failed to act on a bill to take Morse up on his offer, assume control of the telegraph, and continue to operate it under the Post Office Department. Fifteen years later Congress would provide $80,000 for two years, in addition to military support and free access to federal lands, to a private company to extend telegraph service to the Pacific. It is entirely possible that despite early enthusiasm, Congress simply underestimated the potential importance of the telegraph. There is no question that telegraph service grew substantially in the 1850s. But that service was overwhelmingly dominated by business traffic.[37]

Congress assisted Morse in the early development of the telegraph with a grant of $30,000 to experiment on a line between Washington and Baltimore. While it refused to continue to operate the telegraph, Congress would subsidize the operation of a private telegraph company. This subsidy did not extend civic discourse, but business communication.

While the Post Office Act of 1792 advanced information to the public subsidized by business, the Pacific Telegraph Act of 1860 advanced information to business subsidized by the public. The break from the founders is becoming clearer, as current communications policies come into focus.

In an odd twist, it was the 1860 federal subsidy that set the stage for Western Union to monopolize telegraph service. After considerable competition, telegraph service split among a cartel of six telegraph companies, each dominating a different region of the country. This cartel joined to crush their smaller rivals. The two largest companies were the American Telegraph Company, operating in the east, and Western Union, operating in the west. The cartel lobbied Congress for support to expand to California. Disappointed with the offer of $40,000 per year for two years (and the considerably more valuable grant of land, rights of way, and military protection from Native Americans), the cartel, including Western Union, agreed to hold out for more. In a surprise move, Western Union defected from the cartel, becoming the sole bidder for the government funds. Thus, Western Union received the "contract" to expand telegraph service to California—a service Western Union would control. Western Union's double-cross of the wire service cartel consolidated its hold on service to the West, and more important, strengthened its position with the federal government.[38]

By 1861, eight years before the railroads would complete the feat, the telegraph would link the nation from coast to coast. It was the existence of the telegraph line that allowed the railroads to complete their work with greater efficiency and safety. Fulfilling Madison's fears about the problems associated with greater communications, 1861 also saw the beginning of the Civil War.

Anson Stager, Western Union's general manager, was appointed the Union Army's superintendent of military operations. Holding down these two positions, Stager authorized the construction of 15,000 miles of military telegraph, most of which were turned over to Western Union at the war's end.[39] By 1864, Union forces took over the assets and operational control of telegraph companies in the east with lines running north to south. Western Union, left alone, continued to expand in the sparsely settled western territories, and in 1866, with the other telegraph companies near financial disaster, Western Union took on substantial debt, watered its stock, and bought off its rivals. Western Union had become the nation's first truly national private monopoly. Despite occasional attempts by some, such as Senator B. Gratz Brown of Missouri, to nationalize or effectively regulate telegraph service, Western Union remained in the graces of federal representatives by offering them free or reduced rate service.[40]

The Impact of Monopoly on the Press

The first part of the pattern of U.S. communications policy seemed to be set. Did the abdication of government management of a national telegraph system or a private monopoly of that system have an impact on democratic communications?

Around the time Henry David Thoreau wrote from Walden Pond, "[we] are in a great haste to construct a magnetic telegraph from Maine to Texas; but Maine and Texas, it may be, have nothing important to communicate . . . as if the main object were to talk fast and not to talk sensibly,"[41] news about Texas was of special interest to American citizens. Congress admitted Texas to the Union in December 1845, and a few months later war was declared with Mexico. Did Thoreau capture the relevance of the telegraph to democratic communication?

As the nation grew, distance was an even greater problem than it was in the period of Madison. The telegraph reduced that distance. As valuable as postal service was, it remained unreliable. Some merchants had become accustomed to sending several copies of the same message by post in the hopes of increasing the chance that one would be delivered. The telegraph was not only speedier, it was more reliable. Thus, as mentioned earlier, merchants were the dominant users of the telegraph. The cost of telegraphy was prohibitive for ordinary citizens. The fact that private citizens could not afford telegraph service affected not only personal communications, it limited the communication of the citizen associations with which Tocqueville was so impressed. Political communication was still largely conducted face to face in taverns and at public lectures (a great source of public entertainment), and, of course, through newspapers and periodicals. The impact of the telegraph on the newspapers (the dominant public sphere of national democratic discourse in the 1800s) deserves special attention.

The newspapers of the period immediately after the founding were extremely partisan and relatively expensive. Papers such as John Fenno's *Gazette of the United States* published in New York, which backed the Federalists led by Hamilton, and Benjamin Franklin Bache's *Aurora* of Philadelphia, which supported and was supported by Thomas Jefferson, put politics first and commercial advertisements second. These papers were written for the educated elite. Despite their partisanship, "no other class of mailable items enjoyed such favorable rates" as newspapers.[42]

The Whigs and the Jacksonian Democrats also had their partisan backers and attackers among the papers, but as commercial activity increased the newspapers both proliferated and became more commercial. As Tocqueville reports, "three quarters of the enormous sheet are filled with advertisements."[43] These were mainly the plain advertisements of local merchants and other legal and personal notices, without the benefit of an advertising industry. The growing population, connected to a government-subsidized communications system, supported an abundance of publishers. "The most enlightened Americans attribute the little influence of the press to this excessive dissemination of its power," Tocqueville wrote.[44] In other words, the fact that so many Americans were able to communicate equally resulted in a public sphere where no American was able to dominate.

Telegraph service and the race for the latest news from the most distant places helped increase the commercialization of the news. It also created disincentives toward partisanship and incentives to share responsibilities for political newsgathering. These factors furthered the trend toward monopoly—and, most important, increased the ability of a few Americans to dominate the public sphere. The wire services restricted information dissemination and, when they were able, the newspaper cartels restricted both information and access to telegraph service. The constriction on democratic discussion when private interest controlled wire service is in stark contrast to the freeing of democratic discussion under the government-controlled postal service.

In 1846, frustrated by the limitations the telegraph companies placed on the transmission time made available to his operations, Moses Yale Beach, owner of the New York daily the *Sun,* pulled together five of his competitors (the *Tribune, Herald, Journal of Commerce, Courier and Enquirer,* and the *Express*) to form the Associated Press (AP).[45] The New York–based newspaper cartel joined to share the cost of transmitting via telegraph political and congressional news from Washington and to report on the Mexican War.

The founding of the AP furthered a commercializing trend in the newspaper business away from strictly partisan presentations of political information toward a supposed objective journalism. It also furthered a trend toward homogenization of a style of writing more suited to ordinary Americans. AP reporters in major cities gathered stories produced by local papers and sent them to New York, where they were edited, pulled together as a collection of national news, and sent back out to local client newspapers. Subscribing papers were prohibited from independent use of telegraphy; they were barred even from receiving telegraphed stories from their own reporters. Papers that did not subscribe to the AP complained of monopoly.[46]

Francis O. J. Smith, the head of the telegraph companies from Portland, Maine, to New York, declined to carry the AP's traffic and sought to force it to use his own telegraph services to retrieve dispatches from Europe by way of Newfoundland. The AP responded by crying "monopoly" in its editorials and piecing together alternative routes of delivery. The AP also established contracts with smaller telegraph companies in the Northeast in which it received priority over its competitors. The AP contracted for the same exclusivity later when Western Union established its monopoly.[47] Indeed, newspapers that opposed the Western Union telegraph monopoly and supported a return of telegraph service to the U.S. Postal Service found both their Western Union and their AP service in jeopardy or their rates increased.[48] A hundred years would pass before this constraint on news would be corrected.

By 1866 Congress became concerned over the growing influence and reach of Western Union and it passed legislation intended to curb the power of the new national monopoly. The Telegraph Act of 1866 granted telegraph firms the right to string wires along every post route in the country; in return, if Congress so decided, the federal government would be permitted to purchase all the companies' assets at a mutually agreed-upon price. The act also authorized Congress to set rates for federal use of telegraph service.[49] Needless to say, beyond the provision regarding federal rates, the act had little effect.

During the course of the next forty years over seventy bills would be introduced to return control of telegraph service to the Post Office. Perhaps the most persistent lobbyist was Gardiner Greene Hubbard, who, beginning in 1868, called for Congress to pass a Postal Telegraph Bill that would authorize the Post Office Department to operate a telegraph service. As Hubbard would argue, "As a telegraph for business, where dispatch is essential and price is of little account, the Western Union system is unrivaled; but as a telegraph of the people it is a signal failure."[50]

After extensive studies of the government-controlled mail system and Western Union, Hubbard came to these conclusions. Telegraph offices were not always readily accessible to the general public and, even more significantly, their rates were much too high for the average citizen. By contrast, the U.S. postal system offered uniform rates with a relatively efficient and readily accessible delivery system. The U.S. Postal Telegraph Bill, also known as the Hubbard Bill, proposed authorizing Congress to charter a quasi-government corporation identified as the U.S. Postal Telegraph Company, a service of the Post Office Department. This service would not take over existing private telegraph companies, it would compete with them.

Hubbard's extensive research, particularly regarding telegraph rates, and his prior success in civic projects (he led the effort to establish the first U.S. subway/trolley—connecting Boston to Cambridge) earned him a popular following.[51] While he wrote several published magazine articles on the proposal, Hubbard received little newspaper coverage. As Edward Evenson writes:

> Although difficult to prove with documentary evidence, part of his lack of media attention can be attributed to the unique relationship between the Associated Press and the Western Union Telegraph Company.
> Western Union was quick to chastise any newspaper that dared to support or advocate government intervention in the telegraph industry. Newspaper spokespeople, those brave enough to speak out, claimed that it was impossible to establish a newspaper without the consent of the AP and Western Union. Two San Francisco newspapers, the Herald and the Alta California, learned the hard way what happens to those who have the temerity to suggest reforming the telegraph industry. When the Herald violated this canon, it experienced a 250 percent increase in telegraph rates. Under similar circumstances, the Alta suffered the loss of all Western Union telegraph dispatches.[52]

The ability of the AP to turn information into a commodity was directly tied to their exclusive partnership with Western Union. The ability to control what was reported in many papers, and their coordination of time-sensitive, market-sensitive information, would embroil the AP in many controversies by the turn of the coming century.[53] Hubbard would write in 1873, "The abuses of this system are growing, and will increase rapidly until the government interferes to perform the duties for which it was constituted—to protect the people until the rates for the press are fixed by law, equal rights and privileges secured to all, with rates so low that all can use the telegraph. Not until then will a free and independent press be assured to the country."[54]

But Hubbard's bill would never become law. Hubbard was unable to drum up significant popular support for his efforts, given the public's reliance on newspapers operating in league with the AP and Western Union. Western Union and AP control over the news wire market was not their only asset. Western Union also employed a significant lobbying force on Capitol Hill. Unlike the civic-minded Hubbard, Western Union had a privilege it could extend to supportive legislators. Western Union issued franking cards, allowing a congressman to send as many free telegrams as he wished.[55]

Beside lobbying, Western Union and the AP joined to have a powerful impact on politics. As Manahem Blondheim writes in *News over the Wires,* William Henry Smith, a general agent of the AP, former Republican politician, and close friend of presidential candidate Rutherford B. Hayes, began using AP stories to promote Hayes and smear Hayes's Republican rival James Blaine. Despite the fact that the AP withheld reports that would have implicated Hayes and other Republicans in acts of corruption, Hayes still lost the popular vote to Democrat Samuel Tilden. But the electoral-college victory depended upon a resolution of disputed elections in Louisiana, South Carolina, and Florida. Western Union disclosed telegraphs sent between Democrats and Smith, and the AP used these to assist Hayes in anticipating what the Democrats would do. The AP also failed to report protests when a special Congressional Electoral Commission gave the 1876 election to Hayes, but it did report on those Democrats who called for restraint.[56]

The AP could not win the election for Hayes; the party machines remained the dominant force in American politics. But there should be no dispute that the AP linked with Western Union had a dominant voice in the discussion of public affairs in America. As Blondheim writes, "the monopolistic position of the AP in gathering telegraphic news . . . gave it the power to manipulate information."[57] In less than forty years, the public sphere had changed from a place where no news source, no one interest, could dominate discussion to a place dominated by one news source in the hands of one faction—the one Lincoln called capital.

During the mid-1800s the Jacksonian Democrats won their political battle with the Whigs and were able to determine the direction of national policy. The Jacksonians were primarily concerned about the ability of the
old-line aristocracy, which was largely represented by the Whigs, to capture
the federal government, and they supported policies intended to advance
the interests of an expanding western population and white males without
property. Perhaps because they saw the telegraph as mainly a device for
business they chose not to continue its operation by the Post Office. A fiscal
rationale for the continued refusal of the government to take over the telegraph is particularly difficult to accept given the financial support for the
Pacific Telegraph Act of 1860.

The Jacksonian Democrats were able to come to power because of the
expansion of democratic debate made possible by the investment in a public communications infrastructure. The diffusion of information (as Buel
argued) justified expanding suffrage among white males and it aided in
western expansion. Expanded suffrage and an extensive federal communications network west of Appalachia set the stage for this new political force.
The perhaps unintended result of Jacksonian policies, however, was the
suppression of democratic speech and the establishment of a different
elite—the first major national private monopoly. That monopoly, Western
Union, in concert with its partner the AP, was very much focused on guiding public opinion to further its private interests, in opposition to the
Democrats. One unchecked faction now was able to dominate public
debate.

4

The Telephone and
the Trusts (1876–1900)

All that had gone before was useless,
and some of it was worse.

—Henry Adams

A New America—Capital in Command

America was of course a very different nation after the Civil War. The political battles of the Whigs and the Jacksonian Democrats over nullification and the national bank were largely forgotten by 1870, while the core issues of states' rights and federal economic distributions would surface under other guises. Though the confrontations between Whigs and Jacksonian Democrats determined the course of American communications policy, continuing to grapple with the concerns of Clay and Polk was certainly useless in understanding the realities of governance in the late 1800s. The swinging pendulum of the American state, from boom to bust to war and back, would dominate public policy battles over the next fifty years. The Whigs' static preoccupation with the strength of the presidency would seem moot after a long string of weak presidents; however, it would not be the southern slavocracy in control of a powerful senate. To the sustaining disappointment of the Democrats, the federal government would never fail to be a source of economic support captured by a few in power.

There were, of course, other debates the Civil War did resolve. Most important was the resolution of the debate forced upon the nation by John Brown and less fervent abolitionists, and, of course, the related debate over the extension of slavery to newly appropriated aboriginal territory. Also resolved, though grumbling would continue, was the primacy of the federal government over state government. By 1865 the Constitution was amended to abolish slavery, and the Fourteenth Amendment, enacted three years later, would come to be understood to bind states to a set of federal guarantees, such as the right to due process and equal protection of the law.

But in many essential ways America was not a very different country. On September 30, 1859, in Milwaukee before the Wisconsin State Agricultural Society, the former Whig U.S. representative from Illinois, Abraham Lincoln, addressed the debate between those who believed that an aristocracy ("capital") must be placed in a hierarchy over labor and those who believed labor must be free to participate in governance. A core misunderstanding in this debate, said Lincoln, was that "even in all our slave States, except South Carolina, a majority of the whole people of all colors, are neither slaves nor masters. In these Free States, a large majority are neither hirers or hired. Men, with their families—wives, sons and daughters—they work for themselves, on their farms, in their houses and in their shops, taking the whole product to themselves, and asking no favors of capital on the one hand, nor of hirelings or slaves on the other."[1]

Lincoln was right, as usual. As difficult as it may be to imagine such a state today, in the middle part of the nineteenth century most Americans worked for themselves. Early Americans were relatively more economically independent than they would be by the early part of the twentieth century. This economic state was true before and immediately after the Civil War. This is what freedom meant in eighteenth- and nineteenth-century America.

The modern reader is reminded that freedom was not a condition of comfort, it was not what the founders derided as "luxury."[2] Freedom was the state of not being obligated to either landed lord or factory boss, while enjoying the privilege, indeed, the responsibility, of citizenship. It was this strenuous freedom that Jefferson and other founders had in mind as they contemplated democracy. It was the dream of this freedom that justified the genocidal slaughter of Native Americans in the Northeast, the forced removal of Cherokee and Choctaw nations from their lands in the South, and the containment of aboriginal Americans in the West. Free labor, that is, free men required their own land to be independent. The entire system of plantation slavery (with a few whites sitting on the backs of a great mass of black families, while the vast majority of southern whites were landless) contradicted this dream. The destruction of slavery, the expansion to the Pacific Coast, combined with the post, the telegraph, and the railroad to facilitate democratic communications across a continent, made a free republic more possible than ever. But Lincoln, who deeply shared the founders' democratic dream, began to see a future danger.

In a much-quoted letter to a Colonel William F. Elkins, Lincoln wrote: "I see in the near future a crisis approaching that unnerves me and causes me to tremble for the safety of my country . . . corporations have been enthroned and an era of corruption in high places will follow, and the money power of the country will endeavor to prolong its reign by working upon the prejudices of the people until all wealth is aggregated in a few hands and the Republic is destroyed."[3]

Given Lincoln's reputation as a stalwart legal counsel for business interests, it is not difficult to understand the dispute among historians regarding the authenticity of this letter. However, as noted above, Lincoln's attachment was to independent labor, and he would always emphasize the priority of labor to what he called "capital." He would do so in his First Annual Message to Congress on December 3, 1861: "Labor is prior to, and independent of, capital. Capital is only the fruit of labor, and could never have existed if labor had not first existed. Labor is the superior of capital, and deserves much the higher consideration."[4] With the formation of both telegraph and railroad lobbying interests able to secure substantial advantages from local and federal governments, Lincoln had reason to worry that a new powerful business faction would replace the old slavocracy the Civil War was in the process of destroying.

Immediately after the Civil War, roughly 80 percent of Americans lived in rural areas, and while tenuously connected to a market economy they remained largely independent as Lincoln described. By 1900, 40 percent of America was urban, and by 1920 half of all Americans lived in cities and most of them worked for others.[5] This relatively rapid change in the way Americans lived and worked would underlie the politics of the next fifty years after the Civil War, and establish a political philosophy powerful enough to overturn the noble principles of the Declaration of Independence. The shift from an agrarian society dominated by independent labor to an industrial society of wage earners dependent upon corporations led to a reworking of the ideas of both freedom and equality. As they grasped control over the economy, an emerging faction of monopoly/capitalists also grasped control over the new tools of communications—tools that would become essential in determining the course of American debate.

By the 1870s business interests, that faction feared by Lincoln, now controlled a coast-to-coast "electrical" communications system, dominated the newspapers Madison had put so much faith in, and were widely thought to have their hands on the throat of government. Despite these formidable advantages, resentment of "capital" would find its way into independent periodicals carried regularly by the U.S. Post Office, still the largest enterprise in the nation in 1870, with an operating revenue of $18.9 million. Western Union, by contrast, had an operating revenue of $6.7 million.[6] Unlike Western Union, the Post Office Department was still operating on a service-first basis, and continued to emphasize the Madisonian mission of supporting public discussion. As late as 1879, Congress and the Post Office would limit low postal rates to "information of a public character," including arts and science; commercial mail did not apply.[7] Perhaps more important, the taverns, churches, and lecture halls were the places most Americans continued to discuss public policy. In these small places, supported by public information through the mails, agrarian Populists and urban labor would wrestle over the direction of America against the ideas of northern industrialists. It was a battle for the soul of America.

The Gilded Age

Ten years after the Civil War, one hundred years after the Declaration of Independence, America was the most advanced communicating nation in the world. The Post Office delivered mail from the Atlantic to the Pacific and the Great Lakes to the Gulf of Mexico, aided by an overabundance of railroad lines. Telegraphic communication extending political and business information now traveled at lightning speeds coast to coast through over 210,000 miles of wire, dominated by one company, Western Union.

Though most Americans still worked for themselves, the economic and political power had clearly shifted from agrarian states to growing urban areas jammed with small businesses and their employees. This power shift was the result in part of the north-south split of agrarian interests due to the still lingering resentments of the war and Reconstruction. The increase in northern industrial political power was also tied to a dramatic increase in industrial growth after the war. The resulting wealth was not evenly distributed; indeed, it was concentrated in the hands of many of the men, such as Cornelius Vanderbilt, John Astor, Andrew Carnegie, and Jay Gould, who made fortunes in part through their control of the telegraph.[8] These men did not shrink from exercising political influence (political purchase may be only a slight exaggeration) through organizations as brutal and effective as their businesses.

Ulysses S. Grant, the renowned Union general, was ending his second term as president, having presided over an administration marked by corruption and too great a fondness for the faction Lincoln called "capital."

Grant's weak presidency was followed by a series of presidents most of us have forgotten. But as Schudson writes, recent scholars have argued that the years between Lincoln and Theodore Roosevelt deserve some "sympathy and even admiration [because these] were the years of the highest voter turnout in our entire history."[9] Political participation was team sport, an entertaining carnival that also offered jobs. If this period in American history is instructive of anything, it is that simple voter turnout is not the same as a republic operating by the consent of an informed and engaged citizenry. Neither party, whether led by Republicans Hayes, Garfield, Arthur, Harrison, or McKinley or Democrat Cleveland, exercised any real control over the concentration of money and power.

Any writer wishing to understand this period must wrestle with an army of authors from the time, most notably Henry Adams, as well as powerful interpretive historians who reigned in the 1960s, such as Richard Hofstadter and Robert Wiebe, and contemporary scholars. Perhaps no single interpretation of this period has been as powerful as that advanced in 1873 by Samuel Clements (Mark Twain) and Charles Dudley Warner in *The Gilded Age: A Tale of Today*.[10] It is a story of two characters, Colonel Beriah Sellers and Senator Abner Dilworthy, and their part in a bribery scheme involving the federal government and the railroad. *The Gilded Age* drew a portrait of an American society riddled with corruption and scandal. It was not far off the mark, and it resonates still for good reason. The period in American history between Lincoln and Theodore Roosevelt was an age of bosses, such as Tweed and Hanna. But to see the political machines, the increased voter turnout they spurred, the jobs they secured, and the "assessments" they generated, without observing the capitalist faction collecting wealth around them would be sticking one's head in the sand.

The Democrat and Republican parties continued to collect odd sections of the country under their tents. Irish immigrants, silver miners, and southern populists were gathered up by the Democrats. Poor Yankee conservatives, banking interests, and blacks still worshipping Lincoln lined up behind the Republicans. But with a few minor exceptions, both parties were dominated by the big money interest. As Twain would joke in a speech to our British cousins: "I think I can say with pride, that we have some legislatures that bring higher prices than any in the world."[11] The real political battle of the day was not between the parties but between the monopoly capitalists and various reform movements scattered around the country.

Schudson focuses on the "mugwumps,"[12] who were initially identified with Northeast Republicans, but threw their support to the Democrat

Grover Cleveland in 1884. Sandel reminds us of the importance of the Knights of Labor, who sought to create an alternative to emerging capitalism by promoting a cooperative system as "the true remedy for the evils of society . . . the great idea that is destined to break down the present system of centralization, monopoly, and extortion."[13] There were also the Farmers' Alliance, the General Federation of Women's Clubs, and a whole host of other groups struggling to make sense of the new Union. Robert Wiebe wrote several books touching on this period, perhaps the most criticized and most insightful being *The Search for Order*. In it he describes a nation redefining itself and uncertain of its direction; from the bottom class to the elite "like so many free-floating particles, groups of worried citizens tossed about, attached themselves to a cause, then scattered again."[14] This too was the Gilded Age.

During this period the telephone was born.

The Telephone and a Word about Patents

Around Grant's time, February 14, 1876, to be exact, Alexander Graham Bell applied for a patent for an "improvement in Telegraphy." Bell was interested, along with many other more experienced "inventors," in selling a patent to Western Union. Whether Bell's application at the U.S. Patent Office was delivered before Elisha Gray filed a caveat claiming to have invented "the art of transmitting vocal sounds or conversations through an electric current" remains a subject of heated debate.[15] A great deal has been written about the much-disputed Bell patent, which will not be repeated here; however a short note on patent law *as a subsidy* is warranted.

Our first patent commissioner, Thomas Jefferson, wrote:

> If nature has made any one thing less susceptible than all others of exclusive property, it is the action of the thinking power called an idea, which an individual may exclusively possess as long as he keeps it to himself. . . . Inventions then cannot, in nature, be a subject of property. Society may give an exclusive right to the profits arising from them, as an encouragement to men to pursue ideas which may produce utility, but this may or may not be done according to the will and convenience of the society. . . . England was, until we copied her, the only country on earth which ever, by a general law, gave a legal right to the exclusive use of an idea . . . generally speaking, other nations have thought that these monopolies produce more embarrassment than advantage to society.[16]

The giving of a monopoly right to an idea, a patent, in other words, is something a government may or may not provide inventors. There is a balance to be struck in the decision as to whether a monopoly right is an incentive or a disincentive to invention.[17] Without even delving into the debate over whether Bell should have been given patent rights over an idea that was a derivative of other ideas, which he had yet to demonstrate and which required substantial input from others to become useful to the public, we can see that the Bell monopoly over the idea of the telephone was not a "natural" or inherent or self-evident right. It was a form of government largess, a subsidy. It was no less a subsidy than a grant of land to string telegraph cables or lay railroad tracks or provide a license to ferry passengers in a steamship. The question is whether all of us in society benefit when our representatives confer a right to one party as opposed to another (or, perhaps, as opposed to neither). The fact that the government provided a substantial benefit to Bell by granting him (and later the American Telephone and Telegraph [AT&T] holding company) a monopoly right is the main point.

Bell's first line of attack against potential telephone market competitors was to claim patent infringement, initiating over six thousand lawsuits. As a result of this subsidy, the Bell company had the telephone industry in the United States to itself for fourteen years, from 1880 to 1894. Patent claims, along with threatened or real litigation, would serve as a strategy to preserve the monopoly status of subsequent communications monopolies.

Ma Bell and the Independents

Expiration of key Bell patents in the early 1890s meant competition in the telephone industry, and, more important, it meant some entity would attend to providing service to most Americans. In the late 1800s the focus of telephone service was local, urban, and predominantly driven by business. Long-distance service was handled adequately by telegraph and postal service. By 1903, independents provided more service to more communities than Bell. Independents, for our purposes, were both small companies organized by individuals unaffiliated with Bell and so-called mutuals—farmer associations and small towns that established service in mainly rural areas ignored by the private companies.

With an eye on maintaining its advantage in the industry, Bell sponsored research into improvements into telephony. Their technological advantages and their head start in the communications industry, however, would not be sufficient to thwart competition. Like Western Union they would need both state and federal government support to establish a communications monopoly—and they would get it. State and federal regulation would arise initially as a form of support to the Bell monopoly. Later it would be introduced as a means of reform; this dual role of regulation reflected the dominant political shift from populist anger to scientific management as America struggled with what to do with its new industrial giants.

Like the other trusts and industrialists, Bell/AT&T became a vertically integrated company. Not only did it provide local and long-distance service, it conducted research, designed and built the system and all the equipment, and rented the phones customers would use. If a community was not served by AT&T, and AT&T wanted the market, it refused to connect with independents. Thus within a relatively small geographic area there could be several local telephone service providers, using different standards; some were connected to a long-distance network, others were not. Between 1898 and 1907, 57 percent of towns with populations over five thousand were served by non-interconnecting lines.[18]

But before 1894, many of these same towns received no service at all. In 1894, 80 commercial systems were built serving some 15,000 new phones. The next few years saw astounding growth in telephone service: 199 new systems were established in 1895, 207 in 1896. In 1902, Americans received telephone service from over 3,000 non-AT&T-affiliated telephone systems. The number of telephone customers increased 78 percent per year for the first dozen years of competition. In addition, AT&T prices decreased by 47.5 percent for businesses and 64.9 percent for those residential customers in competitive areas.[19] If the goal was simply more telephone service to more people at lower rates, market competition worked. So AT&T's desire to change the goal from expanding the number of customers who had service (what we think of today as universal service) to interconnection (what Vail meant by universal service) made sense, for AT&T. Bell, under the control of the robber baron J. P. Morgan by the early 1900s, asked for regulation at the state level. State legislators, Morgan and Vail thought, would be easier to control than the wily independent competitors.

Kenneth Lipartito argues that AT&T prevailed in its battle with independents in the South not because of its superior technology or its ability to offer long-distance service, but through adroit political maneuvering. AT&T established a strong influence over state legislators, offering not only money but free or reduced rate phone service. It drafted regulation (offered up, of course, by legislators) that set technological standards only AT&T could easily meet, forcing independents to use Bell-patented equipment and raise their costs to provide service. While these "upgrades" undoubtedly improved technical quality, consumers were given no choice as to whether they would prefer a lower cost to a better signal.[20]

When they did not get the local legislative support they sought, AT&T worked to eliminate the ability of local governments to franchise communications service providers. In Wisconsin, for example, they were able to close off the lucrative urban market of Milwaukee, thus limiting the ability of the independents to compete not only in Milwaukee, but in other nearby markets. Moreover, unable to rely on access to the relatively lucrative urban market, independents suffered an inability to acquire capital in financial markets. The independents were played like an overmatched chess opponent. All this was in keeping with the dominant tactics of the day, justified of course by the current popular ideology.

The tactics of market control differed slightly from industry to industry, but the object of eliminating competition through takeover or a marginalized dependence remained fairly constant. Western Union was taken over by financier Jay Gould by purchasing railroads and building up their telegraph subsidiaries to undercut Western Union's market. When Western Union's stock fell, he negotiated to sell his telegraph company to Western Union at an inflated price. He did this in 1877 and once again in 1881. In 1881, as Western Union's stock fell he not only sold his challenging telegraph company, American Union Telegraph, he purchased a controlling share of Western Union. Under Gould's control Western Union bought out its two main rivals and solidified its control over wire service through the remainder of the century.[21] But a single-minded focus on the ruthless capitalists of this era would be misleading if it did not include an appreciation for the federal support of these actions through helpful legislation, direct financial subsidies, and court decisions.[22]

The concentration of wealth resulting from federal subsidies was dramatic. As Kevin Phillips writes: "One analysis in 1890 argued that more than half of the wealth was held by just 1 percent of U.S. families, up from about 29 percent in 1860."[23] This explosive change in equality and government acquiescence, if not obedience, to one faction required a justification that would supersede Lincoln's articulation of a government of the people, by the people, and for the people. It required an adjustment to the founders' notions of a republic based on liberty, equality, and balancing faction. That justification would come dressed up as science.

Spencer and the Laissez-Faire Myth

Laissez-faire, to let the people do as they choose, is a doctrine derived from the seventeenth-century contest between European merchants and the feudal aristocracy. As Walter Lippmann wrote, "It was propounded when men found it necessary to destroy the entrenched ideas of vested interests which opposed the industrial revolution."[24] The idea of laissez-faire was confused with a public policy promoting a lawless operation of markets. No such public policy ever existed, no such market ever existed. A public policy of lawlessness is self-contradictory. The issue is not whether there is a law, or whether there is regulation, but who benefits from the regulation.[25] Laissez-faire in the United States became the rationale for the private interests of merchants to overrule the interests of the public as a whole. The currency of laissez-faire does not derive from Adam Smith, who, as discussed above, clearly delineated between the operation of markets and the operation of nations, between the transaction of goods and transactions between peoples. The still remaining vitality of laissez-faire comes from the ability of people in power to promote their private interest and disguise it as the public interest.

Lippmann, writing in the mid-1930s, argued that for sixty years, "the learned men" have not been "the defenders of established property using their learning to glorify the dominant businessmen." Indeed, "the influential thinkers of the western world have been deeply critical of the existing social order." However, a group he calls "latter-day liberals" became "the apologists for miseries and injustices that were intolerable to the conscience." Moreover, he writes: "Since 1870 the United States Supreme Court has been a rather consistent exponent of latter-day liberalism."[26] Who were these latter-day liberals?

It would not be until the 1860s that Herbert Spencer's writings would be sold in the United States. Between 1860 and 1903, 368,755 books spreading Spencer's "scientific" economic theories would circulate in the United States, thanks in no small measure to the efforts of Andrew Carnegie. Arising from the pastime of Victorian English gentlemen (the observation and collection of birds and insects) and culminating in the "natural selection" theory of evolution advanced by Alfred Russel Wallace and Charles Darwin, it was not a difficult stretch to apply this "science" to the social condition of man. Darwin's science served to buttress many crackpot notions advanced around this time, including the inferiority of women and most notoriously eugenics. Thankfully most of this "scientific" sexism and racism has been banished from the public sphere, but Spencer's laissez-faire economic theories survive and prosper today. As Richard Hofstadter has written: "Spencer's philosophy was admirably suited to the American scene. It was scientific in derivation and comprehensive in scope. It had a reassuring theory of progress based upon biology and physics. It was large enough to be all things to all men, broad enough to satisfy agnostics like Robert Ingersoll and theists like Fiske and Beecher. It offered a comprehensive world-view, united under one generalization everything in nature from protozoa to politics . . . Moreover it was not a technical creed for professionals. Presented in language that tyros in philosophy could understand, it made Spencer the metaphysician of the homemade intellectual, and the prophet of the cracker-barrel agnostic."[27]

While Darwin emphasized natural selection in an evolutionary process and the diversity resulting from distinct habitats, Spencer focused on the "survival of the fittest." Poverty and distress, claimed Spencer, was the natural outcome of weakness, and the opulence of the dominating industrialists is the decree of a "farseeing benevolence"; the strong are meant to prosper, the poor (undeserving or not) are meant to fall away. According to Spencer, government exists solely to protect this fundamental equilibrium, and the state is justified in removing all artificial barriers to this natural law.[28]

Perhaps the best-known American interpreter of the Englishman Spencer was William Graham Sumner, by 1872 a professor of political and social science at Yale. Sumner directly attacked the founders' romantic ideas about liberty and equality and self-government. Liberty was not an inalienable, natural right of man; "those who have the resources of civilization at their command are the only ones who are free," he wrote.[29] As for equality, Sumner dismissed efforts toward a classless society as "survival of the unfittest." Wealthy industrialists, taught Sumner, were "naturally selected agents of society . . . they get high wages and live in luxury, but the bargain is a good one for society."[30] Self-government, he argued, cannot be established by political machinery: indeed, "the more machinery we have the greater the danger to self-government."[31] Needless to say, Spencer and Sumner's "science" was warmly embraced by the then emerging and ruthless class of über-industrialists of the late 1800s—none more effectively so than Andrew Carnegie.

Known now for his philanthropy and libraries, Carnegie was a ruthless industrial competitor who, through savvy and violence (Carnegie and his second-in-command, Henry Frick, pit a private army against the Homestead strikers in 1892, defeating the Amalgamated Iron, Steel and Tin Workers' call for an eight-hour day), built a personal fortune of over $400 million by the time of his death in 1910, outstripped only by oil titan John D. Rockefeller. In his 1889 essay, titled "Wealth," Carnegie viewed great inequality as the necessary result of "the law of competition . . . ensuring the survival of the fittest in every department."[32] However, as we will see, the captains of industry were not blind to the importance of controlling government to ensure the enactment of policies, to bend the law of competition in their favor.

While businessmen promoted the notion that their success was the natural result of free competitive markets, they worked feverishly to eliminate any trace of competition or free markets. Competition was, in fact, a "curse" to be solved. In 1882, Samuel Dodd of Standard Oil found a solution: the trust. Under the watchful eye of John D. Rockefeller, all Standard Oil properties were placed in the hands of a board of trustees. Stockholders received twenty trust certificates for each share of Standard Oil stock and all the profits of the subsidiary companies were sent to the board, which determined the dividends. The trustees also elected the directors and officers of all the subsidiaries. This allowed the Standard Oil Trust to function as a monopoly. Standard Oil also pioneered the holding company, which had the same effect as a trust. The aim was to control price competition through cooperation and coordination of rival businesses, some of which were merely subsidiaries of the same company.[33] Following Rockefeller's example, there were soon railroad trusts and steel trusts and shipping trusts and sugar trusts. By 1893, the Bell patents and subsidiaries would be grouped in a similar trust, a holding company called American Telephone and Telegraph.[34]

The fact that government was not hands off ("laissez-faire"), but very engaged in supporting the interests of the telephone trust was not lost on the independents. As Kevin Phillips writes, government action on behalf of business was so emphatic "by courts, monetary authorities, the military and quasi-military private police, and state legislatures captured by corporations to send millionaire business stalwarts to the U.S. Senate—that any description of laissez-faire might be better replaced by a variation on the unofficial motto of the Mardi Gras: "*laissez les bons temps rouler*"—Let the good times roll![35]

The hold of Spencer's ideas on the practice of public policy in America was clearly evident when Justice Holmes dissented: "The Fourteenth Amendment does not enact Mr. Herbert Spencer's Social Statics . . . a constitution is not intended to embody a particular economic theory." But again, this was a dissent. In 1905, in *Lochner v. New York*,[36] the Supreme Court struck down a New York law that limited the hours a bakery employee could work under the theory that the state law was a violation of due process as an abridgement of the "liberty to contract." They could have been writing from a script written by Carnegie, Sumner, or Spencer.

In the meantime farmers were in a downward spiral. Perhaps their first concern was the effect of a market economy heavily dependent upon what was little more than gambling. Especially troubling were grain speculators; the rise of agricultural futures markets helped to force down the price of farm products even as inflation rose and money, tied to a gold standard, was kept in short supply. As the segment most affected by unstable banks and a rapid succession of economic depressions, farmers felt increasingly helpless in the face of large financial forces beyond their control, and they turned their wrath on "The Trusts." Trusts symbolized the size and power and hidden nature of big business in America; only government action, it was argued, could curb this power. In response to the farmers' demands, both the Democrat and the Republican political parties put antitrust planks into their presidential platforms in 1888. In 1890, the Sherman Anti-Trust Act was passed by a 51–1 vote in the Senate and by a unanimous vote of 242–0 by the House of Representatives. The bill was signed into law by President Benjamin Harrison.

The Sherman Anti-Trust Act, based on the constitutional power of Congress to regulate interstate commerce, declared: "Every contract, combination in the form of trust or otherwise, or conspiracy, in restraint of trade or commerce among the several States, or with foreign nations, is declared to be illegal. Every person who shall make any contract or engage in any combination or conspiracy hereby declared to be illegal shall be deemed guilty of a felony."[37]

The trusts had little to fear. They controlled the state legislatures. The state legislatures picked U.S. senators. The U.S. Senate approved Supreme Court justices. Supreme Court justices determined what the law meant. Industrialists watched happily as the Sherman Anti-Trust Act was used primarily to block strikes and other union activity. Turning the act on its head, the courts agreed that labor unions were a "conspiracy to restrict trade"; thus industrialists were aided by strikebreaking state and federal militia. By 1895, the Supreme Court would rule that many forms of business combination did not constitute "trusts" that restrained interstate trade, and thus could not be prosecuted under federal law.[38]

William Jennings Bryan: Populist

While Republicans were clearly the party of the northern industrial interests, the backroom leaders of the Democratic Party did not advance any concern other than the continuation of patronage politics. Despite Grover Cleveland's reputation as a reformer, he did little in either his first or second administration (interrupted by a defeat to Republican Benjamin Harrison) to jangle the nerves of "capital" or advance the competing interests of farmers or others. His First Inaugural Address was not only vague but careful to calm the fears of Morgan and others. "A due regard for the interests and prosperity of all the people demands that our finances shall be established upon such a sound and sensible basis as shall secure the safety and confidence of business interests and make the wage of labor sure and steady, and that our system of revenue shall be so adjusted as to relieve the people of unnecessary taxation, having a due regard to the interests of capital invested and workingmen employed in American industries, and preventing the accumulation of a surplus in the Treasury to tempt extravagance and waste."[39]

Democratic Party bosses were no less vulnerable to the corrupting power of the wealthy industrialists than were the Republicans, Tammany Hall in New York being only the most famous example of this corruption. While the Democrats spoke of reform on the campaign trail, the Republicans spread rumors about Cleveland's love life.

> Ma, ma, where's my Pa?
> Gone to the White House, ha ha ha!

Cleveland did push some civil service reform, most relevant to our discussion, an 1887 executive order prohibiting the use of postal appointments for raising campaign funds and other political activity. The order was largely ignored.[40] Cleveland also signed legislation establishing the Interstate Commerce Commission, which was promoted as a means to regulate the monopoly railroads. As Howard Zinn writes, railroad attorney Richard Olney (and at one point Cleveland's attorney general) explained: "The Commission . . . is or can be made, of great use to the railroads. It satisfies the popular clamor for a government supervision of railroads, at the same time that the supervision is almost entirely nominal. . . . The part of wisdom is not to destroy the Commission but to utilize it."[41]

The backroom bosses in both parties were strongly in charge of picking their leaders and making certain they did not block the coffers—until, that is, the boy orator from the Plains, William Jennings Bryan. If Carnegie articulated a rationale for a growing aristocracy of ruthless capitalists, Bryan spoke to the angry independent farmers and ranchers in the South and West. Bryan's political philosophy was a direct descendent of Democrats Jefferson and Jackson. But as was true of Jackson, Bryan was the articulate beneficiary of a wave of agrarian anger clearly evident by 1890.

From 1896 to 1913, Bryan was the leader of agrarian forces struggling to hold their place against the rising tide of industrialism. If America was still largely a place of economically independent citizens, Bryan was their man. Bryan's strength was his ability to articulate in sometimes coarse, and sometimes in highly religious language, complex policy proposals and bridge support for them from the South and the West. For thirty years, beginning around 1865, farmers watched the dollar gain in value while the price of their crops or livestock remained steady or shrunk in value. Bryan's answer to these woes was to add silver, along with gold, to the monetary standard. The "free silver" campaign united miners in the West with southern agricultural interests. Others were simply enthralled to hear Bryan.

Some regard his "The Cross of Gold" address before the Democratic Convention of 1896 to be one of the greatest speeches in American history. It prompted an hour of cheering and demonstrations, and is said to have earned Bryan the nomination, pushing the party bosses aside. While a good portion of "The Cross of Gold" was given over to a defense of a bimetallic monetary policy, the heart of it was much broader. "There are two ideas of government. There are those who believe that, if you will only legislate to make the well-to-do prosperous, their prosperity will leak through on those below. The Democratic idea, however, has been that if you legislate to make the masses prosperous, their prosperity will find its way up through every class which rests upon them. You come to us and tell us that the great cities are in favor of the gold standard; we reply that the great cities rest upon our broad and fertile prairies. Burn down your cities and leave our farms, and your cities will spring up again as if by magic; but destroy our farms and the grass will grow in the streets of every city in the country."[42]

Despite being joined by the Populist and National Silver parties, along with Silver Republicans, Bryan's Democrats lost to Republican William McKinley. As popular as Bryan was in the South and West, he was feared in the North, especially among the industrialist class, and perhaps by those who worked for them. In addition, McKinley, with the support of Ohio political boss Mark Hanna, raised $3 to $4 million in campaign contributions. John D. Rockefeller, Cornelius Vanderbilt, J. Pierpont Morgan, and Andrew Carnegie were reportedly his largest patrons. Bryan ended his campaign in debt after raising at most $600,000. McKinley's 7–1 funding advantage meant more money to purchase buttons and flyers and, as was quite common at the time, beer, employer intimidation of workers, police intimidation at the polls, and, of course, votes.[43]

Bryan and the Democrats were generally encouraged by his showing against the powerful Republican machine. Bryan would run again, and lose again, in 1900 and 1908. In addition to a bimetal monetary policy, Bryan also called for tariff reform, control of the trusts, an income tax, direct elections of the Senate, government rather than private issuance of money, and a new group of Supreme Court justices less tied to business interests. All of Bryan's positions, that is, all of these Democratic Party positions, were later embraced by Progressives, who were able to take the industrialists on with only a little more success.

* * *

The interlocking relations between corporations such as AT&T, financial institutions represented by J. P. Morgan, and the various communications industries were really no different than the interlocking relations that characterized American big business from steel to oil. Vertical integration, labor disputes, antitrust activity, bribery of local and federal officials, and the steady accumulation of wealth dominated public affairs in the Gilded Age. Morgan, who would take control over AT&T, and Gould, who had taken over Western Union by 1881, were no different than Carnegie or Rockefeller. In sum, American communication was dominated by the faction Lincoln called "capital" and the founders called "merchants."[44] The balance of interest against interest, the equal political communication of citizens, the liberty to have a real voice in government—the pillars of our republic were under siege.

As movie theaters and radio would not come until the twentieth century, newspapers were the mass media of the day. Despite the development of large regional or national chains, rural newspapers and independent magazines at the turn of the century still found ways to be fiercely competitive. This competition led to an increase in sensationalism as the dailies competed to print the most outrageous stories, true or not, and focus on the most shocking characters in public life. Few characters caught the attention of the newspapers, and thus the public, as did a young New York aristocrat turned cowboy, Theodore Roosevelt. But Roosevelt, and the political philosophy he would embrace, would wait until the new millennium.

As Henry Adams wrote in the first few years of the twentieth century: "The Trusts and Corporations stood for the larger part of the new power that had been created since 1840, and were obnoxious because of their vigorous and unscrupulous energy. They were revolutionary, troubling all the old conventions and values, as the screws of ocean steamers must trouble a school of herring. They tore society to pieces and trampled it under foot. The public had no idea what practical system it could aim at, or what sort of men could manage it. The single problem before it was not so much to control the Trusts as to create the society that could manage the Trusts."[45]

Adams watched the new century and felt Gibbon's despair at the fall of Rome. The ideals, indeed the democracy of his grandfather and Jefferson and Madison and even Lincoln, seemed to have been swept away by forces too powerful to resist. The brutal public philosophy of the day, the philosophy of Spencer and Carnegie did not reflect a society that could manage the trusts, but a society managed by the trusts. In the 25 years between the Civil War and 1890, 26 industrial mergers had been announced; in the next 7 years there were 156. Between 1897 and 1903 alone, over 300 industry consolidations took place, engulfing an estimated 40 percent of the U.S. industrial output. These vast consolidations were vertically integrated with interlocking boards, often resulting in the control over an entire industry by a handful of individuals.[46] This handful of individuals dominated not only steel and steam, but political communication, once managed under the federal postal system, was now firmly in their hands. This state of affairs survived, though challenged, through the Roaring Twenties, until the corruption, boom, and bust realities it imposed resulted in the political upheaval caused by the Great Depression. From this cauldron came radio.

5

From Roosevelt to Roosevelt:
Wireless and Radio (1900–1934)

We gird up our loins as a nation with the stern purpose to
play our part manfully in winning the ultimate triumph, and
therefore we turn scornfully aside from the paths of mere
ease and idleness, and with unfaltering steps tread the
rough road of endeavor, smiting down the wrong and
battling for the right.

—Theodore Roosevelt, September 3, 1901

American Empire and the Wireless

THE RISE OF AMERICAN IMPERIALISM

In the late summer of 1899, Guglielmo Marconi left England after a series of successful demonstrations of a system he developed to transmit telegraph signals without wires. Fitting a steamer with a seventy-five-foot antenna and then sending to the *Dublin Daily Express* a minute-by-minute account of the Kingstown Regatta, Marconi's device allowed readers to learn the progress of the race before the ships were back at port. Learning of this, the *New York Herald* invited Marconi to report on the America's Cup Race in October of that year.

For centuries men have known sea travel, even a few miles out, as a voyage into silence. Flags and light signals were a sailor's tools to communicate, and if a ship went far enough those visual signals would fail. Marconi saw wireless telegraphy, not as a novelty to sell newspapers, but as a way to solve the age-old problem of communication at sea, a problem of both commercial and military importance. At the turn of the century England launched the most impressive navy and commercial fleet in the world, and it was the

British who first understood the value of Marconi's work. In 1899, Britain began installing Marconi's wireless on three of its ships. While the military and commercial applications of Marconi's device were evident, the dramatic impact wireless would have on civic discourse was certainly not.

Upon arrival in New York City on September 11, Marconi witnessed the preparations for a hero's welcome in honor of Rear Admiral George Dewey. In just seven hours of battle, ships under Dewey's command destroyed Spain's Asiatic Squadron. While hundreds of Spanish sailors lost their lives, there was not one American casualty. It was, perhaps, this victory that made the newfound dreams of American imperialism look so easy to realize. Perhaps the new American appetite for empire was what really brought Marconi to New York, just as America was rounding the corner to the twentieth century.

The Spanish American War of 1898 marked a turning point in American history. Within a few months of the war's end, the United States was a world power, exercising control or influence over islands in the Caribbean Sea, the mid-Pacific Ocean, and close to the Asian mainland. As Charles Conant wrote at the time: "Almost as if by magic, the importance of naval power as the advance agent of commercial supremacy has flashed upon the mind of the country. The irresistible tendency to expansion, which leads the growing tree to burst every barrier, which drove the Goths, the Vandals, and finally our Saxon ancestors in successive and irresistible waves over the decadent provinces of Rome, seems again in operation, demanding new outlets for American capital and new opportunities for American enterprise. The new movement is not a matter of sentiment. It is the result of a natural law of economic and race development."[1]

The first few decades of the new century would find the American republic wrestling unsuccessfully with a combined set of interests, called trusts, a faction powerful enough to fundamentally alter the very pillars upon which the government was founded. The challenges facing the nation in 1900 would seem to dwarf even the challenges facing the founders or Lincoln. Capitalism, particularly monopoly capitalism and its engine of avarice, had begun to obscure the dream of a republic of engaged independent citizens. This "spirit" of capitalism had grabbed control over the telegraph and the telephone and was now taking firm control over the newspaper industry. All this, at the very moment a new medium was being developed. This chapter tells that story, and the story of the leaders who would struggle and fail to find room for both an overgrown capitalism and the republic the founders intended.

THE NEWSPAPER WAR

The battle with Spain over Cuba and the Philippines has been called "The Newspaper War" because of the role played by a sensationalist press, particularly those papers published by Joseph Pulitzer and William Randolph Hearst, in drumming up public frenzy. The tactics used by these journalists are at least as much of a tradition of that profession as the so-called muckrakers who would come along in another half-dozen years. Perhaps the most famous story of the time was reported about the famous illustrator, Frederick Remington. Remington was sent to Cuba by Hearst, and when he reported back that there really wasn't much happening, Hearst supposedly cabled back: "You provide the pictures. I'll provide the war." Much like Hearst's reporting of Spain's atrocities in Cuba, the Remington story is an apparent fabrication.[2]

If it is an exaggeration to say Hearst's *Journal* and Pulitzer's *World* caused the Spanish American War, it is not an exaggeration to say they fanned the flames of a war both the McKinley administration and Spain sought to avoid. The story of the "newspaper war" is a story of both the power of a new, more aggressively commercial journalism and a rising American imperialism led by Theodore Roosevelt.

An unsuccessful ten-year struggle in Cuba for independence from Spanish rule began in 1868; there was a second unsuccessful revolt in 1895. Cuban rebels were put in concentration camps and their plight was a source of dramatic, sometimes fictitious human suffering. Hearst found out about the Cuban rebels, quickly dubbed them "freedom fighters," and sent reporters to Cuba to cover the story. Far away from any action, reporters and artists wrote and pictured the expanding story from the comfortable quarters of Havana's luxurious Inglaterra Hotel, fed by the lurid propaganda of Cuban rebel leaders. Pulitzer initially opposed U.S. involvement in Cuba, but he would admit years later that the opportunity for increased circulation caused him to change direction. "Feeding Prisoners to Sharks," blared the *Journal.* "Old men and little boys were cut down and their bodies fed to the dogs," answered the *World.*[3]

On February 15, 1898, an American battleship, the U.S.S. *Maine,* sent to monitor the newspaper story, exploded in Havana harbor. Despite no clear evidence that Spain was at fault, the Hearst *New York Journal and Advertiser* trumpeted the headline: "DESTRUCTION OF THE WAR SHIP MAINE WAS THE WORK OF AN ENEMY," and just below, "Assistant Secretary Roosevelt Convinced the Explosion of the War Ship Was Not an Accident." Pulitzer's *World* was less certain, and featured President William

McKinley's opinion that the explosion must have been an accident. Soon the *World* would claim, falsely, to have found evidence of a mine under the *Maine*, and would write: "The army is ready. The navy is ready. The people are ready. And now the President says 'Wait!'—'Wait' for what?" "Remember the *Maine*" became a popular battle cry.

Reluctantly, President McKinley pressed Spain to abandon its policy of imprisoning rebel leaders. Spain agreed. The calls for war continued. McKinley then demanded that Spain declare an armistice. Spain agreed again. But the calls for war spread from the Hearst and Pulitzer papers through the Associated Press (AP) and on to scores of papers across the country. Citizens were in a fever pitch for war, and their representatives responded. The Senate passed a war resolution on April 19, and war was declared. Somehow the war involved not only Cuba but also Spain's colonial possessions in the Pacific—the Philippines and Guam. And it seemed over in less than four months. Cuba was brought under U.S. influence, but not annexed. Puerto Rico was taken over by the U.S. military. A treaty with Spain was reached, $20 million was paid, and the United States was the proud owner of Guam, the Philippines, and Puerto Rico by December 1898. While the fight to control the Philippines would last several years at the cost of hundreds of thousands of lives,[4] at least Pulitzer's *World* circulation climbed from 600,000 to 800,000 and Hearst's *Journal* from 500,000 to 700,000.

The fierce competition between Hearst and Pulitzer reflected the ethos of the day: profit at any cost. The drive to increase circulation and obtain more advertising revenue transformed the newspaper industry. It is true that the foundations for a commercial press began in the 1830s with the "penny press" of Benjamin Day and James Gordon Bennett. But, as stated earlier, Tocqueville accurately gauged both the abundance of American newspapers and their lack of influence. There were two major differences between the early days of the "penny press" and the era of "yellow journalism": the migration of Americans from isolated rural to concentrated urban communities, and the AP–Western Union combination. The concentration of millions of readers in New York combined with the monopoly power of the AP to create a level of influence never seen by Day or Bennett.

Just as Day's *Sun* and Bennett's *Herald* geared their papers and their editorial policies to entice the majority of readers, "the common man," the papers of Pulitzer and Hearst would follow suit. The yellow journalists covered politics as entertainment, but the real subject matter was crime and sex-related scandals (even if the stories were fiction) pumped up by illustrations, and the real goal was to increase circulation.[5] But Pulitzer and

Hearst were of a different order altogether, because of the hyper-capitalism of the turn of century. It would be a mistake to disconnect editorial positions from the business goals of increasing circulation to increase advertising rates. We have every reason to believe that Hearst and Pulitzer were as sincere in their concern for the common man as they were about the need for war with Spain. Hearst and Pulitzer, despite their convenient "liberal" politics, were charter members of corporate America.

TEDDY AND THE RISE OF THE MILITARY

Martial glory was very much connected to international commercial expansion. Having consolidated interests in the U.S. market, it was past time for American capitalists to join the world stage and project the power to capture, and demonstrate the ability to protect, both foreign markets and foreign goods. No one would do more to make this come true than the young Assistant Secretary of the Navy Theodore Roosevelt. The parade Marconi no doubt witnessed may have been for Dewey, the hero of Manila, but Roosevelt, who resigned his position in the McKinley administration to become captain of the "Roosevelt Rough Riders," and quickly governor of New York, would take center stage. But who was Roosevelt, and what was his vision for America?

As Hofstadter describes: "What Roosevelt stood for, as a counterpoise to the fat materialism of the wealthy and the lurking menace of the masses, were the aggressive, masterful, fighting virtues of the soldier. . . . Despite his sincere loyalty to the democratic game, this herald of modern American militarism and imperialism displayed in his political character many qualities of recent authoritarianism—romantic nationalism, disdain for materialistic ends, worship of strength and the cult of personal leadership, the appeal to the intermediate elements of society, the ideal of standing above classes and class interests, a grandiose sense of destiny, even a touch of racism."[6]

The New Yorker Roosevelt identified strongly with Alexander Hamilton, and had a strongly negative view of Jefferson. Roosevelt thought his rival William Jennings Bryan and Jefferson quite similar. Contemplating Bryan's challenge to William McKinley, Roosevelt wrote to a friend: "If Bryan wins, we have before us some years of social misery, not markedly different from that of any South American republic. . . . Bryan closely resembles Thomas Jefferson, whose accession to the Presidency was a terrible blow to the nation."[7]

To help in Bryan's fall, New York police ensured that protesters without tickets got in Madison Square Garden where Bryan was scheduled to speak, while many of those with tickets were kept out. The police were called "Teddy's Recruits" because Roosevelt served as chairman of the Board of Police Commissioners. Bryan failed to live up to his reputation as a great orator before this hostile crowd.[8] Despite his popularity with the police officers, Roosevelt was unhappy and felt unappreciated as a dedicated civil service reformer of the New York City police. The Republican Party rewarded his service at Madison Square Garden with an appointment as assistant secretary of the navy. In this position Roosevelt led a group dedicated to U.S. imperialism, worked to build up the navy, and made certain Dewey was promoted and ready for war.[9]

As C. Wright Mills observed, America has been, in its short history, ambivalent about the military and the role of those Mills called the "warlords."[10] Having been subjugated by an occupying army, the United States would not have a standing army of any note until after World War II. The fear of a standing army was deeply embedded in the American psyche. For many of the founders it was a fear derived from an understanding of the classics (the collapse of the Roman Senate under Caesar), the fears of an American Cromwell (perhaps Alexander Hamilton? or Aaron Burr?), as well as the very real brutalities demonstrated by the British army in Massachusetts. Providing one example of this fear, Bernard Bailyn quotes a 1768 letter from pamphleteer Andrew Elliot to Thomas Hollis, even before the British red coats would arrive in Massachusetts: "To have a standing army! Good God! What can be worse to a people who have tasted the sweets of liberty?"[11]

Of all the powers given to Congress the raising of a standing army was the most feared by those who opposed the new Constitution. Gary Hart quotes Patrick Henry: "A standing army we shall also have, to execute the execrable commands of a tyranny."[12] At least temporarily, Alexander Hamilton's vision of a nation driven by commerce, engaged in international markets, and backed by a standing army would lose to Madison's determination to avoid international intrigue and to balance the interests of a market-oriented faction against the interests of an agrarian faction. Thus the U.S. Constitution was written to prevent any easy engagement in military action, and, of course, the civilian head of government, the president, was given power over all armed forces. While the concerns of that faction Lincoln called capital were not entirely missing from Jackson's brutal war on Native Americans or the Mexican War, those actions were largely driven by agrarian desires for the settlement of white freemen. The nation would rely upon state militias and volunteer forces to respond to real threats, an arrangement ill-suited to advancing global commercial interests.

Despite the hysteria of rape and colonial brutality faced by the Cubans under Spain, and the racist nonsense of America shouldering the White Man's Burden to civilize the darkies of the world, the action in Cuba and Manila was an international show of force. Roosevelt understood Hamilton to be in favor of a standing army and navy because military might was imperative to protect and advance U.S. commercial interests abroad.[13] Roosevelt's ascension marked the final rise of U.S. capital and the beginnings of its partnership with the military. If it was not a triumph of Hamilton, it was certainly a defeat of Madison.

The experience of the four-month belligerence we call the Spanish American War (forgetting the war against the Filipinos that lasted several years) helped to focus America's need for a modern means of military communication. The first real history of U.S. wireless communications is *History of Communications-Electronics in the United States Navy*. That history suggests that while communications within Dewey's squadrons had been one source of its swift victory, communication between the navy and the army was inadequate. Communication between the armed forces and command in Washington was worse. To inform Washington of his actions, including his victory at Manila Bay, Dewey sent messages via boat to Hong Kong, which were telegraphed across the Eurasian continent and the Atlantic Ocean via British-controlled cable[14]—hardly the position a newly emerging world power, now heady with nationalist pride, wanted to be in.

Marconi was correct in foreseeing a new market in America. But his company would bring two crippling flaws with respect to the U.S. military. Like the telegraph and telephone companies in the United States, Marconi proposed to sell not communicating equipment but the service of communication. At either end of the communication link (ship to ship or ship to shore) the Marconi company would install equipment, furnish an operator, and deliver the communication. Recognizing the difficulty in providing this service to the U.S. Navy, Marconi proposed only equipping naval vessels but with the proviso that they communicate only with Marconi shore operations, except, of course, in emergencies. The fact that the United States was flush with a jingoistic nationalism certainly did not help an Italian in charge of a British company. In short, the proud club of Americans who controlled the U.S. Navy was outraged that a British "monopoly" would attempt to control wireless. As a result the U.S. government began to fund other experimenters to develop wireless equipment it could use instead of Marconi.[15] This logic would have other important repercussions later. But the biggest challenge Roosevelt would face, the challenge of the century just past, would be far more formidable than defeating Spain.

THE BULLY PULPIT VERSUS THE TRUSTS

While some would mistake him for a reforming Progressive, Roosevelt was at heart, and by birthright, a Republican patrician, more inclined toward maintaining order than promoting change on behalf of the poor. In the New York legislature Roosevelt decried "demagogic measures . . . continually brought forward in the interests of the laboring classes." Among the reforms Roosevelt helped to block was one that would have required the cities of New York State to pay their employees not less than $2.00 a day.[16]

His service as a police commissioner brought Roosevelt headlines when he declared his readiness to kill labor strikers and protesters. "We shall guard as zealously the rights of the striker as those of the employer. But when riot is menaced it is different. The mob takes its own chance. Order will be kept at whatever cost. If it comes to shooting we shall shoot to hit. No blank cartridges or firing over the heads of anybody."[17] He also garnered national press for his reforms, including "midnight rambles" in search of policemen not at their posts and requiring all police officers to report for target practice.

While Roosevelt was hardly a friend to labor, he did believe in good government reform. As governor of New York, he called for legislation that would tax corporations on the public franchises they controlled. Through deft maneuvering he was able to move this and other incremental reform legislation, cutting links between corporate power and the political machines they funded. As a result, the Republican boss, Senator Thomas Platt, was happy to see the young governor out of his state.[18]

So Roosevelt, a little reluctantly, was nominated vice-president in the McKinley administration. The vice-presidency seemed to the Republican bosses a safe enough post for the upper-class Rough Rider. Only McKinley's chief fundraiser, Democratic Party Chairman and Ohio Senator Mark Hanna, would protest: "Don't any of you realize that there's only one life between this madman and the Presidency?" It would take six months for Hanna's worst nightmare to come true.

President McKinley was assassinated on September 6, 1901. No doubt it was mere coincidence that Hearst's *Journal* had suggested the idea of assassination in an anti-McKinley editorial a few months before. As George Gordon writes, "The coincidence may have been too much for the public to stomach,"[19] and the advertising revenue for the *Journal* and the other yellow journalists fell briefly. But the nation would have a new leader.

Though promising to follow in McKinley's path, Roosevelt would, in small measure, carry out part of the platform advocated earlier by Bryan, but with a slightly different focus. Roosevelt thought that the agrarian Populists and the Democrats who courted them had to begin to accept the fact that America had moved on, that it was no longer the small agricultural utopia of the founders. America was a dynamic new global colossus with colossal industry at its core. "The captains of industry who have driven the railway systems across the continent, who have built up our commerce, who have developed our manufactures, have on the whole done great good to our people." And yet, "Great corporations exist only because they are created and safeguarded by our institutions; and it is therefore our right and duty to see that they work in harmony with these institutions."[20]

Like Spencer, Roosevelt believed that big business was "the result of an imperative economic law." Unlike Spencer, Roosevelt argued that the way to address business consolidation was to "meet it by a corresponding increase in government power over big business." The solution is "not in attempting to prevent such combinations, but in completely controlling them in the interest of the public welfare."[21] Needless to say, this was a break from the party leaders—and the businessmen they served. Still, legislation to "completely control" the industrialists had little chance of getting through the U.S. Senate.

THE MUCKRAKERS

Despite the odds, voices gathered to challenge the conservative Senate and the bosses. In town halls and taverns citizens learned about the battles between labor and capital; public speakers, such as Mark Twain, commanded the attention of great audiences while they joked and decried the increasing concentration of power and the purchase of politicians. What of the so-called Fourth Estate—the newspapers? With the exception of the unpredictable Hearst and Pulitzer, big business, and the advertising industry that distributed their dollars to the papers, exerted tremendous power to keep the relationship between the trusts and politicians silent.

Will Irwin, who investigated the connections between newspapers, big business, and the party machines for *Collier's* in 1911, reported that while the Chicago papers described the "white slave traffic," they passed over the department store, a prominent and reliable source of advertising dollars, that paid such low wages the female employees worked in brothels to support themselves. While the press liked to paint brave pictures of themselves, they somehow avoided telling how liquor and beer brewers pressured them into opposing prohibition, how Standard Oil seemed to always get good notices, and how a bubonic plague outbreak was hushed up in San Francisco. "Upstairs," Irwin explained, "journalists, willing to risk life itself that they may 'get the story,' to hazard friendship and personal esteem that they may attack special privilege and vested injustice—for such is the spirit and custom of the craft. Downstairs—usually—a publisher frightened at the loss of a hundred dollars of advertising."[22]

While Hearst and Pulitzer commanded truly mass audiences with their newspaper combinations and AP affiliations, they were the exceptions, not the rule. Most papers were local, wary of the influence of and competition from big city papers like the *World* and the *Journal,* and very dependent upon local business advertisements. Most other urban papers divided up the market according to ethnicity (Irish, Italian, German, Jewish) and partisan ideology; some, like the *New York Sun,* were clearly little more than press outlets for power brokers such as the telephone, steel, railroad and banking magnate J. P. Morgan.

Aided by still subsidized postal service rates, an increase in population, an ability to reach a more disbursed audience by rail, and an increased interest among overproducing corporations to market their goods to a national market, the national mass-circulation magazine was ready to initiate, if not establish, the existence of a mass public.[23] Unlike either Hearst or Pulitzer, whose papers would also mix in with their hyperbolic scandals serious investigations of minor municipal and even corporate corruption, the magazines were a different order altogether. The magazines would reassert the power of media to promote what some of us like to think the founders had in mind: the power of reason over might.

Though heavily dependent upon corporate advertisers, magazines like *Collier's* and *McClure's* were closer in spirit to Tom Paine and John Peter Zenger than they were to their contemporary yellow journalism brethren. "Capitalists, workingmen, politicians, citizens—all breaking the law, or letting it be broken. Who is left to uphold it? . . . There is no one left; none but all of us," thundered Samuel Sidney McClure, editor of *McClure's Magazine.*[24] How it must have annoyed Morgan that his railroad, in partnership with the post, was the key to a newborn feature in journalism, the in-depth investigative magazine journalist.

While women were given small space in newspapers, to report on "society" events and soft-feature stories, the magazines soon saw an opportunity to reach a national audience, perhaps largely comprised of women readers, by hiring women writers. In 1894, McClure broke this mold and hired Ida M.

Tarbell. Tarbell was given a long-term contract and paid to spend time in a detailed and complex investigation. This was not the practice of either Pulitzer or Hearst. Unlike the reporters in those papers, Tarbell's audience was national. Between 1902 and 1907, McClure published fifteen investigative articles by Tarbell. In his autobiography he estimated the cost at $4,000 each, and Tarbell earned every penny. She meticulously documented the complicated rise of John D. Rockefeller's monopolistic Standard Oil Company and its unfair anticompetitive business practices. Not even the Republicans could avoid the concern raised over Tarbell's evidence.[25] Moreover, Tarbell was not alone; the magazines spawned a range of investigative journalists, including Lincoln Steffens, David Graham Phillips, and Upton Sinclair, who exposed food adulteration, unscrupulous insurance practices, fraudulent claims for patent medicines, and links between government and vice.

Roosevelt would read the investigative pieces and, in a speech in 1906, expressed agreement with many of the charges of the journalists, but, he argued, some of their methods were sensational and irresponsible. Roosevelt, actually referring to a series in a Hearst paper, compared investigative journalists to a character from Bunyan's *Pilgrim's Progress* who could look no way but downward with a muckrake in his hands and was interested only in raking the filth. According to Tarbell, "Theodore Roosevelt . . . had become uneasy at the effect on the public of the periodical press's increasing criticisms and investigations of business and political abuses."[26]

Despite his uneasiness, Roosevelt and other politicians felt the public's outraged response to the muckrakers' mountain of facts and exposed amorality of the trusts and the political bosses. Legislation would follow: the Pure Food and Drug Act (1906), the Meat Inspection Act (1906), and the Hepburn Act (1906) that strengthened the Interstate Commerce Commission were all attributable to the muckrakers.

The muckrakers were an exception to the rule of the seduction of journalism by the powerful. Their time would not last. The most famous muckrakers believed that financial and business interests, by denying loans and by taking control (through outright purchase or taking over the board of directors), destroyed the leading Progressive magazines. Advertisers became more selective about what sort of environment they wanted their product to appear in, and only publishing trusts such as Hearst's had the sustaining capital to continue. By the 1920s even *McClure's*, purchased by the Crowell Publishing Company in 1911, looked much like the other national magazines filled with what Sinclair would deride as "slush for the women" and hysteria regarding immigration and the "reds."[27] The feisty

S. S. McClure ended his days in poverty, frustrated with what had become of progressive reform.[28]

The decline of the muckrakers is well documented and explained by perhaps the most famous of the group, Upton Sinclair. In a too-long-overlooked book, *The Brass Check* (self-published in 1919), Sinclair demonstrates the deep connections between the press and the trusts: "The methods by which the 'Empire of Business' maintains its control over Journalism are four: First, ownership of the papers; second, ownership of the owners; third, advertising subsidies; and fourth, direct bribery. By these methods there exists in America a control of news and of current comment more absolute than any monopoly in any other industry."[29]

This takeover of mass media by the "Empire of Business," completed with the methodical destruction of the investigative magazines, would not be relinquished, not during the so-called Progressive Era, and not after. As for Roosevelt, while he was given credit as a "trust buster," his main value was his ability to draw newspaper attention to the evils the magazine writers were describing. He is due credit for taking on the Morgan railroad combination, but he left the White House far short of his goal of controlling the combinations.

If Roosevelt did not succeed in his seven-plus years in the White House in resolving the trust problem, he was able to improve upon the work he began as assistant secretary of the navy. By the time of his departure, the U.S. Navy was second only to the navy of Great Britain. Perhaps to mark the end of his administration, Roosevelt sent sixteen battleships, the so-called Great White Fleet, down the Atlantic seaboard, through the newly completed Panama Canal, out into the Pacific and around the world.[30]

Finishing his second term at the young age of fifty, Roosevelt continued over the years to rail at the "malefactors of great wealth" in the Senate and to voice disappointment with his hand-picked successor William Howard Taft.

* * *

The dominance of the trusts and the tactics of anticompetitive behavior could be clearly seen in the actions of AT&T. Despite the increasing competition from the independents, particularly a coalition calling itself the International Independent Telephone Association (ITTA), AT&T continued to establish itself as a monopoly service. The numerous suits brought against AT&T by the ITTA failed to find a sympathetic court, as American justice was still under the influence of the large business faction. But the pressure was on.

CONVINCING THE PUBLIC THAT MONOPOLY IS GOOD

The dominance of the corporate monopoly faction not only determined the business practices of the emerging telephone industry (including who did and who did not get universal service), the rise of vertically integrated national corporations changed the fundamental nature of the American press in the nineteenth century. I wrote earlier of the interrelated impact of private ownership of the telegraph on the press, especially the development of news services. The news services accelerated the increasing interdependence, bureaucratization, and content of papers. The newspaper business employed expensive technologies to produce more and more papers for a growing population: steam presses, linotype, rotogravure were beyond the price range and the capabilities of a couple of men. Starting a newspaper was no longer an inexpensive matter. Dailies and regular periodicals were no longer sponsored by political parties, and they relied less and less on commercial notices, personal ads, or circulation. Newspapers now depended on advertising and the growing advertising agency business, a business formed to serve the industrialist faction.

AT&T, particularly under the direction of Theodore Vail, understood better than most other corporate giants the vulnerability of a press dependent upon advertising. Faced with a hostile press outraged over its anticompetitive business practices, Bell began spending substantial amounts of money advertising in papers where takeovers of independent phone companies were targeted. As Stuart Ewen notes in one example of this practice in Kansas City: "With the lubricant of advertising dollars, [Bell] was soon providing suddenly compliant editors with a diverse range of packaged articles, already typeset and ready to be placed. Ad revenues, James Ellsworth [account executive responsible for the AT&T work at the ad agency The Publicity Bureau] recounted, 'broke the ice'... and the Missouri and Kansas Bell company was 'given access to the news papers of several papers in Kansas City.'"[31]

The seduction of small-town newspapers was just one aspect of AT&T's efforts to overcome its deserved image as a ruthless monopolist. AT&T would demonstrate to a generation of trusts how advertising might be used to manipulate the public and avoid the wrath of reformers.

By 1907, AT&T provided service to roughly 50 percent of all telephones in the United States. This was from a fall of 100 percent in 1893. It had managed to achieve 50 percent through increasingly expensive business tactics, including price-cutting below cost in competitive regions, buyouts of key competitors, and using its financial connections to starve competitors of needed capital. To top things off, the financial panic of 1907 brought the company to the brink of ruin. J. P. Morgan took control and installed Theodore Vail. Morgan and Vail took over at a time when anger over the trusts was rising and advocacy of public ownership was reaching its peak.[32]

Vail's challenge was to convince a public battered by monopolies that the telephone monopoly was a public good. His argument was that telephone service was a "natural monopoly," that universal service—connecting local and long-distance service—could only be achieved with one system. AT&T would shape its image with the slogan: "One Policy, One System, Universal Service."[33]

In addition to the tactics described by Ellsworth above, AT&T offered prizes to local journalists for advertising copy, and began a series of monthly advertisements over the course of the next thirty years to create a positive corporate image. That image would ultimately rely upon depictions of brave telephone linemen and the sisterly telephone operator to replace the image of the business moguls who ran the company. The effort was spectacularly successful.[34] But not even a sophisticated campaign would quell the public concern raised when AT&T announced plans in 1910 to acquire a 30 percent share in its strongest communications competitor, telegraph monopolist Western Union. Despite public relations, regulation was on the way.[35] But it would have to wait until after the election of a new president.

THE DEMOCRATS TAKE CONTROL

The Democratic Party in 1912 was a strange brew of southern racists, western cowboys, Populists from the prairies, and northern immigrants with their corrupt big city bosses as closely tied to big business as the Republicans. Only a personality as magnetic as Bryan seemed able to hold its various elements together, and not even Bryan was able to bring them to victory. But after McKinley, Roosevelt, and Taft, the Republican Party was showing signs of strain and division. Two years into the Taft administration, the Democrats were able to take control of the House of Representatives. Riding a wave of anger at the unstable economy, persistent poverty, and failure to make any lasting progress against the trusts, the majority of voters were hungry for reform. The politician who could convince the public that he was the real reform candidate would win.

John Milton Cooper called the 1912 campaign "a grand moment in American politics."[36] President Taft was in many ways a more aggressive reformer than Roosevelt, but he still led the party most clearly representing the interests of the big business combinations in the North. Eugene Debs was drawing large crowds in his third run as a Socialist. But there was little doubt that the real contest was between Theodore Roosevelt, running as a Progressive, and Woodrow Wilson, the Democratic candidate, known as a reform governor of New Jersey and the former president of Princeton.

Roosevelt opened his campaign arguing that "the old parties are husks, with no real soul within either." He proposed stronger regulations of man-ufacturing and transportation, laws to establish maximum hours and min-imum wages for workers, elimination of child labor, and woman suffrage. Roosevelt drew to himself such progressive luminaries as Jane Addams, Herbert Croly, Walter Lippmann, Dean Acheson, and Felix Frankfurter. However, perhaps in an attempt to draw some of his old Republican base, he denounced "class government" and continued to insist that the approach to the combinations was "to penalize conduct and not size."

In a spirit harkening back to Andrew Jackson, Wilson argued that the nation's problems were the result of "very small, and often deliberately exclusive groups of men who undertook to speak for the whole country."[37] In a series of speeches ultimately collected under the title *The New Freedom*, Wilson laid the problems of America squarely on the shoulders of the trusts.

> If monopoly persists, monopoly will always sit at the helm of government. . . . If there are men in this country big enough to own the government of the United States, they are going to own it; what we have to determine now is whether we are big enough, whether we are men enough, whether we are free enough, to take possession again of the government which is our own. We haven't had free access to it, our minds have not touched it by way of guidance, in half a generation. We have been dreading all along the time when the combined power of high finance would be greater than the power of the government. Have we come to a time when the President of the United States or any man who wished to be the President must doff his cap in the presence of this high finance, and say, "You are our inevitable master, but we will see how we can make the best of it"?[38]

If Wilson did not have the support of the same number of luminaries Roosevelt could boast, he had, perhaps most important, the assistance and support of the still vibrant Bryan. For additional intellectual firepower, he also drew to him the Boston attorney and leading intellectual among reformers, Louis Brandeis. With Brandeis's assistance, Wilson began to focus on the need to restore economic competition as an answer to the trust problem. Wilson would bring together small business and the ordinary citizen. The trust, he declared, is "an arrangement to get rid of competition."[39]

As devoted as the New Yorker Roosevelt was to Hamilton, Wilson, born in Virginia and a graduate of the University of Virginia, identified strongly with Jefferson. Wilson maintained "there is one principle of Jefferson's which no longer can obtain in the practical politics of America . . . [that was the idea] that the best government is that which does as little as possible," and he insisted he was "not afraid of the utmost exercise of the powers of government."[40] But Wilson argued that the core of Jefferson's political philosophy was his insistence on the democratic deliberation of the people to resolve the issues before them. So Wilson rejected regulation that would give great power to a small group of experts to answer those questions the public must determine. "Who have been consulted when important measures of government, like tariff acts, and currency acts, and railroad acts, were under consideration? The people whom the tariff chiefly affects, the people for whom the currency is supposed to exist, the people who pay the duties and ride on the railroads? Oh, no! What do they know about such matters! The gentlemen whose ideas have been sought are the big manufacturers, the bankers, and the heads of the great railroad combinations. The masters of the government of the United States are the combined capitalists and manufacturers of the United States."[41] "[When] it is proposed to set up guardians over those people," he would write, "and to take care of them by a process of tutelage and supervision, in which they play no part, I utter my absolute objection."[42]

> The Roosevelt plan is that there shall be an industrial commission charged with the supervision of the great monopolistic combinations which have been formed under the protection of the tariff, and that the government of the United States shall see to it that these gentlemen who have conquered labor shall be kind to labor. I find, then, the proposition to be this: That there shall be two masters, the great corporation, and over it the government of the United States; and I ask who is going to be master of the government of the United States? It has a master now,—those who in combination control these monopolies. And if the government controlled by the monopolies in its turn controls the monopolies, the partnership is finally consummated.[43]

Wilson's critique resonates strongly today, but he provided no real answer to the challenges to democracy posed by a government dominated by giant corporations. The main ideological difference between Roosevelt and Wilson is plain to see: Roosevelt believed the upper classes could determine what was in the best interests of the people and exhort by word and lead by example. Wilson believed the American public must be educated and informed and put in a position to make the best decisions themselves. Roosevelt remained a Hamiltonian aristocrat, believing that things could be worked out best in the club. Wilson argued alongside Jefferson that the essence of democratic governance was an educated public engaged in self-rule. The Progressive Jeffersonian Wilson however could exercise no more real control over the trusts than the Progressive Hamiltonian Roosevelt. The trusts, with an unwavering public philosophy, would tread water behind Taft and the Republican Party, knowing their time would come again.

The election of 1912 was a resounding success for the Democratic Party. For the first time since before the Civil War, both houses of Congress and the executive branch were finally in their control. In Jeffersonian spirit, Wilson would declare in his inaugural speech: "The firm basis of government is justice, not pity. . . . There can be no equality of opportunity, the first essential of justice in the body politic, if men and women and children be not shielded in their lives, their very vitality, from the consequences of great industrial and social processes which they can not alter, control, or singly cope with. Society must see to it that it does not itself crush or weaken or damage its own constituent parts. The first duty of law is to keep sound the society it serves."[44]

In his first year Wilson, with a firm hand on the tiller of the Democratic Party, pushed through major economic reform, including a graduated income tax, a new banking system establishing the Federal Reserve System (still much in place), and finally the Clayton Anti-Trust Act, which finally put some bite into the previous efforts to control combinations. Shortly after taking office, Wilson's attorney general filed suit against the telephone trust, AT&T. The case was settled out of court in 1913, in an agreement known as the Kingsbury Commitment, negotiated by an AT&T corporate vice-president, Nathan Kingsbury.

Under the Kingsbury Commitment, AT&T agreed to sell its holdings in Western Union, seek prior government approval for additional communications acquisitions, and provide connections to independent companies, so long as those companies met AT&T technical requirements. In the years to follow, progressive reform would also take place at the state level. Between 1912 and 1920, forty-two state public utility commissioners and the District of Columbia adopted policies barring predatory pricing practices.

Except for the forced sale of its shares in Western Union, the Kingsbury Commitment was interpreted by regulators as an agreement to hold the status quo. AT&T was not allowed to grow and kill off competitors, but it was allowed to exchange telephone systems and consolidate territorial dominance. As Brock writes, "This provision allowed Bell and the independents to exchange telephones in order to give each other geographical monopolies. So long as only one company served a given geographical area there was little reason to expect price competition to take place."[45] Thus, while independents were protected from AT&T anticompetitive practices by the Kingsbury Commitment, federal regulators interpreted it as an agreement allowing industry collusion and oligopoly. According to Michael Kellogg, "The government solution, in short, was not the steamy, unsettling cohabitation that marks competition but rather a sort of competitive apartheid, characterized by segregation and quarantine. Markets were carefully carved up: one for the monopoly telegraph company; one for each of the established monopoly local telephone exchanges; one for the Bell's monopoly long-distance operations. Bell might not own everything, but some monopolist or other would dominate each discrete market."[46]

THE *TITANIC* AND WIRELESS

The year 1912 would see not only the first presidential race dominated by proponents of reform, it was also the year radio would at last come under the control of the federal government. From the time Marconi landed in New York in 1899 radio attracted young amateurs. Admiral Evans complained on his return to the United States from the round-the-world trip of the Great White Fleet that his ships were unable to communicate with the Portsmouth Navy Yard because of all the "amateur clamor."[47] The navy lobbied the administration to join the international community and begin regulating what was then called "the ether." Congress responded in 1910 by requiring ships with fifty or more persons aboard to carry radio equipment, but it exerted no other control. By 1911 after winning a patent infringement suit against an American company, United Wireless, Marconi dominated wireless in America.[48]

It would take a popular tragedy to awaken public attention to push Congress to take control over the airwaves, and in 1912 tragedy came. The unsinkable *Titanic*, a symbol of technological arrogance combined with commercial imperative, with millionaires and celebrities on board, sank. The press provided the public vivid stories of the heroism of Marconi operators as they relayed messages to assist the survivors, and they told stories of the incompetence of nearby ships with wireless operators asleep at the switch. Congress responded with the Radio Act of 1912. Thus President

Taft signed into law the first requirement for a federal license to transmit radio signals.[49] While there had been experimentation with sending voice through the "ether," radio signals were still mainly telegraph dots and dashes.

The 1912 act established several important things, first among them that the government had the right to control radio. The act had four major sections: Section One limited federal jurisdiction to radio transmissions outside of the jurisdiction of states, except in the case of interference with licensed interstate transmissions; Section Two required a transmitter to be licensed by the secretary of commerce and labor to a U.S. citizen, and it authorized the president to close or take over any station in time of war or public peril; Section Three mandated that transmission occur under the supervision of someone with an operator's license; and Section Four indicated that the purpose of the act was to prevent or minimize interference, and that the secretary of commerce and labor could grant temporary licenses for experiments. The act also allowed the secretary to assign wavelengths and time limits, and divided the spectrum by function, separating ship, government, and amateur transmission frequencies.

Almost a thousand existing transmitting stations were licensed within the year, including a vast array of educational institutions with many years of experience. The law also contained a fatal flaw: it did not give the secretary the right to refuse a license.[50] Despite this loophole, many amateurs continued to operate without bothering to obtain federal permission.[51] While most users were sending Morse code, a few were actually sending voice signals. Very quickly radio telegraphy was becoming radio telephony was becoming radio.

THE WAR OVER THERE

Two years later and a world away, Austrian Archduke Ferdinand was killed by a Serbian nationalist. The fragile European alliance, which had stood for a hundred years, was shattered and within months the great nations of Europe were at war. While Roosevelt urged immediate preparations for war, Wilson's immediate response was that big defense increases "would mean that we had been thrown off our balance by a war which cannot touch us, whose very existence affords us opportunities for friendship and disinterested service."[52] However, after a German submarine sank a British passenger ship, the *Lusitania,* with 128 Americans on board, Wilson proposed a modest increase in defense expenditures, while refusing to either take sides or commit U.S. forces to the conflict "over there."

Newspaper accounts of the war, supplemented by battlefield photographs, made clear to the public the squalor of trench warfare. While a majority of the press remained faithful to the Republican Party, Wilson enjoyed stronger than usual editorial support for his war policies. Most Americans seemed to agree that it was not their fight. Indeed, much to Wilson's chagrin, one of the Democrats' campaign themes was "he kept us out of the war."

Why then did the United States enter what was then called the Great War?

While U.S. corporations traded happily with both Germany (the Central Powers) and Britain (the Allies), British naval superiority allowed them to blockade all overseas trade to Germany. Thus while the United States professed neutrality, U.S. corporations were put in the position of only trading with the Allies. While disappointed in the substantial loss of "disinterested service" to Germany, U.S. corporations, financed largely by J. P. Morgan, were happy to find themselves in a position as the main supplier to the Allies, and the British debt mounted considerably as the war dragged on. The German response to the British blockade was to launch submarine attacks on all vessels of any kind that might be supplying the Allies—thus, the sinking of the *Lusitania*. The United States protested this action by Germany, gaining temporarily a cease in submarine attacks.

In early January 1917, the German government decided to widen its submarine action against all shipping supplies to the Allies. The German submarine campaign sunk American and Allied ships, killing dozens of U.S. citizens. Wilson broke diplomatic relations with Germany, and while he remained unwilling to commit troops, he sought to protect U.S. commercial ships. Provocation piled upon provocation. In February, to drum up support for a bill to arm ships, Wilson released a captured telegraph from German foreign secretary Arthur Zimmermann to the German embassy in Mexico. Zimmerman instructed his diplomatic envoys to seek an alliance with Mexico offering the recovery of Texas, New Mexico, and Arizona should they join in a war against the United States. Still, Wilson failed to get his "armed neutrality" measure through the Senate before the scheduled March recess. Even as Wilson called Congress back for a special session in April, he agonized about U.S. entry into the war in Europe. If the United States went to war, he told one cabinet member, "you and I will live to see the day when the big interests will be in the saddle."[53]

On April 2, 1917, Wilson addressed Congress. He began slowly recounting the diplomatic efforts toward peace and neutrality, carefully avoiding any mention of U.S. corporations' support of the Allies against the Germans. Then, commenting on German attacks aimed at those supply ships, he declared, "we will not choose the path of submission." Wilson urged Congress to declare war because "the world must be made safe for democracy." But, again, why?

John Milton Cooper suggests: "For all his emotional agony, the president chose war largely through calculations of cost and benefit. Armed neutrality, it rapidly became clear, entailed many of the costs of war, including lives and property lost, and inflamed public passions. But it brought none of the benefits of war, which included psychological release and, most important, the chance to shape the peace settlement."[54]

With France beset by internal disputes, Italy weakened and barely able to contribute to the Allied effort, the collapse of the Russian front and the abdication of the tsar that March, and the British deeply in debt to J. P. Morgan, Wilson saw a looming German victory—even as Germany was weakened with war. As important, he saw an opportunity to determine the peace—but only if America entered the war.

So, on Good Friday, April 6, 1917, the U.S. House of Representatives passed the Senate resolution declaring war against Germany. The result would indeed put the capitalist faction "back in the saddle," and complete the process begun under Roosevelt of embedding military values in a previously isolationist nation. Wilson's call to make the world safe for democracy would have a profound impact on U.S. communications policies and, by extension, the strength of democracy in America.

TAKING OVER RADIO

On the very day the United States declared war with Germany, under authority of a joint resolution of Congress, all amateur radio equipment was ordered shut, dismantled, and sealed. The next day commercial wireless stations were taken over by the navy. Soon the navy and the army were demanding the mass production of wireless equipment. Once again the U.S. commander-in-chief would assume control of the telephone and telegraph systems, placing them under the direction of the Post Office. However valuable those systems might be in the war effort, the army and the navy were most eager for radio transmitters and receivers for ships, airplanes, and land vehicles. They wanted pack transmitters for the trenches and compact receivers for the field. They wanted submarine detectors, radio direction finders, and recording equipment to document and study code transmissions. The problem was that in order to produce this equipment the military authorities had to contend with the patent disputes. Resolution of those disputes, absent intervention, was dependent upon the slow and expensive processes of the U.S. judicial system.

For example, almost all of the equipment desired by the military required vacuum tubes. AT&T purchased the patent rights of such a tube developed by Lee De Forest. However, the U.S. District Court in New York ruled that De Forest's tube, which he called an "Audion," infringed on a detector developed by another inventor who sold his patent rights to Marconi interests. The court ruled, however, that De Forest's improvement was properly patented. To complicate things, Edwin Armstrong claimed a patent on a "feedback" circuit (eventually purchased by Westinghouse) that increased the utility of the De Forest tube.

U.S. manufacturers and patent owners were ordered to make the equipment needed. A letter from Wilson's assistant secretary of the navy, Theodore's nephew, Franklin Roosevelt, guaranteed each contractor "against claims of any and all kinds" in the carrying out of government contracts, and each was told to use "any patented invention necessarily required." Thus, military wants established an industrial policy of cooperation. The previous laissez-faire policy left the result to big business–oriented courts, and too often, to whoever could best afford the cost of extended litigation. The new industrial policy, resulting from the war effort, enabled the vast coordination of radio technology, research, development, and production.[55]

The war also sped up the study of German radio equipment, the advantages of which were quickly integrated into the work of U.S. war contractors. A worker at a Marconi plant in New Jersey, Gustave Bosler, recalls: "It was a miniature affair, but it was a real job, it kicked out. It was about six inches wide, about eight inches high, and about a foot long. It was captured . . . by one of the American boys who struck the German who was working on the transmitter over the head. Blood spattered all over it. That is how I received it." Bosler improved the German transmitter for use by American troops. Presumably the Germans were not included in Roosevelt's guarantee against patent infringement claims.[56]

The U.S. military involvement in the war lasted about seventeen months. The advances in radio technology were so impressive that the navy lobbied for continued control over radio development and over the airwaves. In support of H.R. 13159, Secretary of the Navy Josephus Daniels, an official purportedly very close to President Wilson, testified before the House Committee on Merchant Marine and Fisheries: "[The] passage of this bill will secure for all time to the Navy Department the control of radio in the

United States, and will enable the Navy to continue the splendid work it has carried on during the war. [By returning to the previous state of affairs] we would lose very much by dissipating [our progress] and opening the use of radio communication again to rival companies . . . it is my profound conviction that [radio] must be a monopoly. It is up to the Congress to say whether it is a monopoly for the government or a monopoly for a company."[57] Congressman William Greene praised the navy for its wartime achievements in radio, but reminded his colleagues of the various antitrust laws they had passed and that the United States claimed to be fighting to preserve democracy. "Having just won a fight against autocracy," he argued, "we would start an autocratic movement with this bill."[58] The bill was tabled.

As President Wilson was busy attempting to broker a "peace without victors" in Europe, and becoming increasingly exasperated with the Allies' (particularly the British) heavy-handed demands of the Germans, the Marconi company made a fatal blunder. Marconi agreed to an exclusive purchasing agreement with General Electric (GE) for wireless alternators, in exchange for the exclusive right to use the equipment. Wilson enjoyed his access to the alternators, having used the equipment to keep in touch with events in Europe and in the United States, and having broadcast to all of Europe his "fourteen points" peace plan. In March 1919, Owen Young of GE sent Assistant Secretary of the Navy Roosevelt a copy of the proposed agreement with Marconi, who quickly responded: "before reaching any final agreement with the Marconi companies," confer with the navy.

The idea of Marconi, a British-chartered company, having exclusive use of wireless alternators in the United States had the shock effect Young no doubt intended. Three days later, top navy officials met with Young and a day later they met with the board of directors of GE. Over the course of the next few months a proposal to authorize a GE wireless monopoly was floated and taken off the table. By October, Young and navy brass settled on the idea of creating a separate company in which each of the major patent holders would have a share. The proposal also suggested that not more than 20 percent of the stock would be held by foreigners, and that a U.S. government representative would have a seat on the board. Thus, the Radio Corporation of America (RCA) was born.

The Marconi company, with all of its U.S. stations still in military control, was then "invited" to transfer its assets and operations to RCA. GE purchased all the shares in American Marconi held by the parent Marconi company. GE/RCA quickly formed an alliance with AT&T and Western

RCA Stockholders[59]

	Total Stock	Percent
GE	2,985,626	30.1
Westinghouse	2,000,000	20.6
AT&T	1,000,000	10.3
United Fruit	400,000	4.1
Others	3,302,348	34.9

Electric, whose research arm was joined with the Bell labs. Rear Admiral W. H. G. Bullard was named the government representative on the board. Within two years, RCA was a holding company for all the major patents connected with radio.

Radio was not only dominated by a trust, but a trust strongly associated with the military. Clearly, Wilson failed to keep the "big interests" out of the saddle. His energies and health faded quickly, as did his hopes for a "peace without victors" and for a League of Nations to prevent future World Wars. His Jeffersonian idealism and hopes for lasting progressive reform at home lay, like him, paralyzed and broken, along with the Democratic Party. The nation would return to a string of Republican presidents whose laissez-faire policies would, in ten years, lead the country to the Great Depression.

Radio Arrives (1920–34)

THE ROARING TWENTIES AND TELEPHONE "REFORM"

The year 1920 signaled a major shift in the tectonic plates of democratic engagement. Women finally won a century-long battle for the right to vote with the passage of the Nineteenth Amendment to the Constitution. This expansion of the franchise did not, however, result in any major policy shifts. The vote would not prove a satisfactory answer to a democracy now warped by the overwhelming power of the merchant faction. As Helen Keller, the blind-deaf-mute social visionary, would write to a British suffragist in 1911: "Our democracy is but a name. We vote? What does that mean? It means that we choose between two bodies of real, though not avowed, autocrats. We choose between Tweedledum and Tweedledee."[60]

Another more violent shift overseas would have a more profound impact on U.S. policy. The political theories of Karl Marx were debated prior to U.S. engagement in the war in Europe. Socialist presidential candidate

Eugene Debs gained increasing (though still small) numbers at the ballot box, and socialists gained some measure of influence with a few labor leaders. However, Marx's ideas never took hold in the United States. In addition to denying mail privileges to socialist publications, the United States used the newly passed Espionage Act to prosecute and imprison Americans who spoke against U.S. war policies, including Debs.

Charles Schenck, one of many socialists who opposed the war, was imprisoned for passing out leaflets that stated that conscription was involuntary servitude and unconstitutional. In a unanimous decision written by Oliver Wendell Holmes, the Supreme Court likened Schenck's speech to "falsely shouting fire in a theatre and causing a panic." As a number of legal commentators have noted, the attractiveness of the analogy disguises its weakness.[61] Zinn suggests a more appropriate analogy might have been that Schenck's act was "more like someone shouting . . . to people about to buy tickets and enter a theater, that there was a fire raging inside."[62]

By 1920, Bolsheviks were finally consolidating their power in Russia, bringing to the world stage something more than a theoretical alternative to both feudal aristocracies and democratic republics. The Russian revolution brought a version of Marx's ideas to life in the political structure of a state as imposing as any other on the world stage. The reaction to "communism" would soon come to define the public philosophy of democratic freedom in the United States. The deportation of "aliens" in 1919, and the Red Scare of 1920 leading to the arrest of 2,500 and, some say, the wrongful murder conviction of a shoe factory employee and a fish peddler, Nicola Sacco and Bartolomeo Vanzetti, were only symptoms of a deeper impact this alternative vision would have on American thought. Another, perhaps more important symptom, was the ability of the big business interest to work in concert with jingo nationalists in connecting the labor union movement to "bolshevism." Pointing to Russia, big business conducted a sustained attack on union organizing, resulting in a steady decline in union membership from its high of 5.1 million in 1920 to 3.6 million by 1923.[63]

1920 was also the year that suggested the zenith of the influence of the newspaper industry. Both Democrat James M. Cox and his Republican rival for president, Warren G. Harding, were newspaper publishers. The election of the newspaperman Harding signaled a return to business as usual, with Republican Party bosses back in firm control of all branches of government and petty corruption the order of the day.

The return of the Republican Party to power signaled an important shift as well for the telephone industry, and firmly established another pillar of our modern public philosophy regarding communications: a tolerance for monopoly with the cover of federal regulation.

The nationalization of the telephone industry during World War I had a similar effect as that of the partial nationalization of the telegraph industry during the Civil War. All industry competition was halted, rates were stabilized and increased, and the dominant company, AT&T, developed an especially close relationship with the federal government. The benefits of federal regulation, even nationalization, were clear. As Noobar Danielian writes: "The federal government . . . agreed to pay to AT&T 41/2 percent of the gross operating revenues of the telephone companies as a service fee; to make provisions for depreciation and obsolescence at the high rate of 5.72 percent per plant; to make provision for the amortization of intangible capital; to disburse all interest and dividend requirements; and in addition, to keep the properties in as good a condition as before. Finally, AT&T was given the power to keep a constant watch on the government's performance, to see that all went well with government operation, by providing that the books of the Postmaster General would be at all times open for inspection."[64]

Five months after nationalization, AT&T long-distance rates increased by 20 percent. By the time it was returned to private control, the federal government had approved rate increases for AT&T estimated at $42 million.[65]

AT&T acted quickly to consolidate the favored position it had attained during the war. It began to lobby federal and state legislators, providing a host of economic experts to argue what history disproved, that telephone service was a "natural monopoly," that, in other words, competition is counterproductive in businesses that require great investments to operate efficiently, and if forced to compete they will simply pass on their higher costs to consumers. As stated earlier, AT&T's anticompetitive practices resulted in higher costs for many consumers and a lack of service in rural areas between 1875 and 1894, the early period of AT&T's greatest monopoly power. Once competition arrived in the form of independent telephone companies service improved, particularly to AT&T customers, and consumer prices were lower. This history did not make the "natural monopoly" argument less persuasive to friendly legislators.

During the 1921 debate over the Willis-Graham Act, the Senate Commerce Committee adopted the view that "telephoning is a natural monopoly." A House of Representative committee report noted, "There is nothing to be gained by local competition in the telephone business."[66] The answer according to legislators was federal regulation of this monopoly. The Willis-Graham Act was fully in keeping with both the Teddy Roosevelt Progressives' view of regulatory reform and the pro-business bias of the Harding and Coolidge years. The act allowed AT&T to begin acquiring more local telephone systems without limits, but with the oversight of the Interstate Commerce Commission (ICC).[67] By 1924, AT&T had acquired 223 of the 234 independent telephone companies. By 1934, when the Federal Communications Commission (FCC) took jurisdiction over the telephone industry, the ICC had approved 271 of the 274 purchase requests brought to them by AT&T for review.[68]

This view of regulation was mirrored in the states. A public utilities commission in Michigan in 1921 noted: "Competition resulted in duplication of investment. . . . The policy of the state was to eliminate this by eliminating as far as possible, duplication."[69] In the Midwest and the South especially, state regulatory agencies refused construction requests by independents and encouraged consolidation in the name of "efficient" and "universal service."[70] National long-distance monopoly, and local monopoly telephone service was not only tolerated, in the Roaring Twenties it was embraced.

A NEW FORCE IN MASS MEDIA

What was genuinely new was the birth of a new mass media, a force that would come to dominate, if not determine American political thought in the decades to come.

Broadcasting voice had begun in small limited experiments before the war. The soldiers would come home, many bitten with the radio bug, and with the excess capacity of radio manufacturers lying dormant, Westinghouse looked to develop a market for radio receivers. Thus, KDKA, a Westinghouse-owned station in Pittsburgh, came to broadcast the results of the 1920 election to a small number of groups in homes at the Edgewood Club just outside the city. While the *Detroit News* accomplished the same feat on its station—8MK—KDKA gained far greater national attention for its novel use of wireless technologies. KDKA received more credit in part because rival newspapers had far less interest in the self-promoting activities of another newspaper operation, while Westinghouse's intent was not to sell newspapers but to sell radio receivers.[71]

With the KDKA success heralded as the triumph of American genius in papers across the country, the Department of Commerce formally adopted broadcasting as a separate class of service and began issuing licenses in 1921. From January through November it issued five broadcast licenses, in December twenty-three. By July 1922, an additional 431 stations were licensed to transmit broadcast signals.[72] Still, most radio stations operated unreliably and with limited range, transmitting their signals only a few miles at best. Many of the licensees were local churches, labor unions, or ethnic organizations, directing their programs toward communities not much beyond the neighborhood of the transmitter. Much of what was broadcast reflected the interests of the licensee. Most of it was live and recorded music, but also on the air were religious services, local and national political discussions, and "nationality hours" with news from the homeland, such as Germany or Italy, oftentimes in languages from the homeland as well. Given their limited power—the first 5,000-watt transmitters appeared in 1925 (along with the formation of the RCA subsidiary the National Broadcasting Company), and 10,000-watt stations (low-power stations by today's standards) were not broadcasting until 1928—radio's beginning suggested a medium that would strengthen local institutions and focus on the needs of often isolated local communities. All that would change under the watchful eye of Secretary of Commerce Herbert Hoover.

HOOVER THE "WONDUH BOY"

A little more than two years after Warren Harding took office he was dead at the age of fifty-eight. Aside from the fairly petty corruptions of some cabinet members (most famously, the secretary of the interior, Albert Fall, accepted $100,000 in cash from "friends" in exchange for their access to U.S. oil reserves at Elk Hills, California, and Teapot Dome, Wyoming), Harding's cabinet was filled with men who saw little difference between the obligations of government and the desires of big business. Secretary of the Treasury Andrew Mellon, one of the richest men in America, concocted the Mellon Plan and presented it to the Republican-dominated Congress. The Mellon Plan lowered the top income brackets from 50 to 25 percent (saving Mellon $800,000), while lowering the bottom bracket from 4 to 3 percent. It passed, of course, and caused no scandal. Vice-President Calvin Coolidge also managed to avoid the taint of corruption surrounding the White House, despite his renown as the first vice-president to attend all the cabinet meetings.

Coolidge gained the respect of Republican Party bosses because of his decision, as governor of Massachusetts, to call out the state militia after the police force in Boston went on strike because city officials refused to let them join the American Federation of Labor. When AFL leader Samuel Gompers protested Coolidge's treatment of the police, Coolidge replied: "There is no right to strike against the public safety by anybody, anywhere, any time!" The newspapers, of course, promptly trumpeted their support for this savior. Coolidge's philosophy was made very clear during the first few months of his administration: "The business of America is business." By the middle of his second administration, in 1927, the *Wall Street Journal* could proudly proclaim, "Never before, here or anywhere else, has a government been so completely fused with business."[73]

Harding appointed Hoover to the position of secretary of commerce, and Coolidge kept him on despite an evident jealousy at his accomplishments, derisively calling him the "wonduh boy." Hoover was a liberal Republican, known to have supported Wilson. An engineer by training, and an extraordinarily successful international businessman in the mining industry, Hoover was known as a man who could get things done around the world. His work as chairman of the Commission for Relief in Belgium and as the U.S. Food Administrator under Wilson earned him worldwide fame, with a reputation eclipsed only by Wilson and Roosevelt.

Hoover perhaps more than any other single individual shaped the future of broadcasting in the United States.

Shortly after arriving at his desk in the Department of Commerce, Hoover was overcome with the letters and petitions regarding wireless. It seemed clear that chaos was on the way if something was not done to resolve the conflicting interests. In 1922 Hoover called together the executives of the largest companies: "It is the purpose of this conference to inquire into the critical situation that has now arisen through the astonishing development of the wireless telephone; to advise the Department of Commerce as to the application of its present powers of regulation, and further to formulate such recommendations to Congress as to the legislation necessary."[74] This tendency to look to the executives of the largest corporations for answers as to how they should be regulated by government was typical of Hoover, and it came to dominate the way government would come to regulate the communications industry.

Interference was not the only difficulty facing broadcasters. From the time amateur radio enthusiasts were experimenting with sending voice over the air, they used music. A reasonable interpretation of the copyright law of 1909 suggested that without a license, a broadcaster's use of music "publicly for profit" was a violation of the rights of the copyright holder—even when the broadcast did not result in profit. By 1923 the American Society of Composers, Authors and Publishers (ASCAP) decided that broadcasters had enough of a free ride. In response to ASCAP, the radio operators formed their own organization, the National Association of Broadcasters (NAB),[75] an organization destined to become one of the most potent lobbying organizations in the nation. For the time being, however, most broadcasters, aside from the powerhouses of RCA and Westinghouse, tended to think of themselves not as broadcasters, but as extensions of the school, or church, or union, or local club that sponsored them.

In 1923, Hoover called a second conference, again dominated by the larger interests. While Hoover doubted he had the legal authority to regulate station hours, transmission power, or frequency, the attendees resolved that he should so regulate the industry because of their desire to broadcast with greater power and less interference. Hoover responded with a reallocation of the spectrum that would stand for years to come. Stations were separated into three groups: high-power stations serving large areas would be given different channels/frequencies between 300 and 545 meters on which to operate and suffer no interference; medium-range stations serving smaller areas would operate on various frequencies between 222 and 300 meters; and low-powered stations were relegated to one frequency—360 meters, oftentimes restricted to daytime hours.[76] Somehow the trusts, RCA, AT&T, and Westinghouse, were given the better channels.

This frequency allocation was not simply a matter of separating those with more power and range from those with less. Hoover forced many stations, notably educational and religious stations, to operate at reduced frequency while allowing the major corporations to operate at increased power. The University of Colorado, licensee of station KFAJ, was authorized to operate at 1,000 watts in 1922. After Hoover's second conference it was limited to 100 watts. After GE's station KOA was allowed to increase its power, KFAJ could not even be heard locally. The university concluded that radio as regulated offered no possibility for useful educational service and allowed the license to lapse in 1925.[77]

1923 also saw the circle close between the broadcasters and the military. On the recommendation of Newton Baker, former secretary of war, Major General James Harbord, a man with no experience in either the corporate world or as a broadcaster, was appointed president of RCA.

Hoover called additional radio conferences in 1924 and 1925, and the dominance of the larger interests was ever more apparent. The RCA/GE/AT&T/Westinghouse forces demanded an end to the distribution of licenses, and in 1925 Hoover agreed. While a new license would not be issued, there was nothing, then, to prevent an old license from being sold. This new market was encouraged by the Department of Commerce, so testified a department spokesman before a Senate committee: "We take the position that the license ran to the apparatus, and if there is no good reason to the contrary we will recognize that sale and license the new owner of the apparatus."[78]

In the early 1920s, most of the members of the RCA combination engaged in broadcasting as a way to promote the sale of radio receivers. Among the partners of the combination, the exception was AT&T. AT&T, through its station WEAF, experimented with something it called "toll" broadcasting, allowing individuals and corporations to come into the broadcast "toll" booth and send out, for a fee, any message they wanted. This was the beginning of commercial broadcasting as we think of it today. While others, such as furniture stores and the *Detroit News*, used broadcasting as a sort of publicity gimmick, they were not really engaged in selling air time for others to advertise products or services. The RCA allies began to adopt AT&T's business model, but not without a fight from AT&T. When the dust settled, AT&T agreed to get out of the broadcasting business in exchange for exclusive rights to provide cable lines to the growing number of stations affiliated with the radio trust. Still, the vast majority of broadcasters were not affiliated with RCA. They offered to the public a vast mix of programming, most of it local in nature. By 1926, the radio boom had clearly caught on. Of the 26 million American homes, 5 million had radios.

The large corporate broadcasters believed that their economic model of "toll broadcasting" required both more transmitting power and less interference. RCA-affiliated conferees attending Hoover's second radio conference assured him that the Radio Communications Act of 1912 gave him the power to regulate frequencies and hours of operation. However, when Hoover sought to exercise this power by penalizing the then relatively small Zenith Radio Corporation for operating on an unauthorized frequency, Zenith took him to court. The District Court in Illinois ruled that the 1912 act did not permit him to deny Zenith a license.[79] The fusion of government and business still had the hurdle of passing legal muster. This would not be difficult.

THE FEDERAL RADIO COMMISSION AND THE PUBLIC INTEREST

Congress passed the Radio Act of 1927,[80] reaffirming the intent of the federal government to exercise exclusive control over interstate and foreign radio transmissions and to issue licenses for the use of designated frequencies, reserving all claims of ownership to the public. It created a new body, the Federal Radio Commission (FRC), with legislative, executive, and judicial authority. The five commissioners were to be appointed by the president, with the advice and consent of the Senate, and not more than three of the commissioners were to be members of the same political party, with the chairman selected by the president. Many, though not all, of the powers of the FRC were to revert back to the secretary of commerce after one year. The FRC would continue to have the power to revoke licenses.

In addition to a new "independent" bureaucracy to manage the airwaves, Congress introduced a new term—the *public interest*—which would come to bedevil the government-business partnership. Secretary Hoover actually expressed this concept in a speech before his fourth radio conference: "The ether is a public medium, and its use must be for a public benefit. The use of a radio channel is justified only if there is public benefit. The dominant element for consideration in the radio field is, and always will be, the great body of the listening public, millions in number, country wide in distribution."[81]

It must be noted that Hoover, and many members of the business-government alliance, strongly believed that their cooperation was for the public benefit. Despite his association with Wilson, Hoover was not an idealist about the ability of the common man to join in democratic deliberation about common problems. He was an idealist about the altruistic impulses and talents of the wealthy. If Hoover rejected Wilson's embrace of Jeffersonian democratic idealism, he believed in the part of Jefferson's philosophy Wilson rejected. As Hofstadter wrote: "With Jefferson and the economic individualists he agreed, on the whole, that that government is best which governs least, a conviction that was confirmed by his successes with local and voluntary forms of action. Even as a bureaucrat in Washington he had made it his concern to prime the pump of private business initiative rather than play a paternalistic role."[82]

Despite the pro-business policies of the Coolidge era, there remained Progressives in the Wilson mold with power to influence public philosophy even in the Roaring Twenties. As a number of commenters suggest, this influence reflected both the lasting power of Progressive idealism and the need for some middle ground between the leftist sympathies embodied in the Russian Revolution and the trusts, which though powerful were not popular.

A year after all its members were in place the FRC described the public interest requirement as follows: "[Despite the fact that] the conscience and judgment of a station's management are necessarily personal . . . the station itself must be operated as if owned by the public. . . . It is as if people of a community should own a station and turn it over to the best man in sight with this injunction: 'Manage this station in our interest.' The standing of every station is determined by that conception."[83]

The 1927 Radio Act was updated and enlarged upon in 1934. But its basic structure, from the ostensibly independent nature of the commission to the core notion of the "public interest," continues.

Also of special note in the Radio Act is Section 4 (h), added at the last minute to give the FRC the authority to take into account the changing nature of radio, specifically the advent of national networks, or what the 69th Congress called "chain broadcasting." In March 1927, as the FRC was being formed there were 732 radio broadcast stations in the United States; more than six hundred of them were independent and unaffiliated with the RCA/GE/AT&T trust. These independent stations were run by churches and labor unions, newspapers, hotels, educational institutions, and others.[84] They were not by any means what we today think of as commercial. Even though the National Broadcasting Corporation had begun and generated a great deal of attention, the battle over the role of the independent stations, indeed the battle for broadcasting as a predominately local voice, would rage on through the middle years of the Great Depression.

The early signs were not encouraging. The most pressing challenge facing the FRC was to answer the competing claims of the 733 broadcasters for the ninety available frequencies.[85] Ominously the FRC continued the Hoover precedent of convening meetings dominated by the RCA combination and a few other commercial interests. One Commerce Department official offered the opinion that "the success of radio broadcasting lay in doing away with small and unimportant stations."[86]

In August 1928, the FRC issued General Order 40, which set aside forty "clear channel" frequencies where broadcasters would be able to operate nationwide at very high power, thirty-four channels were set aside for regional broadcasts, and thirty low-power channels in each of the five zones. Twenty-three of the first twenty-five "clear channel" stations were affiliated with NBC, and the 6 percent of stations untouched by the massive reallocation were affiliated with either NBC or the only alternative "chain," the Columbia Broadcasting System. General Order 40 also created a process where anyone could challenge an existing broadcaster for a frequency assignment every three months. Beyond the technical capacities of the opponents, the FRC established a two-step test as the basis for determining the outcome of a challenge. Step one, was the broadcaster inclined to serve itself or listeners?; and step two, were the listeners representative of the entire listening public or a specific audience?

The FRC noted: "There is not room in the broadcast band for every school of thought, religious, political, social, and economic, each to have its separate broadcasting station, its mouthpiece in the ether." While there was general discomfort about the commercialization of the "ether" expressed by politicians of all stripes, the FRC clearly paid close attention to the RCA combination and the other big business interests at its hearings.[87] It stated: "Without advertising, broadcasting would not exist." As Robert McChesney wrote, the FRC position was taken "with apparent disregard for the several score non-commercial stations still in operation."[88] The FRC's position was squarely on the course laid out by Hoover and Coolidge. What was good for America, the listener, was not only business, it was big business. Independent stations had been operating in the absence of advertising support for years; they were in fact still in the majority. Without regard to what the listeners wanted, or what a "free market" might determine on its own, as a direct result of FRC policies, there would be a hundred fewer of these independent broadcast stations on the air by the end of the year.

By 1929, the *Harvard Business Review* would write: "[The] point seems clear that the Federal Radio Commission has interpreted the concept of public interest so as to favor in actual practice one particular group. While talking in terms of the public interest, convenience and necessity the commission actually chose to further the ends of the commercial broadcasters. They form the substantive content of public interest as interpreted by the Commission."[89]

1929 was also the year Herbert Hoover (elected in a landslide) was inaugurated as president, and by October the signal event of the Great Depression shocked the nation. As a number of historians remind us, the crash of the stock market in the late weeks of October did not cause the Great Depression; however, as John Kenneth Galbraith wrote, "this [clarification] puts the wrong face on matters."[90]

Despite assurances from Mellon and Coolidge and Morgan that the economy was sound, the problems of the farmer, the increasing inequality of wealth, the inability of labor unions to influence an increase in wages commensurate with the rise in production efficiencies, and the inability of the British to pay the debt they incurred during the Great War, all contributed to the worsening economic infrastructure in the United States. Thus, while the exposure of overinvestment in fraudulent stocks on Wall Street did not "cause" the Great Depression, as financiers are eager to tell us in any other season, what happens on Wall Street matters to the American economy. Wall Street, more specifically, speculation (radio speculation, Florida land speculation, speculation on the margin), was out of control. Everybody, it seemed, wanted a piece of the dream, in exchange for little work. Hoover had urged Coolidge and Mellon to take some action to control the market, but was rebuffed. The market, he was informed, would take care of itself. So, despite Hoover's personal integrity and competence, and his idealistic belief in the integrity and competence of his fellow business-men, America's most severe economic depression began.

Anyone who followed radio could predict Hoover's reaction to the crash. A month after the crash, November 21, 1929, Hoover called together a con-ference of the nation's business leaders in search of a solution to the prob-lem they had helped create. Needless to say, they were stumped.

A NEW DEAL, BUT WHITHER RADIO REFORM?

After the midterm elections, the Democrats found themselves once more in control of the House of Representatives, and the reform elements in Congress were growing stronger as the economy continued to slide. In 1932, Wilson's former undersecretary of the navy, and Theodore's nephew, Democrat Franklin Delano Roosevelt was elected president.

Under FDR the agrarian interest would be subsidized, the federal gov-ernment would empower labor unions, and stronger controls would be exercised over steel, banking, and other trusts. Given the small resurgence of reform leaders, the great disenchantment with laissez-faire policies and big business in general, and the unhappiness of education, labor, and small businesses with the Federal Radio Commission, why did communications policy fail to undergo the same sort of reform measures contemplated for other economic actors?

First, we should acknowledge that communications reform was a matter of some debate on Capitol Hill. The fact that Democrats took control of the House suggests a disenchantment with the status quo, but as was stated ear-lier they were no less influenced by big business than Republicans. Owen Young, the GE executive who almost single-handedly created RCA and NBC, was a prominent contributor to the Democratic Party. The fact that trust-like corporations had taken control of the airwaves during the Coolidge and Hoover years was wrapped up in a nationalistic frame; pri-vate monopoly control of the airwaves was "the American system." If the public would be given little insight into radio policy matters, the incessant radio commercials could not be so hidden. This commercialism was the focus of most of the debate about radio on Capitol Hill. Given this frame-work (how to curb radio advertising, rather than how to protect diverse political discussion), many members understandably felt they had far more important issues before them. As *Broadcasting,* a pro–big business publica-tion, reported in early 1932, "Only the fact that Congress has been so vitally concerned with major economic problems and legislation has prevented members of the Senate and House from paying more attention to radio matters at this session."[91]

In addition, during this period, the most influential member of Congress with regard to radio was the unreliable, if not unscrupulous, Senator Clarence Dill, a Democrat from Washington state. As McChesney writes, "Dill . . . routinely announced his support for the aims of the broadcast reform movement, although he just as quickly disapproved of any and all specific measures that the reformers might propose."[92] In the final analysis, Dill, along with Hoover, supported the position of the large commercial broadcasters: self-regulation would be sufficient.

Aside from the ire directed at radio advertising, the other major reform effort was to reserve channel space for both labor and educators. Unfortunately, educators, as represented by the National Committee on Education by Radio (NCER), could not be persuaded to support labor. So labor struck a deal on its own with NBC, and any real hope of reform that would reserve channel space for other broadcasters was lost.

Finally, the NAB proved itself a potent lobbying force. According to Representative Thomas Amlie, a first-term reform Republican of Wisconsin, "I have found the Radio interests are well organized. At a convention in my state, the eleven stations assembled adopted a very bitter resolution condemning me in the most outspoken terms for my stand . . . it indicates what any representative is running up against if he attempts to regulate or control the private broadcasters. Members of Congress are dependent upon these stations for many favors."[93]

The inability to construct a compelling frame for reform, an inability to work in coalition, false reform champions on the Hill, combined with effective opposition, closed off the opportunity to reform the infant industry of commercial broadcasting even while so many other reform efforts would be revived. What of the second President Roosevelt?

Franklin Roosevelt was no supporter of broadcast reform, particularly not initially. Not only was he reportedly close to Owen Young, a tie established in his days as assistant secretary of the navy, as indicated earlier, Roosevelt played a critical role in promoting wireless as a monopoly. Moreover, Roosevelt would have been at the very least ambivalent about dismantling the mechanism through which he could give his fireside talks to the public.

The 1934 Communications Act was passed, adopting the basic framework of the 1927 Radio Act. Its only real novelty was the addition of all electronic communications services (an idea of Senator James Couzens dating back to 1929)[94] to the jurisdiction of a new and more permanent agency, the FCC. Given the failure of independent stations, labor, and educators to work together, it should come as no surprise that a proposal to reserve 25 percent of channels for education was defeated that same year.[95] While some commentators suggest that the establishment of the FCC was essential to aggressive federal regulation of the telegraph and telephone industries,[96] the most important fact about those services was their destruction of any competitor, and so the telephone monopolies would remain firmly in place for another fifty years.

While broadcast radio began the decade of the 1920s as a technology supporting local diverse communications, by the mid-1930s it served as a tool to concentrate power in distant places, by-passing local leaders and institutions. Roosevelt was not the first or the only voice. Father Charles Coughlin and Louisiana Senator Huey Long, both of whom Roosevelt considered dangerous, were also on the air. But the most dominant messengers were of course the trusts, promoting consumption as freedom, along with the twin myths of Horatio Alger and the independent cowboy, and their silence about racism and sexism. Radio, which started as a medium of two-way communications, had become a powerful tool of propaganda, where compelling voices could reach out to millions, without interruption or rejoinder. As David Kennedy would write in his book on Roosevelt and the Depression, *Freedom From Fear:* "The radio created a political environment unimaginably distant from the give-and take of the town meeting, which Thomas Jefferson had praised as 'the best school of political liberty the world ever saw.'"[97]

RADIO AND THE SECOND NEW DEAL

There would come, during the so-called Second New Deal, some efforts toward broadcast reform from the first truly progressive individual to oversee broadcasting, James Lawrence Fly, and by Senator Harry Truman. But the dominant strain during these and the Roosevelt war years was the increasingly close connection between the government, especially the military, and the commercial broadcast industry.

First, Chairman Fly. On September 1, 1939, James Lawrence Fly, a Democrat from Texas who had served as general counsel for the Tennessee Valley Authority (TVA), was appointed by President Roosevelt to serve as the fourth chairman of the FCC. William Leuchtenburg, perhaps the most comprehensive of the Roosevelt administration chroniclers, called the TVA "the most spectacularly successful of the New Deal agencies, not only because of its achievements in power and flood control [but because its various programs altered] the mores of the region."[98] Fly was the man in charge of protecting it against attack in courts. Unlike many other Roosevelt New Deal programs, the TVA succeeded. The TVA was also in keeping with the new Brandeis-influenced emphasis of the New Deal on controlling monopoly and promoting decentralization.[99] A determination to address this concern is what Roosevelt, in the person of Fly, would bring to communications policy.

Much of Roosevelt's success in his first two elections has been attributed to his ability to get his message out, despite the influential newspaper publishers, who were as a group almost rabidly against him and his policies. His advantage was the relatively new medium of broadcast radio. But in the late 1930s Roosevelt noticed the increasing interest of newspaper publishers in acquiring radio stations. In 1940, a third of all radio stations were controlled by the newspaper industry, and in over ninety communities the newspaper/radio combination was the only mass media in town.[100] This concern would ultimately result in the prohibition against newspaper/broadcast cross-ownership some thirty-five years later.[101] But Fly's first focus was on a proceeding begun the year before he joined the FCC, a review of the networks (called "chains") and their influence over local stations.

The initial *Report on Chain Broadcasting* was released in 1941 and savagely attacked by the broadcasters. The FCC slightly amended it and ordered it to be put into effect in 1942. The report found that NBC used its two networks, the red and the blue, to suppress competition. It also found that the CBS contract with affiliates, wherein it held an option to take over any period in the affiliate's schedule, amounted to a surrender of control and a violation of the station's license to serve its community. To correct these abuses, the FCC ordered that "No license shall be issued to a standard broadcast station affiliated with a network organization which maintains more than one network." The FCC also ruled that the local station had the unquestioned right to reject any network offering, and that the network option was limited to three hours within each of four segments of the broadcast day (8:00 a.m. to 1:00 p.m.; 1:00 p.m. to 6:00 p.m.; 6:00 p.m. to 11:00 p.m.; 11:00 p.m. to 8:00 a.m.).[102]

William Paley, CBS president, called it a "wrecking operation." Niles Trammel, NBC president, predicted "chaos." The networks took the FCC to court, but they did not stop at that. Suddenly, Representative Martin Dies, chairman of the House Committee on Un-American Activities, took an interest in the FCC, claiming that it harbored government subversives.

Representative Eugene Cox, a member of the House Rules Committee, arranged for a special committee to investigate the FCC, calling Fly "the most dangerous man in Washington," and later announced plans to impeach him. The House Committee on Interstate and Foreign Commerce held several hearings on a bill to void the Report on Chain Broadcasting. The House Appropriations Committee voted to cut the FCC budget by 25 percent, attaching it as a rider on another (veto proof) bill authorizing pay to thousands of other federal employees.[103]

Had any government official ever faced such a withering attack from so many directions? In the short life of either the FRC or the FCC, no chairman of that body had ever faced anything like it. But Fly held on. In 1943, the Supreme Court ruled in favor of the FCC.[104] *NBC v. U.S.* was a sweeping victory for the nine-year-old commission. After a review of the relatively new history of federal regulation of the airwaves, and the still recent experiences of interference that prompted the establishment of the FCC, Justice Felix Frankfurter, writing for the court, ruled that the FCC had the authority to establish regulations in line with what they determined was in the public interest. As to whether such regulations interfered with the broadcasters, free speech rights, Frankfurther wrote:

> The Regulations, even if valid in all other respects, must fall because they abridge, say the appellants, their right of free speech. If that be so, it would follow that every person whose application for a license to operate a station is denied by the Commission is thereby denied his constitutional right of free speech. Freedom of utterance is abridged to many who wish to use the limited facilities of radio. Unlike other modes of expression, radio inherently is not available to all. That is its unique characteristic, and that is why, unlike other modes of expression, it is subject to governmental regulation. Because it cannot be used by all, some who wish to use it must be denied. . . . The right of free speech does not include, however, the right to use the facilities of radio without a license. The licensing system established by Congress in the Communications Act of 1934 was a proper exercise of its power over commerce. The standard it provided for the licensing of stations was the "public interest, convenience, or necessity." Denial of a station license on that ground, if valid under the Act, is not a denial of free speech.[105]

NBC was forced to sell its blue network, and thus ABC was created. Fly's focus was not on content, but on local control and the anticompetitive practices of the large chains and station groups. The next commissioner to draw as much negative attention from the broadcasters was another southern Democrat, Clifford Durr, serving under FCC Chairman Paul Porter. Durr's focus was the local broadcasters' promise of service in the public interest as compared to its actual programming record, and he put his staff to work comparing the next group of twenty-two stations up for renewal. The commission was so shocked at the discrepancies (instead of airing either local or network public service programs, stations such as KIEV, Glendale, California, devoted 88 percent of its time to recorded music interrupted by 1,034 commercial announcements and eight public service announcements) it provided only temporary licenses instead of the usual three-year renewal.

Chairman Porter called for a report on local broadcasting, and in 1946 the FCC released *Public Service Responsibility of Broadcast Licensees* (called the "Blue Book" because of the color of its cover). The Blue Book drew its power by comparing the NAB Code and the statements of the leaders of the commercial broadcasting industry with the actual performance of the stations. It then defined the public interest as requiring unsponsored programs, local live programs, programs devoted to the discussion of local public issues, and reasonable limitations on advertising.[106] Durr would face the same outrage that greeted Fly. Members of Congress called for impeachment, committees demanded investigations and alleged ties to Communists, amendments to the Communications Act were proposed. Porter was transferred from the FCC to the Office of Price Administration, and was replaced by Charles R. Denny.

Denny was no Fly. After assuring that he would not "bleach" the Blue Book, he soon announced that programming was ultimately up to the licensees, and they, not the FCC, "are the ones whom listeners should hold responsible."[107] By 1947, Denny was serving as the vice-president and general counsel of NBC.[108]

The power of the broadcast lobby was firmly established. This power mainly involved the power to manipulate Congress into harassing FCC officials and cutting the agency's funding, but it also included the ability to seduce those same officials with high-paying and prestigious positions. The general public, emerging from World War II increasingly dependent upon broadcasting as a source of social connection and political information, had little idea of these behind the scenes debates. The public did not think of broadcasters as politically powerful or threatening; broadcasters were Bing Crosby and Ed Murrow.

While the Chain Broadcasting Report remained the law of the land, affirmed, along with the notion of the public interest, by the Supreme

Court, the networks remained in de facto control over what local stations aired. But even here, Congress would have the last word. NBC's friends in Congress created a special tax break allowing the company to avoid any taxes on the gain realized from the forced sale of its network.[109] This would not be the first or last tax benefit created to support privately owned media. That brings us to Senator Harry Truman and another major linchpin of federal communications policy.

TAX POLICY AS SUBSIDY

The decision to tax, more specifically whom and what to tax, has been at the core of government policy as far back as the Romans. Taxation without representation, or more specifically, the taxes on paper and commodities such as tea levied by the British sparked the colonial revolt, and the inability of the federal government to tax (raise revenue from) the states to pay off the Revolutionary War debt was the fundamental reason the Articles of Confederation were abandoned and the Constitution was drafted. War (notably the War of 1812, the Civil War, World War I) was the usual reason the federal government exercised its authority to tax (excise tax, direct income tax, tariff); the Great Depression was an exception. Among the many mechanisms used to solve the economic puzzle of the Great Depression was an increase in taxes. For some, like Senator Huey Long, it was not enough. Other (perhaps more responsible) legislators tried to make intelligent tax policy, policy that would stimulate investment and redistribute wealth through government services. These policies were at the core of the New Deal, and earned Roosevelt the lasting hatred of the wealthy.

If there was any industry in America prospering in the hard years of the Depression, it was the broadcasting industry. One FCC commissioner, George Henry Payne (a Republican Progressive and follower of Theodore Roosevelt), thought things were so good for the broadcasters, he proposed a tax on broadcasting stations on the basis of the amount of power used.[110] The proposal did not make it very far.

With a war rationing on paper limiting the amount of ads a newspaper or magazine could run, business only got better for the broadcasters after Pearl Harbor. In 1942, the commercial broadcast industry was pretty much all that there was (only about thirty noncommercial broadcasters remained on the scene), other broadcasters having been soundly defeated in the 1920s and 1930s. Advertising revenues were climbing. Why? Even though Congress enacted an excess-profits tax, with tax rates up to 90 percent, to counter the sort of gouging that had occurred in both the Civil War and World War I, advertising was fully deductible as a necessary business expense—even for businesses whose only market was the federal government.

Senator Truman, chairman of a committee investigating the defense program (known as the "Truman Committee"), wondered, along with Thurman Arnold, the assistant attorney general, and Donald Nelson of the War Production Board, why advertising was a necessary business expense. The advertising industry, at the time fond of calling itself "the information industry," claimed advertising was necessary to keep visible before the public. Truman's response to this was that if they had to advertise, they should pay for it "out of their own pockets." After all, all Americans were now being asked to sacrifice and to do without many of the goods being advertised. Soon the IRS announced an investigation into excess deduction of business expenses.

Truman, like Fly and Durr, barely knew what hit him. In addition to fierce lobbying by the NAB, the advertising industry swung into action. As luck would have it, government agencies anxious to ration goods, sell war bonds, indeed anxious to sell the war effort, turned to the information industry and broadcasters to get the message out. The War Advertising Council (the precursor to the Ad Council) swung into action and within weeks of the announcement of the IRS investigation, radio ads were on the air urging every American to do his or her part for the war effort. By 1943, a War Advertising Council brochure, titled "This is the Army Hitler Forgot!" claimed $100 million in "talent and time" already contributed to the war effort. Truman did not stand a chance.[111]

*   *   *

One other item of note before we leave the Roosevelt years. While the federal government retained the right to close down and take over all radio operations, as it did in World War I, it only closed down small experimental and ham operators. Byron Price of the AP and John Harold Ryan, a general manager for the Storer group stations, were appointed to lead an Office of Censorship. A voluntary system of censorship was established. Despite serious problems (such as the reporting of one location where atomic research was being conducted, and the broadcast of Axis propaganda by Italian- and German-language speakers) the system survived.[112] Despite the problems caused by the occasional progressive irritant insistent upon defining "the public interest," close relations with Congress, the president, and the swelling of former military men within the ranks of broadcasters kept the commercial operations in business and largely in control.

The American public philosophy of communications was now set, and seemingly entrenched. Federal investment and subsidies would foster the early development of a communications industry; those subsidies would continue as the federal government abdicated any role of operating the industry, with the important exception of military uses; industry monopoly or oligopoly would be tolerated; and the "public interest" would be left to weak and irregularly enforced regulation. The dominance of giant corporations over communications policy, invisible behind the attractive screens devised by an army of publicity agents, would continue, except for one brief moment in our history.

6

From Truman to Eisenhower:
The Birth of Television (1935–1959)

> The American government today is not merely a
> framework within which contending pressures jockey
> for position and make politics. . . . There is no effective
> countervailing power against the coalition of the big
> businessmen—who, as political outsiders, now occupy
> the command posts—and the ascendant military men—
> who with such grave voices now speak so frequently in
> the higher councils. Those having real power in the
> American state today are not merely brokers of power,
> resolvers of conflict, or compromisers of varied and
> clashing interest—they represent and indeed embody
> quite specific national interests and policies.
>
> —C. Wright Mills, 1956

The Military-Industrial Complex

Perhaps the single most important jolt to American democratic balance
after World War II was the rise of the military and its union with the industrial faction in the cause of U.S. imperialism. The careful balance struck by
the founders was knocked off kilter by this joint force, and neither agrarian Populists nor Labor would be able to offset this faction's power over
government. If there was any chance that such a combined force could be
countered, it was effectively eliminated by the domination of the trusts
over mass media, particularly that faction's control of a medium that
would come to capture and hold the attention of the public like no
other—television. The domination of corporate America over public discourse effectively stifled Labor and any other political agenda that did not
fit comfortably with a pax-Americana hidden beneath that odd macabre
dance we called the Cold War.[1] But the priorities of the military-industrial

complex would be effectively challenged by the civil rights struggles waged on behalf of black Americans. While what has been called the Second Reconstruction would get a significant push from Truman, it would not culminate and would not affect the nation's communications policies until after the Eisenhower years.

It should be noted that this was not, particularly at first, an easy partnership. U.S. imperial ambitions and militarism, stoked by Theodore Roosevelt and Hearst, was at the start a point of contention within the financial-industrial faction. While Ohio industrialist–political boss Mark Hanna was most famously identified as opposed to "that damned cowboy," Carnegie and the others, so effective as behind-the-curtain-wizards of the political machines, saw little profit in conflict, market or otherwise. An aversion to conflict was, after all, one of the driving forces behind their ruthless capitalism. War, another name for competition, was wasteful; better to bribe and merge and grow and control. The trusts carried through on this tendency selling to both Allied and German powers in those years before America joined the conflict in both World Wars. As Susan Douglas points out in her book on the early years of radio, military leaders were at first quite suspicious of the contribution organizations such as Westinghouse and General Electric (GE) could make to their profession.[2]

But the need to protect Morgan's loans to England combined with Wilson's romantic vision of a world peace bartered by America offered, in the end, a brutal lesson: sacrificing the sons of the poor created an opportunity for huge profits, as well as the manly joy of exercising the martial arts. Even industrialists vehemently opposed to Franklin Roosevelt's redistribution of their wealth through taxation and government projects saw war with Japan and Germany as an opportunity to relive the postwar boom they experienced after the first war to end all wars. By the end of World War II the industrialist faction harbored little of the dovish reticence they had expressed at the turn of the century. Indeed, their interests would be so joined with those Mills called the warriors that President Dwight Eisenhower would soon warn the nation about the dangers of "a military-industrial complex." This joining of forces was most expertly demonstrated in the early history of the new mass medium of broadcast radio, epitomized by Marconi protégé and RCA leader David Sarnoff's final ascension to the rank of general.

This rise of the military among the nation's leaders signaled, among other changes, a shift in the industrial takeover of research and development in electronic media. Sometimes this takeover was done for military (if not nationalistic) purposes and with military assistance, sometimes not.

After the Gilded Age the center of extraordinary scientific progress shifted from entrepreneurial tinkerers like Morse and Bell and Marconi to national corporations such as AT&T and RCA by the onset of World War II. In addition to the atomic bomb, massive research investments driven by military needs would produce developments in radar and computers that would bring tremendous advances in communications technologies. After the war, control over the development of communications technology would change hands from largely national corporations to a complex partnership between the captains of global industries and U.S. warlords. Support for the prerogatives of this partnership would direct federal communications policy through to the present.

The factions contending with this powerful partnership would not be the agrarian force epitomized by Bryan's Populists, nor would an "Industrial Democracy" led by small business Progressives arise as Brandeis hoped.[3] Pragmatic labor leaders and intellectual leftists unleashed by Franklin Roosevelt in both the first and second New Deal would be the main forces to contend with the military-industrial complex. The remnants of this political force would be hopelessly outmatched until they were joined by a group of second-class citizens soon to be emboldened by the Roosevelt Supreme Court and President Harry Truman's decision to finally do something about apartheid in America. Television would be nurtured in the environment of this particular political wind.

The Lost Balance and Lost Understandings

What had become of Madison's dream of a popular government enabled by a set of communications policies that would promote the circulation of popular information? By the time of Truman, the postal system continued to enjoy widespread support, and it continued to subsidize the distribution of newspapers. But newspapers had undergone a radical change from partisan leaflets to commercial organs deeply integrated within the faction of big business. The telegraph, once part of the postal system, grew to become a giant private monopoly with the substantial assistance of federal subsidies, but by the 1940s it was but a shadow of its former self. Still, Western Union spawned two giant monopolies that still had a tremendous impact on communications in America: the Associated Press (AP) and AT&T. The first part of our current public philosophy of communications policy was put in place: investment followed by abandonment to private industry, continued subsidy, and an ineffective response to monopolization.

The second part of that public philosophy can be most generously characterized as an attempt to correct some of the clear problems resulting from our deviation from the citizen-focused communications policy established by the founders. Those problems included private restrictions on popular information, anticompetitive practices, and the effects of rampant commercialism in both chain radio and newspapers. But even the "correction" of imposing public interest obligations on the media trusts was a task dominated by the trusts themselves, most notably under Coolidge and Hoover.

What the media conglomerates accomplished, cloaked in the public interest, was the near elimination of competition in the telecommunications industry and the banishment from "the ether" of those voices that did not speak on behalf of corporations. Our federal representatives encouraged commercial advertising through both licensing and tax policies, while labor unions, churches, and even educational institutions were squeezed from the radio band. These noncommercial operators were called "propaganda stations," as if the jingoistic trumpeting of consumerism was not propaganda. Moreover, mass media, particularly network radio, dominated the public sphere like no form of communication before and disrupted local leadership and local conversation, shifting the public's focus from the local to the national, from the commons to the isolation of one's home.

Still, New Deal programs such as the Tennessee Valley Authority (TVA) and the Public Works Agency set the stage for limited government support of the capacity of citizens to have access to electrical communications services.[4] While promoting democracy was always one of the many justifications given for taxpayer support of business interests in communications, considerations of what an informed citizen required nearly vanished from the public debate. If Adams and Jefferson once dreamed of a public sphere akin to the ancient republics, Holmes would reframe the founders' goal as a "marketplace of ideas." If you could afford to participate in the market, and if you did not advocate an overthrow of the market, you were, for the most part, able to join. Otherwise, your role was to consume, passively. The merchants were clearly in charge.

If few citizens had the opportunity to do much more than listen to others in this oddly undemocratic communications environment, by the 1950s more citizens had access to the ballot box, despite the continuing prohibition of black political participation in the South. But political equality was no longer the ability to make an argument in town hall, or form an association toward effective collective action. Political equality had become simply a matter of one man (or woman) one vote, and then get out of the way of the experts. In addition to this dramatic shift in the idea of equality, in the aftermath of World War II and the end of the Great Depression, Americans influenced by commercial mass media would learn to embrace very different notions of liberty than their forbears. Liberty would no longer be viewed as the ability to participate in a community of self-governors. Nor would it be viewed as the ability to move west and start over again in "virgin" territory. Despite the extraordinary expansion of administrative agencies during the New Deal, Franklin Roosevelt's ideal of freedom from hunger and want would not take center stage either. Liberty after World War II would come to be synonymous with the purchase of an automobile, or access to a mortgage and the ability to take advantage of a world of choices trumpeted in the privately controlled public sphere of commercial mass media.

Why Is There No Socialism in the United States?

Roosevelt's notion of liberty was not abandoned entirely. Harry Truman attempted to carry it forward, as did a far more adept politician and Roosevelt acolyte, Lyndon Johnson. But neither Truman nor Johnson succeeded. Why?

There is a large body of historical analysis that asks this question in different forms. These questions posit an "American exceptionalism" in so far as our paltry welfare state is concerned. Perhaps the most popular phrasing is: Why is there no socialism in the United States? Or as Eric Foner reformulates the question: "Why is the United States the only advanced capitalist nation whose political system lacks a social democratic presence and whose working class lacks socialist class consciousness?" Why is there such a "disjuncture of industrial relations and political practice in the United States?"[5] In other words, why do people in serious conflict with and in such a different economic situation than their employer vote for people who act in their employer's interest?

The easiest answer to this question is that American capitalism meets the needs of American workers. Someone suggesting this answer would argue that the American worker, unlike workers in England or France or Germany or Italy, is and has been happy with the status quo. Such an answer, of course, ignores the long history of labor unrest in the United States. Even while progressive taxation and programs such as the GI Bill helped reduce disparities in wealth and access to higher educational opportunities, as Howard Zinn catalogues in *A People's History of the United States*, there would be regular strikes and work stoppages in those places where labor was allowed to organize throughout the nineteenth and twentieth centuries.[6] The myth of the happy American worker has been banished from respectable history.

Another suggested answer to this question is the impact of racism in America on class consciousness.[7] The assumption behind this is that poor white Americans feel less inclined to identify with their poor brethren, thought to be overwhelmingly black and brown, and more inclined to identify and support their more affluent white neighbors and employers. The dream of American prosperity is colored white, the nightmare of American poverty is a darker hue. As Alexander von Humboldt wrote: "In America, the skin, more or less white, is what dictates the class that an individual occupies in society. A white, even if he rides barefoot on horseback, considers himself to be a member of the nobility of the country."[8] The argument suggests that but for the peculiarly virulent strain of racism in America, there would be class consciousness and a political party that truly represents labor. While I am not convinced that racism alone explains the stinginess of social support in America (and I offer below as an additional reason our unique public philosophy of communications), American racism is a much better answer to the problem than so many others posed in the past.

We have not thus far examined the political impact of racial politics on the development of communications policy. Because racism and the efforts to eliminate this disease played such an important role in shaping modern communications policy, we will add a few words on this subject here.

A Brief History of Racism and Communications

The term *racism* has come to provoke such an emotional response among Americans it tends to obscure its utility in describing a potent political force. While modern anthropologists today tend to view race as a not very scientific construct, historians understand racism as a shameful fact. In a very useful summary of racist practice, George Fredrickson suggests that "racism exists when one ethnic group . . . dominates, excludes, or seeks to eliminate another on the basis of differences that it believes are hereditary or unalterable."[9] Thus the deliberate federal policies of extinction of Native Americans, the enslavement of blacks, the ghetto-like exclusion and internment of Asian immigrants, and domination of Americans originally from Mexico and Puerto Rico are racist to the extent to which these practices are justified by a belief that these groups are inherently different from whites.

Resentment by Native Americans of whites who have taken their land by force is not racism. A black slave attacking her or his master is not a racist. A law requiring the use of race to correct discrimination is not racist.

Our focus is not on the psychology of racism or the impact of racist content on society. Our focus is on racism as a source of political power that so shaped the practices and mechanisms of communication, that one group, those considered white, was allowed to dominate members of nonwhite groups.

If the founders put forward a communication policy regarding race it was obfuscation and silence. Jefferson's original condemnation of the racist practice of slavery in the Declaration of Independence was struck from that document by committee.[10] Despite references to "other persons" and beings "held to service or labour" the Constitution avoided the term *slaves* or *slavery*, and it avoided clarity about just what "other persons" were to be counted as three-fifths. In 1790, in perhaps his last public act, the abolitionist Benjamin Franklin forwarded to the first Congress a petition to consider the gradual elimination of slavery. The aged revolutionary founder's pleas were met with howls of protest that the issue was even raised, with the result that Madison managed to establish a precedent under which the issue of black emancipation would not even be debated in Congress for another forty years.[11]

If the founders were intent upon artful avoidance regarding their racism, Chief Justice Roger Taney would speak for them in the now infamous Dred Scott case. According to Taney's review of history, "neither the class of persons who had been imported as slaves, nor their descendants, whether they had become free or not, were then acknowledged as a part of the people . . . they had for more than a century before been regarded as beings of an inferior race, and altogether unfit to associate with the white race, either in social or political relations, and so far inferior that they had no rights which the white man was bound to respect."[12] A small town lawyer-politician, living in a state that prohibited free blacks from entering, would be stirred by the Supreme Court's decision to argue that the treatment of blacks had actually gotten worse since the nation's founding. Lincoln argued: "In some trifling particulars, the condition of that race had been ameliorated; but, as a whole, in this country, the change between then and now is decidedly the other way; and their ultimate destiny has never appeared so hopeless as in the last three or four years. In two of the five States—New Jersey and North Carolina—that then gave the free Negro the right of voting, the right has since been taken away; and in a third—New York—it has been greatly abridged."[13] According to Lincoln, the Constitution reflected a series of compromises regarding the morality of slavery, forestalling any prohibition of the slave trade until 1808, but refusing to even identify (and embrace) the enslavement of blacks. Lincoln would argue before and during the Civil War that the signers of the Declaration of Independence really meant that "all men are created equal," but to hold a union together that could embrace the abolitionist Franklin and the slaveholder Jefferson, the corrupting compromise of silence was the price.

Regarding the founders' communications system, the first argument against state control of the mail as a guarantor of political equality was the treatment of abolitionist newspapers by the Jackson administration until the Civil War. In 1835, New York abolitionists, frustrated in Congress, sought to stir the conscience of their fellow citizens in the South by mass mailing newspapers that argued against slavery. But political discussion of the fate of blacks was prohibited by law in many southern states. A group of relatively prominent men in Charleston, South Carolina, calling themselves "Lynch Men," broke into the Charleston post office and burned the mailing in a bonfire on the Parade Grounds along with effigies of three leading abolitionists.[14] Instead of defending federal prerogatives against this act of state nullification, President Jackson urged Congress to enact legislation barring abolitionist material from the mail. Lawmakers would not comply. Unable to bend Congress to his will, Jackson and his administration simply refused to prosecute postmasters in southern states for censoring abolitionist mail, and so would every other administration until abolition was accomplished with the defeat of the Confederacy.[15]

Still, for abolitionists, including black abolitionists such as Frederick Douglass, access to postal service was a tremendous benefit to their cause, even if that access was limited to communicating in the North and West. Douglass's *North Star,* first published in 1847, would not be the first newspaper by a black American; *Freedom's Journal,* published and printed by Samuel Cornish and John Russwurm, would precede it by twenty years.[16] Even political discussion by "other persons," by those who "had no rights which the white man was bound to respect," was supported before the Civil War by the federal postal service.

*   *   *

As horrific as slavery was, as terrible an era as the dark pre–Civil War period was, Fredrickson identifies the period after Reconstruction, circa 1880 up until the 1950s, as the nadir of American racism. The harsh backlash against black assertion of political equality was, according to many scholars, the·

time white supremacy "attained its fullest ideological and institutional development."[17] The operations of the Post Office Department mirrored the racism of American society.

Mary Frances Berry tells the story of the brutal treatment suffered by Callie House at the hands of the Post Office Department. In the late 1800s House led the National Ex-Slave Mutual Relief, Bounty and Pension Association, a group dedicated to getting Congress to provide reparations to African Americans formerly held in bondage. Not only was the association's and House's mail opened by the Post Office, delivery service was denied, and after seventeen years of harassment House was tried and imprisoned for mail fraud. Those who ran the Post Office Department believed it was fraudulent to assist "ignorant, illiterate" freedmen to organize and petition for reparations, because they believed such a petition had no chance of succeeding in Congress.[18]

If the mid-eighteenth-century public sphere was infested with religious ("Christian") justifications for the oppression of blacks, Asian immigrants, and Native Americans, a more modern and tenacious set of scientific myths regarding "white" superiority would take hold in the nineteenth century. Ronald Takaki argues that racism in the United States, that is, the subjugation of Native Americans and Mexicans within newly appropriated territory, and the oppression of Chinese immigrants and black Americans into second-class objects of menial labor, took root in nineteenth-century America.[19] Wherever one picks up the story, the fact that state-enforced economic oppression of nonwhites was so pervasive after Reconstruction would limit the opportunities of oppressed minorities to provide or take advantage of communications services completely tied to economic position. This limitation was exacerbated by the federal abdication of serving the communication needs of citizens beyond post service.

As John Coward demonstrates in his book, *The Newspaper Indian*, the ruthless attack on Native Americans in the West was supported by a distortion of events conveyed to readers in the East. "By reducing the amount and variety of routine Western news, the telegraph contributed to the one-dimensional nature of Indian war reporting."[20] The telegraph dispatches of stereotypes regarding Asian immigrants, the racist stereotypes conveyed by yellow journalists, and Rudyard Kipling's racist poetry helped to justify U.S. brutality in the Pacific.[21]

Still, the racial politics of the Progressive Republican Theodore Roosevelt were, at least at home, less incendiary than those of the Progressive Democrat Wilson. Roosevelt may have embraced the "white man's burden," but he seemed to think the "darker races" were capable of improving. Roosevelt's sharing a meal with Booker T. Washington at the White House was a scandal in the white press,[22] but in the growing black press it was a moment of celebration. As for the so-called muckrakers, with the exception of Ray Stannard Baker, who examined the horrible state of race relations in America in an article in *McClure's* and in his book *Following the Color Line*, their wrath was focused on the trusts; for the "negro" they counseled patience and education.[23] As for Wilson, the first Congress of his administration, dominated by southern Democrats, proposed a greater number of bills discriminating against blacks than any previous administration. When those bills failed to pass, Wilson issued an executive order segregating eating and restroom facilities, and began phasing out the few black federal civil service employees the Republicans left behind.[24] Wilson did not sup with Booker T. Washington or any other black leader, but, ignoring the protests of the newly formed National Association for the Advancement of Colored People (NAACP), he did screen D. W. Griffith's spectacular romance of the Ku Klux Klan (KKK), *Birth of a Nation*. Wilson proclaimed it "history writ with lightning, and my only regret is that it is all so terribly true." Black Americans cried openly at the popular film's racist caricature of them, while white audiences, North and South, cheered. The film is associated not only with a rise in the ranks of the terrorist KKK, but with a rash of white on black violence in major cities, including Boston and Philadelphia.[25]

* * *

Given the dominant white image of black Americans, the fact that blacks were largely ignored by the major urban press and national magazines of the early 1900s seemed a blessing. It was also an opportunity for a growing black press. Black-owned papers such as the *Chicago Defender* had a national readership; some such as the Baltimore-based *Afro-American* even established a chain of newspapers, and the NAACP *Crisis* magazine served their substantial membership for decades.[26] This was all possible because the Post Office provided service and discounted rates to all newspapers, no matter the color of the owner.

Black newspapers continued to prosper, even through the early days of radio, in part because African Americans were rarely represented on the air. The absence of blacks on radio may have come as a surprise to many, given the wildly popular program "Amos and Andy," whose black caricatures were portrayed by two whites, Freeman Fisher Gosden (Amos) and Charles J. Correll (Andy). The "Amos and Andy" program was the most popular program on radio for many years, embedding a stereotype of happy and incompetent black Americans, the flip side of the wild-eyed rapists who drove white Americans to frenzy in *Birth of a Nation*. On a rare occasion a real black person, such as the entertainers Duke Ellington and Paul Robeson, were allowed to sing or play music on the radio. But there would be no black Father Coughlin. There was occasionally a local program, such as "The All-Negro Hour," which featured black performers exclusively on white-owned radio station WSBC in Chicago. In addition to substantial black audiences, many stations featuring black performers drew a sizable white audience. But there would not be a black person in management in broadcasting, nor a black-owned radio station until 1949, when Jesse B. Blayton Sr. purchased 1,000-watt station WERD in Atlanta and hired his son Jesse Blayton Jr. as station manager.[27] However, it would be another twenty years, and a radical shift in race politics, before even small efforts were made to address the communications inequities whites imposed on "other persons." Here our story dovetails with World War II and the dreams of American empire.

The International Liability of Racism

Fredrickson distinguishes between an overtly racist system and a society in which prejudice leads to social stratification. The United States typified both as immigrant Irish, Jews, Eastern Europeans, and others were certainly subject to prejudice but not to the racism nonwhite groups, particularly blacks, faced. Fredrickson offers five features present in a racist regime:

1. There is an explicitly racist government ideology. High-ranking officials proclaim that the subordinated groups' differences are permanent and to dissent from this ideology is dangerous.
2. The ideal of race purity is expressed in laws forbidding interracial marriage.
3. Segregation is mandated by law.
4. The subordinated group is prevented from exercising the right to vote.
5. Economic opportunity is limited, keeping the majority of the subordinated group in poverty.[28]

These characteristics fit three societies, South Africa under apartheid (1948–90), Nazi Germany (1933–45), and the United States, except for a small portion of New England (1776–1866 and 1877–1967). The brutality of the Nazis and the more recent fall of apartheid in South Africa should not obscure the peculiar longevity and recurrence of overt racism in America. I have argued previously that after the Civil War (with the nullification of the constitutional advantage of whites "representing" three-fifths of blacks), the largely agrarian South lost its dominance over public policy to northern industrialists. However, after the brief period of Reconstruction and the introduction of Jim Crow laws, the South regained substantial political power, particularly in Congress and in the Democratic Party, and its priority was the maintenance of its racist regime. Not even Theodore Roosevelt would attempt to do more than tweak that interest by breaking bread with Booker T—once. What I mean to point out here is that during the periods of overt racism in America our communications policies were formed. These policies and the institutions that both formed these policies and were formed by them would have consequences resulting in white privilege.

The shocking brutality of the Nazis' Final Solution was an embarrassment to a racist America. As Fredrickson writes, "Within the United States, there was a growing realization among those concerned with international relations that Jim Crow not only was analogous to Nazi treatment of the Jews and thus morally indefensible but was also contrary to the national interest."[29]

This was especially true if the national interest included advancing American business interests and, particularly, free market capitalism in the face of newly prominent and expansionist communist powers in China and the Soviet Union. The battle for the hearts and minds of noncommunist Asia, Africa, or even Latin America would be all the more difficult to wage if America could not correct its persistent racism.

W. E. B. Du Bois argued that black soldiers fighting for democracy abroad would create added moral pressure upon America to live up to its ideals at home as early as World War I. Once war was over, he pushed home the point in his famous May 1919 *Crisis* editorial.

> It was right for us to fight. The faults of *our* country are *our* faults. Under similar circumstances, we would fight again. But by the God of Heaven, we are cowards and jackasses if now that the war is over, we do not marshal every ounce of our brain and brawn to fight a sterner, longer, more unbending battle against the forces of hell in our own land.
>
> We *return*.
> We *return from fighting*.
> We *return fighting*.
>
> Make way for Democracy! We saved it in France, and by the Great Jehovah, we will save it in the United States of America, or know the reason why.[30]

But the time and circumstances were not yet ripe. Du Bois was charged with subversion after this editorial, but not convicted. The mailing privileges of *Crisis* magazine were temporarily suspended. In addition, the disruption of returning black soldiers in 1919 led to a rise in lynchings and a rash of frenzied white on black violence north and south. Government officials either stood aside or actually joined in the antiblack violence. Clearly, fighting and dying for democracy was not sufficient. International competition with the avowed antiracist communist nations and the revulsion toward Nazi racism would increase the stakes.

A. Philip Randolph understood the vulnerability of America's expressed outrage at Nazism and the potential embarrassment to America's claims to moral superiority, as he threatened to march on Washington in 1941 protesting discrimination in the armed forces. He understood that it was his determination to carry through on that threat that led President Roosevelt to issue an executive order forbidding race discrimination in war and government industries.[31]

In addition to the pressure to set an international example, the NAACP's legal attack on segregation would have the Roosevelt-packed Supreme Court to help it chip away at the edifice of Jim Crow. First, in 1938, *Missouri ex rel Gaines* (the state must provide equal education); then, in 1944, *Smith v. Allwright* (white primaries ruled unconstitutional); in 1946, *Morgan v. Virginia* (segregated bus travel on interstate ruled unconstitutional), and in 1948, *Sipuel v. Oklahoma* (the state must provide equal opportunity to study law) and *Shelley v. Kraemer* (restrictive racial covenants on property are unenforceable). But it would be President Harry Truman who would send shock waves through the South and set the stage for a major political shift with important ramifications for communications policy.

Give 'Em Hell, Harry!

In 1945, President Roosevelt died in office, not long after he had been elected to an unprecedented fourth term. In 1946, with Democrats weakened, barely able to refer to Harry Truman as Mr. President, Republicans triumphed in the congressional elections. With control of Congress Republicans immediately launched a series of investigations against the Truman administration, alleging communist infiltration and corruption. Complicating Truman's chances for reelection in 1948 was the defection of liberal Democrats, who opposed his willingness to fight China's expansion into Korea and his hardline opposition to the Soviet Union. Many of these liberals supported the candidacy of Henry A. Wallace, who was running as the Progressive Party candidate for president.

But nothing threatened the patched-together coalition Roosevelt made of the Democrats as much as Truman's decision to do something about discrimination against black Americans. In 1946, President Truman issued an executive order creating a Committee on Civil Rights. In 1947, Truman urged Congress to adopt a civil rights program including anti–poll tax and anti-lynching measures. He was turned down. In 1948, Truman issued an executive order integrating the armed forces. This was the last straw for fellow Democrat Strom Thurmond. At the head of the States Rights Party, Thurmond would campaign as a protector of race purity: "I wanna tell you, ladies and gentlemen, that there's not enough troops in the army to force the southern people to break down segregation and admit the nigger race into our theatres, into our swimming pools, into our homes, and into our churches."[32]

With the Dixiecrats in open revolt over his civil rights policies and the Republicans pouring money into radio stations and advertising agencies in support of Thomas E. Dewey, Truman was in the battle of his life. But unlike Roosevelt, who felt he could use the young medium of radio and go over the heads of the conservative newspaper publishers, Truman believed corporate interests had taken hold of radio. As he wrote in his memoirs, "The figures showed that approximately ninety per cent of the press and radio opposed me and supported other candidates. This was to be expected, as most were owned, operated, or subsidized by the same private interests that always benefited from Republican economic policies. Even the segments of the press and radio which were not directly controlled by anti-administration interests depended to a great extent upon the advertising revenue which came from the wealthy, and often selfish, private groups. . . . As far as I was concerned, they had sold out to the special interests, and that is why I referred to them in my campaign speeches as the 'kept press and paid radio.'"[33]

Truman conducted a campaign reminiscent of William Jennings Bryan, barreling across the country and blasting the "do-nothing, good-for-nothing Republican Congress." As he hammered away at Republican support for the antilabor Taft-Hartley Act, passed over his veto, and other conservative targets, including a media taken over by corporate interests, crowds responded with "Give 'em hell, Harry!"

* * *

The disenchantment of southern racists like Strom Thurmond with the Democrats begun under the Truman administration and completed with the Johnson administration was a major shift of political power. The ugly transformation of the party of Lincoln to the party of Coolidge and Hoover and finally to the party of the Goldwater right and the Dixiecrats gives support to the identification of racism as a reason for America's comparatively stingy social support system. As Lyndon Johnson predicted, the Dixiecrats, however poor, would rather join the party of big business than continue an association with labor and the left and relinquish what Derrick Bell would call the property value of whiteness. A sizeable faction of southern whites would never forgive their former partners in the Franklin Roosevelt coalition for the betrayal of extending political equality to black Americans.

While the new technology of television would arise in this period and come to dominate the media landscape, overtaking even radio for the nation's attention, government policies were derived from patterns established for radio. The 1934 Communications Act was amended to include the new service of television. Television was regulated by the FCC in the same laissez-faire manner, dominated by the same white male leaders of national corporations, with the same impact on local discourse. The public interest remained more theoretical nicety than enforceable obligation, and the tax break on advertising ensured that the money would roll in. One important exception to that pattern occurred in the 1950s: the reservation of channel space for educational broadcasters. While the resurgence of anticommunist hysteria also swept the nation during the 1950s, having a particularly ugly effect on broadcasting, so-called McCarthyism (as if the anticommunist hysteria could be blamed on one publicity-seeking politician) would expose the fundamentally conservative nature of the communications industry but would not alter either the structure of the broadcast industry or the federal policies with which it was blessed.

Frieda Hennock and the Beginning of Noncommercial Broadcasting

On June 27, 1945, the Federal Communications Commission (FCC) moved the frequency assignment for FM (frequency modulation) radio from between 42 and 50 megacycles to ninety channels between 88 and 106 megacycles, and it reserved twenty of those channels for noncommercial educational FM.[34] This decision was the culmination of the second round in the battle waged between educational stations and commercial stations begun in the late 1920s. The educators, joined under the banner of the National Association of Educational Broadcasters (NAEB), made major compromises to achieve this qualified victory. Perhaps the most significant was the agreement to not compete for advertising dollars—thus the association with educational broadcasting and noncommercial broadcasting. Another compromise was the assignment of FM to a higher band than AM (amplified modulation), resulting in an immediate loss of an audience that had already invested in radios manufactured to receive only the lower designation of frequencies. Still, the NAEB was encouraged to fight for a reservation of channel space in television, and in 1948 they were given two gifts to help them in that cause. The first gift was the first woman commissioner, Frieda B. Hennock, and the second was a freeze on television licensing.

Field tests for television began in 1936, and three years later commercial television was launched with an impressive debut at the New York World's Fair. By late 1948, when the freeze was declared, there were about a hundred television stations on the air. New York and Los Angeles had seven stations competing for audiences, twenty-four cities had two stations, but in other urban areas, such as Houston and Pittsburgh, there was only one. Despite the spotty coverage, it was becoming clear that audience and advertiser interest in television would soon easily surpass radio. Television was also having a damaging effect on the movie business; by the end of the freeze movie attendance dropped between 20 and 40 percent in those cities with television stations, while attendance held steady or rose in cities without television.[35] The three-year freeze would give the educational broadcasters time to organize.

While Commissioner Hennock was only one of seven commissioners, she focused relentlessly on establishing a space for noncommercial television. Eric Barnouw suggests that Hennock benefited from the public revulsion to the Nazis. Despite the difficulty Truman faced with nearly every appointment and measure he put before a Republican Congress, members not wanting to be branded anti-Semitic confirmed her quickly.[36]

The idea of using television for educational purposes drew little support in the Northeast. Stuck in a limited framework, professional educators divided over the utility of a television in the classroom or the ability of television to convey what a teacher was trained to do. But reservation of public airwaves for education resonated in western and midwestern states with their land-grant colleges and broader ideas of continuing education. Southern states saw educational television as a way to provide "equal" education while maintaining segregated classrooms.[37] Hennock envisioned something else; she saw a purpose even larger than the one proposed by educational broadcasters. Hennock argued that noncommercial television might be "a beneficial complement to commercial broadcasting." Not dependent upon advertisers, it could "provide greater diversity in television programming [and] competition and public responsibility in broadcasting."[38]

Competition was not at all what the commercial broadcasters had in mind, and they fought ferociously over the proposed reservation of space for educational television. Given the struggle for survival experienced by noncommercial radio stations, some at the FCC doubted that educators could keep a noncommercial television station on the air. In the end, the commissioners believed they had little to lose and much to gain by granting the educators their wish. If the noncommercial television stations failed, the FCC could say they were given a chance. If they succeeded, the FCC could claim to have served the public interest. In 1952, the commission reserved 242 frequencies, with the stipulation that they be used to meet the educational needs of communities and that the stations be noncommercial and nonprofit enterprises.[39] If this was a foot in the door, commercial broadcasters would continue to press against that door with all the political weight they could muster. *Broadcasting*, the mouthpiece for the commercial industry, summed up the industry position when it wrote: "One day the FCC must take another look at the Communications Act in relation to these socialistic reservations."[40]

The Fairness Doctrine and Murrow

In 1949, in a decision referred to as *In the Matter of Editorializing by Broadcast Licensees*, the FCC codified a policy to promote the presentation of differing sides of controversial issues; it was called the Fairness Doctrine.[41] The Fairness Doctrine was derived from the FCC and court application of the 1928 General Rule 40, a policy discussed earlier, which gave licensing priority to commercial stations over noncommercial stations. The FCC also cited *Associated Press v. United States*.[42] As we discussed above, the AP established a monopoly that, in concert with Western Union, restricted the flow of news. The Roosevelt Justice Department charged the AP with violation of the Sherman Anti-Trust Act, focusing with special concern on AP by-laws that prohibited all AP members from selling news to nonmembers and that granted each member powers to block its nonmember competitors from membership. In ruling against the AP, Justice Hugo Black noted that the First Amendment "rests on the assumption that the widest possible dissemination of information from diverse and antagonistic sources is essential to the welfare of the public."

The broad understanding of the Fairness Doctrine is that it required broadcasters to present controversial issues of public importance, and that such issues must be presented in a fair and balanced manner.[43] Ten years later Congress amended the 1934 Communications Act by adding: "Nothing in the foregoing sentence shall be construed as relieving broadcasters . . . from the obligation imposed upon them in this chapter to operate in the public interest and to afford reasonable opportunity for the discussion of conflicting views on issues of public importance."[44] The FCC operated with the understanding that Congress had thus codified the Fairness Doctrine, and it made no attempt to alter that doctrine for many years.[45]

Commissioner Hennock dissented from the *Editorializing* decision on the ground that the standard as laid out "in the report is virtually impossible of enforcement."[46] But the still vague (perhaps necessarily so) standard was only one of the problems. Another problem was that the commission was hopelessly understaffed to monitor content effectively, particularly given the explosion in broadcast licensees. It was no longer overseeing a few hundred AM broadcasters; now it had FM broadcasting and television as well. Despite requiring stations to keep logs, and issuing rules to clarify licensing and other policies, the FCC simply could not effectively police the so-called trustees of the public interest.

The Fairness Doctrine was a powerful symbol; even the National Association of Broadcasters adopted much of its language in their Code of Conduct. But the Fairness Doctrine, like earlier attempts at regulation, would not correct the fundamental error of leaving the responsibility of informing a democratic citizenry in the hands of commerce. Commercial pressures would push the broadcast industry away from the presentation of "controversial issues." These pressures are painfully demonstrated in the finest hours of early television and modern journalism.

In October 1953, Edward R. Murrow notified CBS management and air force officials that he planned to televise on his half-hour prime-time documentary program, "See It Now," a program about the forced resignation of Lieutenant Milo Radulovich. Radulovich was forced out because his father and sister were accused of communist sympathies. It would be the first of five "See It Now" broadcasts that gently, soberly, questioned communist hysteria in the United States.

The air force declined to participate in the program. Such a decision usually meant that the program would be cancelled, as CBS and most other broadcasters had adopted a policy of carrying "both" sides of an issue. Murrow regarded this as allowing one party to veto a discussion by simply deciding not to participate. He repeated his intention to go ahead with the broadcast. An air force general and a lieutenant colonel met with Murrow, joined by Murrow's partner at CBS, Fred Friendly. The general assumed that Murrow, a recipient of the Distinguished Service to Airpower award, would not go ahead with the broadcast. Murrow was silent, but pressed on.

Murrow had a special relationship with CBS. His World War II broadcasts from London and his shaping of the CBS news team established the network's leadership in broadcast news. He was a member of the CBS board of directors. In addition to his television work on "See It Now," he continued as a radio newscaster on the air Monday through Friday evening. Because of his years of service at CBS, and his celebrity, he had more autonomy and clout than any other newsman in America working at a network. But when Murrow and Friendly asked for publicity support for the planned program, CBS management declined. Murrow and Friendly paid, from their own pockets, for an advertisement in the *New York Times. The Case Against Milo Radulovich, AO589839,* aired on October 20, 1953.

As Radulovich said in the program: "The actual charge against me is that I had maintained a close and continuing relationship with my dad and my sister over the years. . . . If I am going to be judged by my relatives, are my children going to be asked to denounce me? . . . I see a chain reaction that has no end."

In closing the program Murrow offered the air force studio facilities to respond. On November 23, "See It Now" aired a program on the tensions between those who wanted to begin an American Civil Liberties Union (ACLU) chapter in Indianapolis and those who denounced the ACLU. That same night, Secretary of the Air Force Harold Talbott in a filmed statement aired before the show announced that he reviewed the case of Lieutenant Radulovich and directed that he be returned to his former status with the air force. It was a clear victory for Murrow, but pressures from anticommunist groups were increasing, aimed not only at CBS but at "See It Now" sponsor Alcoa.[47]

There would be three more programs on American communist hysteria. In 1954, one featured the Republican senator from Wisconsin, Joseph McCarthy, bullying government employees with unsubstantiated charges of communist sympathy; another featured McCarthy bullying Murrow with similar unsubstantiated charges, including a vague charge that traitors had delayed the development of the hydrogen bomb. In 1955, Murrow broadcast a long interview with Robert Oppenheimer, the man considered most responsible for the scientific research that led to the atomic bomb. Oppenheimer had been stripped of his security clearance after McCarthy's charges. While Oppenheimer would not discuss the specifics of the security ruling against him, he made a passionate case for open communications.

> Oppenheimer: The trouble with secrecy isn't that it inhibits science [or] that it doesn't give the public a sense of participation. The trouble with secrecy is that it denies to the Government itself the wisdom and the resources of the whole community, of the whole country. And the only way you can do this is to let almost anyone say what he thinks . . . and to let men deny what they think is false. . . . You have to have a free and uncorrupted communication . . . that is why we are all the time saying, "Does this really have to be secret? Couldn't we say more about that? Are we really acting in a wise way?" . . . Not because we are not aware of the dangers of the world we live in, but because these dangers cannot be met any other way.

> Murrow: Well, if I may say so, I think you were speaking there not only for your profession, but for mine—if it is a profession.[48]

By the end of the 1954–55 season, after four years with Murrow, Alcoa decided it had had enough. As Friendly explained it: "Aluminum salesmen had difficulty explaining to irate customers why their company felt it necessary to sponsor programs *against* McCarthy and *for* Oppenheimer, *against* cigarettes and *for* 'socialized medicine.'"[49] The last straw was a program that drew attention to a Texas land scandal at the same time that Alcoa was enlarging its operations in Texas. Still, in a deserved tribute to Alcoa, Jack Gould of the *New York Times* argued: "That *See It Now* is changing sponsors or going [without sponsors] is not so nearly disturbing as the fact that television still has only one *See It Now*."[50] The program continued, irregularly scheduled though longer, offering substantial fare such as the famous "Harvest of Shame" documentary on the plight of migrant farm workers. But it would not last, and there would be nothing like it to come again.

The "See It Now" broadcasts on the anticommunist hysteria typified by the junior Republican senator from Wisconsin would over the years provide a sort of luster to American media. Those broadcasts would support the simplistic notions of the power of a "free press." In short, the argument goes, because Murrow could show McCarthy for what he was demonstrated the power and privileges of television in America. However, the fact that McCarthy and a legion of others like him in the Republican Party could so dominate public discourse as to drive Americans crazy with fears about "commies" is the result of the American system of communications. The fact that Murrow lost his financial support, and the American public lost

"See It Now," as a direct result of his brave stand, exposes the true nature of American communications policy.

In 1958, Murrow would deliver a searing indictment of the young medium of television to the Radio and Television News Directors Association. "The top management of the networks," he said, "with a few notable exceptions, has been trained in advertising, research, sales, or show business. But by the nature of the corporate structure, they also make the final and crucial decisions having to do with news and public affairs. Frequently they have neither the time nor the competence to do this." Looking to the future, Murrow predicted historians would look at the television film of his time and see "evidence of decadence, escapism and insulation from the realities of the world in which we live."[51] Unfortunately, we look at Murrow's time as the Golden Age of Television.

By the time he was done, Murrow and his partner Fred Friendly believed the only answer to the challenge of American communication and American democracy was another network, more like the BBC than the commercially driven operations in America. But that story will have to wait until a Texas broadcaster by the name of Lyndon Johnson would become president. In some small measure, it would have to wait for the push of civil rights activists struggling against racism, north and south. Again, this newly powerful political force was emboldened by Truman's civil rights activity and the Roosevelt-packed Supreme Court, and bolstered by the ongoing U.S. struggle against the Soviet Union and China over which economic system would dominate the world, capitalism or communism—a struggle soon to be taken over by the general of generals, Dwight David (Ike) Eisenhower.

I Like Ike, but Impeach Warren

By 1952, the liberal Democrats led by Harry Truman, with their pesky appointments like Hennock, were out of power. A coalition of Republicans and southern Dixiecrats ruled Congress and conservative big-business Republicans were after a long absence finally back in charge of the executive branch.

With the help of the first presidential campaign run by an advertising agency, Batton, Barton, Burstine & Osborn, Eisenhower defeated his Democratic opponent Adlai Stevenson to take the White House.[52] The key to victory was to provide the country with a genial general who could resolve the conflict in Korea, continue the red-baiting, and lay at Truman's lap the blame for the corruption of petty officials.

Eisenhower began his campaign with the statement: "The aim of this crusade is to sweep from office an administration which has fastened on every one of us the wastefulness, the arrogance and corruption in high places, the heavy burden and the anxieties which are the bitter fruit of a party too long in power."[53] Still, Ike preferred to campaign as a genial non-partisan leader, leaving Republicans in Congress and his running mate, Richard Nixon, to join McCarthy's red-baiting and decry the petty scandals caused by minor officials in the IRS and an agency called the Reconstruction Finance Committee. With a weakness for alliteration Nixon would yell "no administration with the greedy, gouging, grumbling history of the Truman regime" can be trusted.[54]

None of the congressional charges of corruption were successfully pinned on Truman or any other top Truman official, but it didn't help matters that Stevenson distanced himself from the Truman administration.[55] The press-driven anticommunist hysteria was especially damaging to a national political debate over post–World War II policies. The sensational claims of "Reds" taking over the government was like blood in the water, or money in the bank. It would prove too powerful for a press more interested in profit than fact to resist. It was a story that drew readers. The habit of reporting what top government officials were saying while ignoring whether what they were saying was true (such as the shifting numbers of commie infiltrators) would be a difficult habit to break.

Nixon's claims of Truman corruption would come back to haunt him when similarly petty charges were hurled at him for accepting gifts, endangering his vice-presidential spot. But the Republican Party purchased television time and Nixon would immortalize his dog Checkers and draw on the sympathy of viewers. But, all of the dramatics of the campaign may have masked a deeper truth, suggested by Walter Lippmann: "By 1952 this country and the Western world had had all the dynamism, all the innovation, all the crusading that human nature can take. . . . It had become imperative that this country collect itself, that it consolidate itself, that it restore its confidence in itself, that it find a way to quiet its frayed nerves, to allay its suspicions, and that it regain its composure and its equanimity. That was the wellspring of the Eisenhower movement."[56] The majority of the press, including the *New York Times*, endorsed Eisenhower and Nixon.

Once in office, Eisenhower chose cabinet members that demonstrated that big business was back in charge. Eight of the nine members of Eisenhower's cabinet were millionaire corporate executives; three of them had ties to General Motors, prompting Stevenson to say, "The New Dealers have all left Washington to make way for the car dealers."[57] It is perhaps no surprise that the major achievement of the Eisenhower administration was the Federal-Aid Highway Act of 1956.[58]

Serious corruption among top Eisenhower officials would soon come to light. In 1955, Harold Talbott, Eisenhower's secretary of the air force, was found to have used air force stationery to conduct a private consulting business, and to have directed government contracts to a firm in which he was a partner. Eisenhower quickly dismissed him. In 1958, Eisenhower's chief of staff, Sherman Adams, accepted a vicuna coat from a Boston businessman seeking to influence the White House. He, too, was forced to resign. But neither of these incidents matched the corruption of Eisenhower's FCC commissioner, John C. Doerfer.

Doerfer understood his position as an advocate for commercial broadcasters, strongly recommending that broadcast licenses be made permanent. He was a popular commissioner with the industry. The commercial broadcasters strongly urged he be given the chairmanship, and in 1957 Eisenhower complied. Doerfer once made a trip to give two speeches to two different broadcasting groups, and collected full fees for the same travel from both groups and the government. He also took a week-long yacht trip to Bimini at the expense of broadcaster George Storer, at a time when Storer had a case before the commission. A House FCC oversight committee hired Bernard Schwartz to conduct a probe, and then tried to stifle Schwartz's testimony. Schwartz leaked his findings to the *New York Times*. Doerfer was forced to resign in 1960, along with fellow Commissioner Richard Mack, who had accepted a bribe for his vote on a disputed Florida channel.[59]

As for Eisenhower's pledge to do something about communism, hundreds of federal employees were fired under his expanded loyalty-security program. With his approval, Congress passed a law designed to outlaw the American Communist Party. Eisenhower also kept his word and went to Korea, and accepted a stalemate. Even after a brief economic slump in the middle of his first term, the press and the public clearly liked Ike. By 1955, the economy was experiencing a small boom, employment was rising, and prices were stable. Another wave of big business mergers swept across the nation, but this time the consolidation was not only within related industries; a relatively new form of trust, the international conglomeration, was rising. Corporations were pulling under one roof a wide variety of industries. International Telephone and Telegraph, for example, purchased Sheraton Hotels, Continental Baking, Hartford Fire Insurance, Avis, and other companies. But unions were able to win increasingly favorable collective bargaining contracts from employers, including automatic pay increases to protect wages from inflationary erosion and, in some cases, provision for guaranteed annual wages. This renewed prosperity led many workers to forget their union-won victories and defy their liberal civil rights–oriented leaders and vote Republican.

It was, in fact, a Republican who would provide momentum to a movement not even Ike could stop. In 1953, Eisenhower appointed the enormously popular California Republican Earl Warren as the new chief justice of the Supreme Court. Only a few years after his appointment of Warren, Eisenhower said it "was the biggest damn fool thing I ever did." As was mentioned earlier, there were a number of Supreme Court cases that whittled away at Jim Crow, or more specifically the giant oak of *Plessy v. Ferguson,* which legitimized segregation under the lie "separate but equal." But no court decision stirred the jubilant hopes of black Americans as did *Brown v. Board of Education.* When a unanimous Supreme Court ruled in 1954 that "separate educational facilities are inherently unequal," it seemed as if a new day had begun in America.

To his credit, Eisenhower did order the protection of those few black children attempting to enter school in Little Rock, Arkansas, and he would sign the tepid Civil Rights Act of 1957—the first such law passed since 1875, thanks to the legislative skills of Lyndon Johnson.

Despite these acts or because of them, at the close of the Eisenhower years, black Americans were becoming increasingly restless. The meaning of the language about ending the segregation of American schools "with all deliberate speed" was becoming clearer. As Wiley Branton, the chief counsel for the plaintiffs in the Little Rock, Arkansas school case, would later say, "desegregation wasn't very speedy, but it was very, very deliberate."[60]

W. E. B. Du Bois, who had suffered through the disappointment of Wilson and Roosevelt, who was hounded during the communist hysteria years of Truman, had now heard President Eisenhower in 1958 urge blacks to be patient in pressing for full citizenship. Du Bois would soon declare himself a Communist, a certain sign that this ardent Victorian democrat had given up all hope that America was capable of overcoming its racism or achieving democracy. One reason for this, he was now convinced, was the dominance of one faction over all other sectors in American society—big business. "The organized effort of American industry to usurp government surpasses anything in modern history. . . . From the use of psychology to spread truth has come the use of organized gathering of news to guide public opinion, then deliberately to mislead it by scientific advertising and propaganda. . . .

Mass capitalistic control of books and periodicals, news gathering and distribution, radio, cinema, and television has made the throttling of democracy possible and the distortion of education and failure of justice widespread."[61]

If most black Americans would not join Du Bois and turn their backs on American capitalism, neither would they be patient—and with the help of a new medium, they would work to alter the racist regime of the American South forever. In their protests and litigation they would also come to alter communications policy.

7

Kennedy, Johnson, and Satellites (1960–1968)

The new era of human relationships in which we live is
one marked by mass production for remote markets, by
cable and telephone, by cheap printing, by railway and
steam navigation. Since the aims, desires, and purposes
created by a machine age do not connect with tradition,
there are two sets of rival ideals, and those which have
actual instrumentalities at their disposal have the
advantage.... Conditions have changed, but every aspect
of life, from religion and education to property and trade,
shows that nothing approaching a transformation has
taken place in ideas and ideals. The ties which hold men
together in action are numerous, tough and subtle. But
they are invisible and intangible. The thoughts and
aspirations congruous with them are not communicated....
Without such communication the public will remain
shadowy and formless, seeking spasmodically for itself,
but seizing and holding its shadow rather than
its substance. Till the Great Society is converted into a
Great Community, the Public will remain in eclipse.
Communication can alone create a great community.

—John Dewey, *The Public and Its Problems*, 1927

The Search for the Public

The 1960s saw the last gasp of the Roosevelt Progressives. It was the last
decade when merchants turned trusts turned international conglomerations would be well contested by the remnants of the old Roosevelt coalition: eastern intellectuals, Labor, newly empowered minority groups, and
poor people. Aided by the most liberal court the nation has ever seen, and
by the emotional power resulting from grief and guilt over a martyred

leader, this new left coalition made more progress toward establishing a government for the common man than even Roosevelt could accomplish in the midst of the Great Depression. It is no surprise that during the Johnson reawakening of what Sandel calls the "Procedural Republic" the public service broadcasting institutions came into being in the United States.

However, unlike public service broadcasting in Europe, the American model was conceived at a time when the priorities of hegemony promoted by the military-industrial complex dominated all other considerations of national policy. To understand that time, as Sandel suggests, as merely the continuation of the Roosevelt expansion of the administrative state is to ignore the core importance of the military-industrial complex as a political faction. Education, social services, race relations, and, of course, budgetary considerations were all viewed through the prism of America as alternative to China and Russia. In this prism, totalitarianism was equated with socialism and democracy equated with industrial capitalism. As much as Johnson may have wanted to follow in the footsteps of his hero Franklin Roosevelt, he was in fact trapped by military-industrial prerogatives in a way that Roosevelt had never been. Roosevelt, like Lincoln, was clearly a civilian commander in charge of the military. More important, with the Great Depression having demonstrated the failure of laissez-faire economic policies, Roosevelt had a much easier hand vis-à-vis the industrial faction. Johnson was a political lion caged by the anticommunist framework of the military-industrial complex in a boom time. Commercial mass media was an integral part of that complex and that boom. Johnson would be destroyed in this cage, and the opportunity for social reform, including communications reform, would be lost. In Dewey's sense, Johnson sought to communicate the ties that bound citizens and connect them with the ideals of political equality, freedom to participate in governance, and the check and balance of diverse interest. But neither Johnson nor the coalition he empowered was in control of the necessary instrumentalities of communication.

In a sense, the 1960s can be seen as an awakening from the private consumer culture of the Eisenhower years into a search for what John Dewey called the Great Community. From Kennedy's call to public service, to the rise of dozens of groups demanding an end to racism or a say in administrative decisions, to Johnson's empowerment of community groups or private commissions, to the rioters provoked by police brutality, to the antiwar protesters, it was a time when the role of associations would come under political debate. How could the federal government promote democratic self-governance among citizens acting in local communities? What was the political relationship between citizens and private institutions—including media?

No less important than the battle over these questions was the new field of public debate. If radio helped move the public sphere into the private home, television would secure that space. Television proved itself ideally suited to the gripping immediacy of American political drama, and it would provide, still in its infancy, the greatest platform for protest the nation had ever known. This was no longer a quiet and orderly time for trusting in genial generals, or a time of the backroom deals of rowdy but staged machine politics. It was a time when the country seemed either on the precipice of chaos—or on the verge of a truly inclusive communicating democracy.

Sputnik over the Vast Wasteland

On October 4, 1957, the Soviet Union launched into space a two hundred-pound beeping metallic sphere about the size of a basketball. They called it *Sputnik I*. The harmless artificial satellite orbited the earth, passing over the United States, roughly every hundred minutes. The American elite, busy looking for Communists but certain of American scientific superiority, was caught off guard. On November 3, *Sputnik II* was launched, carrying the first live earthling in space, a dog named Laika. The U.S. establishment was in shock. While the United States had spent time improving on the destructive force of the atomic bomb, as mentioned above, they now feared that the Soviets' ability to launch satellites also demonstrated an ability to launch missiles carrying atomic (or maybe even hydrogen!) weapons not only to their neighbors in Europe but directly to the United States, providing barely enough time to retreat to the backyard bomb shelter.

While scientific research into launching objects into space began as early as 1955 in the United States, *Sputnik* suggested that the Soviets were far ahead of the rest of the world. Immediately after the first *Sputnik* launch, the U.S. Defense Department responded to the political furor by funding a U.S. satellite project, led by the ex-Nazi Wernher von Braun.[1] The race was on.

On January 31, 1958, the United States successfully launched a small satellite called *Explorer I*. In July 1958, Congress passed the National Aeronautics and Space Act (commonly called the "Space Act"), which created the National Aeronautics and Space Administration (NASA) as of October 1, 1958.[2] But Eisenhower remained cautious about any dramatic increases in military spending. Democratic presidential candidate John F. Kennedy would attack the Eisenhower administration for its complacency and allege, without any foundation, a missile gap between the United States and its Russian nemesis.

Kennedy, the handsome and privileged son of an ambitious Massachusetts businessman turned Roosevelt reformer, posed as the vigorous leader of a new generation. It was perhaps Kennedy's excitement of the spending glands of industrial and military leaders that led Eisenhower to sour on the forces that had sponsored him earlier. In his farewell address, he would warn the nation "against the acquisition of unwarranted influence, whether sought or unsought, by the military-industrial complex. The potential for the disastrous rise of misplaced power exists and will persist."[3]

After a close election victory, Kennedy in his inaugural address claimed that the "torch has been passed to a new generation" while assuring the world that America was willing to "pay any price" to battle communism. He also inspired Americans to public service, to "ask what you can do for your country."[4] It was a call to reach beyond the accumulation of consumer goods and the comforts of the new suburbs, it was a call back to citizenship. These early days in a new decade were a time of romantic hope for dormant democratic ideals mixed with the real and present fear of nuclear war.

A few months into his administration, Kennedy made a special address "on Urgent National Needs" to Congress.

> Recognizing the head start obtained by the Soviets with their large rocket engines, which gives them many months of lead time, and recognizing the likelihood that they will exploit this lead for some time to come in still more impressive successes, we nevertheless are required to make new efforts on our own. For while we cannot guarantee that we shall one day be first, we can guarantee that any failure to make this effort will make us last. . . .
>
> I therefore ask the Congress, above and beyond the increases I have earlier requested for space activities, to provide the funds which are needed to meet the following national goals:
>
> I believe that this nation should commit itself to achieving the goal, before this decade is out, of landing a man on the moon and returning him safely to earth.[5]

A strongly divided Congress would accomplish little the new president would request, but they did provide the support necessary to create the satellite industry. A quick glimpse behind the curtain of power reveals the clear and steady influence of the forces Eisenhower warned against. Just as Congress provided support for the telegraph, telephone, and broadcast industries, they would provide support for the satellite industry.[6] Quite contrary to the myth of industry genius and independence, big business was supported by taxpayer dollars to advance the nation's "privately controlled" communications system. This result satisfied the interests of both industry and the military.

While AT&T would build its own medium-orbit satellite, there is no doubt that it benefited not only from prior government research but by the millions of taxpayer dollars invested in putting its satellite in orbit. By the middle of 1961, the federal government, through NASA, awarded lucrative contracts to RCA to build a medium-orbit (4,000 miles high) communication satellite, and billionaire Howard Hughes (Hughes Aircraft) to build a twenty-four-hour (20,000 miles high) satellite for the military. The Communications Satellite Act of 1962 created a private corporation, the Communications Satellite Corporation (COMSAT); half of the stock was to be offered to the public, while the other half would be owned by AT&T. Three members of the COMSAT board would be chosen by the president, six by the public stock-holders, and the other six by communications companies.[7] In addition to AT&T, communications board members represented RCA, Western Union, and IT&T. In 1964, the United States entered into a treaty with other American allies to establish a new international organization, the International Telecommunications Satellite Organization (INTELSAT), which would ultimately assume ownership of the satellites and responsibility for management of the global system, but all management functions were delegated to COMSAT. By the end of 1965, INTELSAT was providing telephone and television service critical to both commercial and defense sectors.[8]

Satellite communications would come to have a dramatic impact on our communications environment, but that impact would not be for another two decades beyond the 1960s. In perhaps the most famous speech about television, President Kennedy's designated chairman of the Federal Communications Commission, Newton Minow, noted that: "Ours has been called the jet age, the atomic age, the space age. It is also, I submit, the television age." Indeed, by 1960 television had transformed American democracy; it was the place Americans learned about their neighbors and the people who would lead them, it was the new public square. While there were fewer than 17,000 television sets in American homes in 1946, by 1960 three-quarters of the 53 million American families owned at least one television. According to Minow, in 1960 the television industry "profit before taxes was $243,900,000—an average return on revenue of 19.2 percent. . . . This, despite a recession." Minow congratulated the industry on its financial health, but noted that he was concerned about what Americans were being exposed to by "the most powerful voice in America," and he extended an invitation to the nation's television broadcasters: "[Sit] down in front of your television set when your station goes on the air and stay there without a book, magazine, newspaper, profit-and-loss sheet or rating book to distract you—and keep your eyes glued to that set until the station signs off. I can assure you that you will observe a vast wasteland."[9]

Within weeks six thousand letters poured into the commission, overwhelmingly in favor of Minow's characterization of television. Much of the public dissatisfaction with television, indeed with broadcasting in general, undoubtedly resulted from the "quiz show" and "payola" and Federal Communications Commission (FCC) bribery scandals that made newspaper headlines only a year earlier.[10] But, for broadcasters, perhaps the most chilling portion of the new chairman's speech was his vow that license "renewal will not be pro forma."

In 1960, after nineteen days of congressional hearings and testimony from more than ninety witnesses, the FCC released a "Statement of Policy re: Commission en banc Programming Inquiry." The so-called 1960 Programming Policy Statement clarified for the broadcasters and the public the "major elements usually necessary to the public interest":

1. Opportunity for local self-expression
2. The development and use of local talent
3. Programs for children
4. Religious programs
5. Educational programs
6. Public affairs programs
7. Editorialization by licensees
8. Political broadcasts
9. Agricultural programs
10. News programs
11. Weather and market services
12. Sports programs
13. Service to minority groups
14. Entertainment programming[11]

Unlike the Blue Book, the 1960 Program Statement would by the following year have an FCC chairman dedicated to enforcing the public interest obligations of broadcasters. In order to compare a station's public interest promise to their community of license with their performance in that com-

munity, Minow vowed to draw on the FCC's "fine reserve of monitors"—
the viewing public. For the next two years, he became the second most visible member of Kennedy's New Frontier; only the president made more
appearances on television and radio.[12]

But not since the early days of the Franklin Roosevelt administration had
a president commanded the attention of the media the way Kennedy did. If
Ike was the likable general, Kennedy was American royalty as celebrity. We
saw him and his beautiful wife and perfect family, one boy and one girl, on
magazine covers and television. We saw the president laughing, sometimes
at himself, and we saw him concerned about the trouble we were in, sometimes the trouble he put us in. In my household, the most profound television appearance Kennedy made was his 1963 speech explaining why he
called out the Alabama National Guard to ensure the peaceful admission of
"two clearly qualified young Alabama residents who happened to have been
born Negro. . . . Today we are committed to a worldwide struggle to promote and protect the rights of all who wish to be free. When Americans are
sent to Vietnam or West Berlin, we do not ask for whites only. It ought to be
possible, therefore, for American students of any color to attend any public
institution they select without having to be backed up by troops. . . . The
fires of frustration and discord are burning in every city, North and South,
where legal remedies are not at hand. Redress is sought in the streets, in
demonstrations, parades, and protests which create tensions and threaten
violence and threaten lives."

Kennedy went on to describe the inequities facing blacks in America and
contrasted these inequities with American ideals of equality and freedom.
He called on Congress to pass legislation to authorize the federal government "to participate more fully in lawsuits to end segregation in public education."[13] Clearly the military-industrial complex was not pushing for *this*
legislation, and Kennedy would be denied.

By the climactic year of 1963, when FCC Chairman Minow stepped
down, the Roper polling organization reported that the majority of Americans relied upon television, not newspapers, as their main source of news.[14]
While no license had been denied and no major policy initiated to improve
upon "the vast wasteland," television would demonstrate why it was pro-
foundly important to the nation. In the summer of that year, A. Philip Randolph's threat to bring thousands of activists to Washington to demand an
end to second-class citizenship for black Americans was finally made real.
Television had brought the nation compelling pictures over the years of the
southern Negro movement to desegregate public facilities and schools, and

had found a charismatic spokesman in a young Baptist minister who led successful protests in Alabama in the nonviolent, but quite confrontational style of Mahatma Gandhi. Randolph would introduce the Reverend Dr. Martin Luther King Jr. to the crowd gathered before the Lincoln Memorial, indeed, to the nation watching on television. King's speech that day, in the shadow of Lincoln, using the words of Jefferson, continues to ring in the American conscience.

Later that year, television would broadcast another event that echoes still, the assassination of President Kennedy and the murder of the man arrested in that assassination, Lee Harvey Oswald. If American television had once been dominated by fixed quiz shows and superficial comedies, American television was about to change. If the money-losing, often unsponsored news and public affairs programs were once given only a little room in the broadcast day, as concession to their public interest obligations, news and public affairs programs would come to dominate American television. With a nation glued to their sets for the latest bulletin or the latest funeral, all doubts about the power of television and its place as America's public square were answered. If no one else wondered whether this private system of commercial communications, the so-called American system, was the best protector of America's democratic hopes, King, who had benefited so much from national television exposure, was wondering.

Reverend Parker and Red Lion

The Reverend Dr. Everett Parker was a former broadcaster for church groups in Chicago and with NBC, and since 1954, he served as the director of the United Church of Christ's (UCC) Office of Communication. Parker knew the Reverend Andrew Young, who trained people in voter education for the UCC in Dorchester, Georgia, and was at the time working closely with Dr. King. In 1963, the three men met at the National Arts Club in New York City and Parker asked what he could do to help with the Negro movement. King's reply was "please try to do something about the television stations." King had especially wanted the UCC to tackle the station in Birmingham, Alabama. As King argued in his famous *Letter from the Birmingham Jail,* he saw the core work of the Negro movement, not to create tension, but "merely to bring to the surface the hidden tension that is already alive. We bring it out in the open, where it can be seen and dealt with. Like a boil that can never be cured so long as it is covered up but must be opened with all its ugliness to the natural medicines of air and light, injustice must be exposed, with all the tension its exposure creates, to the light of human conscience and the air of national opinion before it can be cured."[15] King understood that his success rested in the hands of the gatekeepers of what Madison called "popular information," and that television was a new and important gatekeeper. He also knew, sitting in that jail in Birmingham, that racist practices continued to prevail because they went unreported on television.

Parker and an associate, Ray Gibbons, who headed the UCC's Council for Social Action, toured the South, and decided to focus on the television stations in Jackson, Mississippi. One of those stations, WLBT, was licensed to broadcast the most powerful signal in the South. Blacks made up 40 percent of the population of the county in which the station was located, and 45 percent of the population in its five-county service area. WLBT had already been under investigation by the FCC because of complaints that it had encouraged the resistance to the enrollment of James Meredith, the first black student at the University of Mississippi.

Mississippi was a courageous choice. The very word struck fear in the heart of the most committed activists. In one bloody week in June 1963 Fannie Lou Hamer, Lawrence Guyot, June Johnson, and many others were jailed and beaten by police in Winona, Mississippi, and the director of the National Association for the Advancement of Colored People's (NAACP's) Mississippi branch, Medgar Evers, was murdered outside of his home. At the beginning of the summer of 1964, a time Mississippi voting rights organizers would call Freedom Summer, James Chaney, Michael Schwerner, and Andrew Goodman were killed and their bodies buried in an earthen dam near Philadelphia, Mississippi. All during that summer churches were burned and civil rights workers beaten, jailed, and harassed. Monitoring television, particularly a television station rumored to be in league with the worst of the white terrorist groups in Mississippi, was dangerous work.[16]

Parker's monitors found a series of problems. The station used only white performers. Except for crime, newscasts ignored the black community. When whites were referred to they were called Mister or Miss—blacks were not. The station's public service announcements addressed concerns of the white community, but not the black community. Black people attempted to buy air time, but were denied. Of special importance, WLBT carried news of the "official attempts by the state of Mississippi" to maintain segregation, but did not present any statement on behalf of those working toward voting rights and integration. When the networks would

air a documentary program on the Negro movement, or featured an interview with someone like NAACP lawyer Thurgood Marshall, the station
would cut the signal and put up the sign: "Sorry Cable Trouble." Among this
long list of violations, the UCC charged that WLBT was in clear violation of
the Fairness Doctrine.

The UCC took this evidence to the FCC when the three-year license
period for stations in Jackson was to expire in 1965. The FCC voted 4–2 in
May 1965 to renew for a full three-year term the licenses of WJTV and several other stations when their managements promised to make improvements, and it expressed concern about the allegations against WLBT and
issued a one-year license. Perhaps most important, the FCC ruled that neither the UCC nor the local petitioners had a right to bring their complaint
to the commission. In legalese, the plaintiffs did not have standing. But the
commissioners rejected a staff recommendation to conduct its own hearing
and gather its own evidence because they did not want to further inflame
the racial tensions in Mississippi.

The UCC appealed the FCC decision to the U.S. Court of Appeals for the
District of Columbia in August 1965, drawing a conservative panel headed
by Warren Burger.

Lead attorney Earle K. Moore decided to attack the precedent that viewers had no right to challenge a station license, and argued that church members Aaron Henry and Robert Smith, as viewers of WLBT, were "parties
aggrieved, entitled to appeal." What could the term *public interest* mean,
argued Moore, if the public did not have the right to protect its interest?
Burger and the court agreed, unanimously. Writing for the court, in 1966,
Burger shook the broadcasting industry to its core: "in order to safeguard
the public interest in broadcasting . . . we hold that some 'audience participation' must be allowed in license renewal proceedings."[17] Some have called
this ruling the Magna Carta of the public interest.

The FCC held a hearing looking at WLBT, ignored the evidence gathered
by the UCC, and renewed the station's license. Burger, who delayed his elevation to the position of chief justice of the U.S. Supreme Court in 1969, was
livid. "A curious neutrality-in-favor of the licensee seems to have guided the
examiner in his conduct of the evidentiary hearing," he wrote. Both the FCC
examiner and the commission "exhibited at best a reluctant tolerance of this
court's mandate and at worst a profound hostility to the participation of the
public."[18] With that, in 1969, the court took away the WLBT license, and
ordered the commission to invite new applicants to apply.

1969 was also the year the Supreme Court, still under the guidance of Earl Warren, issued the decision upholding the Fairness Doctrine in *Red Lion v. FCC*. The circumstances of that case also began in 1964.

On November 27, 1964, a Pennsylvania radio station operated by the Red Lion Broadcasting Company aired a fifteen-minute broadcast by the Reverend Billy James Hargis as part of a "Christian Crusade" series. Hargis discussed a book by Fred J. Cook entitled *Goldwater—Extremist on the Right*, and said that Cook had been fired by the *New York World Telegram* for making false charges against city officials, that he worked for the *Nation* (a magazine he called "Communist-affiliated"), that he defended Alger Hiss and attacked J. Edgar Hoover, the FBI, and the Central Intelligence Agency; and that he had now written a "book to smear and destroy Barry Goldwater." Cook heard of the broadcast and demanded free reply time under the personal attack rules of the Fairness Doctrine. The station refused and was then ordered by the FCC to provide reply time whether or not Cook would pay for it.

The FCC decision was upheld by the Court of Appeals for the DC Circuit[19] and after a short time the FCC decided to specify with more clarity its rules related to political editorials. The Radio Television News Directors Association (RTNDA) filed suit, claiming that the FCC's Fairness Doctrine was a violation of the First Amendment. The RTNDA suit was upheld by the Court of Appeals for the Seventh Circuit.[20]

These conflicting decisions over the same set of underlying rules brought the Warren Court into the dispute. The Court ruled that FCC authority over licensees was consistent with the First Amendment because it protected the speech interests of the public. On behalf of the majority, Justice White wrote, "the people as a whole retain their interest in free speech by radio and their collective right to have the medium function consistently with the ends and purposes of the First Amendment. *It is the right of the viewers and listeners, not the right of the broadcasters, which is paramount*" (emphasis added).[21]

*   *   *

The WLBT and Red Lion decisions had a profound impact on the FCC's review of program content in future license renewals and on the equal employment practices of the licensees. Rules were established that required stations to find out what issues were important to be discussed by the various segments in the community, to report on how the licensee was addressing those ascertained interests,[22] and to let under-represented groups know about employment opportunities.[23]

Public Broadcasting and the Kerner Commission

In his famous "vast wasteland" speech, Chairman Minow vowed to do all he could "to help educational television," and before he left he lobbied Congress to support the Educational Television Facilities Act of 1962, which authorized federal grants for construction of educational television stations. In 1958, under the National Defense Education Act, $18 million was allocated for "research and experimentation in the new media," and in the first two years thirty-one grants were made supporting educational television.[24] None of this suggested to educational broadcasters that they would be able to rely upon the government for support. Even in Minow's "vast wasteland" speech there was no hint that "educational" stations could be anything more than an instructional service, providing lectures. It would take a new administration to advance Frieda Hennock's suggestions that noncommercial broadcasting could be a vibrant alternative, indeed perhaps even a competitor to commercial broadcasting.

When the freeze on television licenses was lifted in 1952, KTBC-TV, Austin, Texas, licensed to a Mrs. Lyndon B. Johnson, was among the first to go on the air. The wife of the rising young leader in the U.S. Senate was making extraordinary profits at the Austin station even before it went on the air Thanksgiving Day 1952.[25] Whether it was the programming or the fact that advertisers wanted to be close to the man who seemed able to dole out so many favors from Washington, one could only guess. What was certain was that Lyndon Johnson understood the power of television and how to get things done in Washington.

With the nation in shock and grief over the assassination of President Kennedy, Johnson used the skills that earned him Robert Caro's title "Master of the Senate" to push through Congress programs stalled only a few months earlier. While cloaking his action as carrying out the work of the martyred Kennedy, Johnson did much more. Pushing Kennedy's tax bill, Johnson linked it to an economic stimulus package and began a "war on poverty," more formally known as the Economic Opportunity Act of 1964. Then there was the Civil Rights Act of 1964, a great advance over Kennedy's proposed civil rights legislation. Surrounded by black leaders, a president from the South signed a bill outlawing segregation in southern public facilities. If Jim Crow was not dead, he was in his death throes. There was no mistaking the fact that Johnson was involved in turning both of these controversial bills into law. But he was just getting started. By the time the 89th Congress wrapped up in October 1966, it had produced more law than any other in American history, including the 1965 Voting Rights Act and an ambitious interrelated set of domestic reforms Johnson called the Great Society. In 1967, LBJ signed into law the Public Broadcasting Act, creating the Corporation for Public Broadcasting (CPB). Finally, America would have a real alternative to commercial broadcasting—or would it?

So much has been made of the role of the Ford and Carnegie foundations in establishing public broadcasting that the close connection between both these foundations and the Johnson administration has been obscured. As much as intellectuals would like to think that public policies change as a result of a few smart people deciding what the proper policy should be, the birth of the public broadcasting "system" as we know it was (like Medicare, and the Department of Housing and Urban Development, and the National Endowment for the Arts) the result of the raw-edged political skills of President Johnson. PBS may have been fussed and cooed over by a few academics and foundation executives, but its mother was the federal government, the same mother who brought us RCA. As RCA would enter the world with all the advantages wealthy parents could bestow, PBS was the unwanted child of wealthy parents near divorce.

As stated earlier, the reservation of channel space for educational broadcasters was possible in part because they accepted the poison pill of no financial support, agreeing to drop the goal of competing with commercial stations for advertising dollars. At a time when direct government support was easily labeled "socialistic" for all efforts except those designed to defeat communism (such as the Voice of America), educational broadcasters were forced to rely upon private philanthropy. Only a few stations were able to eke out a survival in this situation; none of these stations was able to compete for an audience.

James Day tells the stories of the stumbling beginnings of educational television in Houston and Los Angeles, both made possible by the generous philanthropy of Texas oil millionaires. But most of the educational stations still on the air in the mid-1960s owed their existence to matching construction grants made by what was then the nation's largest philanthropy, the Ford Foundation. Their best programming came from another Ford grantee, the National Education Radio and Television Production Center in New York. But the Ford Foundation commitment was increased considerably when Johnson's former national security advisor, McGeorge Bundy, was appointed to lead Ford. Bundy brought on board Ed Murrow's former partner at CBS, Fred Friendly.[26] Friendly saw that one of the "problems" with educational television was that it was not like CBS, it was not a network. One of the impediments to this solution was the exorbitant price charged by AT&T for connecting lines. The new technology of satellite was the obvious solution, and at least a part of Friendly's obsession with satellite "interconnection" was incorporated in the Public Broadcasting Act. The other part, the part that suggested that fees for commercial communications' use of satellites be targeted to support public broadcasting, was ignored.

While the participation of the Ford Foundation preceded Johnson, and was only given a push by a close Johnson associate, the work of the Carnegie Commission had Johnson's hands all over it. In fact, when Ralph Lowell, the wealthy patriarch of Boston's WGBH, proposed a presidential commission to study the problem of educational broadcasting, Johnson declined. But he offered his support if a privately financed commission could be arranged. Lowell went to the Carnegie Corporation, whose president, John Gardner, was a close advisor to LBJ. Gardner provided a half-million-dollar grant for the study. All of the Carnegie commissioners were approved by LBJ assistant Douglass Cater. One, Jesse C. Kellam, was especially close to Johnson. Kellam, a former high school football coach, managed Johnson's Texas station, KTCB, and was a trustee for all the Johnson family broadcast interests.[27]

During the deliberations of the quasi-governmental commission, educational broadcasters came to compromise their narrow educational purposes to fully embrace two politically significant, if ultimately falsely descriptive concepts, noncommercial and public. Given his close ties to the commission, it should have come as no surprise that a month after receiving the report from the Carnegie Commission, President Johnson summed up the state of educational television, shifting the emphasis from education to noncommercial: "Practically all noncommercial stations have serious shortages of the facilities, equipment, money, and staff they need to present programs of high quality. There are not enough stations. Interconnections between stations are inadequate and seldom permit the timely scheduling of current programs. Noncommercial television today is reaching only a fraction of its potential audience—and achieving only a fraction of its potential worth."[28]

To address these problems Johnson proposed an appropriation of roughly $20 million to support all of the Carnegie recommendations, except two. The Carnegie Commission recommended a relatively independent board for a quasi-public broadcasting corporation, and it recommended an annual budget of $100 million for public broadcasting in 1967, to be funded by a tax on the sale of television sets.[29]

The Carnegie Commission called for a Corporation for Public Television,[30] with a board of twelve citizens; six of these "public-spirited" people would be appointed by the president, and six would be appointed by the other six. Some of the board members would serve six-year terms, others would serve two-year terms. What the commission had in mind was a board somewhat removed from partisan politics. Instead, Congress and the president established a fifteen-member board (later pared to nine) all appointed by the president and all serving six-year terms.[31]

A tax on television sets was only recently lifted after the Korean War. But no measure was put into place to fund noncommercial broadcasting at the level or with the independence from politics Johnson's "Carnegie" advisors suggested. Upon signing the bill that created the Corporation for Public Broadcasting, Johnson would remark: "It will get part of its support from our Government." While that was undoubtedly true, the next lines in that paragraph would not be: "But it will be carefully guarded from Government or from party control. It will be free, and it will be independent—and it will belong to all of our people."[32] According to Day, Johnson promised to deliver legislation for long-range insulated funding within a year (thinking perhaps that he would run for another term), but within a year Johnson was packing his bags.[33]

In a way, not at all as well-managed as the birth of "public broadcasting," Johnson was also responsible for the readiness of "all of our people" to challenge not only the comfortable white halls of educational broadcasting, but to challenge the lily-white world of commercial broadcasting as well. The 1960s was a time of giddy hope and profound anger, and Johnson, stirring the deep well of America's promise and problems, fathered both.

The Great Society programs, particularly Sargent Shriver's Office of Equal Opportunity, did not merely dole out money to the needy. Johnson understood that to solve the problem of poverty, the Gordian knot of powerlessness would have to be cut. As Shriver testified, the War on Poverty "embraces entire neighborhoods, communities, cities, and states. It is an attempt to change institutions as well as people. It must deal with the culture of poverty."[34] The Great Society program reached over the heads of entrenched local power, both business and government, to provide resources and guidance to the local poor. The Johnson administration required "maximum feasible participation" by local people engaged in "autonomous and self-managed organizations which are competent to exert political influence on behalf of their own self-interest." While this notion harks back to the founders and Tocqueville, it was a radical proposition in modern America.

As the philosopher John Dewey wrote, by 1927 "local communities without intent or forecast found their affairs conditioned by remote and invisible organizations. The scope of the latter's activities was so vast and their impact upon face-to-face associations so pervasive and unremitting that it is no exaggeration to speak of 'a new age of human relations.'"[35] The administrative state created by the New Deal and extended by both Truman and Eisenhower did not change "human relations" in the forty-year interim.

In modern America, the culture of poverty benefits certain people in power, and those "remote and invisible organizations" would not take handing power over to poor people, whether in Newark or Appalachia or Mississippi, without a fight. While the real power behind those powerful organizations was often cloaked, there were local actors at the ready to maintain the status quo. As Bruce Schulman would write, "local actors [had] an unusually large bag of tricks for frustrating national policy."[36] Local governments designed projects without representatives of the relevant communities, often ignoring the core needs of the neighborhoods federal funds were appropriated to address. The federal government rejected such plans, and would not provide funds until minorities and poor people were included on boards and given real responsibilities.

In addition to the Office of Equal Opportunity under Shriver, the Community Relations Service (CRS), established in the Department of Justice by the 1964 Civil Rights Act, supported meetings between minority groups and local power players—including the local news media. The CRS Office of Media Relations helped minority groups organize and share tactics with each other, and they brought them in touch with public interest law groups and officials at the Federal Communications Commission.[37] These were times of hope, times when it seemed even the poorest mother and father could dream of a better life, a life out of or spent improving the ghetto or the barrio or the abandoned coal town. The hopes stirred by the New Frontier, and King's Dream, and the Great Society would meet the reality of American racism and the intransigence of power and spill over into the streets.

The signs of the strain began to show as early as 1963 with violence in Birmingham, Savannah, Chicago, and Philadelphia. In 1964, white segregationists attacked civil rights demonstrators in St. Augustine, Florida, protests against police violence erupted into riots in New York City and Jersey City and Elizabeth and Paterson and Chicago and Philadelphia. In 1965, whites attacked black demonstrators in Selma and Bogalusa, Louisiana, and the worst race riot in twenty years erupted in the Los Angeles neighborhood of Watts. Los Angeles again in 1966, Chicago again, Cleveland, and forty other disorders and riots were reported in 1966. The riots continued in 1967: Detroit, Houston, Tampa, Newark, Cincinnati, Atlanta, Plainfield, New Jersey.[38] The riots actually seemed to have a positive effect in shaking up entrenched power, in hastening reform in Newark and Philadelphia and New York and Detroit, but they could not continue without tearing the nation apart.

In the hot summer of 1967, Johnson formed a National Advisory Commission on Civil Disorders, led by Illinois Governor Otto Kerner. This is how the president charged the commission:

> The civil peace has been shattered in a number of cities. The American people are deeply disturbed. They are baffled and dismayed by the wholesale looting and violence that has occurred both in small towns and great metropolitan centers. No society can tolerate massive violence, any more than a body can tolerate massive disease. And we in America shall not tolerate it.
>
> But just saying that does not solve the problem. We need to know the answers, I think to three basic questions about these riots:
> —What happened?
> —Why did it happen?
> —What can be done to prevent it from happening again?

President Johnson asked another question: "What effect do the mass media have on the riots?"[39]

The Kerner Commission responded with what was pretty much old news for black Americans. "Our Nation is moving toward two societies, one black, one white—separate and unequal." Regarding the media, the commission reported that "important segments of the media failed to report adequately on the causes and consequences of civil disorders and on the underlying problems of race relations. They have not communicated to the majority of their audience—which is white—a sense of the degradation, misery, and hopelessness of life in the ghetto."

The commission recommended expanded coverage of the black community, integration of the news staffs, and training and recruitment of black journalists. Combined with new equal employment opportunity laws at the FCC, Reverend Parker and Earl Moore's work in establishing the right of citizens to petition the FCC, and a renewed vigor to enforce the Fairness Doctrine, the Kerner Commission recommendations actually had some small impact on segregated media.

In conclusion, the commission noted: "To pursue our present course will involve the continuing polarization of the American community and, ultimately, the destruction of basic democratic values. [The alternative course] will require a commitment to national action—compassionate, massive, and sustained, backed by the resources of the most powerful and the richest nation on this earth."[40]

But the nation was in the middle of an escalating war in Vietnam, and it would not afford guns and butter.

Direct U.S. involvement in the war between the people in North and South Vietnam may be marked at 1955, when the Eisenhower administration began to send aid directly to the government in Saigon and agreed to train the South Vietnamese army. The rationale, and certainly indirect support, may be marked as far back as the so-called Truman Doctrine, which was the set of precepts that led Truman to commit U.S. forces, without congressional approval, to Korea: contain communism at all cost. Of course, that doctrine was directly related to the anticommunism hysteria of the time, generated by the press. When Vice-President Johnson visited South Vietnam in 1961, there were fewer than seven hundred U.S. advisors there, but by mid-1962 the number of U.S. advisors had increased to 12,000. In February 1965, North Vietnamese troops attacked American installations; the United States retaliated with aerial bombing and by the spring the first combat troops arrived to protect the airstrips from which the U.S. bombers took off. By the end of that year U.S. troops in Vietnam would number 200,000. What we think of as the war in Vietnam may have begun much earlier, but by 1965 it was clearly Lyndon Johnson's war.[41]

While television news, most notably a former Murrow associate Eric Sevareid, expressed reservations about the escalating U.S. involvement in Vietnam as early as 1966, there was no question of what Barnouw would call "the very completeness of military-industrial control over television."[42] The dominant sense of the press at the time still tracked the anticommunist hysteria from the 1940s and 1950s: a loss to the Communists in Vietnam would be a blow to American interests. Johnson, who had prickly relationships with the press, as did every Democratic president before him, was determined not to be called soft on communism. Convinced that the press would turn the public even more against him, understanding that a show of toughness has always played well with the press, and with the military convincing him that the North Vietnamese would either be defeated or would agree to peace if he committed more troops and more aerial bombing raids, Johnson committed more troops and bombing raids. The press supported his actions, and reported as fact the predictions of imminent victory. Then, in 1968 on the Vietnamese New Year (Tet), with a half-million American soldiers in action, the North Vietnamese conducted an impressive military campaign, storming the American embassy. While the Tet offensive ended in defeat for the communist forces, it demonstrated to Americans, who had been watching the confusing scenes of war on the television sets in their living rooms, that victory was not imminent. The fact that establishment faith had been shaken was most obvious when CBS newscaster Walter Cronkite called for the de-escalation of U.S. military presence in Vietnam. [43]

In the end, as Johnson admitted, "That bitch of a war, killed the lady I really loved—the Great Society."[44] Soon student protests against the war would be joined by King, and John Kennedy's brother, Robert. Johnson declared he would not accept a nomination as president. King was assassinated, then Robert. Youthful protesters battled Chicago police outside the Democratic Convention, as a shaken nation watched. The forces of backlash and retrenchment would again take the reins of public policy. Richard Nixon would return the Republicans to power, this time disguised as peacemakers.

8

From Nixon to Reagan: Backlash and Cable (1968–1991)

> My friends, some years ago, the federal
> government declared war on poverty, and poverty won.
> —President Ronald Reagan, State of the Union
> Address to Congress, January 25, 1988

The Backlash

The turbulence of the 1960s and the resulting disruption to American racism and sexism and warrior imperialism would seem to contradict Mills's assertion that there is no countervailing power against the military-industrial elite. It might also seem to contradict the assertion of this book that U.S. communications policy has failed our democracy. The nonviolent and violent protests of black Americans, north and south, so embarrassing to the U.S. elite's claims of egalitarian democracy, inspired protests among Mexican Americans and Asian Americans and women and young people. Those protests, the voice of poor and working-class Americans, were heard and included in policy deliberations. Surely the Voting Rights Act and the Great Society and public broadcasting and even Johnson's downfall—resulting from the misadventure in Vietnam—are proof of American democracy, proof that a power elite could be contested, proof that Dewey's public did exist and mattered, proof, even, that the American system of communications was sufficient to the goals of self-governance and policy making based on the consent of the sovereign people.

Mills cannot be dismissed so easily. He suggests that a power elite comprised of economic, military, and political forces makes "consequential" policy in a way that violates the intent of the founders of our democracy. The Washington, D.C. antiwar rally of the Students for a Democratic Society took place in 1965, clearly challenging a core interest of the power elite. But, Mills would point out, that the war dragged on until 1975. Mills's view of what is consequential, focusing on war and the economy (including the welfare state), *is* too narrow from the perspective of a black American who may not have been allowed to vote before 1965 or a woman who was not allowed to control her own womb before 1973. I suspect Mills would grant the importance and the success of these movements, but would argue that these social advances do not conflict with the core interests of the power elite. The fact that some important issues—issues that may reside outside the core concerns of the power elite—appear to be subject to democratic processes does not diminish his point about democratic failure. Just because a bully takes your apple and leaves your sandwich does not make him less a bully, nor does it mean you have not been robbed.

But, perhaps, there was an uglier shift taking place in American politics. Perhaps, in the 1980s the bully realized he could take your sandwich too if he could find a way to blame the poor black kid. President Johnson's War on Poverty was inspired by Michael Harrington's book about another unseen America, an America neglected by the postwar boom of the late-1950s.[1] The poverty rate was 22.2 percent in 1960, according to official Census Bureau figures. By 1969 the poverty rate had fallen to 12.1 percent, and hovered between 11.1 and 12.6 percent through the 1970s. Federal programs reducing poverty were working.[2]

Beginning in 1976, the former governor of California, a minor movie actor who had turned to giving speeches on behalf of General Electric (GE), began running for president. In his campaign speeches Ronald Reagan told the story of a black woman living on the South Side of Chicago. According to Reagan: "She has 80 names, 30 addresses, 12 Social Security cards and is collecting veteran's benefits on four non-existing deceased husbands. And she is collecting Social Security on her cards. She's got Medicaid, getting food stamps, and she is collecting welfare under each of her names." In some stories Reagan would call her a "welfare queen" and claimed she was driving around in a Cadillac. There were convicted welfare frauds in the United States, some white, some black, but no one matching Reagan's description was ever found.[3]

Reagan's departure from the facts was seen as a brave reclamation project in some circles. Poor working whites embraced him and the certainty that they were being taken advantage of. Here was an explanation for the difficulty of their existence. Oddly, the answer to the black welfare queen was a sizable tax cut for the wealthy. As school lunch programs, and job training programs, and other social services were being taken away from them, struggling middle-class white Americans flocked to the Republican Party. Poverty rates began to climb back up, to 15.2 percent in 1983.[4] But there was more money for both the wealthy and for the military. The budget deficit in the Carter years was approximately $250 billion; it rose to over $1.4 trillion under Reagan. But, it was "morning again in America." At least for a few.

But our focus is communications policy, and our story is just as dramatic as the rise in poverty and the budget deficit. The policies of Minow under Kennedy and Johnson's Great Society initiatives created a more democratic, a more accountable set of communications policies. Moreover, the social protests of the 1960s were a sort of giant gathering of unruly citizens taking the public stage. The ability of marches and protesters, peaceful and not, to have an impact on policy deliberations can be attributed to the confluence of two important factors: (1) the widely shared belief in government as a solution to national problems that carried over from Roosevelt's New Deal experiments and American success in World War II; and (2) the relative youth of television as a regulated source of public information.

The first factor is fairly obvious as we look back: Eisenhower's support for a government-constructed national highway system, Kennedy's call to public service and commitment to landing a man on the moon, and Johnson's Great Society initiatives were all infused with an optimism that the federal government was a solution to problems. Even in an age that has become deeply cynical about government efficacy, it is not difficult to see why protesters would march on Washington to alert the problem solvers about problems needing solutions. The second factor may not be so obvious.

Minow's complaint about the vast wasteland of television had power not only because of the belief that government might actually solve the apparent problems of a medium obsessed with commercials and game shows, Minow's complaint had power because television broadcasters then understood their licenses to obligate them to serve the public interest. Even networks, unlicensed by the federal government, acted as if they were responsible to act, at least in part, as public servants. If the networks were not prepared to go as far as Murrow would lead them, they still broadcast serious documentaries and children's programs. Undoubtedly it was at least in part a response to a time when even American business recognized a public service duty, but it was also a time when the federal government seemed to be looking around to correct injustices. The Fairness Doctrine and the 1960 Programming Policy Statement may have been rarely enforced, but they were not collecting dust on the shelves of the law firms that represented the broadcasters. The television license was almost never revoked, but that did not mean that broadcasters did not make efforts to ensure that their license would be approved at the next renewal hearing only three years away. If only because of the threat of government action, the regulatory regime both contained television's excesses and encouraged its contribution to public debate.

Johnson sought to unite the country in support of minorities and the poor and ended up sacrificing the coalition that called itself the Democratic Party. In the process he unleashed tremendous forces demanding a rights-based role in the affairs of state. The 1960s seems as far away now as the Gilded Age or the Roaring Twenties. The period that followed darkened American optimism and dismantled the small protections that were erected to protect and advance democratic debate. The backlash of Nixon and Reagan shaped our present.

Nixon and Public Broadcasting

Cronkite's insistence on holding the scraps of Murrow's legacy and calling attention to the problems with the war in Vietnam made him just one of the many "enemies" targeted by Richard Nixon. While Nixon deputies threatened to use the Federal Communications Commission (FCC) to take away the local stations owned by CBS, there was little he could do to the most trusted man in America. But he did have some power over the infant system of public broadcasting. As was typical of Nixon, his attack on public broadcasting was well-planned, sustained, and often indirect; he offered support and then encouraged division.

As Bruce Schulman writes: "Not for nothing did Nixon earn the nickname Tricky Dick. . . . He fooled many observers, then and now, because he pursued [an] attack on public life in a particularly devious sort of way. Unlike Barry Goldwater before him or Ronald Reagan after him, Nixon never took on big government directly. He rarely assailed the liberal establishment he so furiously hated and so openly resented. He did not attack liberal programs or the agencies and political networks that undergirded them. Rather, he subtly, cunningly undermined them . . . by stripping its bases of support and its sources of funds."[5]

One of Nixon's key targets in his attack on public broadcasting was the Ford Foundation. The opening salvo directed against the Ford Foundation was the Tax Reform Act of 1969. As Waldemar Nielsen argues in his book *Golden Donors,* there were much needed reform elements in the act,[6] includ-

ing a requirement that foundations pay out 6 percent of their assets annu-
ally, and limits on the share of private businesses that an individual foundation can own. What Nielsen soft-pedals are the limitations the act placed on
a foundation's ability to influence legislation or support political campaigns.
Prior to the act the only sanction available to punish a foundation was the
extreme and rarely used revocation of the charity's organizational charter.
What Nixon's minions pushed was a set of penalties far more likely to be
imposed: a system of penalty taxes levied not only against the private foundation, but against the foundation manager.[7] These limitations and penalties aimed at foundations, particularly the Ford Foundation led by the
Kennedy-Johnson associate McGeorge Bundy, undercut financial support
for those organizations and movements in contention with big business.

At the first meeting between Nixon, Albert L. Cole (Nixon's first
appointee to the Corporation for Public Broadcasting [CPB]), and the CPB
Chairman Frank Pace, Nixon indicated support for public broadcasting but
identified what he saw as a key problem: Ford Foundation support for public affairs programs.[8] The foundation's influence could not be disputed. The
major supplier of national public affairs programs was National Educational Television (NET), a New York–based public affairs production house
largely funded by Ford. NET public affairs programs, such as *The Great
American Dream Machine, NET Journal,* and the monthly program *Black
Journal,* provided a glimpse of the content missing from commercial
broadcasters (including Cronkite's show). In his book, *Vanishing Vision,*
James Day, a former president of NET, listed some of NET's offerings to the
Public Broadcasting Service in 1970, PBS's first season.

> Frederick Wiseman's *Hospital* was an unblinking portrait of an East Harlem
> hospital emergency room on a busy Saturday night. . . . Bob Fresco's *Trial:
> The City and the County of Denver vs. Lauren R. Watson* provided national
> television with its first actual courtroom trial. Jack Willis's *Hard Times in the
> Country* examined the question of why consumers were paying more for
> farm products while farmers were earning less. Dick McCutchen's *The Three
> R's . . . and Sex Education* stepped carefully around the minefield of sex edu-
> cation in our public schools. *The Long Walk* gave the Navajo nation a chance
> to speak out candidly about the effects of government policy on the Native
> American. And a jailhouse interview with Black Panther leader Bobby Seale
> raised questions many wish had never been asked.[9]

It was not only that NET programs were, in the jargon of the day, anti-
establishment, nor was it only that Ford was led by "Mac" Bundy; the Ford

Foundation stood for the eastern elite Nixon had learned to deeply resent all of his life.

Nixon's attempt to wrest control of public affairs programming on PBS began with coercing CPB to move production responsibility away from NET. In July 1971, CPB announced the creation of the National Public Affairs Center for Television (NPACT) to be located in Washington, D.C. Unfortunately, NPACT hired long-time NBC journalist Sander Vanocur, a journalist who spoke out against Democrat President Johnson's escalation of the war in Vietnam, but Nixon remembered him as "a Kennedy sympathizer." Upon learning of the NPACT's new staff, Nixon ordered that "all funds for public broadcasting be cut immediately."[10] But Nixon's point person on communications, Clay Whitehead, the director of the Office of Telecommunications Policy, suggested another approach. In a memo to White House Chief of Staff H. R. Haldeman, Whitehead suggested: "We will quietly solicit critical articles regarding Vanocur's salary coming from public funds. . . . We will quietly encourage local station managers throughout the country to put pressure on NPACT and CPB to put balance in their programming or risk the possibility of local stations not carrying these programs."[11]

At a meeting of the National Association of Educational Broadcasters (NAEB) in 1971 Whitehead charged public broadcasters with betraying the goals of the Carnegie Commission by creating PBS, by seeking ratings success, and by turning over control of programs to the Ford Foundation. And he added: "Do any of you honestly know whether public broadcasting—structured as it is today and moving in the direction it seems to be headed—can ever fulfill the promise envisioned for it or conform to the policy set for it? If it can't, then permanent financing will always be somewhere off in the distant future."[12] In 1971, the Nixon administration supported a one-year funding bill of $35 million, the same amount appropriated the year before, and $10 million less than had been authorized by Congress. In January of the following year, White House aides working through Congressman William Springer contacted the new Republican head of CPB to let him know that "there was not a chance to get any appropriation of any kind . . . passed in the Congress . . . if [public broadcasting] were to continue news, news commentary and news analysis."[13] Vanocur was let go that year, and so were Bill Moyers, Elizabeth Drew, and William Buckley.

Representative Torbert Macdonald, chairman of the House Communications Subcommittee, suggested an approach to meet the Nixon administration halfway. He introduced a five-year appropriation, offering $65 million the first year and $90 million the second, with 30 percent of the funding to be earmarked for the local stations. First this proposal was cut to two-year funding, and then on June 30, 1972, four days after the Senate adopted it, Nixon vetoed the bill. In his veto message he cited "serious and widespread concern expressed in Congress and within the public broadcasting system itself, that an organization, originally intended only to serve the local stations, is becoming instead the center of power and the focal point of control for the entire public broadcast system."[14] Four days before he announced his veto he met with thirty commercial broadcasters who complained about anticommercials on PBS, as well as competition from PBS. One meeting participant remembered Nixon disparaging "government-sponsored broadcasting" abroad, saying reports that it produced high-quality programming "was a bunch of crap."[15]

On the day of the veto, CPB board Chairman Frank Pace resigned. In ten days, CPB President John Macy, who had done so much to work with the Nixon administration, resigned; much of his staff would follow. Soon CPB's board and staff would strip PBS of programming authority, and provide a preliminary list of approved programs more in line with the tastes of the Nixon administration.[16]

Nixon's combined attack on private foundations and public broadcasting intimidated both institutions, and created a climate of caution and self-censorship. Despite the brave talk about all the good that foundations can still do, the aggressive political activity of corporate America is work most mainstream foundations stay clear of, thus limiting the ability of nonprofit organizations to counter big business influence over policy. While Nixon left public broadcasting weakened and divided against itself, he was only exploiting the problems (political appointees and inadequate funding subject to political control) left behind by Johnson.

While CPB received substantially more support during the Carter administration—the federal appropriation for CPB jumped from $92.3 million in 1975 to $197.6 million in 1981—the incoming Republicans would make CPB a target in their strategy to "defund the left." Reagan first proposed cutting CPB funding in half, but the Democratic-controlled Congress would not go along. As a result of the stalemate, funding dipped to $163.7 million by 1984. Reagan would have a much larger imprint on the CPB board.[17] Nixon showed the way, and he had other lessons to teach.

Nixon Reforms the Post Office

Winton M. "Red" Blount, a wealthy Republican scion of Alabama, was president of the U.S. Chamber of Commerce of the United States when Nixon tapped him for a bold assignment—to eliminate Benjamin Franklin's office. Within four months, May 1969, he proposed the removal of the postmaster general from the executive cabinet and, more important, the termination of the Post Office's operation as a government-subsidized public service.

The Post Office would be given a similar name, the U.S. Postal Service. The stated mission would be the same: "to bind the Nation together through the personal, educational, literary, and business correspondence of the people." But the U.S. Postal Service is a different animal altogether than the Post Office.

The burdens faced by the Post Office had grown enormously, as the nation and the nation's population had grown. There was no comparing the nation or the government James Madison understood with this new colossus. Despite the advent of the telegraph, the telephone, radio, and television, Americans were still relying in part on the mail for the "popular information" Madison believed was so essential to self-governance. Members of Congress still enjoyed the privilege of free mail service to report to constituents in their districts. And while the postal service still restricted mail, when the occasion warranted, to prevent American minds from the "pollution" of pornography or communism, the incredible increase in direct mail advertisements expanded considerably in the post–World War II years. Despite the increase in volume between 1945 and 1970, postal service was being handled in pretty much the same way it was handled when Lincoln was president. The Post Office operated on a mix of tax revenue appropriated by Congress and the collection of postal fees. Postage rates did not correspond to the cost of service; some Americans paid more (generally merchants and personal correspondents) and some paid less (generally newspapers) and some paid nothing (national office holders).[18]

Despite the increased workload and decaying buildings and disgruntled and underpaid employees, congressional leaders, influenced by a commercial publishing industry still subsidized to provide "popular information" to the public, were reluctant to allow an increase in postage rates. Arguments for the privatization of postal service were raised and quashed in 1968. A majority in Congress viewed privatization as a complete break with the service-first philosophy that had guided postal policy for over a hundred years. As Texas Senator Ralph Yarborough argued, "Reform is not spelled c-o-r-p-o-r-a-t-i-o-n."[19] The vast majority of Americans were satisfied with postal service. But the money to resolve the increased pressures on postal service was not appropriated. Congressional failure to respond to this problem led to increasing unionization of postal employees, with increasing threats of work stoppages. In March 1970, the threats were carried out and approximately 152,000 postal employees in 671 locations shut the postal system down. Blount agreed to negotiate with the unions and continued to press Congress for a lasting resolution.

On August 12, 1970, Nixon signed Public Law 91–375, and the new U.S. Postal Service began operations on July 1971. The postmaster general was removed from the executive cabinet. Operational authority over the post was vested in the executive branch, with an eleven-member board of governors, rather than Congress. A new Postal Rate Commission of five members would recommend rates. All these new officers would be appointed by the president with the Senate's consent, except two—the postmaster general and the deputy postmaster general (who would be appointed by the board of governors). The new law allowed Congress to appropriate tax dollars to pay for its mailing privileges. Most important, the new law allowed for borrowing money from the public but phased out the general public service subsidy. In other words, instead of a service directly overseen by the elected legislators representing citizens the new service would be operated by the burgeoning administrative state attached to the executive branch of government.[20]

Putting aside this radical rewriting of the Constitution without amendment, the new law demonstrated first and foremost the fact that political leaders had completely lost any sense of responsibility for maintaining a system guaranteeing to each citizen an equal ability to communicate political information. The effect of the Nixon treatment of the founders' Post Office was predictable: by the late 1990s small independent newspapers, the same sort of papers Madison was so eager to distribute throughout the nation, were paying higher rates for post service than mass circulation magazines and newspapers.[21] Soon the U.S. Postal Service would contemplate a "Postal Ad Network," which would support post service by providing advertising space on mail trucks, post office lobbies, and the U.S. Postal Service web site.[22]

Watergate and Its Legacy

Nixon continued and expanded many of the Great Society programs, even as he undercut them through something his lieutenants called "devolution." For Nixon's new friends in the South "devolution" had a more familiar name—states' rights. While Johnson reached over the heads of oppressive state and local governments, Nixon would reduce the budget for the Office of Equal Opportunity and eliminate the Community Relations Service, but provide greater funding for the states to supposedly do the same work. Under the guise of offering more money for community programs, Nixon undermined those programs by providing support directly to local officials intent upon thwarting the community participation called for by Johnson. Nixon's embrace of economic advancement for minorities in America, embodied in the conflicting notions of "affirmative action" and "benign neglect," had the same effect as Nixon's embrace of tax reform for foundations, public broadcasting, and the Post Office.

The quest for the integration of schools and buses and lunch counters by southern "Negroes" moved north, and facing resistance and backlash black activists rejected the nonviolent cries of "We Shall Overcome Someday" and opted for "Black Power" and "Burn, Baby, Burn." The American melting pot cracked and splintered into Mexican Americans, Asian Americans, Native Americans, and, more important to the Nixon coalition, the so-called silent majority of working class Irish Americans, Italian Americans, Polish Americans, and on and on.

But, perhaps, the key activity of the Nixon administration that simultaneously strengthened the right and undermined all those who sought to use the federal government to encourage democratic engagement, was the collection of criminal acts we have learned to call "Watergate."

The bungled burglary and ransacking of the Democratic National Committee Headquarters in the Watergate office-apartment complex in Washington, D.C., was the tip of a much larger iceberg of unconstitutional activities, some of which still remain to be uncovered. Dirty tricks, enemies lists, abuse of surveillance and tax power, smear campaigns, all led to the criminal indictment and/or resignation of the president, attorney general, chief of staff, and other top officials in the White House. Vice-President Agnew resigned as a result of an unrelated investigation by the U.S. attorney in Baltimore for allegedly receiving payoffs when Agnew was governor of Maryland, and ultimately pleaded "no contest" and received a fine of $10,000 and three years' probation.

Despite assurances from Gerald Ford—the first unelected vice-president to ascend to the presidency—that "our Constitutional system works," the vast majority of Americans clearly understood that our democratic republic was broken. Although a few too many of us were convinced that the press, particularly a couple of cub reporters at the *Washington Post*, caused Nixon's unraveling, the press, as a whole, was very slow to pick up the darkness emanating from the White House. So slow in fact that Nixon had little trouble winning reelection after several years of illegal conduct in the White

House. Nixon's final triumph was that his apologists and collaborators, from Henry Kissinger to Pat Buchanan to Diane Sawyer to William Safire, all became an integral part of the modern press establishment, as did the Republican conservative Bob Woodward.

As a result of Watergate, many Americans lost hope in government and turned away and inward. This confused and tangled mass of enclaves and ethnicities and white suburbs was ripe for the politics of divide and conquer. The great white majority of Americans hungered for the simple truths of a simpler time. At first they turned to a decent peanut farmer from Georgia who promised never to lie to them. But advice about the setting of the thermostat and the limits of American empire proved uncomfortable, and so they turned to a man who understood the importance of, well, the simple truths from that simple time so long ago and far away. To the surprise of many on the left who could not believe America could trust a Goldwater-Republican, big business and the reactionary right understood the national ego as a deflated balloon and proceeded to fill the American dreamspace abandoned by the protesters and the idealists, and brought us Ronald Reagan.

The radical Reagan right would join with libertarians and rip out the heart of the structure regulating broadcast media in the public interest, and shift the ground of communications policy debate even further away from considerations of democracy and toward a narrow ideological view of what they called "the market." If government was too entrenched in its support of old-line players (such as broadcasters and Ma Bell), the courts would serve as the leverage or the excuse to shuffle the deck. In the 1980s, Ronald Reagan and Gordon Gekko taught us that "greed is good."[23]

Public Interest via Private Litigation

If the period after World War II was the period for civil rights and social justice groups (Tocqueville would call them "associations") to exert influence over public policy, the period following would see modern corporations regain their dominance over the nation's agenda. Appropriately enough, the early targets were other more entrenched merchants.

In the early 1960s several large corporations began to complain to the FCC about the long-distance telephone service and rates charged by AT&T. They sought to establish their own communications links using microwave transmission. The FCC determined that there were not enough microwave bands to go around, but it did spur the development of the first substantial competition to AT&T for business service since the early 1900s. In 1963,

Microwave Communications, Inc. (later MCI) requested permission to build a microwave telecommunications system between St. Louis and Chicago. The commission would approve the application in 1969, but would limit MCI and other specialized carriers to private line services. In 1972 MCI began commercial operation of its service to executive networks (Execunet). MCI, a major contributor to both political parties, continued to file court actions against the FCC limitations and AT&T.

In 1974, the Nixon Department of Justice filed a comprehensive antitrust suit against AT&T, requesting the divestiture of all the Bell Operating Companies. The core complaint in the action was fifty years old: Ma Bell was clearly a monopoly and had clearly engaged in anticompetitive activities as long ago as the early days of the trusts. It was merely the most extreme example of the tolerance for communications monopolies that became a core part of the U.S. public philosophy regarding communications. The Nixon administration could file suit with little fear of quick consequences. In fact, the trial *U.S. v. AT&T* would not begin until 1981.

But in 1977 and 1978, at MCI's urging, a U.S. appellate court reversed FCC limitations on the services specialized carriers could provide, and ruled that AT&T and its local telephone companies must permit the other long-distance carriers to interconnect to their local networks.[24] In 1979, AT&T filed a statement (a tariff) at the FCC justifying a raise in the cost they would charge for an unaffiliated "specialized" carrier's interconnection with AT&T's local network—the increase was 300 percent. MCI and other specialized carriers, most serving private business, had poor connections into the Bell local networks owned by AT&T. Led by MCI, the private carriers pushed the federal government to crack down on AT&T's anticompetitive behavior.

On January 15, 1981, the *U.S. v. AT&T* antitrust trial began, but was immediately recessed. Despite rumors of a settlement, negotiations between the Department of Justice and AT&T apparently broke down and the trial was resumed on March 4. When the Justice Department concluded its case AT&T immediately moved for a dismissal, but U.S. District Judge Harold Greene concluded that "the testimony and the documentary evidence adduced by the government demonstrate that the Bell System has violated the antitrust laws in a number of ways over a lengthy period of time." The trial continued, but AT&T understood Greene's ruling and the rulings in a variety of other cases it was losing, and decided it was time to get serious about settlement negotiations. On January 8, 1982, AT&T agreed to settlement terms proposed by the Justice Department. Those terms required the breakup of the Bell System and the new regional Bell companies to provide equal access to all long-distance companies, including MCI.

In July 1983, Greene approved a modified final plan, reorganizing AT&T.[25] It took sustained political and legal pressure by private telecommunications companies established to serve business to make the government enforce the law. This was a bad omen for any individual without substantial financial resources expecting her or his representatives to operate on behalf of the public good.

The Birth of Cable and Public Access

Local and long-distance service was not the only communications industry restructured at the behest of entrepreneurs through court action and in defiance of the FCC. In 1972, Charles Dolan and Gerald Levin of Sterling Manhattan Cable created the nation's first pay-TV-network: Home Box Office (HBO). In its first year, HBO would transmit via microwave to its fourteen cable system affiliates in Pennsylvania and upstate New York, movies, New York Knicks basketball, New York Rangers hockey, and miscellaneous sports events. But on September 30, 1975, HBO distributed via satellite the Muhammad Ali versus Joe Frazier fight live from the Philippines ("The Thrilla from Manila") to other cable operators (United Artists and American Television and Communication Corp.) and their customers in Vero Beach and Fort Pierce, Florida, and Jackson, Miss.[26] This, perhaps more than any other development, signaled the birth of cable television as we understand it today.

Cable is hardly a new medium. The carriage of television programs to homes by cable is almost as old as television sent over the airwaves. The first cable operators began in 1948 with a service known as Community Antennae Television (CATV). Many of the early CATV operations were owned and operated by the municipal or regional government authorities, with the limited purpose of providing television signals to households in mountains, valleys, or geographically remote areas where reception was poor. Antennas erected on mountain tops or tall buildings were wired and those wires connected to a central location and then on to homes. But in 1962, H&B Microwave began importing the signal of Chicago's WGN to the Dubuque, Iowa CATV.[27] The battle between cable and broadcasters was on.

The response of the broadcasters, particularly the more powerful and established VHF licensees, was to go to the government and ask that this new competition be stopped. The importation of distant signals they argued would destroy the public interest tenets of "localism."[28] So the FCC responded by expanding its jurisdiction and placing limits on the ability of cable systems to deliver distant television signals, whether they were movies, sports, or old reruns.[29] The effect of these policies was to briefly limit cable's development. But the potential financial rewards were too obvious, and banks and other speculators would fund a series of court challenges to the FCC limitations.

The FCC asserted jurisdiction over cable television as early as 1962, and issued cable regulations in 1965 and 1966. In 1968, the U.S. Supreme Court ruled that the FCC's jurisdiction over cable television is "reasonably ancillary to the effective performance of the Commission's responsibility for regulating broadcasting."[30] In 1972, the FCC issued a comprehensive set of regulations concerning (1) signal carriage, (2) access and nonbroadcast activities, (3) technical standards, and (4) federal/state/local arrangements.[31] But the cable industry began to grow as a financial and political power, and the tide began to turn against the broadcasters in the mid-1970s. The courts ruled that while the FCC had the authority to oversee cable, it did not have the power to limit the cable operators to local television broadcasts,[32] and in the late 1970s the court would determine that rules limiting pay television were invalid.[33]

These hard-fought, expensive cases would pave the way for Dolan and Levin and HBO. In 1976, an Atlanta billboard company owner put the programming of his independent (not affiliated with a network) UHF station on satellite and offered it to cable operators nationwide.[34] Ted Turner was just beginning to take the communications world by storm, soon he would offer cable operators a twenty-four-hour network devoted to hard and developing news stories from around the world.[35] In 1978, Bill Rasmussen convinced Getty Oil to put up the money to fund a cable sports network, ESPN, and the backbone of television as we understand it today was in place.[36]

I have emphasized the growth of cable as a battle between two large economic forces. The established broadcasters, given their control of the FCC, were able to slow cable's introduction. A few entrepreneurs, with hundreds of thousands of dollars to spend on lawyers and legislators, were able to push their way into a field they understood held tremendous opportunity for profit. But there is another way to view the development of cable television, and it begins not in the Nixon era, but in the Johnson era.

FCC Commissioner Nicholas Johnson, one of the few truly maverick progressives to serve on the commission, suggested that rather than destroying localism CATV could actually generate more local programming. In an article published in 1967 in the *Saturday Review*, Johnson argued that cable's capacity to carry "a wide variety of programming aimed at a wide variety of audiences" coupled with its ability to operate as a "large close-circuit system" might allow it to serve select geographic portions of a city "which may correspond to particular social, economic, or other special interest groupings. . . . Whereas a local broadcaster may not be able to justify programming aimed just at ballet enthusiasts, or the local Negro community, or *aficionados* of sports cars, a regional or even a national cable network might be developed which could enhance its appeal significantly through such specialized programming." However, Johnson cautioned that without appropriate regulation, the public service potential of cable would be lost.[37]

Johnson's "large close-circuit system" soon began to be referred to as "wired cities." It was a perfect fit in the whole range of President Johnson's Great Society initiatives. CATV could be used to bring urban citizens in on the resolution of urban problems. The federally funded National Academy of Engineers established a panel, chaired by Peter Goldmark, charged with investigating how the application of cable and telecommunications might improve city living and stimulate regional development. In 1968, the Goldmark panel reported that cable could be central to the development of "broadband communication networks" that could support a variety of social services. A Johnson task force embraced the report and urged the telecommunications and cable industries to "encourage the growth of communications of all kinds within localities."[38]

By 1970, Ralph Smith, a journalist for *Nation* magazine, would write excitedly about the democratic possibilities inherent in cable television, eventually publishing a book in 1972 titled *The Wired Nation: Cable TV, the Electronic Communications Highway.* Two things especially excited the Goldmark panel and Smith: (1) cable, like telephone service, had the inherent capability to provide two-way, interactive, communication; and (2) cable television sent multiple signals at once, which might allow local governments and associations to have their own channels or programs.

PEG (or public access, education, and government) channels were born of the democratic impulses spurred by the Great Society efforts of the Johnson administration. Unfortunately, just as a reservation of channels would not be sufficient to support the promise of public broadcasting, mere access without a mechanism for substantial and reliable funding would marginalize the democratic potential of public access to cable. What happened to PEG during the antidemocratic period of backlash between Nixon and Reagan is a study in the failure of the American public philosophy regarding communications.

In 1968, Cable TV, Incorporated, provided a channel operated by the Dale City, Virginia Junior Chamber of Commerce, making it, according to a Rand report, "the first community-operated closed-circuit television channel in the United States."[39] But public and government access to municipally franchised (licensed) cable operations began to generate national attention in Manhattan. According to Ralph Engelman, Fred Friendly, advisor to the Ford Foundation and chairman of New York Mayor John Lindsay's Advisory Task Force on CATV and Telecommunications, recommended that the city require franchised (locally licensed) cable companies to set aside two channels the public could lease for a minor fee. A number of black activists, most notably Ossie Davis, protested that Friendly's proposal would limit the access of poor people. Thus, free public access to cable was achieved.[40] But a number of fathers can claim public access: Theodora Sklover, director of Open Channel, Inc., had been lobbying for public access in the heavily cabled neighborhood of Inwood, New York, since 1969. Monroe Price, deputy director of the Sloan Commission on Cable Communications, analyzed the challenges and potentials of public access in 1970. Other groups, such as the United Church of Christ, Office of Communications, the Filmmakers' Cooperative, and the Markle Foundation, were proposing public access before New York established a franchise agreement in July 1970 with Sterling Information Services and the Teleprompter Corporation. Despite the many cooks, the requirement to make four channels available for lease—two controlled by the city government and the remaining two controlled by the public—would become a beacon to many "free speech" advocates across the nation.[41] Public access programming began a year later in July 1971.[42]

In 1972, the FCC proposed rules requiring all cable operators in the top hundred television markets to provide at least twenty channels and to reserve four of them for public, educational, and governmental access. Those rules were slightly altered (including the revision of certain technical requirements, and the inclusion of all cable systems having 3,500 or more subscribers) in 1975,[43] and again in 1976.[44] Up in arms about these impositions into their agreements with local communities, the cable industry supported a court case brought by a relatively small cable operator, Midwest Video Corporation, which eventually made its way to the Supreme Court. In a 5–3 decision, the Court ruled that "the FCC exceeded the limits of its authority in promulgating its access rules," and that "[authority] to compel cable operators to provide common carriage of public-originated transmissions must come specifically from Congress."[45]

Legislative support for the right of municipalities to require PEG channels would eventually come, but in a compromise that revealed the lopsided political power of the newly organized cable industry, as compared with the fractured and disorganized community of public access advocates.

QUBE and C-SPAN

By the mid-1970s the entrepreneurs who were wrestling with the broadcast-dominated FCC began competing among themselves to provide CATV service to urban areas. Cable operators negotiated agreements with municipalities for the use of public streets and alleys so they could get their service to the homes of potential customers. As these franchise agreements came up for renewal the different operators began to look for ways to separate themselves from their competition. In 1975, Steve Ross, president of Warner Communications, a division of the Warner Brothers motion picture company, was staying at the Otani Hotel in Tokyo where he watched a hotel-operated cable system with interactive capabilities. He asked Pioneer, the Japanese company that had developed the hotel system, if they could provide a similar service over a city-wide cable operation. In December 1977, the first commercial interactive cable television operation was providing service in the state capital and college town of Columbus, Ohio, calling itself QUBE.

QUBE offered thirty video and thirty audio channels, which was a high number at the time. Ten of the video channels were reserved for broadcast television channels, ten were allocated to pay-per-view channels (like HBO), and ten channels were dedicated to original interactive programming. According to Paul Dempsey, former chief engineer for QUBE in Columbus, "QUBE was the first to offer first-run movies on a pay-per-view basis, other than a few hotels. PPV sports events were popular, too, especially Ohio State University football games."[46] That pay-per-view service became the satellite service On-Demand. They also produced a program called "QUBE Consumer," featuring a local consumer investigative reporter. The program host would take live phone calls in the studio and ask viewers to respond to questions. Live interactive programs featured Speaker of the House "Tip" O'Neill, George H. W. Bush, and local leaders available to respond to the viewing audience in town meetings that covered zoning problems or college drinking. Educators used QUBE, allowing students to talk with teachers through their television at home. Two other programs produced by QUBE continue today: the program for young people, "Pinwheel," grew into its own cable channel, Nickelodeon; and a program dedicated to the music of teenagers, "Sight on Sound," evolved into Music Television, also known as MTV.[47]

Ross's hunch was that the promise of interactive television would make Warner very competitive in the bidding wars for cable franchises. After running QUBE in Columbus, Warner won franchise bids to build similar systems in Houston, Milwaukee, and the suburbs of Chicago and St. Louis. They also won franchises for sixty-channel QUBE systems in Cincinnati, Dallas, and Pittsburgh. Every local QUBE operation was connected to the other QUBE systems, and programming was shared nationally, by satellite. If a national QUBE talk show posed a question, all subscribers on the entire QUBE network could be polled in seconds, with the poll results available almost instantly.

If the interactive features of QUBE were not the system's most popular, they certainly added luster to a well-subscribed, popular cable service. Unlike broadcast television, cable received revenue from multiple sources, including advertising, regular cable subscribers, and pay-per-view users. But these were extraordinarily expensive systems to build. Because cable operations, particularly new systems, require enormous initial investments of capital long before any revenue starts, Warner was hard-pressed competing against systems such as TeleCommunications Inc. (TCI) not only for franchise agreements, but for financing on Wall Street. TCI, led by a ruthless monopolist, John Malone, who liked being called doctor, would become notorious for its failure to keep to its franchise agreements and its lack of investment in cable infrastructure. Malone made a point of telling his audiences on Wall Street that, despite the evidence of QUBE, interactive cable could not work. "Cable never was, should not have been, and never will be . . . an efficient way to return signals from the home. . . . The technology is poorly equipped, and to make the technology work overburdens the facility with so much, not only capital, but operating expense on a continuing basis as to render it very very unacceptable."[48] In other words, unlike old movies or passive one-way shows, interactive programming cuts into profit margins.

Warner's QUBE was doing reasonably well, but attracting financing in light of its comparatively lower margin of profit was difficult. According to Dempsey, "Warner Cable would not have been able to keep on going past 1980 if we had not received an infusion of capital from American Express."[49] With a new financial partner on board, Warner-Amex Cable brought in Drew Lewis, soon to be the U.S. secretary of transportation under Ronald Reagan. As was typical of business practice during the Reagan years, Lewis split the cable company in half, canceled the QUBE national network, cut local programming, sold MTV and Nickelodeon to Viacom in a deal valued at $685 million, and then sold the sixty-channel Pittsburgh and Dallas systems to TCI. Warner bought out Amex in 1984 and two years later Lewis resigned. By 1994, all the QUBE systems were closed.

According to Columbia University communications professor James Carey, "Warner-Amex used QUBE as a marketing tool to help win cable franchises in a number of cities, and once it had those franchises, it let QUBE die a slow death."[50] That indictment is perhaps too harsh. QUBE could not expand in the absence of regular infusions of capital for infrastructure development. While Amex seemed to provide the answer to access to capital, Amex managers, described by the Warner QUBE team as "conservative bankers," were not a good mix with the company. The decision to sell On-Demand, Nickelodeon, and MTV meant a quick infusion of revenue but a loss of an extraordinary future revenue stream. QUBE was killed by the modern business attitude that demands quick profit, but the fact that a means of communication useful to democratic dialogue depended solely upon a market dominated by a combination of get rich quick financial investors and monopolists is the result of political decisions, not public taste.

A number of writers looking at the death of QUBE and the still struggling public access operations suggest that the core problem is that the public really is not interested in this sort of programming. There is no denying that wrestling and pornography draw larger audiences than civic debates, but that does not suggest that regulation should protect wrestling and pornography. Returning briefly to Madison, the subsidy provided for the circulation of newspapers was not based on the argument that newspapers were what most people wanted. The subsidy was created based on the argument that civic dialogue was necessary for an informed citizenry. We should be able to rise above the confusion between what is interesting to a majority of the public and what is in the public interest.

One such programming experiment, which also serves to keep the cable industry in the good graces of Congress, is the Cable-Satellite Public Affairs Network—C-SPAN. On March 19, 1979, C-SPAN was given access to the cameras in the chambers of the U.S. House of Representatives (equipment owned and operated by Congress, thus making certain to avoid showing the more than occasional empty chamber during a member's passionate speech) to cablecast live to 3.5 million households. By 1982 C-SPAN began twenty-four-hour-a-day programming, including coverage of a variety of public affairs events when Congress is not meeting. C-SPAN is a private, nonprofit company, created, funded, and directed by the cable television industry. It receives no government funding, and while cable operators are not mandated to carry C-SPAN, 97 percent of all cable customers have access to C-SPAN.

The cable industry invested $384 million between 1979 and 2002 in C-SPAN—every penny of it comes from the cable customers as a part of their monthly cable bill. Considering the amount of money it takes to run a cable network, that is not a lot over a twenty-three-year period. Sometimes the lack of resources is painfully obvious. Still, C-SPAN estimates that 28.5 million Americans watch C-SPAN each week. Perhaps more important, C-SPAN viewers vote.[51]

Despite C-SPAN's apparent success, there is no guarantee that cable operators will continue to carry it. In 1996, John Malone's TCI, then the nation's largest system of cable operators, threatened to cancel C-SPAN. It was saved only after a savvy campaign by founder Brian Lamb, which alerted not only viewers but members of Congress.[52] Other less direct threats have also limited C-SPAN's audience. According to Lamb, C-SPAN is "getting hit" by legislation that protects broadcasters' right to cable carriage and requires cable operators (like AOL/TimeWarner, which owns CNN and other cable networks) to carry competitors like FOX, and does not require carriage of C-SPAN. As Lamb told a National Press Club audience in 1997, "in the last two or three years, we've been hit in over 9.9 million homes where there's less C-SPAN than there used to be."[53]

1984: The Dismantling

Still, C-SPAN's public service contribution to Congress paid off in 1984. After intensive lobbying by the cable industry, Congress enacted the first comprehensive amendment to the 1934 Communications Act.[54] The Cable Communications Policy Act of 1984, sponsored by that erstwhile foe of "liberal media," Senator Barry Goldwater, gave notice to the telecommunications and broadcast industry that there was another major player on the block.[55] The news was not particularly good for municipalities or public access advocates. The 1984 Cable Act seemed to assure the existence of public access channels, stating: "This Act . . . Authorizes a Federal, State, or local governmental entity empowered to grant a cable franchise (franchising authority) to establish and enforce franchise requirements for the designation or use of channel capacity for public, educational, or governmental use. Prohibits a cable operator from exercising any editorial control over such use of channel capacity."[56] Like much other legislation enacted under the influence of big business, the 1984 Cable Act took away from local communities much more than it would give back. As Mark Herring would argue, "the Cable Act, in fact, provided a windfall for cable operators."[57]

While allowing municipalities to require government and community access in their negotiations with private cable companies that were using their streets to provide communications services for a fee, Congress took away local authority to determine subscriber rates or the amount the cable companies had to pay local authorities. These prohibitions on local power, of course, limited the amount of funding local communities could apply to the channels the federal government now allowed them to negotiate.

Soon after the new rules went into effect cable companies hiked subscribers' cable rates. Between 1987 and 1988, cable prices rose 25 percent. Little of that money went into public access channels. Instead, with new regulation (mystifyingly called "deregulation") protecting cable companies from the locals, a bidding war began for cable properties. As corporations took on greater amounts of debt to pay the escalating purchase prices for the extraordinarily valuable cable franchise, cable prices continued to rise to pay off the debt, and companies sought to get out of any obligation to support or even provide public access. Some companies simply announced they could not afford to meet their obligation and cut off funds for public access. By 1990, only 16.5 percent of cable systems around the country offered public access. The vast majority of these were poorly funded and in no position to offer viewers a viable alternative to commercial programming. Once again, considerations of what information citizens might need to make democratic choices were not a part of the calculation of cable policy.[58]

The year 1984, made so famous in George Orwell's dystopian novel about a totalitarian state supported by mass media control and surveillance, would not be a good year for the Great Society advances toward democratic communications. Dismantlement began, in Orwellian fashion, when the Reagan Justice Department used the antitrust laws to "force"—perhaps to give cover to—the National Association of Broadcasters' elimination of its own code of conduct in 1982. But the real bloodletting would begin with Mark Fowler.

Appointed by Reagan to the chairmanship of the FCC in 1981, Fowler, who shared credit for a paper with Daniel L. Brenner titled "A Marketplace Approach to Broadcast Regulation,"[59] has become widely known as the FCC commissioner who said, "television is just a toaster with pictures."[60] Under Fowler the FCC made broadcast license renewal much easier, issuing a shortened renewal form (the so-called postcard renewal),[61] and abolished the core elements of the Fairness Doctrine that required broadcasters to present a balanced airing of controversial public issues. One of the key arguments was that the long-held rationale of the inability of the federal government to issue a broadcast license to everyone who wanted one was no longer valid because of thirty-channel cable operations.[62] This bit of confusion over scarcity was really all a Reagan-packed court would need to undermine the public interest obligations established by the FCC under Kennedy.

Not even children were safe from the Reagan FCC. Despite countless studies demonstrating that people mimic behaviors shown on television, despite the 1972 Surgeon General's report, "Television and Growing Up: The Impact of Televised Violence," the Reagan FCC effectively destroyed regulations that called for educational programming for children and limited the number of commercials that could run during children's shows. The result, of course, was an unfettered market and a dramatic increase in the level of violence and sexual behavior and commercials on television to which children were exposed. Toy-based programs aimed at children increased from thirteen in 1980 to more than seventy by 1987, and the amount of commercials children saw per year doubled from twenty thousand in the late 1970s to about forty thousand in 1987.[63]

1984 was a high-water year for the Reagan right, with the Cable Act and the seemingly innocuous FCC ruling that revised "programming rules."[64] As conservative Brookings commentator Robert Crandall noted with apparent glee: "In 1984 the commission eliminated its nonsensical 'ascertainment' requirements for television station licensees. Under this policy station owners were supposed to canvas their communities to ascertain the breadth of interest in various types of programs and events. They were then supposed to structure their program offerings to reflect the findings. . . . Mercifully, the FCC eliminated most of the silly programming, commercial-minute limitation, and ascertainment requirements from the excess baggage of television regulation."[65]

As much as Crandall would like to give Reagan and the Fowler FCC credit for dismantling the public interest regime and adopting a marketplace approach to broadcast regulation, that process actually began earlier under Carter and the FCC under Charles Ferris[66] with the elimination of the ascertainment requirement for radio licensees.[67]

Like many other programs established in the wake of the Great Society, the ascertainment procedure proposed by the Federal Communications Bar

Association was overly detailed but hardly nonsensical. As Crandall suggests, too many broadcasters simply didn't take seriously the promise to meet their license obligation to serve the local public interest. Too many broadcasters viewed themselves merely as businessmen, and their only obligation was to the stockholders. Too often, "the FCC simply buried ascertainment reports, dusting them off only occasionally when it received either a petition to deny the renewal of a license or a competitive application for the license."[68] However, the notion that a stop sign is useless because some drivers ignore it or because police officers don't catch every violator is too nonsensical to debate.

Some broadcasters valued, at least at the time, both the ascertainment process and the information derived from that process. I worked for some of these broadcasters in the late 1970s and early 1980s (Cosmos, Storer, NBC) and conducted ascertainment reports. Many valuable local programs, even some on Sunday morning, were created to reflect the wide range of interests expressed by the community. Still, to see the ascertainment requirement as merely a means to provide broadcasters information about their "market," including the market for public information, is to understand it in far too narrow a context.

Whatever it might have meant in the years between 1927 and 1966, the public interest regime (including the Fairness Doctrine and the limitation on network influence over local programming) was not founded upon public engagement. Viewers and listeners, the public, were not even allowed to play a role in the licensing process until 1966.[69] Ascertainment was a fundamentally democratic process requiring the temporary federal licensees of local public property to consult with the local public over how best to act in the local interest. In this process local citizens were empowered to engage in a deliberation over what issues were important for their community to consider, and many of them were informed for the first time by powerful institutions (radio and television stations) in their community that their opinion mattered. Ascertainment was a tool that treated local broadcasting like a public sphere, not a market, a place where citizens would not only find out about products but discuss public issues. As a flawed tool, disruptive to established power, the ascertainment process was directly connected to Johnson's Great Society project.

The cynical Reagan backlash against government provided a space for laissez-faire ideologues, modern-day Spencers, like Crandall, to dominate policy discourse in Washington, to lay flat all the laws that stood between market priorities and democratic discourse.

The Liberal Media

One of the key difficulties in understanding modern communications policy or modern politics is the set of labels too many writers give to a rather limited spectrum of opinion (from right to left: conservative-moderate-liberal-radical, or hawk-dove), along with the assumption that Democrats occupy the left and Republicans are on the right. One of the values of studying history is that it allows us to see the limitations of this trap and to see both the human complexity and the play of interests (or factions) weaving through political debate and policy making.

Was President Johnson's escalation of the war in Vietnam (based upon the fictitious provocation identified with the Gulf of Tonkin) the policy of a liberal or a conservative? Was Nixon's pledge to end the war in Vietnam (while secretly expanding the war into Cambodia) the policy of a hawk or a dove? What about Nixon's support for "states' rights" (gaining sympathy with southerners angry with federal intrusion into state enforced racism), or his support for expanded racial preference policies he called "affirmative action"? Does this make Nixon liberal or conservative? The fact that these labels are not helpful does not mean politics cannot be understood. Nixon's great contribution to our public dialogue was to blur the lines of public debate, to sow confusion and division among the masses, while keeping a clear bead on those he would call his enemies.

The joining of labor and remnants of the socialist and largely immigrant left with minorities, aging protesters from the 1960s, feminists, and environmentalists constitutes a substantial block of power, struggling for representation largely through the Democratic Party. Former Dixiecrats and John Birchers have joined with a growing military class and a large segment of religious fundamentalists to form the core of the modern Republican Party. Both of these parties incorporate major segments of the business elite. Given the importance of money in gaining access to the channels of communication in our society, the business elite dominate the direction of both parties. But the so-called campaign finance reform problem is not merely, not even fundamentally about capping soft-money contributions—it is a problem of communications policy.

To argue, as a truckload of writers do, that the international conglomerates calling themselves General Electric or Disney or Viacom or News Corporation or AOL/TimeWarner are liberal is nonsensical. It makes almost as much sense to call them American. Some have suggested that a few questionable studies showing that a majority of news reporters vote for

Democrats prove that the media is liberal. This suggestion misunderstands the complex and shifting coalition that is the Democratic Party, and it overestimates the importance of a working journalist's voting behavior in the construction of a product designed to benefit a giant international conglomerate. The same can be said for the less widely held view that the media is conservative.

Major mass media operating in the United States represent the interests of an international corporate community. Sometimes the players in this community conflict, just as the interests of Carnegie or Morgan sometimes conflicted with the interests of Rockefeller or Hearst. These conflicts are important to us all; their resolution may determine the degree of services the government provides to the rest of us (should federal dollars support Head Start or not?), or the level of investment in nuclear or conventional arms. But in the most important ways the interests of the international corporate community are singular. Whether the members of this community are in the entertainment business, or the automobile or banking or oil or agricultural business, they are interested in increasing their profit margins at almost any cost. They are interested in getting government to construct a regulatory environment that allows them to limit risk and increase their return to shareholders. They do not care whether their labor comes from China or Nigeria or Mexico or Poland or South Carolina, as long as it is cheap. General Electric and TimeWarner and Disney are one faction, they belong to the same faction as Haliburton Oil and CitiCorp. If they together do not control our national conversation, the public information Madison deemed so important to a popular government, they certainly dominate that conversation.

As stated earlier, factions are not parties. The Republican Party, for example, is made up of several factions, including most prominently the Religious Right and the former Dixiecrats. The Religious Right may howl about abortion and homosexuals, and the Dixiecrats may scream about affirmative action and illegal immigrants, but neither of these groups should be confused with the faction that determines tax or military policy.

What I have just described is a form of Mills's theory of the structure of U.S. society. There is a power elite, and there has always been this sort of elite in American society, and it has always included the most wealthy. But now it is in less conflict with itself than it was when it was made up of agrarian slaveholders and preindustrial merchants. Now it is made up of the very wealthy leaders of international corporations all driven by the same principles. There is also, as Mills suggested, a middle level of power where most of the politicians and unions and church groups and others contest policy. At this middle level of power, those who call themselves conservatives have become much better at using media, and one of the tools employed in this task is the notion of a liberal media.

As we have seen, since the dawn of the trusts in America, the party in power most closely associated with the trusts has benefited from the fact that American mass media—Hearst, the Associated Press, the Radio Corporation of America—was also a collection of trusts. So-called conservatives battling in the middle levels of power are able to corral the occasional idealistic reporter, like Murrow, by demanding a conservative "balance." At the same time, these same forces have driven out so-called leftist ideas, such as a national health care plan or greater support for the poor, by branding them "communistic" or "un-American."

The old Red-baiter Richard Nixon would blame his enemies for calling attention to illegal bombing, domestic spying, and dirty tricks, and he would blame the media. Despite the long-standing support by the vast majority of newspaper publishers for the Republican Party, despite the dominance of big-business interests over broadcasting, there was a sharp difference between the Eisenhower and Hoover GOP and this new coalition Nixon shaped from the racist southern Dixiecrats, the Goldwater/John Birchers in the West, the reactionary working-class whites in middle America, and the East Coast Bush-Rockefeller elite. The East Coast elite (the presidents George Bush, for example) which once dominated the party of Lincoln embraced Nixon's noxious coalition because it allowed them to dominate the executive branch and exercise control over their core concerns of economic policy and the military apparatus to protect international interests such as access to oil, cheap labor, and open markets.

In his victory over that elite in 1964, Goldwater understandably attacked the East Coast media for not taking his bellicose and racist campaign seriously. Nixon, never on good terms with reporters (upon losing a bid in yet another Red-baiting campaign for a U.S. Senate seat in California, Nixon said goodbye to reporters: "Think how much you'll miss, you won't have Dick Nixon to kick around anymore"), sensed the anxiety that much of television's offerings created among his coalition. Blaming the messenger would prove to be a good tactic. Assigning one of his right-wing propagandists fond of alliteration, William Safire (now with the "liberal" New York Times), to assist Vice-President Spiro Agnew, the Nixon administration went on the attack against the "nattering nabobs of negativism." The right would adopt "the media" as a favorite whipping boy, even while they developed sophisticated mass media techniques.

Ronald Reagan and his handlers accomplished a mastery over media—from feeding journalists pretty pictures to override ugly messages to tightly scripted news conferences to limiting access to war zones.[70] What the Reagan publicists understood was that they could turn the frustration of a large number of Americans against the very mechanism instituted to secure their rights (in the words of the Declaration of Independence)—the government—while promoting the president as a celebrity, more symbol than substantive executive.

But the so-called great communicator was buttressed by more than a highly trained staff of public relations experts; there was also a cadre of well-funded organizations (Cato, American Enterprise Institute, the Heritage Foundation, etc.) dedicated to promoting the ideas of quack social theorists (Charles Murray), obscure economists (Arthur Laffer), and college polemicists (Dinesh D'Souza).[71] When this intensive effort is combined with comic hate-filled rantings from popular radio hosts and a proliferation of magazines and television screamers, the result is a radical tilting of mainstream political discussion far to the right. One of the most valuable tools in this arsenal is the constant whining that the media is liberal.

But all this organizing talent and money might be frustrated if American communications policy reflected the design set out by Madison. If we understood communications as central to our republic, and required that it reflect a system of balancing interest against interest, political equality, and freedom to participate, no one interest would be able to dominate the means of communicating public issues. The greatest damage done in the Nixon-Reagan era has been to the Roosevelt-Johnson optimism that government can and must reflect us, and that government, not the market, is the means to restore the democratic promise of liberty and equality to all.

9

The Internet: Communications Policy
in the Clinton Era (1992–2000)

> Roper: So now you'd give the Devil benefit of law!
>
> More: Yes. What would you do? Cut a great road
> through the law to get after the Devil?
>
> Roper: I'd cut down every law in England to do that!
>
> More: Oh? And when the last law was down, and
> the Devil turned round on you—where would you hide,
> Roper, the laws all being flat? This country's planted
> thick with laws from coast to coast—man's laws, not
> God's—and if you cut them down—and you're just
> the man to do it—do you really think you could stand
> upright in the winds that would blow then? Yes, I'd give
> the Devil benefit of law, for my own safety's sake.
>
> —Robert Bolt, *A Man for All Seasons*

Deregulation: The Devil Turns Round

In the Reagan years, America was like a drunken bully reluctant to go home. Reagan's botched military adventure in Beirut, his failed assassination attempt against Libyan leader Muammar Qaddafi, and a bungled operation to fund a private war against the democratically elected government of Nicaragua through the illegal sale of arms to Iran brought immediate embarrassment to his administration. Reagan's support for Saddam Hussein, the Taliban, Al Qaeda, and Manuel Noriega would haunt us long after he was gone. But as luck would have it, in 1985 the Soviet Union was under the leadership of a bold reformer, Mikhail Gorbachev. Gorbachev pushed a number of political reforms (glasnost), and economic reforms (perestroika) that would lead to the collapse of the Soviet Union by the time he stepped down in 1991. With the "evil empire" no longer competing in the arms race, the United States had an opportunity to redirect spending from the military to projects at home. In the face of the astronomical Reagan budget deficits, junk-bond shenanigans on Wall Street, a banking crisis, and rising health care costs, it was time for the bully to come home.[1]

Reagan's vice-president, George H. W. Bush, was burdened by his predecessor's military and fiscal legacies, without the benefit of Reagan's press manipulators. After bravely signing legislation raising taxes in 1990 (brave because he had to face his own irresponsible taunt "Read my lips: no new taxes"), Bush was criticized for not being sufficiently sensitive to middle-class Americans suffering under Reagan economic policies. America was ready for a president focused on domestic problems, and so a young charismatic governor from Arkansas, William Jefferson Clinton, was elected.

Clinton was a "new Democrat," which seems to mean that he was successful at being a wide variety of different things to different people. He was for gun control, and for putting more police on the streets. He was for affirmative action, and for ending welfare as we know it. He was for fiscal restraint and closing corporate loopholes, but strongly believed in the power of market forces. He would close the revolving door between government officials and corporations, but open the doors to the Lincoln bedroom to campaign contributors. He called for "an America where 'family values' live in our actions, not just in our speeches," and had an extramarital affair with a White House intern half his age.[2] Combine all of this with the vehemence of well-funded enemies (denouncing him for everything from financial fraud to murder to expensive hair cuts), eager to feed scandal-hungry reporters (including the "liberal" *Washington Post* and *New York Times*),[3] and you have a noxious and confusing political environment.

In the midst of this would come the first major reform of communications policy in over seventy years. On February 8, 1996, a week after a tremendous show of support in both the Republican-controlled House and Senate, President Clinton signed into law the Telecommunications Act of 1996. What popular information the American public received about this major updating of communications law focused on its purported benefit to U.S. consumers. As Senator Pressler, who introduced the legislation, explained: "Passage of the Telecommunications Act of 1996 was my highest legislative priority in the first session of the 104th Congress. On Feb. 8, that priority became law. Thanks to my bill, the communications industry will see an explosion in new investment and development. Who are the winners? The consumers. There will be more services and new products at lower costs. All of this economic activity will mean new jobs. Competition is the key for this development. My bill unlocked the regulatory handcuffs restricting the communications industry."[4] Characteristically, upon signing the act, President Clinton noted the expectation of increased competition and the benefit to consumers, but almost as if he were referring to a different piece of legislation, he also mentioned: "This bill protects consumers against monopolies. It guarantees the diversity of voices our democracy depends upon. Perhaps most of all, it enhances the common good."[5]

To be kind, President Clinton was badly mistaken. In less than five years it became clear that the 1996 Telecommunications Act helped to usher in an unprecedented wave of media mergers, further empowering the already dominant voices in our public sphere. In many ways the Telecommunications Act of 1996 is a mirror of the Clinton years. It provided a grab bag of initiatives to address a wide variety of mostly economic concerns, but it did not advance a coherent policy connecting communications policy and civic engagement.

As he would do with welfare, Clinton embraced the right-wing call for "deregulation" of the communications industry. To some extent the Telecommunications Act did eliminate regulations, particularly those barriers that served to protect the business interests of different segments of the communications industry from the encroachment of other segments of the industry. For example, telephone companies were allowed to compete with cable companies in delivery of video service. However, the removal of these "economic barriers" entailed the creation of a whole new set of regulations. So "deregulation" resulted in increased regulation.

If the term *deregulation* has a meaning beyond rhetoric, it can be found in practice.[6] In practice, no one in the communications industry really wanted to cut down core "economic" laws. The patent laws, the copyright laws, the tax laws, the federal laws preempting the power of states and municipalities, laws protecting broadcasters from signal interference, laws requiring the cable industry to carry broadcasting signals, laws setting telecommunications standards, all of the laws protecting the core interests of the communications industry were certainly not cut down. The issue, of course, is not whether there is regulation, but who benefits from the regulation, and how they benefit. Open, equal, democratic communication did not result from "deregulation."

*   *   *

The reader who has followed this brief history of U.S. communications policy will not be surprised by the themes of this chapter: massive public investments handed over to private industry with only the most superficial regulatory controls, tolerance for monopoly, and only token concern over the impact of new technology on enabling civic engagement or advancing political equality. The challenges this philosophy poses to our democratic principles could not be more stark in our present. But before we more fully examine the 1996 Telecommunications Act, we should back up to the dawn of the new "medium" of communications that act was, at least in part, meant to take into account—the Internet.

The Dawn of Our Digital Age—and Al Gore

What many of us think of as the Internet (still so new we continue to capitalize it) is really a combination of codes and computer devices operating (often simultaneously) through spectrum, satellite, cable, and telephone communications systems. Just like television (cable, broadcast, and satellite) and telephone (wired and cellular) the Internet is a communications *system* in the broadest sense. Just like broadcasting (radio and television) and the telephone, the Internet has many "inventors" and one major institution that supported its early development and subsequent growth—the federal government. Just like every medium of communication, the Internet is subject to the U.S. public philosophy of communications. Because that public philosophy now thwarts democracy, not even the powerful tool of the Internet will advance the democratic goals of liberty and equality.

The Internet, as most of us use it, is really two things: the personal computer and the system that computer is sometimes connected to.[7] If you take away the personal computer, the communications system that allows computers to communicate would be meaningless to most of us. So the Internet was meaningless to most of us for most of its history.

Computers are far more complex than the word *computer* would suggest. Modern computing is much more than counting. Modern computers re-create reality in ways that are useful. For example, computers allow us to respond in intelligent ways to calculations by representing those calculations as pictures and sounds. While calculators deployed to crack enemy code were one of the many uses of tabulating/computers in World War II, relatively sophisticated devices that worked in close interaction with humans to locate and target fast-moving aircraft and invisible submarines are another early use of computers. For good reason, the U.S. Department of Defense was the greatest funder of computer research and development.[8]

Just as the launch of *Sputnik* spurred the space race and the U.S. satellite program, it also spurred great investments in computer technology. Many of these investments were given over to contractors specifically created to serve the military, such as the RAND Corporation. Other investments were in academic institutions such as the Massachusetts Institute of Technology (MIT) or the University of California at Los Angeles, both of which conducted research in association with the DOD-funded Advanced Research Projects Agency (ARPA).

By the 1960s, the U.S. military and its supporters in the academy were using giant computers to solve a variety of problems. Even though many of the problems were related, each computer operated with a unique set of codes, with the data locked in one location, resulting in duplication and rising expenses. In addition, computers were the means of control over the many nuclear missiles spread across North America, and the military was concerned that the nation's telecommunications system, the privately controlled AT&T, would not survive a missile attack.[9] Thus, establishing standards and technologies for linking computers and making those linkages relatively safe from attack became a priority for the military and its contractors. The result was the splitting of digital code (ones and zeroes in unique combinations) into small blocks or packets embedded with information about code placement that could be sent and received from redundant lines and connecting points and then reassembled. As so often happens, several "inventors" were finding similar solutions to the same problem: MIT (1961–67), RAND (1962–65), and the National Physical Laboratory (NPL) in Britain (1964–67). The word *packet* was adopted from the work at NPL. Standard operating systems, methods for building code, and a host of other developments followed.[10]

The military, its contractors, and a few academic institutions immediately benefited from the early ARPANET, established as a physical network in 1969, linking UCLA, the Stanford Research Institute, the University of California at Santa Barbara, and the University of Utah. But its use as a popular communications device was not apparent until 1972, with the first e-mail, developed as an unauthorized use (a hack), at the military contractor Bolt Beranek and Newman (BBN) and MIT. But computer use was still limited to institutions connected with the military that could afford extraordinarily expensive equipment sometimes taking up entire rooms.

Much like the early radios, a number of young tinkerers were fascinated by computers. A few manufacturers targeted this market, selling computer kits through advertising in magazines like *Popular Science*. Two of these early kits were the Scelbi (SCientific, ELectronic and BIological) "personal computer" designed by the Scelbi Computer Consulting Company, and the

Mark-8 designed by Jonathan Titus. Ed Roberts, the owner of a small company in New Mexico, Micro Instrumentation Telemetry Systems (MITS), designed a personal computer kit he called the Altair 8800. The Altair was the computer Paul Allen and Bill Gates would work on to begin developing the Microsoft operating system.[11] Perhaps the first small computer that was useful beyond exciting the imagination of hobbyists was made by International Business Machines (IBM), a long-time supplier of computational equipment for business and military. The IBM 5100 Portable Computer was first introduced in September 1975. At fifty pounds and at a price that ranged between $8,975 and $19,975 it was designed for professional business use. But in 1977, a new company created a sensation by introducing the first "personal computer," the Apple II. The Apple II could display color graphics and it included two game paddles—all for $1,298. IBM would introduce its own PC in 1981 (no game paddles), and the race for the home market was on.[12]

After nearly ten years of development at the renamed Defense Advanced Research Projects Agency (DARPA), a team of computer scientists, led by Robert Kahn and Vinton Cerf, created the common language and protocols for all computers (TCP/IP) on the growing (by 1981–213) number of host computers on ARPANET. By 1982, this networked collection of computers would be referred to as an "internet."

In 1986, the junior U.S. senator from Tennessee rose to support legislation authorizing enhanced computer research activity of the National Science Foundation. Specifically, he wanted to speak on two amendments to the act, both reflecting what would come to be hallmarks of his public service: "Within this Bill I have two amendments, the Computer Network Study and the Greenhouse Effect Report. The first amendment was originally introduced with Senator Gordon as S. 2594 [introduced June 24, 1986, as the Supercomputer Network Study Act of 1986]. It calls for a 2-year study of the critical problems and current and future options regarding communications networks for research computers. The second amendment requires the President to submit a report to Congress on the actions taken to establish an international year of the greenhouse effect."[13]

Public Law 99–383 was eventually passed in late August 1986, and the National Science Foundation (NSF) would take up the task proposed by Senator Al Gore. The NSF had been interested in the field of computer science since the late 1970s, and proposed creating a network for the academic community of computer scientists in 1974. In 1979, computer scientists from six universities met at Madison, Wisconsin, to discuss setting up something they called the Computer Science Network (CSNET). This ultimately led to five-year funding from NSF beginning in 1980, and allowed non-military-related uses of computer networking for the first time. By 1985, NSF was sufficiently convinced of the importance of computer networking to support connecting five supercomputer centers as a robust "backbone" network, the NSFNET. Commercial network traffic was prohibited on the NSFNET.

By the time of Al Gore's speech, nearly all the country's academic institutions interested in computer science, as well as a few private-sector research sites were connected, but continued funding and research on NSFNET exposed academic and research communities to the potential for ubiquitous wide-area networking. By the end of 1989 ARPANET dissolved and NSFNET became the backbone of the Internet.

The Internet was created not by market forces or the private sector; the Internet was created by the federal government. Its development was initiated at a time when Americans believed in government. But as Gore recognized, while the early Internet was being used exclusively for military purposes, it had the potential to increase the communications capabilities of many more Americans. Inspired by his father, Al Gore Sr.—also a U.S. senator from Tennessee, who had co-authored the Federal-Aid Highway Act of 1956[14]—Al Gore Jr. introduced the idea of the "information superhighway" in 1992 while campaigning for vice-president. Gore argued that an information superhighway "ought to be built by the federal government" much like the interstate highway system. However, a year later, then Vice-President Gore announced that "unlike the interstates, the information highways will be built, paid for, and funded by the private sector." He also announced the administration's support of removal of "judicial and legislative restrictions on all types of telecommunications companies: cable, telephone, utilities, television, and satellite." The vice-president's representatives denied any connection between the financial largess of the communications industry to the Democrats and the vice-president's 180-degree turnaround on the role of private industry.[15]

Courting private industry to assist in extending the power of new communications technologies to all Americans is understandable. But Gore's new position diminished the thirty-year history of the government in building, paying for, and funding the Internet. Instead of noting that history and alerting the public to the benefits of federal research and development, Gore fed the misconception advanced by the Republican right that only the private industry was sufficiently competent to improve our lives. Moreover, as private industry is given credit for building the road, the demands of private industry to determine the rules of that road are also strengthened. While citizens are blinded to the benefits of government support, and the role of their tax dollars, that make the road possible, they remain blind to their right to benefit from their contribution.

Gore's spokespersons may deny any connection between the campaign contributions from Silicon Valley and the new emphasis on private industry, but that denial only increases public cynicism. The public is only too aware that in modern America all politicians are beholden to wealthy corporations and individuals who are willing and able to finance the increasingly expensive campaigns. Our representatives face daily pressures to raise money and, if they are to remain in office, they must also remain aware of the need to placate the rich captains of global industries who provide the bulk of that money. While Republicans pointed with glee to the nightly rents charged for sleeping in the Lincoln bedroom by Messrs. Clinton and Gore, their joy was no doubt born of a deep appreciation of the pickle those erstwhile liberal democrats were in. One cannot rise to govern in our present lived democracy without lowering oneself to grovel for money to purchase the attention of citizens. In America the delivery of "popular information" is controlled by private corporations, and they are pleased to offer this service to our democracy to the highest bidder.

Communications Reform in the Clinton Years

Americans have every reason to suspect that the provisions of the 1996 Telecommunications Act were meant to mollify, if not to please, a communications industry dominated by global conglomerates.[16] The influence of this global industry over the national legislative process was hinted at in the scandal over the book deal offered to Georgia Republican Newt Gingrich, the then Speaker of the House, by the international media magnate Rupert Murdoch. But that book deal was the tip of the iceberg.

According to Charles Lewis of the Center for Public Integrity, Senate Leader Bob Dole received hundreds of thousands of dollars before the 1996 act from communications companies such as TCI and Time/Warner in direct contributions and through support of Dole fronts such as the Better America Foundation.[17] As Ken Auletta reported in the New Yorker, AT&T spent nearly $1.3 million in soft-money contributions to both parties in 1994 alone.[18] The political action committees of the broadcasting industry, long considered the most powerful special interest group in the country, contributed over $1.3 million during the 1995–96 election cycle. For the first six months of 1996, the broadcast industry spent at least $10.7 million in lobbying Congress, the Clinton administration, and the Federal Communications Commission (FCC).[19]

The making of modern legislation is an ugly process of bargaining between those who have the greatest financial ability to influence representatives. While there are always a few legislators who genuinely deliberate the issues and consider the long-term consequences of their vote, keeping all of their constituents in mind, these Mr. Smiths do not represent the character of our current politics. Efforts to reform the campaign funding process have not yet succeeded and a story or two occasionally surfaces about the issue. But there have been precious few "news" stories on campaign finance reform focusing on the political power of the various communications lobbies. As Charles Lewis has said, it would be like a bank robber announcing to the public that he was in the process of robbing the bank.[20] The debate, or lack thereof, over the 1996 Telecommunications Act is a prime example of why private industry alone cannot be trusted to control the public sphere.

The problem is not merely whether News Corporation or General Electric (GE) contributes money and legal expertise in drafting legislation; more disturbing is the fact that they can limit the amount of information the public can receive about legislation they favor or legislation they oppose. Up in arms about the lack of debate and the lack of news coverage regarding that portion of the act giving, rather than auctioning, to existing broadcasters additional spectrum to send digital signals, Republican Majority Leader (and 1996 presidential candidate) Bob Dole put it this way: "Here we are, trying to balance the budget, cutting welfare, cutting other programs, and about to give a big handout here to the rich, the powerful. We have not seen a single story on any of the networks about this issue. We see a lot of stories on the networks about some Member of Congress going somewhere on a 'junket,' they always like to say on the networks. But I have not seen anybody, except for CNN, not a single story on what could be the biggest giveaway of the century—not one. You will not see it on the networks. You probably will not see it in any newspaper that owns television because this affects them."[21] Actually, the *Washington Post*, which owns several television stations, ran several articles and editorials on the act.[22] But Dole's point was not far from the truth. As Dean Alger told Bill Moyers in the 1999 PBS documentary, "Free Speech for Sale," in the nine months during which the Telecommunications Act was being debated, from May 1995 to February 1996, the three major networks (ABC, CBS, and NBC) carried a total of nineteen minutes on the Telecommunications Act, with no mention of those provisions related to broadcasters.[23] A public dependent upon local and national television news[24] had either no information about this important legislation, or the information it received was drowned out in celebrity trivia in the typical fashion of modern news shows or distorted in ads threatening a "TV Tax."[25] Media coverage about the manipulation of our democracy by global media has not improved. The ability of private global media to censor or dominate important national public discussion about media and the unwillingness of elected representatives to change this state of affairs should concern all citizens in a democracy.

What was at stake in this major communications reform of 1996 was much more fundamental than whether to give or auction spectrum to broadcasters or how to protect children from Internet pornography[26] or whether interconnection and unbundling policies would generate competition in the telecommunications market. What was in play was how effectively the broad and dynamic communications industry would be regulated by the state. What was at issue was no less than whether the capabilities of each citizen to participate effectively in society (to engage in, among other activities, political dialogue) would be extended or curtailed. But this frame, this way of understanding communications policy, was mostly absent from the debate.

The industry compromise that became the Telecommunications Act of 1996 was sold to the American public by its promoters, the communications industry, as a great consumer victory. Competition, it was reported, would reduce prices and provide more services. The early promises of competition and reduced prices have failed to materialize, as has the promise of new jobs. Prices, particularly cable prices, have gone up.[27] Employment growth is negligible and wages are depressed, particularly in the telephone industry.[28] But something more fundamental and dangerous has occurred.

The Church of the Free Market and Technology Nirvana

Far more troubling than the broken promises to consumers has been the shift in the public debate. As noted above, that shift away from the public interest and toward an egalitarian myth of the market[29] began during the Reagan years of the 1980s, but in the 1990s it was joined with the notion that what was being called "technology" would itself solve our problems. This is well demonstrated by a manifesto funded by the right-wing Progress and Freedom Foundation, "Cyberspace and the American Dream: A Magna Carta for the Knowledge Age." Under the signatures of Esther Dyson, Alvin Toffler,

George Keyworth, and George Gilder, the "Magna Carta" is a relentlessly upbeat stew of cyberspeak, utopian fantasy, and laissez-faire economics.[30]

Alvin Toffler, along with George Gilder and Esther Dyson, view the advent of new communications technology as the inevitable advent of a new order, a "third wave" resulting in the obsolescence of "all our congresses, parliaments . . . our courts and our regulatory agencies—in short, all the tools we use to make and enforce collective decision."[31] So, technology will not only make our smiles brighter, it will eliminate the need for all the messy mechanisms of democracy. As Neil Postman argues, "anyone who has studied the history of technology knows that technological change is always a Faustian bargain: Technology giveth and technology taketh away, and not always in equal measure. A new technology sometimes creates more than it destroys. Sometimes, it destroys more than it creates."[32] Postman also suggests that the modern hype of technology actually serves to pacify the poor (the "losers") with the promise of better, less complicated tomorrows, as it further empowers those in power (the "winners") today.[33]

These are the two dominant solutions offered to correct our society today: the so-called free market and the inevitable progress of what we call science. While these ideas are offered as new realities, replacing the dinosaur structures of the New Deal and the Great Society, as we have seen these nostrums are as old as the Gilded Age, promoted by the same set of interests and just as wrong today as they were then.

Despite the dominant paradigms of modern communications policy, a paradigm as old as the republic itself was given new life in the 1996 Telecommunications Act, government support for all citizens to have access to communications services. While the term *universal service* was first invented by the public relations apparatus at AT&T to justify the need for government support for one set of technical standards, that is, AT&T-developed standards, for all local and long-distance telephone communications, the term has come to mean support for poor people so they too can access telephone service.

Section 254 of the Telecommunications Act re-created and organized a previously confusing set of cross-subsidies and low-income support programs. The act mandated that all telecommunications carriers were to contribute to a Universal Service Fund. That fund would continue to support telephone access for rural and high-cost areas as well as for the poor (Lifeline and Link-Up), and provide support for access to advanced telecommunications service to beneficiaries including K-12 schools, libraries, and rural health care facilities. The act left most of the details up to the FCC.

Lifeline and Link-Up help provide basic phone service to the poor. These programs are funded at about $500 million per year. The so-called high-cost subsidy supports carriers offering telephone service in rural and high-cost areas. There are different levels of support depending on the size of the carrier and the cost of service within a specific area. Small carriers receive greater amounts of support than large carriers. This program is funded at about $2.5 billion per year.

Because so much attention, and funding, supports schools, the fact that libraries are also included is often given little attention. As with schools, the FCC provides discounts on the purchase of telecommunications services, Internet access, and internal connections to eligible libraries. Eligibility is determined by a formula that looks at libraries' eligibility for subsidies and other support and their geographic location. As of November 2, 2000, more than 4,500 libraries had received about $77 million in discounted services, according to the American Library Association.[34]

A July 1999 report from the Commerce Department's National Telecommunications and Information Administration[35] found that 70 percent of rural libraries and 80 percent of libraries serving low-income communities provide public Internet access. The report also demonstrated the importance to individuals of providing such access. Libraries provided access to the Internet for 60 percent of Hispanics and 21.9 percent of the unemployed. Rural African Americans rely on libraries for Internet access more than any other group, according to the report.

The Telecommunications Act of 1996 also includes provisions for improving access to advanced telecommunications service for rural hospitals, clinics, and physicians. Public and nonprofit rural health care providers are provided discounts that can make their rates about the same as those paid in urban areas. This program is funded at about $400 million per year, but initial participation has been far below that of schools and libraries.

The Universal Service Fund fee has emerged through a brutal political battle. Republicans and their media allies (particularly Rush Limbaugh and "economist" James Glassman) called it the "Gore Tax" after the telecommunications companies decided to report to consumers the percentage of their payments that would go toward the universal service contribution. As if these subsidies had not existed before, or as if consumers would not be equally upset to learn what percentage of their bill went to pay for lobbying. The Democrats called the Universal Service Fund the "E-Rate"—as in the education rate, ignoring of course the fact that it supported the less politically popular poor. Still, the universal service program has been the one qualified success of the Telecommunications Act.

* * *

It would be easy to dismiss the act as another Clinton-Gingrich era corruption, a revision of over sixty years of law purchased by the telecommunications and broadcast industry. There is evidence to support that view.[36] It would also be easy to extol it as a compromise between competing stakeholders reached, after too long a delay, to bring an industry radically altered by new technology into the present. There is a little evidence to support this view, generally expounded by the major news organizations that bothered to report on the act and that view public engagement (democratic deliberation, in other words) in these sorts of issues as a naive and meddlesome notion at best.[37] Those nominally responsible for bringing the act into being and interpreting it characterize it as a boon to consumers, an expert piece of legislative drafting that would encourage competition and thus promote better and more varied services for lower prices. There is some evidence to support this intent.[38] There is no evidence to support the view that the act's mechanisms to introduce competition have reduced the market power of existing telecommunications monopolies or spurred the growth of new competitors.[39]

The 1996 Telecommunications Act is a fairly predictable bit of legislation fully consistent with the development of our public philosophy of turning over to trusts a powerful tool necessary to the operation of our democratic republic. It is a cousin to the Pacific Telegraph Act, and the Willis-Graham Act, and General Order 40 of the Federal Radio Commission, and all of the other foundations of our communications policy, except, of course, the Post Office Act of 1792.

The Joke Is on Us

One final note about Al Gore and the Internet will serve to illustrate the fact that censoring information from the public that might damage their corporate interests is not the only impact major mass media has on public debate. Major mass media (from Rush Limbaugh to the *New York Times*) also tend to trivialize political activity and through this trivialization limit public discussion.

One of the major factors in the growth of the Internet was the language protocol, TCP/IP, developed by Vinton Cerf, Robert Kahn, and a few others.

If the Internet can be said to have founders, Cerf and Kahn certainly belong in the pantheon. In a paper published on the Internet, Cerf and Kahn included Al Gore among the founders:

> Al Gore was the first political leader to recognize the importance of the Internet and to promote and support its development.
>
> As far back as the 1970s Congressman Gore promoted the idea of high speed telecommunications as an engine for both economic growth and the improvement of our educational system. He was the first elected official to grasp the potential of computer communications to have a broader impact than just improving the conduct of science and scholarship. Though easily forgotten, now, at the time this was an unproven and controversial concept. . . . When the Internet was still in the early stages of its deployment, Congressman Gore provided intellectual leadership by helping create the vision of the potential benefits of high speed computing and communication. As an example, he sponsored hearings on how advanced technologies might be put to use in areas like coordinating the response of government agencies to natural disasters and other crises.
>
> As a Senator in the 1980s Gore urged government agencies to consolidate what at the time were several dozen different and unconnected networks into an "Interagency Network." Working in a bi-partisan manner with officials in Ronald Reagan and George Bush's administrations, Gore secured the passage of the High Performance Computing and Communications Act in 1991. This "Gore Act" supported the National Research and Education Network (NREN) initiative that became one of the major vehicles for the spread of the Internet beyond the field of computer science.[40]

In 1999, then Vice-President Al Gore was asked by Wolf Blitzer, a talk show host on CNN, "Why should Democrats, looking at the Democratic nomination process, support you instead of Bill Bradley, a friend of yours, a former colleague in the Senate? What do you have to bring to this that he doesn't necessarily bring to this process?" Gore responded: "During my service in the United States Congress, I took the initiative in creating the Internet. I took the initiative in moving forward a whole range of initiatives that have proven to be important to our country's economic growth and environmental protection, improvements in our educational system."

Gore clearly introduced legislative initiatives to support NSFNET, the backbone of the Internet as we know it. He was clearly far ahead of Bradley or frankly any other U.S. politician in recognizing the potential of the Internet and in doing everything a legislator could do to see that potential realized. Somehow, his rather awkward response in a relatively obscure cable talk show has become a purported boast that he "invented" the Internet. This claim was repeated in dozens of newspapers and television news shows and by late night comedians.[41] *Wired* magazine, which focuses on the Internet and digital technologies, a source one would think should know better, even claims to have been the first to report this falsehood.[42] Presidential candidate George W. Bush took advantage of the perception by running a campaign ad where a female voice remarks, "If Al Gore invented the Internet, then I invented the remote control." The fact that Bush took advantage of this false characterization is, unfortunately, what we have come to expect of politicians.

But certainly when Truth and Falsehood do battle in the public arena, Truth will win out. Eventually. Maybe. The American public may not know much about greenhouse effects or the role of legislation in supporting relatively obscure scientific research, but they can make character judgments. As Steve and Cokie Roberts reported in a January 2000 column: "When Gore does try to assert himself, it often backfires—witness his claim that he helped invent the Internet. 'He sounded naive when he said that; he was just trying to make himself look good,' says Mike, a telephone lineman. 'I just don't trust him; he doesn't know his facts.'"[43]

As Richard Wiggins points out, newspaper reporters, television commentators, politicians, late night comedians all repeated the lie that Gore said he invented the Internet, and the endless repetition created the impression that Gore is a liar and a braggart. Let me repeat—this was an impression unsupported by the facts. Let us make the giant assumption that Mike the Lineman actually exists, and Steve and Cokie are smart enough to understand what Al Gore did as a legislator, and let us assume that they are not partisan hacks. We are left with, at the very least, a repeated trivialization of the work of legislators to initiate public funding for scientific research. This trivialization of public policy makes an informed debate impossible.

But then, given our public philosophy regarding communications, we have no reason to expect more. Despite the recent romanticism about what we call the press, the major sources of our public information are private citizens dependent on the largess of global corporations. These corporations have no real responsibility to speak the truth. They are accountable only to their shareholders regarding the amount of profit they make, and toward that end their goal is to entertain and keep us coming back. Neither citizens nor consumers are the primary audience for Viacom, News Corporation, General Electric, Disney, or the *New York Times*. Their primary audience is other corporations who advertise and provide them services to run their business. They are not subject to being voted out of office. They are not driven by moral concerns over the impact of their actions on our democracy.

Let me tease out two additional points here: (1) media is a seamless web for most Americans (a snippet of an interview on cable television is picked up by radio talk show hosts, newspaper columnists, web sites and late night television network comedians) representing reality; and (2) the fact that Al Gore's legislative record is on the Internet and the Blitzer interview was transcribed and available to the public did not help either Al Gore, Steve and Cokie the "journalists," or, more important, Mike the lineman.

A Complex Interrelated Media Environment

Before leaving the 1990s and our history of communications policy, a brief discussion of communications and race will serve to demonstrate the complex character of our current media environment.

As stated earlier, for the vast majority of its two centuries of independence America has been a deeply racist nation. Even after the end of slavery, African Americans were relegated to a second-class status enforced not only by social norms but by state and federal governmental action, north and south. This status severely limited political, economic, housing, and educational opportunities for African Americans while it privileged Americans who could claim the status of whiteness. This racist regime was not effectively altered until the 1960s with the passage of the 1964 Civil Rights Act and the 1965 Voting Rights Act. Thus, early attempts to address American racism came some thirty years after "the American system" of broadcasting was developed. To be blunt about it, the cultural norms of radio and television and the legal structures that grew around them were established in a society permeated by racism—by assumptions of white supremacy. Whatever promise broadcast media held to create an environment of brotherhood and equality, to promote and protect a true diversity of expression in the public sphere, would be stunted in such an environment.

Racism in America was altered in the 1960s but it was not destroyed. Efforts to correct the racism of white media would not occur until after civil rights activity directed at broadcasting, most notably the case a local NAACP leader, Aaron Henry, and the United Church of Christ brought against the government agency created to license broadcasters, the Federal Communications Commission.[44] Legislation and FCC decisions designed to promote black voices in broadcasting followed this civil rights litigation.

Federal efforts to correct racist practices, including those related to communications, provoked a severe backlash. The demands of oppressed blacks were met with antibusing protests, charges of reverse discrimination, white flight from the cities, and, perhaps most important, political realignments. The once-solid South dominated by racist Democrats like Strom Thurmond and Jesse Helms shifted in the 1980s to support the Goldwater-Reagan right of the Republican Party. It is the Republican Party that has come to dominate our national policies and our awkward discourse on race and communications.

In 1971, racial minorities, a third of the nation, were licensed to only ten (yes, ten) of the approximately 7,500 radio stations and held no licenses to operate the thousand television stations in the nation.[45] If black Americans were visible or heard in the public debate, their participation was largely limited to noncontroversial entertainments, caricature inventions such as "Amos and Andy," or news and public affairs programs controlled by whites. Early attempts to correct this problem focused on establishing guidelines to promote and monitor equal hiring practices in the broadcast industry,[46] but to little effect.

In 1978, under the leadership of President Carter, the FCC adopted a *Statement of Policy on Minority Ownership of Broadcasting Facilities,* noting that despite its policies discouraging employment discrimination among broadcast licensees "the views of racial minorities continue to be inadequately represented in the broadcast media. This situation is detrimental not only to the minority audience but to all of the viewing and listening public." The commission proposed two sets of policies: (1) to consider minority participation as a factor in comparative license proceedings; and (2) to encourage broadcast licensees to sell to minority buyers through a distress sale (a broadcaster whose license may not be transferred because he is in jeopardy of losing it may transfer it to a minority applicant) or a tax certificate (a broadcaster may sell to a minority and defer any gain realized from the sale).[47] That year, minority broadcast ownership climbed to nearly one hundred—still less than one percent of the nation's broadcast licensees.[48]

By 1986, all minorities combined were licensed to just 2.1 percent of the more than 11,000 radio and television stations in the United States.[49] In 1990, a Supreme Court still dominated by New Deal and Great Society appointees ruled in *Metro Broadcasting, Inc. v. FCC*[50] that the FCC minority ownership programs were mandated by Congress and were constitutional because they serve the important governmental objective of promoting program diversity. The Reagan appointees on that court, Rehnquist, Scalia, O'Connor, and

Kennedy, dissented. But with the help of the black arch-conservative Clarence Thomas, appointed by President George H. W. Bush, the *Metro Broadcasting* dissenters have dominated the Court since 1990. Presidents Reagan and Bush packed not only the Supreme Court but appellate and lower courts.

By 1994, in response to the Reagan-Bush court ruling questioning the inclusion of a government preference for minority applicants, the FCC suspended comparative hearings, a process that forced broadcasters to demonstrate why they should be given a license as compared to other petitioners.[51] By 1998, citing a decision by the Reagan-Bush majority on the Supreme Court overturning a federal affirmative action program,[52] the Reagan appointees on the Court of Appeals in the District of Columbia declared the FCC's Equal Employment Opportunity (EEO) rules to be unconstitutional. The FCC EEO rules never made much of a difference in licensing and merely encouraged broadcasters to inform women and minorities when employment opportunities were available and to report on the number of women and minorities employed.[53]

The Reagan backlash was apparent not only in the courts, it created a sort of anti–affirmative action frenzy in both the press and the Republican-dominated Congress. In their book, *The Black Image in the White Mind*, Robert Entman and Andrew Rojecki report on a framework used by print and broadcast journalists that distorted the issue of affirmative action (calling the complex set of programs either quotas or racial preferences, while ignoring white women as beneficiaries) and exaggerated the conflict over the issue between blacks and whites: "The most comprehensive review of survey data concludes that Whites' attitudes on affirmative action remained virtually unchanged between 1965 and 1995, despite journalists' and politicians' frequent claims of a massive shift in the mid-1990's. . . . The failure of the issue to catch on in the 1996 election campaign despite the expectations of many pundits and politicians suggests White Americans were much less exercised over the issue than the news media depicted."[54] Concerned about the political backlash of a tax policy tarred by the black brush of "affirmative action,"[55] Congress voted to eliminate (and President Clinton did not veto) section 1071 of the tax code in 1995.[56] While this effectively killed the tax certificate used to promote minority ownership in the communications industry, it also eliminated the use of the tax certificate for a wide variety of purposes to which it had been applied since 1943. Two years after the tax certificate was eliminated there was a drop in the number of black broadcast licensees. Of the 11,475 U.S. commercial broadcast operations, black ownership decreased from 218 stations in 1992 to 193, or 1.7 percent, of commercial broadcast stations in 1997.[57]

By the late 1990s, Justice Scalia's dissent in *Metro Broadcasting* now reflected the sentiment of those who would determine policies that shaped the public sphere: "I cannot agree with the Court that the Constitution permits the Government to discriminate among its citizens on the basis of race in order to serve interests so trivial as 'broadcast diversity.'"

The Promise and Failure of Cable

The apparent inability of African Americans to secure legislation or regulation or court interpretation that might provide a means to communicate to mass audiences might seem to leave the mass media image of black Americans securely in the hands of whites. But the story is more complicated than that. During the twenty-year period 1978–98, while African Americans were winning and then losing efforts to correct their severe under-representation among the federal licensees for broadcast operations, an alternative to broadcast television was gaining momentum. Cable television offered the promise of interactive television and multichannel television providing a new opportunity for under-represented groups to have their own platform and engage in civic discussion.

The excitement of cable was evident in a new movement centered around public access. However, while there are some notable public access successes, most public access operations failed for lack of sufficient revenue to attract talented producers, audiences, or political support.[58]

Instead of investing in robust infrastructure that served all communities,[59] TeleCommunications Inc. (TCI)—for many years the largest multiple cable systems operator—invested in content. One of TCI chief John Malone's successes was BET, the idea of Robert Johnson. Johnson, a black Washington lobbyist, convinced Malone to put up the bulk of capital to support a Black Entertainment Television cable network to run on TCI. With Malone's backing, Johnson created a successful cable television network featuring the violent and sexually suggestive rap and hip-hop music videos MTV was reluctant to run. The dominant image of blacks in America would not be improved through BET.[60]

But cable's development, as distinct from cable's promise, would portend a trend even more disturbing than BET's music videos—the segregation of American viewing. While America was no longer limited to three networks, all dominated by white males, we were becoming a nation fractured into a multitude of audiences. Not only our neighborhoods would be segregated, with segregated churches and schools[61]; our news and entertainments are segregated now as well. One example of this segregation can be seen in the viewing choices of white and black viewers. The newer broadcast television networks, Fox and Warner Brothers (WB), programmed their prime-time schedule to attract previously neglected black audiences. Among the top twenty most watched programs by black or white audiences, only six were shared in common. WB's "The Steve Harvey Show," the most popular show among blacks, is rarely watched by whites.[62]

The Black Image and the White Media

Roughly thirty years after the Kerner Commission reported that the white press failed to communicate to white audiences "a sense of the degradation, misery, and hopelessness of life in the ghetto,"[63] the *Washington Post* reported: "Whether out of hostility, indifference or simple lack of knowledge, large numbers of white Americans incorrectly believe that blacks are as well off as whites in terms of their jobs, incomes, schooling and health care . . . 40 to 60 percent of all whites say that the average black American is faring about as well and perhaps even better than the average white in these areas. In fact, government statistics show that blacks have narrowed the gap, but continue to lag significantly behind whites."[64]

Whatever progress that was achieved toward an integrated society has been lost. A variety of factors have resegregated America into the two unequal nations, one black and one white, about which the Kerner Commission warned.[65] Whites and blacks do not know each other personally. Given the resegregation of America, where do the perceptions of white Americans about black Americans come from? Television. More particularly, the dominant source of information about others in our society today comes from local television news, and local television news tells a tale of black violence.[66] As Entman and Rojecki wrote: "Television news often portrays an urban America nearly out of control: night after night the news overflows with victims and perpetrators of violence." While the news shows victims who are most likely white, the criminals are disproportionately black. Moreover, unlike whites, blacks tend not to be portrayed as individuals, are more often portrayed in handcuffs and chains, and are not seen as helpers or police officers.[67]

The ugly portrayal of black Americans on local television occurs despite the ever-present black anchor or the increase in black television news directors, reaching 3 percent in 2000.[68] As a former television reporter and producer I can personally attest to the lack of influence an anchor person has on news stories, and to the difficulty in including a nonwhite perspective. Aside from the simple resistance to go beyond stock footage, or the "perp walk" offered by police stations, there remains the not-too-subtle pressure to conform to the status quo. As Av Westin reported: "I feel confident in declaring that racism is alive and well in many television newsrooms around the country. Race is a substantial factor in assigning stories and deciding whom and what to include . . . pieces involving minorities are routinely dismissed with such code phrases as 'It's not a good story for us.'"[69]

As Entman and Rojecki suggest, while black anchor persons have no real impact on the stories they tell, their "very presence suggests that if Blacks just keep quiet and work hard, the system will indeed allow them to progress." Whites are able to retain negative stereotypes about blacks while being comforted by black performers that they are really without racial animosities.[70] While network news is not as important a source of information about blacks as local news, it is still relied upon more than cable news, newspapers, or other sources of information. While crime is not as prevalent, the expert so relied upon by news shows is overwhelmingly white and male. A recent study of the network news programs showed that 92 percent of U.S. sources were white and 7 percent were black.[71]

The combination of exaggerating both black violence and white expertise leads to the quite understandable set of warped perceptions the *Washington Post* article revealed. It also leads to a lack of support for policies that might create conditions of equality.[72]

What I've tried to describe here is a circle, perhaps a spiral, from which there seems no escape. Black Americans, as second-class citizens in the early age of radio and television, had little opportunity to participate as licensees when the broadcast media controlled the public sphere. When cable television opened up opportunities the nation was undergoing a backlash against government action intended to correct long-standing inequalities based upon race. The inability to alter communications in the arena where the dominant discourse takes place amounts to an inability to correct stereotypes and the warped perception a majority of white Americans hold regarding blacks. Black economic and political advance is held hostage to what Cornel West calls "the structural dynamics of corporate market institutions that affect all Americans."[73]

The Antigovernment Culture

Cornel West is correct to point out that black Americans are affected by the same cultural institutions that affect all Americans, and in many of the same ways. Beyond the challenges posed by a group of men who consider broadcast diversity trivial, beyond the splintering of the audience into a hundred self-segregating pieces, perhaps the most damaging cultural impact of the Reagan years was a turn away from the common understanding that government is the solution to problems we cannot resolve as individuals. This was an understanding in full flower during the Roosevelt New Deal, given power because the vast majority of Americans shared in the suffering of the Great Depression—a largely forgotten economic catastrophe that resulted from decades of unchecked pro-business policies, or (in more modern terms) reliance on market forces.

Those unchecked pro-business policies were supported by the Horatio Alger tales that dominated mass media at the time, just as our current television programs celebrate the wealthy and downplay or ignore structural poverty. Calvin Coolidge's witticisms about the business of America being business are oddly familiar today. What Holmes called the social statics of Herbert Spencer is an uncomfortable parallel to the policy papers of the right-wing think tanks crowded around the White House and Congress.

Computer, satellite, and Internet technologies were made possible by the investment of the federal government. But our present culture, dominated by private industry, extols the market and pleads for the government to get off our backs. The ridicule of government as some sort of incompetent foreign object by the very people who seek the reins of government power has helped to create a disengaged citizenry, whose "pursuit of happiness" is the collection of consumer luxuries.

The Internet and Black America

Every technical advance in communications has sparked great optimism about its impact on democracy, if not peace and human understanding. The Internet is no different. Only a few years ago Microsoft founder Bill Gates offered lavish predictions about how new Internet technology would improve our lives, including making us "better citizens." In his book, *The Road Ahead*, Gates envisions that "politicians will be able to see immediate representative surveys of public opinion. Constituents will be able to tap out a quick letter to their congressional representatives and find out what her positions are and how she's voting on this or that issue. . . . Even if the model of political decision-making doesn't change explicitly, the network will bestow power on groups of citizens who want to organize to promote causes or candidates."[74]

Is the Internet the public sphere we have been waiting for? Will government web sites or e-mails create a place for all Americans to deliberate issues of concern to their communities, local and national? While I have studied, written, and spoken widely on the communications challenges faced by African Americans, I hope the reader will be mindful that similar challenges are faced by the poor, by rural Americans, by women, and by other so-called ethnic and racial groups.

Regarding the gap between blacks and whites in Internet access and use, the so-called digital divide, I will say only what the reader already knows, namely, that the gap exists, like all the other gaps between blacks and whites. That gap was extensively documented by the National Telecommunications and Information Administration when it was under the leadership of a young black man, Larry Irving, during the Clinton period.[75] Even if we adopt the stance of the new Bush administration and suppose that the digital divide is closing and that we are indeed a nation on-line,[76] our public philosophy of communications policy will preclude the Internet from serving as a public sphere where all Americans can participate equally in a deliberative democracy.

In the first instance, it must be recognized that the Internet is only part of a complex media environment, and (excuse the pun) for the foreseeable future it is only a bit player. That environment is composed of billboards and newspapers and the mail and radio and, most important, television. Whether it is cable or broadcast, network or local, television is the overwhelmingly dominant place Americans get their information. In a survey by Harris Interactive the day after the attack on the World Trade Center and the Pentagon, television was "the primary source of information for 78% of Americans *with online access* in the 24 hours immediately following the attacks, followed by radio at 15% and the Internet at 3%" (emphasis added). Three weeks later the group reported that the Internet was the primary source for 8 percent of the population, while there was no statistically significant change in the figures for television (76 percent).[77] In 2002, a nationwide survey by the Pew Research Center and the Pew Internet and American Life Project found that the Internet was a principal source of campaign news for 11 percent of on-line users and 7 percent of the general public. Television remained by far the leading source of election information, with roughly half of on-line users and the general public listing it as their main resource. Moreover, roughly half of on-line election news consumers (52 percent) went most often to the web sites associated with television, such as ABC News or CNN, or with major newspapers, such as the *New York Times*.[78]

The Internet works most effectively in conjunction with other media. This is easily seen in the newspaper articles, billboards, and radio, and television programs and advertisements directing us to web sites. Perhaps more than any other medium, the Internet reminds us to consider the entire communications environment as an integrated inter-related whole. Thus, those who control other media, particularly television, will continue to dominate Internet discourse.

Beyond the fact that major news organizations dominate both the overall media landscape and the Internet, the ability of people to select only that news or entertainment that interests them further exacerbates the difficulties marginalized groups such as Latinos and Asian Americans have in being heard by the larger public. If black and white Americans rarely watch the same television programs, it is not likely that white Americans will regularly sample the wide array of web sites designed to present, as Melanet suggests, "the Uncut Black Experience."[79] The fragmentation of the American audience seen in radio and cable is only exacerbated by a device that allows users not only to find a source they identify with, but to target only the specific information they want from that source. Cass Sunstein calls this the "Daily Me" and warns against the impact of this political isolation on democratic engagement.[80]

As Sunstein points out, there is substantial merit in web sites that promote in-group deliberation. The Internet allows Americans the ability to consider the wide range of issues that concern them, to debate these issues in a place that is not hostile, and to organize among other like-minded Americans. African Americans, Latinos, women have long had their own newspapers and magazines that reflected their own experiences, and that were rarely read by others outside their group. But, as important and valuable as this is, it is not active participation in the larger conversation involving all Americans. Absent participation in the larger conversation, marginalized Americans with unique concerns and contributions to that conversation will remain on the margins.

Data, Data Everywhere, But Not a Stop to Think

One of the great conundrums of what some call the "Information Age" is the increasing abundance of available data and the decreasing lack of knowledge among the public. To see the problem clearly one need only think of the children's rhyme about being thirsty while surrounded by only sea water. Data is not the popular information Madison was so concerned to promote. But this is not to deny either the potential or the very real advantages provided by access to the Internet.

The Internet is an incredible tool, allowing far more access than ever before to legislation and other public information and government conduct. The Library of Congress, the National Archives, and a wide range of administrative agencies provide not only final documents on-line but records of debates and the iterative process of legislative, judicial, and administrative decisions, and notice about action being considered. While some of this information has obviously been written with narrow partisan goals in mind, it is clearly an advance over what was possible in a world of paper records requiring on-site viewing.

However, the record of federal government efforts to restrict and privatize public information has been well documented over the past fifteen years by the American Library Association Washington Office (ALA).[81] The ALA reports that "while government information is more accessible through computer networks and the Freedom of Information Act, there are still barriers to public access." Moreover, as a Senate investigation revealed in 2002, federal agencies "have had particular difficulty complying with the Federal Records Act with respect to electronic records, including records posted on the Internet."[82]

As OMB Watch reports, private companies seeking to sell public information have begun putting pressure on state legislators to limit public access to electronic databases.[83] The value of government information is made clear, however, by the efforts of the environmental groups. Since the collection and release of "community right-to-know information" by the Environmental Protection Agency, releases of toxic chemicals have declined by 43 percent nationwide.[84] But terrorist attacks have sped up efforts by the Bush administration to remove from government web sites greater amounts of public information.[85]

Even while more and more information is being kept from the American public, the amount of available data is overwhelming. The very abundance of even nontrivial information creates a sort of barrier to its effective use. Much of the work of Washington lawyers is tracking the daily activity of Congress and the myriad of specialized administrative agencies, such as the FCC, or the Department of Housing and Urban Development, to make certain that their clients are informed on a timely basis of any activity that may impact their interests. This is not work even the best of newspapers are able to do effectively.[86] Except for the extraordinary work of associations such as the Association for the Advancement of Retired Persons (AARP) or the

Consumer Federation of America or OMB Watch, the public would have little clue as to the vast amount of work that goes on in its name and is made possible by its financial support.

While many of the nonprofit associations make the government information they collect and analyze on behalf of the public available on web sites, they rarely, and usually only in emergencies, have the resources to conduct effective public awareness campaigns that require television, radio, newspapers, and oftentimes direct mail efforts to reach a public already oversaturated with "information."

Whether because of government secrecy, or journalistic inability, incompetence, or bias, too many Americans do not have access to the information necessary to form rational policy choices. As Herbert Schiller argues, "inequality of access and impoverished content of information are deepening the already pervasive national social crisis. The ability to understand, much less overcome, increasingly critical national problems is thwarted, either by a growing flood of mind-numbing trivia and sensationalist material or by an absence of basic, contextualized social information."[87]

The problem of being overwhelmed with information may also characterize the experience of many of our representatives. E-mail, while of some use to local government officials, has not been found to be an effective way to communicate with federal officials. In a survey conducted by the Pew Internet Project in cooperation with the National League of Cities, congressional representatives report being swamped by e-mail and dismiss constituent e-mails as not very meaningful. On the other hand, a large majority of local officials find e-mail an effective way to communicate with constituents. Seventy-nine percent of all municipal officials surveyed said they have received e-mail from citizens or local groups about civic issues. Some 25 percent receive e-mail from constituents every day. Sixty-one percent of online local officials use e-mail to communicate with citizens at least weekly, while 21 percent report doing so every day.[88]

Still, officials at all levels report that face-to-face or telephone contact is a more effective way to communicate with constituents. As the late Senator Paul Simon remarked, a representative is more likely to meet with or take a call from a constituent who has donated to a campaign than from one who has not.[89] Advanced communications technologies do not limit the ability of office holders to continue to preference those wealthy individuals and corporations with established power. In his study of the impact of the Internet on political participation, Richard Davis argues that the Internet does not bestow new power to previously disaffected groups, as Gates suggested; it merely adds to the tools of those who already feel empowered in our society.[90]

* * *

All things being equal, will the Internet provide an opportunity for marginalized Americans to participate fully in the deliberation of national policies? Will it ameliorate the fact that less than 2 percent of those licensed to operate our most dominant medium are African American? Will the ability to e-mail and access the Library of Congress on-line allow a poor but intelligent mother to have the same impact on tax policy as the Heritage Foundation? No, no, and no. Of course not.

Americans have long had great faith in the power of technology, and faith that limiting government censorship would be sufficient to protect democratic speech. This faith may even be older than the renewed religious frenzy over "the market." Over sixty years ago, John Dewey cautioned us about this tendency in our culture.

> It is no longer possible to hold the simple faith of the Enlightenment that assured advance of science will produce free institutions by dispelling ignorance and superstition: the sources of human servitude and the pillars of oppressive government. The progress of natural science has been even more rapid and extensive than could have been anticipated. . . . It has put at the disposal of dictators means of controlling opinion and sentiment of a potency which reduces to a mere shadow all previous agencies at the command of despotic rulers. For negative censorship it has substituted means of propaganda of ideas and alleged information on a scale that reaches every individual, reiterated day after day by every organ of publicity and communication, old and new.[91]

That was before television or the Internet. For most of us, including African Americans, the situation has not changed. If we are to have a vital democratic public sphere to which all Americans have an equal access, it will not be because of technological triumph.

But it is worth noting that the challenges of restricted information created by monopolies such as Associated Press and the Radio Corporation of America are very different than the challenges of today. The oligarchies that control the major organs of communication do not have the same ability to restrict "popular information." Their power comes from their ability to dominate the conversation in a very crowded public arena. They no longer have the only megaphone in the hall, they just have the most powerful megaphone with the ability to drown out any competitors.

10

The End of History

Yet I could not rid myself of the notion that the
Englishmen and Americans who had successfully
overthrown tyranny and founded flourishing free societies
had a more genuine experience and a deeper insight
than men of a sheltered age. It was true that they had
lived before the age of manufacture with power-driven
machinery, that they traveled by horse and buggy rather
than by airplane; but they had dealt at first hand with
tyrants and revolutions and social disorder. They had
known how to orient their spirits, gather together their
faculties, and challenge the turbulence and tyranny of their
times. Might it not be that they had possessed an insight
which we have lost, and that, if we are to be worthy of our
inheritance from them we must recollect and repossess and
reanimate their ancient and half-forgotten faith?

—Walter Lippmann, *The Good Society*

An Insight Which We Have Lost

In 1792 the American experiment in democracy was still new and fragile. A
second government was established, a Bill of Rights was added to the Constitution, and, despite strong disagreements among the various factions,
foreign debts were being paid and the location of the nation's capital was
decided. The work of binding the nation together remained, and to accomplish that task Congress, led by James Madison, decided to subsidize the
delivery of newspapers throughout the country, and laid the foundation for
a communications network that would dwarf all other parts of the federal
government. In doing this, the founders suggested to us the core importance of communications to a republic. "Might it not be that they had possessed an insight which we have lost?"

Our brief tour of the history of American communications policy reveals a clear and recurrent public philosophy governing the role that communications (what we today call media and technology) plays in our lived democracy. While "free speech" jurisprudence and antitrust regulation are often noted, these areas of law are most consistently applied as protections for those who have control over the means of communication, rather than as protections of the goal of ensuring citizens have access to popular information to engage in democratic deliberation. Free speech norms are useful and should be preserved, but these norms have been distorted in the main to protect corporate and commercial speech and campaign expenditures. Likewise normative American values against bigness run deep, but they have been largely overrun by practice.

Our lived philosophy of communications can be broken into one major and one minor theme. The major theme is: (1) Substantial taxpayer investment in the research and development of new communications technology. Federal investment was vital for the telegraph, radio during World War I, computer technologies during World War II, and satellite and Internet technologies during the Cold War. (2) Federal government abandonment of control over that technology to private industry (except for military purposes). We have seen this again with the telegraph, radio, computer, and satellite technologies. (3) Continuing public subsidy of private industry. We have seen direct subsidies of all communications industries, perhaps most prominently the telegraph industry and satellite industry, patent and regulations subsidies benefiting the telephone industry and the broadcast industries, and tax regulation subsidizing both the broadcast and cable industry. (4) A tolerance of private monopoly or oligopoly control over national communications systems. We have seen this with all communications industries, most clearly with the first monopoly, Western Union, and then AT&T, and fairly recently with the monopolization of the broadcast and cable industries.

The second and minor theme of this philosophy is limited government regulation of these "private" businesses "in the public interest," along with limited government subsidy to support the communications capabilities of citizens. We have seen this theme in the willingness of AT&T to be regulated at first by the Interstate Commerce Commission (ICC) and then the Federal Communications Commission (FCC), by the call for regulation of the "ether" by commercial broadcasters, and by the request for uniformity of cable franchise regulation by the private cable operations—all in what they called the public interest. We have seen the fairly weak support of first educational and then public service broadcasting, and inconsistent "universal service" support for schools and the poor for access to telephone service.

Our public philosophy of communications policy is coherent, even if it is not at all reflective of the framework established by the founders in their support of the Post Office. Our public philosophy supports a vibrant commercial market in communications, and it supports a vibrant consumer market. Perhaps this is good. However, this philosophy does not merely fail to serve civic needs, it actually undermines political equality and the deliberation of citizens. Citizens recognize themselves as consumers, they do not recognize themselves as a responsible sovereign concerned that their representatives act in their interest. Our public philosophy is that of a modern consumer society; it does not carry the hallmarks of a democratic republic.

Is the United States of America a Democratic Republic?

If a democratic republic is a government where the ultimate power, the right and liberty of collective decision-making, resides equally in all citizens, where interests are checked and balanced to thwart the domination of any one faction, and where policy is executed by representatives acting with the consent of citizens, the United States of America is not a democratic republic.

There are many who would point to the expansion of suffrage to include those without property, African Americans formerly held in slavery, other nonwhite groups, and women as marks of greater progress, and I would agree. I would not agree that expansion of the right to vote alone means that we are closer to the ideals of our democratic experiment.

There are those who would point to the great material prosperity of the United States and the generally high standard of living enjoyed by most Americans as proof that the sacrifices made to the republican form of government were both necessary and good. Putting aside for only a moment the severe inequalities of wealth in the United States, I would agree with the founders that material luxuries are not substitutes for the core promise of our republic—political freedom. As Hannah Arendt has famously written, "Political freedom, generally speaking, means the right 'to be a participator in government,' or it means nothing."[1] Moreover, the severe inequalities of wealth indicate severe inequalities of political freedom.

There are those who would argue that the democratic republic I have described is an ideal, a romantic nostalgia at best. I would argue that the society that Tocqueville described, that Lincoln defended, and that Franklin

Roosevelt and Johnson attempted to revive was, even with its flaws, far closer to the ideal of a democratic republic than our present society. While a republic of engaged and informed citizens may be an ideal, the goal should be to move closer toward that ideal rather than watch it recede in our rearview mirror.

Sandel agrees that we are further away from the founders' ideals of a republic today, and argues that a philosophic struggle to maintain greater consumer prosperity, under the terms of John Maynard Keynes and American progressives, has led to a rights-centered procedural republic with too little appreciation for civic duty. He faults left-wing promoters of welfare rights and blames intellectuals such as John Rawls who, Sandel argues, claims that "the right is prior to the good."[2] He also faults right-wing promoters of economic noninterference such as Milton Friedman.[3] There is no evidence that either Rawls or Friedman have been anything other than an intellectual sideshow providing an occasional academic gloss to the power politics exercised at the middle or elite levels of power. If our government could be described even as a republic focused on providing equal procedural safeguards to a set of nonarbitrary rights, we would be much closer to the founders' ideals than we are today. The inability of the vast majority of Americans who live on the poorer end of the scale to secure what citizens in most other democracies take for granted—basic health care and equality in the courts[4]—speaks volumes about our so-called procedural republic.

There is a popular fallacy that labor unions and church groups and civic associations, such as the National Association for the Advancement of Colored People (NAACP) or the American Association of Retired Persons (AARP), serve as an effective countervailing balance to Corporate America. Despite the ability to get occasional press attention, and despite the occasional legislative victory, the real power these nonprofit associations in America have does not compare to the power of Haliburton Oil or Archer Daniels Midland or General Electric.[5] It's not even close. Moreover, as Putnam has observed, membership in the most politically effective organizations, such as AARP, amount to making small, if regular, contributions to a Washington-based group of advocates—these are not associations of engaged citizens.[6]

Some argue that in today's environment the sort of associations Tocqueville described are inadequate to the task of competing with modern industry or the bloated administrative state that has become our government, and that church, union, and national civic association leaders are able to better negotiate on behalf of the interests of citizens, however disengaged citizens may be from determining the policy direction of the organization itself. Michael Schudson and others suggest this is "an efficient use of civic energy."[7] Perhaps. Unfortunately, this model also fails to provide the lessons necessary to be an effective citizen. Moreover, absent citizen oversight, the leaders of church, union, and national civic associations are just as susceptible to the corrupting power of corporate influence as government officials.

There is also a fallacy that competition between corporations such as Viacom and News Corporation is itself a sort of balance. This fallacy fails to understand that despite the political differences between Sumner Redstone and Rupert Murdoch, Viacom and News Corporation join together to influence legislation and politicians to protect their common interests around tax policy and communication regulation. While they do sometimes compete fiercely for audience share, they are as likely to invest in joint partnerships to share the risks inherent in business. Anyone who believes that one party is the beneficiary of the lobbying dollars spent by these corporate interests would be sadly mistaken. While Republicans have traditionally gotten the lion's share of support from corporate interest, Democrats are also at this trough; if they were not, they would have vanished into obscurity and been replaced by another party long ago.[8] Some say they have been replaced by another party, they just call themselves Democrats.

Again, it is not only that those with the most amount of money to spend on television commercials have the clearest path to the "marketplace of ideas"; it is that those with the most amount of money *own and control* television—the mechanism that dominates that marketplace. Unlike the post, all Americans simply do not have access to television to communicate to their fellow citizens. The balance of factions in a deliberative democracy as intended by the founders is out of whack.

The fact that the dominant mechanism of deliberation, of acquiring and conveying popular information in the American republic is controlled by that set of interests most feared by Tocqueville and Lincoln is the one most important cause of our democracy's dysfunction. If the federal government was able to provide all Americans with an equal ability to participate in the public sphere no one interest would be able to dominate that sphere. An equal ability to communicate in a democratic republic is what Madison had in mind when he argued for support for the U.S. Post Office for the circulation of newspapers.

Readers familiar with other literature regarding communication and democracy may have been slightly startled to see a long quote from Walter Lippmann open this chapter.[9] In his books *Public Opinion* and *The Phantom Public*, Lippmann, borrowing heavily from William James, argued against the idea of citizen omnipotence and the efficacy of journalism. According to Lippmann, "the real environment is too big, too complex, and too fleeting for direct acquaintance," even by reporters whose job it is to capture policy making and report on it.[10] In *The Phantom Public*, Lippmann argues that "what the public does is not to express its opinions but to align itself for or against a proposal. We must abandon the notion that democratic government can be the direct expression of the will of the people."[11] I agree with Lippmann that we must acknowledge the limitations of reporters to reflect with complete accuracy the action of policy making. I also agree that our government, particularly at the national level, cannot be the "direct expression" of the will of the people. But neither of these cautions negates Madison's idea of the importance of either a sovereign people, or the importance of that sovereign's access to popular information.

The ability of a human being to capture adequately a reality outside himself is limited. James would write: "The spectator's judgment is sure to miss the root of the matter, and to possess no truth. The subject judged knows a part of the world of reality which the judging spectator fails to see."[12] I do not take Lippmann to mean more than this. But I take Madison's view of popular information to mean something different than an accurate reporting of policy making. As discussed above, Madison seemed to think that policy making was a process, and that the sharing of opinion, however differently constructed, however necessarily limited, was a legitimate part of that process. The partisan press of Madison's day could hardly be confused with objective, much less accurate reporters. I take Madison, and James and Lippmann, to suggest we do the best we can to discuss the reality we know and that this badly informed discussion is popular information.

Madison did not seem to confuse the idea of a direct democracy with a representative republic. I do not understand Lippmann to suggest anything other than the fact that government representatives act on behalf of the people who elect them. Representatives do not do only that which their electors have already decided upon. Citizens decide, in Madison's words, on the "comparative merits and demerits of the candidates" seeking to represent them, and the policies they are considering. Lippmann's writings on public opinion seem less about a despair in relationship to Madison's "popular government," and more about dissuading those he calls "mystical democrats" from their embrace of "the omnicompetent, sovereign citizen."[13] Lippmann challenges us to doubt the wisdom of "public opinion" and is concerned about what needs to be done to educate citizens to be better citizens. "Education for citizenship, for membership in the public, ought, therefore, to be distinct from education for public office. Citizenship involve[s] a radically different relation to affairs, requires different intellectual habits and different methods of action. . . . It needs for its direction a new intellectual method which shall provide it with its own usable canons of judgment."[14] I do not take Lippmann's caution about the limits of reporters or the limits of citizens as a disagreement with the Madisonian conception of democracy and the important role of popular information. I agree wholeheartedly with his suggestion that the founders may have something to teach us.

Whatever one might want to call our present lived democracy, it does not reflect the core tenets of the republic established by the founders. Despite access to satellite radio and the latest shampoo and the ability to purchase stock on-line and the right to vote, factions are not checked and balanced against each other and the average citizen is not an effective participant in her or his own governance, not even to the point of being able to ensure the merits or demerits of her or his representative.

Civic Engagement and Civic Literacy

In his book *Bowling Alone,* sociologist Robert Putnam has carefully documented the disturbing decline in civic engagement in the United States since the 1960s. "[Since] the mid-1960's, the weight of the evidence suggests, despite the rapid rise in levels of education Americans have become perhaps 10–15 percent less likely to vote, roughly 35 percent less likely to attend public meetings, both partisan and nonpartisan, and roughly 40 percent less engaged in party politics and indeed in political and civic organizations of all sorts."[15]

Putnam is interested in a wide range of social activity, including religious activity, and attributes the cause of this civic disengagement to a loss of "social capital"—the skills and civic virtues, including trust, which develop through community interaction. While our focus on the impact of our communications policies on democratic deliberation and self-governance is, perhaps, more narrow than Putnam's, his conclusions about "what killed civic engagement" are instructive. He names pressures on time and money, suburbanization and commuting, generational change, and electronic entertainment—particularly television. He notes that there is some "overlap between generational change and the long term effects of television," and guesses that television combined with the television generation may be 40 percent of the reason for civic disengagement.[16]

In addition, Putnam's identification of a civic generation, born between 1910 and 1940, correlates with our look at the period where broadcasting was born along with the measures designed, at least in part, to correct the laissez-faire practices of the Gilded Age. As we have seen, the rejection by this generation of previous policies promoted by the faction Lincoln called capital coincided not only with a return to civic engagement but federal investment in technologies from computers to satellites. As Putnam documents, this civic generation (spanning the time of the great stock market crash to the election of President Kennedy) was more engaged in civic activity than either their parents or their children.[17] But to say the loss of this engagement results from a "generational trend" is to make it seem natural, an inevitable part of the nation's life cycle, rather than the shift in political power from the Harding and Coolidge gang to Roosevelt-Johnson and back to Nixon-Reagan. Putnam's confusion between generational differences and the cause of a decline in civic engagement avoids an analysis of power politics. Moreover, Putnam's assertions regarding a decline in civic engagement focus us on too short a time frame, despite his references to Tocqueville. Still, when Putnam compares the Gilded Age generation with our own, and analyzes the failure of early Progressive reformers to confront capital and chides their ultimately antidemocratic reliance on professional managers and technological triumph, he provides a much better clue to understanding our present problems.[18] Of particular importance to our discussion is Putnam's reminder about the Panglossian belief of some Progressives, notably Herbert Croly, that new communications technology would inevitably generate greater civic participation.[19]

One final note about Putnam. In analyzing the impact of electronic media, Putnam notes a difference between entertainment and public affairs. While entertainment programs tend to discourage civic engagement (along with a host of other bad effects), public affairs programs tend to encourage civic engagement. Putnam also notes the fact that television dominates an increasingly complex media environment that includes newspapers, radio, and the Internet.[20] Whatever problems I or others may have about Putnam's data crunching and analysis, his assessment of the United States as a deeply disaffected and disengaged polity with an electronic media that contributes to the problems is insightful and must be confronted.

Henry Milner's work on civic literacy is, perhaps, closer to our core concerns. Milner argues that policies that promote civic literacy—"the knowledge and ability capacity of citizens to make sense of their political world"—can generate informed political engagement and lead to more equitable policies.[21] This was Madison's argument for subsidizing the Post Office, absent his view of factions and Montesquieu's lessons on balancing those factions.[22]

Despite Milner's attention to the efficacy of newspaper subsidies in fostering civic literacy, he does not suggest, as Neil Postman has on occasion, that television is inherently destructive to promoting civic literacy. Milner also suggests that those countries with strong public service broadcasting institutions do a much better job of promoting informed civic engagement than the United States. The key for Milner is not merely the distinction between entertainment and public affairs made by Putnam, it is between commercial and noncommercial (public service) television. Milner, again, is not only concerned about civic engagement; he is concerned about informed engagement. A number of studies support the view that public service television (the U.S. version is too weak and too dependent upon sponsors to qualify as such) provides more substantive reporting and analysis, and public service viewers are more likely to be politically knowledgeable and less likely to be misled and misinformed.[23] Despite the distracting laurels we bestow upon ourselves for "our" free press, we should not be surprised that the population of every industrial country that subsidizes the press, whether newspapers or broadcasting, has a much more politically informed population than the United States. The very purpose of a press subsidized by taxpayer support is to provide the "popular information" Madison argued was so essential to democracy. The purpose of commercial press, whether the *New York Times* or Fox News, is to provide space for advertisements and a profitable return on the investment of their shareholders. While commercial advertisers and stock investors make certain to get what they pay for, the citizen is left out in the cold.

The American Plan

The supposed champion of broadcast regulation, fickle opponent of commercialism, and co-author of the 1927 Radio Act, Senator Clarence Dill, visited Europe in 1931 to observe broadcasting there and reported that he found the BBC "stiff and bureaucratic." Dill liked what he called broadcasting "by the American Plan."[24] There should be little doubt that the BBC has had its troubles, particularly with government interference and bureaucratic infighting, over its now eighty-year history.[25] While Dill had no CPB or PBS to compare to the BBC, his comparison was on the right track. There is really no comparison between public broadcasting in the United

States and public service broadcasting in Europe or almost any other democracy. The most frequent method to convey the dissimilarity is the amount of public funds that go to support the institutions.

In the United Kingdom, each household pays 10 pounds (roughly $16.50) per month for a TV license.[26] In 2001 this worked out to be roughly $69.08 per person over the course of the year. Over the same period of time, the U.S. government appropriation to the Corporation for Public Broadcasting and the Public Telecommunications Facilities Program (PTFP) totaled $364.7 million. This comes to $1.30 per person per year.[27] Even if one adds the individual and state contributions to local public radio and television stations the contributions increase to approximately $7.00 per person per year. The difference in financial support is reflected in the robustness of the operations and the role the different systems play in each country's public sphere. While the British enjoy privately operated commercial broadcasting, the BBC clearly dominates the public sphere in that country. Conversely, privately operated commercial broadcasting clearly dominates the public sphere in the United States.[28]

But, again, the comparison between the BBC and CPB or PBS is wrongheaded, Dill had the apples and oranges in the proper perspective. Our history allows us to see the American Plan more clearly. If one compares all the federal subsidies afforded private broadcasters, including a tax structure that encourages advertising, free licenses, regulatory protections, research and development, and direct support through federal advertising, the hidden public expenditures (or relief of legitimate tax burdens that might otherwise be imposed) supporting private U.S. broadcasting begins to seem at least as generous as the much more open tax of the British TV license subsidizing the BBC.

Comparing commercial broadcasting in the United States with public service broadcasting in the United Kingdom also reveals a stark contrast in what Madison called popular information. This was clearly evident in recent coverage leading up to, during, and in the aftermath of the U.S. invasion of Iraq. The leading figure of the U.S. executive branch did not grant interviews with the media prior to the war, but the leading figure of the British executive did open himself to questions as to why British citizens should risk their lives to invade Iraq. The BBC interviewer, Jeremy Paxman, and, more important, members of the public on hand asked direct and pointed questions.[29] Prime Minister Tony Blair was treated as if he were a public servant responsible to the people. When President George Bush allowed himself to be questioned after the war, NBC anchorman Tom

Brokaw (promoted for his ability to establish "a calming force"[30]) treated him as if he were a celebrity or a king due extraordinary reverence.[31]

In a series of articles on the U.S. coverage of the U.S. war against Iraq, economist and *New York Times* columnist Paul Krugman has noted the very different coverage provided by the BBC.

> A funny thing happened during the Iraq war: many Americans turned to the BBC for their TV news. They were looking for an alternative point of view— something they couldn't find on domestic networks, which, in the words of the BBC's director general, "wrapped themselves in the American flag and substituted patriotism for impartiality."
>
> Leave aside the rights and wrongs of the war itself, and consider the paradox. The BCC is owned by the British government, and one might have expected it to support that government's policies. In fact, however, it tried hard—too hard, its critics say—to stay impartial. America's TV networks are privately owned, yet they behaved like state-run media.
>
> What explains this paradox? . . . [Because] networks aren't government-owned, they aren't subject to the kind of scrutiny faced by the BBC, which must take care not to seem like a tool of the ruling party.[32]

Krugman's observation of the controlling influence, the check and balance through government operation, of opposing stakeholders upon the BBC was exactly the sort of dynamic at play in the early days of the U.S. Post Office. The result is an informed British public more critical of its chief executive, indeed more critical of all its representatives, and more critical of the dominant press.[33] The failure of the so-called American Plan could not be more evident.[34] It could not be, in fact, less reflective of the original American Plan.

Why Is There No Socialism in America—Redux

We are finally ready to pose an explanation for American exceptionalism. What, then, accounts for the oddly passive current nature of America's working poor? Why, as a majority in a democracy, do the middle class and the poor seem unable to even secure the gains made under Roosevelt? Despite extraordinary resources and productivity, the pre–Great Depression extremes of conspicuous wealth and grinding poverty have returned to America. These extremes are unique among all other "developed" countries. Despite the vast number of working families living at the margins, there is less social welfare, more limited national health care, less comprehensive unemployment insurance, and weaker higher educational support than in any of the other capitalist countries that America spent so much money rebuilding after World War II. Why?

In his book, *Civic Literacy: How Informed Citizens Make Democracy Work,* Henry Milner provides the evidence to back Madison's political theory regarding the importance of information and voice in a democracy and why it was essential for the federal government to support the communication capacity of citizens. In those countries where the national government generously funds public service media institutions, most notably the Scandinavian countries of Sweden, Norway, Finland, and Denmark, civic literacy—knowledge about policy and governance—is high. In those countries that provide little support for public service media institutions, civic literacy is low. In states that generously fund public service media, voting rates are high. In states that support public service media, the social safety net (health care, child welfare, housing assistance, educational resources, etc.) for the majority of the population is strong.[35] It should not be surprising that where there is a strong state-supported public sphere, there are also regulations that control political campaigning. Denmark, for example, restricts campaign television commercials to public service channels with equal time provided to all parties. The United States represents the other end of the scale.[36]

If there is any truth to American "exceptionalism," the public philosophy that has come to guide our media, and the power of those political forces that seem to control both media and public policy, may be its foundation. There are weak social supports in America because our public sphere is dominated by private corporate interests opposed to those supports.

PART III

Reclaiming Our Republic

11

A Few Lessons

Our exhaustive ownership review demonstrated that the
United States boasts the most diverse media marketplace
in the world and is by no means concentrated and the
rules adopted in that proceeding are well-designed to
prevent any media company from having excess power
over competition or viewpoints. During the proceeding
and in the months that followed, however, we heard
the voice of public concern about the media loud
and clear. Localism is at the core of these concerns,
and we are going to tackle it head on.

—FCC Chairman Michael Powell

As should be clear through our historical summary, communications policy in the United States is determined largely at the federal level. This is true even while those mass media corporations that exert the greatest influence over the greatest number of U.S. citizens are largely global conglomerates. In other words, the News Corporation, Viacom, Disney, General Electric (GE), and AOL/TimeWarner are international corporations, doing business around the world on behalf of thousands of shareholders who claim citizenship in a wide array of nation-states. In order to advance their business plans in the United States these companies focus their attention on the federal government. GE and Viacom spend millions of dollars deploying an army of lawyers, engineers, and economists to influence the Federal Communications Commission (FCC), various congressional committees, and specific legislators, and to file various pleadings before federal courts. This was the work I did as an attorney on behalf of large corporations in Washington. Any suggestion that the small group of understaffed public interest attorneys dependent upon fickle foundations serves as an effective counter-balance to the corporate interest would be pure nonsense.

What the public interest attorney has on her or his side is the residue of the American promise of equality and fairness still lingering in the public heart. There remains a sense that even private corporations have obligations to act for the larger good, that free speech means that everyone gets a turn to speak, that every serious candidate for elected office and every serious policy proposal will be heard, that if a public official says something untrue the press will report it, that most journalists will try to get the facts straight. The Fairness Doctrine may be dead, but most Americans would be shocked to think that fairness is gone too. This sense is a powerful ally, even if it does not exactly conform to our lived public philosophy of communications policy.

In the summer of 2003, the FCC on a party-line vote (three Republicans against two Democrats) reversed nearly thirty years of communications law and eliminated rules designed to preserve a diversity of local voices. Despite hearing from hundreds of thousands of Americans opposed to a relaxation of ownership rules, the Bush FCC made it possible for one company to own a newspaper and television station in the same community, to own more than one television station in the same community, and to own a greater number of stations nationwide.[1] GE/NBC, Fox, Viacom/CBS, Disney/ABC were in favor of the change, as were the *New York Times*, the *Washington Post*, the *Wall Street Journal*, and most other media (liberal and otherwise) around the country.[2] But the public uproar over the FCC action did not go away.

Lawmakers in the House and the Senate heard from their constituents and voted to block the FCC rules.[3] Perhaps caught by the vehemence of the public outcry, the FCC chairman responded by creating a task force to "tackle head on" the problem of "localism." FCC Commissioner Michael Copps, a Democrat, who had fought for open and well-publicized public hearings on the media ownership rules was hardly amused.

> This proposal is a day late and a dollar short. It highlights the failures of the recent decision to dismantle ownership protections. To say that protecting localism was not germane to that decision boggles the mind. The ownership protections, as well as the other public interest protections that the Commission has dismantled over the past years, are all designed to promote localism, diversity and competition. We should have heeded the calls from over 2 million Americans and so many Members of Congress expressing concern about the impact of media concentration on localism and diversity *before* we rushed to a vote. We should have vetted these issues before we voted. Instead, we voted; now we are going to vet. This is a policy of "ready, fire, aim!"[4]

Commissioner Copps is being kind to call Commissioner Powell's proposal for a task force on localism a policy. Powell's late embrace of localism and public hearings on the obligations of broadcasters was a cover-up, a blatant attempt to soothe a ruffled public. Nothing in Powell's votes as a commissioner or actions as chairman suggested he could even see a public beyond the gaggle of attorneys who feted him on behalf of "important" corporations. If there is a lesson in this farce, it is only that there remains a latent power in the public's notions about how we should be managing our media.

To be sure broadcast licenses are granted on condition of service to local communities, cable franchise agreements are negotiated by local communities, and telephone companies are subject to local zoning regulation. This split federal/state/municipal oversight of international media conglomerates requires them to operate through local subsidiaries, such as your local radio and television stations and your local cable and telephone company. So these international companies must devote some resources to attend to the purchase and persuasion of state and municipal regulators. Nonetheless, all of this "localism" is subject to federal limitations. Broadcasters serve local communities but the terms of their licenses are set by the FCC. Cable companies are local, but the terms of the franchise agreements are restricted by Congress. Telephone companies are local, but local and state regulation of rates and interconnection are all restricted by federal authorities. These federal regulations were created (sometimes under the misleading term *deregulation*), as we have seen, at the behest of the corporations.

For most of our history, the one reliable source of local news was the daily newspaper. As Ben Bagdikian writes: "After World War II, mass advertising steadily destroyed competitive dailies; monopoly became the norm. In the new suburbs there were new dailies, but far from the number that had grown in American cities in the past. The new monopoly corporations in the central cities pushed outward to the suburbs, preempting the best advertising that might otherwise have supported a new local daily. Existing papers did not cover the new communities journalistically. In 1920 there were 2,722 urban places and 2,400 daily papers in the country. By 1980 there were 8,765 urban places and only 1,745 dailies. Today [1983] more than 7,000 American cities have no daily paper of their own."[5]

In the absence of a local newspaper, a local radio news program, a local television station that covers local government, a local cable operation with the resources to actually cover local events, the vast majority of Americans live in communities where they have no popular information about either their local or state representatives. Still, there remains some room for the development of local communications policies that might actually serve local community interests.

Why is it important to focus on what happens in local communities given the power of the federal government? Local governments are the places citizens learn about politics in practice. Even if local politics is more mediated, that is, less immediate and more interpreted by others than it was in the middle of the twentieth century, there remain more opportunities to see the direct impact of your vote, and to talk with policy makers, and to propose solutions in your local community than there are at the federal level. It may be useful to the reader to see that a few communities still struggle, sometimes with success, to establish a communications environment that serves an engaged community.

The Communications Conundrum of Cambridge

We begin with a cautionary tale. If there would be anyplace where local democracy was supported and thriving, one might suspect to find it in the most famous college town in New England. New England is, after all, the home of the town meeting,[6] the birthplace of local civic engagement and the struggle for American freedom and equality. Who could forget the stirring speeches of Samuel Adams, the Boston Massacre, the midnight ride of Paul Revere? If there is a place where rational discourse and the engaged citizen thrive surely it must be Cambridge—home not only to the college of presidents, Harvard University, but home to at least one of the parents of the Internet—MIT.

Harvard University and MIT dominate many perceptions of Cambridge, but the community is much more than a two-college town, or even a four-college town when you include Lesley University and Cambridge College. Though only roughly six and a half square miles in total acreage, Cambridge contains a broad diversity of cultures, challenges, and advantages. While two-thirds of the roughly 105,000 Cambridge residents identify themselves as white, Cambridge is one of the most racially and ethnically diverse communities in all of New England. Twelve percent black, 12 percent Asian American, Cambridge is also home to a substantial Hispanic population (7.4 percent), and a large population of recent immigrants from South America, particularly Brazil.[7] More than one-fifth of Cambridge residents are foreign-born.

The diversity of Cambridge is reflected in its public schools, with students from 64 nations, from families speaking 46 different languages.[8] Despite its reputation as a college town, only one-fifth of Cambridge residents are college students, and less than 10 percent of the land use in Cambridge is for educational purposes.[9] While 54 percent of the population has graduated from college (as compared to roughly 30 percent for Boston, and 20 percent for the United States[10]), 30 percent of the seniors in the Cambridge public high school (Cambridge Rindge and Latin) failed to pass Massachusetts's student achievement test in 2001.[11]

Aside from the employment provided by its educational institutions, Cambridge is home to one-third of the state's biomedical employers, and former factory buildings in which ladders and soap were manufactured now house computer technology and other twenty-first-century industries. Employment is high (unemployment in 2001 was at 3.4 percent[12]) as is the median family income in Cambridge—at $59,423. Still, 12.6 percent of families with children 18 and younger live below the official poverty line. Over 20 percent of all households report earnings of less than $25,000 per year.[13] A look at the Cambridge neighborhoods reveals stark income disparities. The median family income ranges from nearly $141,000 in census track 3542 bounded by the Charles River, Fresh Pond to the west, and Harvard, to roughly $24,700 in census track 3524 near Kendall Square and MIT.[14]

During the summer and fall of 2003, I oversaw a project, the MIT Community Lab, which examined the communications environment in Cambridge, and interviewed a diverse set of seventy Cambridge leaders to get their sense of social capital, civic engagement, and major issues in Cambridge, including media. The study borrowed heavily from a set of ideas advanced by Robert Putnam—most notably, that "a society of many virtuous but isolated individuals is not necessarily rich in social capital,"[15] and that media services play an important role in both curbing and encouraging the development of social capital and civic engagement. Television, for example, can create a community of common experience, or it can isolate us from real human interaction by providing a steady supply of entertaining distractions.[16] The Internet can offer the benefits of access to an incredible bank of information and opportunities for expression, while giving us the tools to isolate ourselves and communicate with only those people who share our interests.[17] What we found, in short, is that the current communications environment in Cambridge reflects neither the needs of the city nor the values of the city's leaders, but like fish swimming in polluted water these leaders cannot imagine a better environment.

Cambridge is bombarded by commercial media, including at least sixteen daily and weekly newspapers, twenty-five local broadcast radio stations, and ten local broadcast television stations that report on some local events.[18] Yet, most of these media outlets focus on Boston, or what they refer to as the greater Boston market. In addition to the *Cambridge Tab* (a free weekly paper focusing on Cambridge human interest stories, arts, and entertainment) there is one weekly newspaper devoted to Cambridge news and civic affairs, the *Cambridge Chronicle*. The *Chronicle* and the *Tab* belong to a chain of "community papers" owned by the Herald Media. In 2003, the relatively new editor for the *Chronicle* and *Tab*, Michelle Babineau, expressed the view that there is enough information going on in Cambridge to fill a daily. But those decisions are in the hands of Herald Media, which also owns another daily serving Cambridge, *The Boston Herald*. The other major newspaper is the *Boston Globe* (owned by the New York Times Co.). Both the *Globe* and the *Herald* run occasional small stories about Cambridge, but no newspaper devotes itself to the daily life of a very active city. The closest Cambridge comes to a daily paper is the occasionally daily *Harvard Crimson*, a paper that devotes equal time to Harvard and national affairs.

There is no regular television or radio station focused on the Cambridge community, though there are three radio stations located in Cambridge: a small independent AM radio station, a Harvard station, and an MIT station. None of the Cambridge radio stations focus on Cambridge, and none have the resources to do so. Viacom/Infinity of New York operates five of the other twenty radio stations beaming signals to Cambridge, including the most popular news talk station WBZ; Greater Media of New Jersey operates four; and Entercom of Pennsylvania operates three stations. There are no television stations based in Cambridge, and of the ten broadcast television stations available over the air three are owned by Viacom.

The local cable public access operation, Cambridge Community TV (CCTV), is underfunded and understaffed. The city government mediates the relationship between CCTV and Comcast/AT&T, the current parent company of the local cable franchisee. In concert with the *Chronicle*, CCTV provided the only substantive coverage of Cambridge political issues and choices during the 2003 election. But neither the *Chronicle* nor CCTV has the resources to hire the best talent, conduct in-depth investigations of local politics, produce attractive programs, or effectively promote their coverage. The cable channels dedicated to government and education purposes are barely used, and when they are, the production quality is so poor some leaders find it distracting. Business leaders, religious leaders, and political leaders asserted that "there is no way to effectively communicate with the public at large."

Cambridge leaders agreed that the lack of affordable housing and the dismal performance of the public school were the two biggest problems facing Cambridge, but none could recall a discussion of these issues in the local media. Two weeks prior to the local city council election my students monitored the most popular local television program (The 11 o'clock News on WHDH), the most listened to radio program (8:00 a.m. on WBZ) and the most read newspaper (the *Sunday Boston Globe*). WBZ radio devoted 103 stories totaling one hour and 48 minutes to a category we called Greater Boston, mostly crime and fires and a few public interest stories. Not one story in that 2 weeks was about anything in Cambridge. WHDH aired 110 stories totaling one hour 32 minutes about Greater Boston, and devoted 3 stories totaling one minute 10 seconds—that's three stories each averaging 25 seconds, to Cambridge. None of these stories were about the election or issues Cambridge leaders deemed most important to Cambridge. The *Boston Globe* did mention the election and gave it a few column inches, 8 to be exact, in its Sunday edition.

As one of my research assistants observed: "Perhaps one of the most interesting results of the questionnaire was the repeated opinion that local media in Cambridge was not only poor, but severely inadequate in serving the needs of any person or group in the city. While many leaders recognized the effect of poor media as a major issue, there were few actions that leaders could recall as having effectively addressed this problem. Indeed, only a handful of leaders even cited the condition of local media when asked about major problems or concerns in the city. More disturbing, however, was the widespread acceptance that receiving irrelevant, inaccurate, incomplete or outdated information from local media sources would continue to be the norm."[19]

Perhaps as a result of the lack of information about Cambridge, many neighborhood groups have established their own e-mail lists and web-based communications to share information about important events. As valuable as this resource is, it does not bring neighborhood groups together within the city. The local web site or e-mail list works as an effective local bond, but it does not bridge the interests of one neighborhood to another.[20] While the City of Cambridge manages public bulletin boards and kiosks and operates a robust web site and an e-mail service to city employees, these communications sources are underutilized, poorly staffed, uncoordinated, underfunded, and badly distributed.

The local media environment at once overwhelms Cambridge with sensational commercial fare and obscures important local information. Given the fact that this environment is dominated by commerce, most of the large number of complaints about communications in Cambridge focus on the cost and quality of media, particularly cable television service. The notion that the city government may have a duty to maintain an effective communications structure for purposes of democratic engagement (if not for purposes of health, safety, education, or economic infrastructure) is not even a passing thought shared between the guardians of the local democracy.

But the consumer complaints have frustrated both the city manager and the city councilors of Cambridge. In his June 27, 2002 letter denying the transfer request of AT&T and Comcast, City Manager Robert Healy noted AT&T's "willful misinterpretation" of the negotiated discount for Cambridge seniors, the "bait and switch" tactics of AT&T salespersons, inappropriate charges for cable boxes, poor response to customers, and poor quality service. As Healy noted: "I have never observed community relations and customer service to be at a lower ebb."[21] Despite these concerns, the Massachusetts Department of Telecommunications and Energy (DTE) overruled the city manager's denial of the transfer request. This state of affairs may be what prompted the City of Cambridge Policy Order Resolution O-22 requesting "that the City Manager . . . report on other communities that have a municipal cable channel and the steps involved to create a municipal cable channel."[22]

In these frustrations with cable service, Cambridge is not unlike many other cities in Massachusetts or across the country.[23] While some of these other cities have taken the initiative to ensure competition in their communities, there is no effective competitive alternative to Comcast in Cambridge. As the DTE notes: "In Massachusetts, the FCC has declared the following communities subject to effective competition: Arlington, Boston, Dedham, Lexington, Needham, Newton and Somerville."[24] Absent even a threat of competition, Cambridge will continue to suffer the burden of a monopoly that has clearly indicated a disregard for not only Cambridge customers, but the agreement negotiated in good faith with the Cambridge city manager.

Government control of water, power, transportation, and communications services is a common feature of most industrial societies. While municipal ownership of services deemed vital to public health, safety, civic engagement, and mobility has a long history in the United States, it is the exception and not the rule. Of the roughly thirty thousand municipalities in the United States, approximately five hundred are operating a cable and/or broadband telecommunications service. Most of the municipalities, or collection of municipalities, operating or considering operating telecommunications systems are also providing some utility service, usually electric power, to their communities. For example, the town of Shrewsbury, Massachusetts, about thirty miles west of Cambridge has owned its own water system since 1905, and its own Light Department since 1908. Shrewsbury, a town one-quarter the size of Cambridge, has run its own cable television operation since 1983.

Because of frustrations with lack of service to their communities or the perception of broken promises by local cable or telecommunications companies, there is a small movement underway in communities across the country toward municipal ownership of advanced telecommunications facilities. Berkshire County, Massachusetts, is one such community. To address concerns that it was not being served adequately by private communications operations, Berkshire received a $250,000 grant from the State of Massachusetts to conduct a planning study to determine the feasibility of operating what is now known as Berkshire Connect, a telecommunications service that aggregates local demand to negotiate low rates from private companies.[25]

As the Berkshire Connect example suggests, there are many different forms that government involvement may take. One town can own and operate a combined cable and telecommunications operation. That town might vest the operation of a telecommunications system in an independent but wholly owned public utility. The town may collaborate with other towns or other entities (such as an academic institution, a private corporation, or a citizens' group) in ownership and operation. The choices and permutations are as varied as the range of services and the number of communities in the United States.

Federal law does not prohibit municipalities from operating their own telecommunications system, but a few state legislatures, such as Missouri, Nevada, Texas, and Pennsylvania limit or prohibit municipally operated telecommunications services.[26] There are no such limits in Massachusetts. While the city franchise agreement with licensee MediaOne (parent owner is now Comcast) extends to 2010, that agreement does not keep the city from awarding a license to another party, perhaps even one associated with the city.

Despite its frustrations with its communications environment, it is highly unlikely that the City of Cambridge will address its very real needs. The city has adopted a strong city manager/weak city council form of government, with the mayor chosen from among the city council members by the city council. With the political power concentrated in the hands of a resourceful city manager, even most leaders feel disconnected from the operation of city government. The fact that they have no strong place to join the community in a discussion of the problems of Cambridge, and their failure to even understand that communication is a problem, leave many local leaders dispirited and angry. The vaunted educators at Harvard and MIT are largely content to study and recommend policies for communities far away from their home base.

In contrast, some communities do recognize the connection between the health of their local democracies and the vitality of their local communications environment, and some even have educational institutions engaged in the challenges of their local community. Here is a very brief look at a few of them.

The Blacksburg Electronic Village

Beginning in 1979, professors and students in the Urban Affairs and Urban Planning programs at the Virginia Polytechnic Institute and State University (Virginia Tech) began to consider how computer networks might be used if focused on the needs of communities. In 1989, after receiving little interest from the local telephone and cable companies, officials at Virginia Tech engaged officials in the Town of Blacksburg, Virginia, in a discussion over the possibilities and benefits of a community electronic network project.

The initial goals for the proposed project were: (1) to create a community testing ground for the twenty-first-century learning environment; and (2) to create replicable community models for low-priced access and advanced, high-bandwidth communication and for universal network and computer literacy.

In the fall of 1990, after a public discussion of the proposed network, Bell Atlantic executives proposed collaborating with the university to create a state-of-the-art system to provide the same communications capabilities to off-campus students that were available to students on campus. Virginia Tech folded these discussions into the talks it was having with Blacksburg town officials. In January 1992, the chief executive officers of Blacksburg, Virginia Tech, and Bell Atlantic announced their collaboration to determine the feasibility of an "electronic village."

What is an electronic village? An electronic village is an interactive communications network based on Internet technologies and designed for multiple and varied users. The Blacksburg Electronic Village (BEV) is about as good an example of an electronic village as one can find. People can get

and share information about government or civic activity, they can advertise and sell products, they can find a babysitter or a boyfriend, they can create art or play games, they can engage in mindless gossip in chat rooms or
they can learn physics from college professors.

By the fall of 1995, BEV was clearly a successful experiment. Roughly half
the population was on-line, the majority of Blacksburg businesses were
advertising on the Internet, television cameras had become as familiar a
sight as national stories proliferated about "America's most wired town,"
and the National Telecommunications Infrastructure Administration
awarded Virginia Tech with a six-figure grant. By the following spring, Virginia Tech announced it would no longer sign up users who were not affiliated with the university, and private industry stepped up to respond to the
increasing demand. As of 1997, Blacksburg could claim one of the most
computer-literate communities in the nation.[27]

Our focus, of course, is whether an interactive communications network
supports democratic engagement, whether it provides the "popular information" so necessary to self-governance. As indicated earlier, the Internet is
an important new communications tool in an increasingly noisy media
environment; it may even be an essential tool in this environment, but it is
not the dominant tool. Nor, as we have discussed, is the Internet alone a
panacea for the structural problem we are wrestling with; in other words,
the Internet does not negate the ability of one faction of our society to
dominate citizen deliberation. Still, as an important and perhaps even an
essential tool, Blacksburg provides an important lesson on what is necessary to maintain an electronic village open to all citizens.

Aside from the continued active engagement of Virginia Tech, a key to
the success of BEV is citizen engagement. Citizen engagement was an early
element in the formation of BEV, through the Blacksburg Telecommunications Advisory Committee (BTAC). BTAC is a citizen committee formed in
1983 out of frustration with the local cable service. Virginia Tech is represented on the nine-member committee, and so are retirees, business leaders, and other citizen representatives. When the Blacksburg Town Council
decided to embrace Virginia Tech's electronic village initiative they charged
BTAC with oversight of the local government component.

BTAC suggested ways to improve the town's web site, helping the town's
site developers to order information by topics rather than city departments.
BEV provides basic information about the town of Blacksburg, such as a
directory of local officials, a list of fire stations and their locations, as well as
town and university activity calendars. BEV also provides a wide variety of

"e-government" services, such as the ability to reserve a picnic shelter, request a police report, obtain a dog license, or pay water and sewer bills. In addition to helping make certain BEV worked to serve the needs of citizens, the citizens committee was an important link in educating fellow citizens about the benefits of an electronic village.

Why Blacksburg? Blacksburg, Virginia, is a small (nineteen square miles with a population of a little over 39,500) relatively homogeneous (90 percent white) rural town in southern Virginia. The only thing of special note about the town is BEV. Nothing about the town suggests that it is an ideal location for such an experiment in communications technology. The old Bell Atlantic, now Verizon, was not especially concerned about Blacksburg. There are no significant high-tech industries demanding advanced communications services in Blacksburg. The population of Blacksburg is not full of wealthy individuals seeking the latest in technology—also known as first adapters. What is unusual about Blacksburg is an engaged university: Virginia Tech. There should be no doubt that Virginia Tech and Blacksburg have developed a symbiotic relationship. Blacksburg is overwhelmed by the presence of Virginia Tech students, a population now exceeding 25,000. With approximately 8,500 employees, Virginia Tech is the town's major employer. The next largest employer is Federal-Mogul Corp., with 565 employees.

The initial goals of BEV were the goals of urban planners and communications technologists. Despite the emphasis of some in the community and at Virginia Tech on the role of private industry in creating the electronic village, neither private industry nor what is obliquely referred to as "the market" was a major element of BEV's creation or "success." Nor has BEV had any major impact on Blacksburg's economy; the median family income in Blacksburg has not risen more than a few thousand dollars above $32,243 where it stood in 1990, and industry has not flocked to the small town. Still, the benefits of a strong democracy of educated and engaged citizens are clearly worthwhile.

Chicago Access Network

As we noted earlier, the cable public access movement has failed to live up to the glowing promise born during the Johnson years. Characterized too often by nearly unwatchable cable channels, there are still some communities that have been able to turn local access into vibrant community forums for democratic deliberation. One such community is Chicago.

Cable television came relatively late to Chicago. It has been suggested to me that in a roundabout way James "Big Jim" Thompson was the cause. It seems the future Illinois governor got his big push by successfully prosecuting aldermen tied to the corrupt Democratic machine of long-time mayor Richard Daley. Thompson, a U.S. attorney, began a purge of corruption in Chicago that lasted nearly twenty-five years. Every sort of official, from Governor Otto Kerner, to Representative Dan Rostenkowski, to nearly fifty aldermen and over a dozen judges, did jail time. Some allegations seemed to have involved bribes to aldermen by cable companies looking to lock up an exclusive franchise. As a result of the turnover, and the heightened scrutiny, cable television came a little late to Chicago.[28]

When it seemed clear that cable was going to come, media activists in Chicago were already in the midst of organizing activity directed at local television stations. They decided to turn their focus on making certain a strong public access operation was part of the deal. Chicago is a city of rough and tumble politics, and reformers from Jane Addams to Saul Alinsky have established a tradition of engagement among community activists. The core of that tradition is building diverse coalitions and conducting research.

In August 1981, the mayor convened five Chicago civic organizations, the Chicago Cable Television Study Commission, to advise the city on cable franchising agreements. These organizations were Business and Professional People for the Public Interest (BPI), the Chicago Urban League, the Church Federation of Greater Chicago, the Roger Baldwin Foundation of the American Civil Liberties Union, and the Citizens Committee on the Media. This last group included over fifty nonprofit organizations, media activists, and representatives from labor, church, and minority organizations. Gordon Quinn, a documentary filmmaker and media activist involved in this early organizing effort, describes this as an exciting time of hope and activism in the city. According to Quinn the media activists, seasoned by their experience with the local broadcasters, understood how important it was to get a well-funded channel that would give a priority to the voice of nonprofits, organizations whose views could rarely get a full airing on local television.[29]

The Chicago Cable Television Study Commission was also able to take in the ten years of lessons of big and small cities across the country that had negotiated their own franchise agreements with some of the same cable companies, such as Tele-Communications Inc. (TCI) and Westinghouse, seeking a franchise in Chicago. On February 10, 1982, the Chicago Cable Communications Ordinance was passed. A centerpiece of the ordinance is the establishment and funding of an independent nonprofit to administer

Chicago's public access channels. That entity, under the name of Chicago Access Network Television, was established in 1983. On March 18, 1984, Chicago granted franchises to construct and operate cable television systems: Group W Cable of Chicago (a Westinghouse subsidiary) was assigned Areas 2 and 3. Chicago Cable Communications (a TCI subsidiary) was assigned Area 4. Stellar/Continental was assigned Area 5. On February 20, 1985, Communications and Cable of Chicago (a TCI subsidiary) was granted a franchise for Area 1 and acquired Stellar/Continental's franchise.[30]

While the cable companies have changed hands several times over the course of the last twenty years, Chicago Access Network TV has remained and thrived. In part this is because they never forgot the lessons of community engagement and research. "PEG centers that are successful tap into the pulse of their community," according to Barbara Popovic, CAN TV's executive director. "We are not satisfied to simply offer communications tools, we want to see those tools put to work broadening the voices and issues on local television. We really have three goals. One, serving as a platform for local communications, that is, giving people a platform to discuss issues important to them. Two, serving the non-profit community by covering their issues and events and offering easy to use service like the ability to call in and place a bulletin board ad. And, three, address the needs and unmet interests of the viewers. That means aggressively reaching out to organizations and communities to get their voices heard."[31]

"You Have A Right," is one example of a successful CAN TV program. It's a call-in talk show produced by the Chicago chapter of the ACLU, an organization involved in starting CAN TV, and it demonstrates the power of good cable access programs. A program on racial profiling and the ACLU's call for increased data collection by the local police department is fairly typical. Young and not so young African American men called in with reports of repeatedly being stopped by local police officers and searched for drugs and weapons. Adam Schwartz, the ACLU attorney on hand that day, said he gets calls like this every week, and that he hopes people will continue to contact the local ACLU to report on these incidents. Another caller argued that the ACLU was "ganging up on the cops," and their efforts would result in demoralizing the police force. Schwartz responded that many police departments and police organizations have endorsed data collection efforts, noting that "you need data collection to distinguish between those who are doing their jobs well and those who are not."[32]

Ed Yohnka, the driving force at the ACLU behind the cable access program, admits that taping a show is a lot of work. "We tape 13 weeks, then take a 13 week break and then do another round," he says. "We provide the graphics and the content, and CAN TV does the rest. Volunteers are a big part of the production team." But the benefits are worth it; according to Yohnka, the people of Chicago see the ACLU as an approachable human organization that confronts issues city residents care about. Other longtime supporters and users of the Chicago Access Network are unions and civil rights groups.[33]

Like most public access systems across the country, CAN TV is always at risk of losing its core funding or having some of its channels taken away. In Chicago, CAN TV's relationships with hundreds of community organizations allow it to communicate effectively with local politicians. But aside from the pressure these groups can bring, CAN TV also has direct links to local politicians. While the incumbent mayor dominates the local government channel, many Chicago aldermen communicate with their constituents through CAN TV. Chicago Alderwoman Freddrenna Lyle told the *Chicago Tribune* that "unless someone gets indicted or they throw a brick through somebody's window, there is no coverage, by the big TV stations." Lyle has used CAN TV to reach voters, and to be reached by her constituents. "You can't buy this kind of coverage," she says.[34] Not only are alderman regular guests on programs such as "North Town News," 50th Ward Alderman Bernard Stone has his own public access program where he takes call-in questions from viewers.[35]

When a relatively new cable company, RCN, defaulted on its 2002 payment to CAN TV, it was pressure from the Chicago City Council that helped turn the tide. One day before the council was expected to pass a resolution calling for stiff daily penalties, RCN paid CAN TV $645,000 plus interest. The sponsor of the resolution: Bernard Stone.[36]

In addition to CAN TV's engagement with community groups and local politicians, it has funded independent research to establish its effectiveness. According to a study by CJ Research,

- eight out of ten nonprofit executive directors are aware of CAN TV
- eighty-nine percent of those who don't work with CAN TV think it is valuable to the community, and ninety-three who do work with CAN TV think it's valuable
- seventy-nine percent of nonclients express interest in using CAN TV in the future
- less than 5 percent of Chicago nonprofits think commercial television is doing a good job serving the community[37]

CAN TV's commitment to voice combined with political savvy and community support has resulted in a yearly operating budget of $2.7 million, which in turns makes better programs possible.[38]

Municipal Ownership

Of the roughly thirty thousand municipalities in the United States, as of 2003 approximately five hundred were operating a cable/broadband telecommunications service. Because of frustrations with lack of service to their communities or the perception of broken promises by local cable or telecommunications companies, there is a small movement underway toward municipal ownership of advanced telecommunications facilities. While a few state legislatures have been convinced by the telecommunications industry to limit or prohibit municipalities from operating their own telecommunications systems, federal law does not.[39] One of the main barriers to this movement is not the law, but the grip of the laissez-faire religion. But even this grip has come undone in the wake of ever-increasing cable rates and poor service. One of the shining lights in this movement is Click! operated by the city of Tacoma, Washington.

TACOMA, WASHINGTON

Tacoma, Washington, is a mid-sized city resting between the state capital of Olympia and Seattle. Known for too long as a backyard to Seattle, reeking with industry (the phrase "the aroma of Tacoma" is a local pun), the third largest city in Washington State boasts a strong public sphere, near universal access to cable and advanced telecommunications services, a very competitive telecommunications environment, and, not coincidentally, the largest municipally owned telecommunications system in the United States. The advanced telecommunications service is called Click! Network and its roots stretch back to 1893, the peak of the robber barons and ruthless industrialists. Unlike many other cities, it seems Tacoma never forgot the lessons of that era.

Populist and Progressive reformers struggled to come to terms with the growing political power of the eastern industrialists they called trusts. Of particular concern was the concentrated political and economic power of the railroads. European immigrants first began to settle in what was to become Tacoma in 1852. The Indian Wars of 1855–56 paved the way for white European control of the Puget Sound region, and while there were a lumber mill, a U.S. Post Office, and telegraph service, white domination of the area did not begin in earnest until the federally subsidized Northern Pacific Railroad arrived in 1883.[40]

Charles B. Wright, selected by the Northern Pacific directors to head a subsidiary they called the Tacoma Land Company, managed to secure for himself an agreement with the elected officials of the city to be the exclusive provider of water and electricity for the boom town. Thus, in 1884 the Tacoma Light and Water Company was formed.[41]

This extraordinary grant of an exclusive license for a vital public service was not unusual in developing western territories. The so-called boom towns were desperate to copy the utility infrastructure established in eastern cities, and a quick way to do it was to convince an eastern industrialist to apply his expertise and access to capital in the new territory. Providing an exclusive right to provide services in exchange for modern infrastructure may have seemed a good deal. Moreover, a popular theory of the time was that certain businesses, such as those providing water and electricity, were "natural monopolies." In other words, the financial investment in infrastructure required to provide such services was too high and the margin of profit too low to encourage competition. Thus, providing an exclusive right to do something that would have become exclusive at some point in the future may have seemed an easy bargain to make. The long experience of caveat emptor (let the buyer beware) many citizens had with exorbitant fees charged by a variety of merchants for shoddy, or even dangerous, goods was somehow lost in the shared dream of great riches to come. The inevitable and widespread abuses of exclusive franchise authority and grants of land (only recently captured in a deadly battle with indigenous people) generated enough public anger to lead to a Washington State constitutional ban on such public generosity to private interests. That ban would come too late for Tacoma.

By 1889 it became clear to Tacoma residents that they had made a bad deal. The street lights were not bright and there were not enough of them. There was no electricity service to the homes and too little electricity to serve the lumber mills properly. Water service was either inconsistent or nonexistent, and the water that did arrive ranged from poor quality to poisonous. The price charged for these essential services was high. In the meantime, Wright, who liked to refer to himself as the "Father of Tacoma," had returned to Philadelphia.[42]

By 1890, the Tacoma City Council began to negotiate with Wright to purchase Tacoma Light and Water. After a face-to-face meeting in Philadelphia, the proud parent agreed to accept the sum of $ 1.75 million in exchange for an inadequate "natural monopoly" to provide light and water to a desperate community living on the other side of the continent. The citizens agreed, by a vote of 3195 to 1956, and the City of Tacoma was in the utility business.[43]

It would not be long before the citizens of Tacoma applied their experience with water and light to other basic infrastructure services valuable to the public such as light rail and waste management. But municipal ownership alone did not end either poor service or corruption. In the 1950s citizens voted to separate certain utility management (specifically rail, power, and water) from direct political control by establishing a separate department of government, Tacoma Power (TP), overseen by a public utilities board. The board, appointed by the mayor with the approval of the city council, would be responsible for hiring and oversight of the professional staff that operated the various units of TP.[44]

In the mid-1990s it was clear that telecommunications services were becoming an infrastructure as important to business and community as water and light and transportation. While both Seattle and Olympia seemed to be getting adequate telecommunications services, Tacoma was not. According to Diane Lachel, government and community relations manager of Click!Network, in some communities near Tacoma, U.S. West would provide residential/rural customers cell phones because it was not going to provide wireline service. In addition, the city council would regularly receive complaints about the ever-rising cost of cable service and criticism about public access service and programming.[45]

Perhaps the most serious concern was the potential damage to Tacoma's economy. Lachel said it would take a business twelve to eighteen months to get a telephone connection. Tacoma businesses with great telecommunications needs, such as Frank Russell Company's billing service and Total Renal Care, were considering moving. Indeed, TP's own telecommunications needs were not being met. TP serves nine jurisdictions in an 180-square-mile area and needed to be able to gather information from around its service area. Available high-speed (ISDN) service was both too expensive and provided insufficient coverage. Neither U.S. West nor TCI Cable had plans to upgrade service.[46]

In 1995, TP funded a study on telecommunications development by Stanford Research Inc., and followed that up in 1996 with more research on local market potential and a business plan. TP, now a well-endowed utility actually selling excess power on the national market, proposed investing $50 million to establish an advanced telecommunications network that would serve its own needs and the communications needs of the citizens of Tacoma. The profits from the operation of the network would be reinvested back into the utility and would pay a regular return to support other non-utility city services such as the courts and fire protection.[47]

Despite citizen complaints, and despite the frustrating personal experiences city officials had with both TCI and U.S. West, former Mayor Bill Baarsma said the decision to approve the TP plan was the toughest in his career—but the wisest. Baarsma and other city officials were not concerned about TP competence, that was clearly proven; they were concerned about lawsuits that might be filed by TCI or other private interests opposed to municipal ownership. Leo Hindery, a TCI official, stormed out of the room, turning over a chair, calling the council incompetent, and threatening a court action. No court action was filed. Despite the fact that it is an asset and a branch of the city government, TP still had to negotiate a cable and telecommunications services franchise agreement with the City of Tacoma. Because of concerns that the private companies would sue, the franchise negotiations with the city were determinedly at arm's length. Some of the negotiators describe them as the most difficult negotiations they have ever engaged in.[48]

The negotiations and the investment (a reported $90 million to date) have paid off. Since the launch of Click! Network, over a hundred high-tech communications businesses have located in Tacoma. In addition, in response to the competition from the city AT&T has laid new fiber optics, provided cable TV and high-speed Internet, and reduced the rate schedules for cable TV. The monthly charge for AT&T's basic cable services in the Tacoma area is $26, which is $2 higher than Click! but 20 percent lower than what it charges in Seattle.[49]

But the advantages go far beyond low cable rates, or a modern telecommunications infrastructure that provides clean pictures. The Click! Network supports a vibrant public access channel, with not only coverage of the council and public utility and board of education meetings, but political discussion programs and programs attending to the various interests of Tacoma's diverse community. The advanced telecommunications infrastructure makes it easier to maintain other infrastructure from transportation to water to the electric grid, and it supports educational and medical and legal and government services. It really is the super public infrastructure of the present.[50]

A variety of "think tanks" supported by the cable and telecommunications industry have published reports attacking the idea that a local government should operate a communications service.[51] The arguments include: (1) the telecommunications business is too complex to be operated by local governments; (2) local governments will lose money and tax citizens for their mistakes; (3) it is not fair for the government to compete with business; and (4) the government will interfere in citizen speech and privacy rights. There is no evidence that municipal operation of telecommunications service has resulted in any loss of free speech or privacy. In fact, the greater local accountability and transparency of public utility companies is a strong guard against the real possibility of these abuses in the future. Most of the arguments focus not on the speech of citizens, but on the economic options of large corporations. Our focus is not on what is good for the market, but what is good for citizen speech. Nonetheless, the attacks on Click! Network are worth noting as they have been cited as evidence of failure.[52]

Paul Guppy of the Washington Policy Institute in Seattle, Washington, prepared a report for the Progress & Freedom Foundation on the "disappointing results of Tacoma's foray into the telecommunications business." Guppy's charges are either misleading or unsupported. A wide variety of entirely predictable and inconsequential circumstances out of the Tacoma Public Utility's control prevented Click! Network from beginning operation when they initially proposed, yet Guppy would have us believe that this is evidence of TP's incompetence. But the most damaging charge is a 50 percent surcharge in local electric bills as a result of Click! Network charges.[53] According to Diane Lachel the surcharge was not initiated because of Click! but because of the extraordinary high costs of electricity resulting from the energy crisis impacting California and the Pacific Northwest in the winter of 2000–2001. At the beginning of the "energy crisis," Click! was already constructed.[54] The energy crisis was brought about by the deregulation of energy markets and the manipulation of that market by entities like Enron.[55]

Guppy's claims to the contrary, Click! Network is serving a third of the homes the network passes, is operating in the black, is providing timely service that was unavailable prior to its start, and forces private telecommunications companies to keep their prices lower than the prices they charge in Seattle.[56]

As mentioned above hundreds of local governments in the United States have already established their own telecommunications services. The private telecommunications industry has fought this by filing court actions and lobbying state legislatures to pass laws that would prohibit or discourage local governments from running their own telecommunications operations. Ten states have such laws in place.[57]

As mentioned above, private telecommunications companies argue that municipal ownership is unfair competition, noting that municipalities possess the ability to issue tax-exempt bonds and obtain business and zoning privileges. Lachel, who claims to be a staunch supporter of the values of private enterprise, argues that Tacoma did not go into the telecom business "just to make money, we went into the business because the telecom and cable companies were not providing adequate service. They had their chance."[58]

In fact, the continued presence of AT&T suggests that they still have their chance. The main difference is that while private industry looks at Tacoma as only a consumer market to reward individual shareholders with ever higher profits, Tacoma Power's core mission is to serve the community—all of the community, not just those select businesses or neighborhoods that might be the most lucrative. With 670 miles of fiber and coaxial cable lining every street in Tacoma, anyone who wants high-speed Internet service and cable television can get it. Just like water and light.

* * *

We began this chapter with a cautionary tale and we shall end it with one. Corporate interests are extraordinarily capable of battling against reform movements—and they don't play nice.

TRI-CITIES, ILLINOIS

Geneva, St. Charles, and Batavia are three small towns in Illinois snug against the Fox River about an hour or so from Chicago. Like Tacoma, the three cities have provided residents electricity. Batavia, for example, began generating its own electricity around 1890 to support its street lighting system and serve its growing population. Today, Batavia purchases energy from Commonwealth Edison and resells it to residents. This arrangement ensures low rates, reliable service, and local control. It was this spirit that led the three cities to join together to explore whether they might exercise greater control over the cable and telecommunications services provided to Tri-City residents.

In 2001, the three cities funded a poll that indicated that roughly half of all residents were very unhappy with the telecommunications services provided by SBC and AT&T Cable (now Comcast). At around that same time, the City of Geneva was building a fiber optic network to link all of its municipal buildings, electric substations, schools, as well as Kane County operations located in Geneva. Upon completion of Geneva's network, plans called for the interconnection with the similar networks already completed in Batavia and St. Charles.

In the summer of 2002, the three cities acting together hired United Telesystems, Inc. (UTI) to prepare a feasibility study to determine whether it was cost-effective to operate their own telecommunications system. UTI reported that it was. UTI suggested that there was no need to monopolize the provision of telecommunications services, such as the three cities had done with providing electric service. In fact, they proposed competing directly with Comcast and SBC, and showed that the Tri-Cities could ensure all residents had the services they wanted at an affordable cost. The plan for a $62 million municipal broadband network was provided to residents on line, and offered as a referendum for the citizens of the Tri-Cities to decide.[59] That's where the trouble started.

According to Geneva Mayor Kevin Burns, "We were out-manned, out-resourced, out-spent and out-maneuvered. Our campaign was rooted in truth, our opponents' in anything but."[60] SBC and Comcast demonstrated they had learned the lessons handed down a century ago by Vail and AT&T. Local newspapers were filled with advertising that looked like news, "informing" local residents that the proposed municipal service was unrealistic and unnecessary, a waste of taxpayer money. They also funded a telephone blitz disguised as a survey, asking area residents questions such as "Should tax money be allowed to provide pornographic movies for residents?"

The citizen group Fiber for Our Future took on the responsibility for informing the public about the referendum, but apparently failed to understand they had jumped into a fierce political power struggle. As Peter Collins, Geneva's information systems supervisor, put it: "Unfortunately, we were outspent on marketing (Fiber for Our Future—$3,000, SBC & Comcast—God only knows) and failed to undo the 'strong-arming' and lies laid out by our competitors." The referendum was defeated, with roughly 60 percent of the community against and 40 percent in favor.

Officials in the Tri-Cities have vowed to bring the matter up again.[61] In the meantime, both SBC and Comcast have stepped up efforts to provide better service to the communities.

There are citizens across the country who understand the connection between communications and democracy. Whether they are creating electronic villages or better-supported public access cable operations or communications operations run by and subject to the vote of local municipalities, they are reinventing the structural relationship that Madison had in mind when the founders supported the Post Office and subsidized the distribution of newspapers. There are hundreds of these groups in every state of the Union, and many enlightened local elected leaders who share the views of these citizen groups about the importance of communication to a strong democratic community. However, as much as many of us wish it were so, these local groups do not as yet constitute a movement to establish communications rules that might actually bring about the vibrant deliberating republic of informed citizens the founders had in mind.

Moreover, many of these groups are not associated with the myriad other organizations competing for attention and public, foundation, and corporate funding. Too often environmental activists, women and minority leaders, clergy, consumer groups, and others see the work of "media reform" activists as just another voice in the public arena, and a rather unimportant voice at that. Indeed, the notion that communication and the principle of equal political communication are fundamental to the ability of civil rights activists or consumer groups or environmental activists is completely overlooked. Madison's lesson that democracy *is* communication is lost on the very groups that need to understand that lesson most. Indeed, too often media activists see themselves as a minor and sometimes rather harmless concern. Not only are they disconnected from other activists, they split off from each other into groups concerned about programs for children, access to cable, cost of communications services, the images of minorities, media literacy, journalism standards, public broadcasting reform, and so on.

All of these fissures occur in a society where the dominant media and messages remain largely controlled by international corporations. While "media" activists are divided as to their goals, underfunded, and confused about whether they intend to influence markets, parents, or politicians, the communications corporations are not so burdened. Communications corporations compete sometimes fiercely for market share, but they understand that their goal is to make greater profits. To that end they join their considerable financial resources, and are clear that they mean to influence everyone, from citizen to government official, in an effort to shape the market.

The reader is reminded here that this book is less about reforming media than reforming democracy by putting the equal communications ability of citizens back into the center of our republic as the founders of that republic intended. The fact that citizen communication has become captured by international corporations is our main point. We are just as concerned about the inability of people on welfare to deliberate over welfare reform and the relative silence of the environmental activists as compared to the automobile and oil lobby, as we are concerned about the challenges mindful parents face when confronting Jerry Springer. Democratic governance is the problem. Communications inequality is the reason the American republic is broken.

But, frankly, if a movement is to take hold that will create a communications system that best serves democracy it will require radical goals and tactics, tactics that begin to tackle the hold corporations have on federal levers of power. That is the subject of our next and final chapter.

12

Reclaiming Our Republic

Our democracy, or rather the republic of the founders, has been corrupted because one faction, international business, has come to dominate civic deliberation. The fact that global corporations dominate discourse in the United States is not the result of the fairly popular but ultimately amorphous notions of the natural and inevitable preeminence of the economy—sometimes referred to as the "free market" or "the almighty dollar." Nor is this dominance the result of the vastly overstated importance of "new technologies." If military dictatorships and nation-states run by religious clerics are not inevitable, neither is it inevitable that our democratic deliberations are managed by market forces or scientific invention. If the capitalist market and technological development have come first in our considerations of communications policy, it is only because those responsible to the sovereign people to make communications policy have put democracy second.

This book is fundamentally concerned about the condition of the American republic. I mean here to put the republic first. The overwhelming evidence of the lack of basic civic literacy,[1] the declining rate of voter participation,[2] and the disengagement of the average American from local civic activity[3] should alarm every friend of democracy. The fact that life and death decisions (decisions about the quality of our air or the availability of health care or whether or not we should go to war) are being made either out of public sight or sold to us like toothpaste should shake us to our bones. Our public conversation is missing the sort of genuine public deliberation the founders of the republic had in mind. We are in this situation because we have given corporations the power to largely determine the flow of public information Madison thought so necessary to democracy.

It is not as if the sickness in our democracy has gone unnoticed. Michael Sandel points to efforts on the right to initiate a dialogue about civility and Christian virtue and efforts on the left to restore the New Deal priorities of economic subsidy as two separate means of restoring our republic.[4] As Sandel points out, neither of these efforts goes to the heart of the matter, neither of them is really focused on how to equip and engage Americans to become effective citizens.

Former Senator Gary Hart suggests that we revisit Jefferson's proposal to constitutionalize a ward system, a subdivision of counties within the states, so that "every citizen can attend, when called on, and act in person." Every citizen would be empowered in these wards to deliberate and decide "all things relating to themselves exclusively. A justice, chosen by themselves, in each, a constable, a military company, a patrol, a school, the care of their own poor, their own portion of the public roads," and the like.[5] The purpose behind such a system is clearly not efficiency, but the creation of responsible citizens through the practice of local democratic engagement.

Sandel also recommends Jefferson's design for a ward republic and sees it in part as antidote to the increasing and understandable pull of international concerns. Too often, he argues, this preoccupation with global concerns creates a cosmopolitan, a so-called citizen of the world who belongs to no particular community. As Sandel writes: "The cosmopolitan ethic is wrong, not for asserting that we have certain obligations to humanity as a whole but rather for insisting that the more universal communities we inhabit must always take precedence over more particular ones."[6] I take Sandel's point, and have experienced the problem with cosmopolitans in Cambridge, but I suggest that young people protesting slave labor in Asia or the imposition of trade deals upon countries in Africa are right to see the connection between the global and the local. If citizens can be born because they are committed to doing what they can to stop the evils of global capitalism by taking action in their local community, I embrace them. I think these sorts of citizens hold the key to our challenge. For that challenge is at core to find a way to act with conviction where we can have a lasting impact—upon the hearts and minds in our local communities.

Hart's advocacy for a reconsideration of Jefferson's wards is instructive because it focuses, rightly, on governance structure. He is particularly convincing in his call to return greater responsibility for public schools to local citizens: "Since the local public school has been a traditional venue for the dissemination of civic values, the weakening of community administration of public education also weakens the inter-generational link by which community civic values are conveyed. For Jefferson, schools were centers for training citizens, and participation in political life was itself an education."[7]

Schools should be centers for training citizens. The engagement of local citizens in the challenges of paying for and educating their children is fertile ground for civic engagement and the continuing political education of adults. But the challenges faced by local schools and local governments are not only the nationalization of standards or the attention paid to an ever-widening sphere of interests and influences; school boards are also challenged by the fact that they have little or no influence over the local public arena—the places where school standards should be debated. As mentioned above, citizens of Cambridge, Massachusetts, are incensed over the problems of local schools, but there has almost never been a debate or any extensive deliberation of the problems with the schools where most people get their information—local television.

People do not participate in local elections, including school board elections, because the popular information—the reporting, if any, about those elections—is driven, like all other reporting, by commercial concerns.[8] The backdrops to the staged presidential events, the rousing speechifying of politicians in Washington, the latest bombing in Jerusalem, the earthquake in Guatemala, and the bloated belly in Africa are much more compelling than the local hearing on test scores or street lights.

As long as the means by which potential citizens (what else do you call the majority of nonvoters in the United States?) receive and share information comes filtered through business concerns, any effort to restore the republic will be stunted. What neither Hart nor Sandel seems to appreciate is that communication is the most basic infrastructure of a democracy. The ability of citizens to share and receive information is, with all due apologies to Jefferson, even more fundamental to democracy than public schools. In the absence of a public debate, public education will continue to serve our children badly. Still, I embrace Hart's suggested reforms. I also agree with Sandel that a compelling public philosophy that embraces both our diversity and our common interests is vital to repair our republic. What I suggest here is that Hart and Jefferson's wards and Sandel's public philosophy require the sort of public debate that only a vibrant and fair system of communications can guarantee. Thus, our democratic infrastructure, our system of communication, must be our first concern.

On the Other Hand

The lessons offered in the previous chapter begin to point the way toward reestablishing the robust public sphere Tocqueville described. But if those lessons or the lessons of the extended history have led the reader to think my focus is media reform or media justice, those lessons clearly do not go far enough. This book is about restoring and updating a vision of our democracy that puts an informed and engaged public in the vital center of our government. This book advocates expanding the number of thoughtful and articulate citizens, and argues that this is the first priority of our republic. My concern is our republic, but the means of restoring that republic is to establish a set of communication policies that put the health of democracy first and in the hands of citizens. The fact that this essential democratic work, this communications policy work, has been put in the hands of global corporations is, quite literally, dumb-founding.

Far too many media critics do not even approach the problem of our broken public arena with an understanding of social or governance structure. Their arguments range from media bias[9] to the increased speed of public conversation resulting from technology and commercial pressure[10] to the weakness of the Democratic Party.[11] I have no problems with media bias—it should be expected and anticipated, and the romantic ideals of objectivity should be abandoned and honest bias should be admitted. The problem and the joke of Fox "News" is not that it is right-wing but that it pretends to be "fair and balanced." Yellow journalism was not born in the era of twenty-four-hour news and instant analysis but at the same time, and due to the same forces, as corporate and commercial ascendancy. There is nothing about the technology that requires instant analysis or the seven-second sound bite, and as Upton Sinclair pointed out, it is not only that journalists seek to please business through advertising, journalists are part of the same fraternity as the corporate elite. The news that the Democratic Party is only another representative of the corporate elite is as old as Grover Cleveland, with the same core cause, the control of the public arena by the business faction.

The dominant debate over media reform is too piecemeal and timid to ensure that "a people who mean to be their own governors" can "arm themselves with the power knowledge gives." Three hours a week of educational programs for children, the right to download music from the Internet, an understandable system that rates sex and violence, forcing one company to allow another company onto "its" communications infrastructure, limiting national media reach to only 33 million Americans, and muzzling Janet Jackson and Howard Stern will not alter the control big business exercises over public information.

Media reform is useful if it sows the ground with the seeds of republican duty and engagement. I would call these seeds revolutionary if they were not first planted two hundred years ago by James Madison. If media reform merely creates a subsidy for poor people to partake of minimal communications services in a market controlled by powerful corporations, it does not go far enough. If media reform merely allows a few more people, perhaps more women and minorities, to enter the game, it does not go far enough. If media reform creates an electronic village or a cable public access operation or even a municipally run advanced telecommunications system, but fails to put the promotion of civic engagement at the center of these creations, it does not go far enough.

The Brass Check Revisited

I have had a number of students suggest that the problems of mass media can only be addressed if people rely more upon the Internet and begin to build their own web sites. We have already discussed some of the challenges to any reliance upon the Internet, borrowing heavily from Cass Sunstein's book *republic.com*. But the core impulse behind this approach should not be dismissed so easily. It does have noble historic precedents and it contains elements of a call to civic engagement that should not only be respected but should be incorporated into any set of communications policies that put democracy at the center. My main objection to this emphasis is certainly not that the individual voice should not be exercised; in fact, it is the exercise of the individual voice that prepares the citizen for effective participation in the public sphere. Nor is my main objection that a web site is bound to be inconsequentially lost in a wide sea of other more powerful voices. While invisibility is a near certainty it is true that individual voices have found a way through the clamor of public debate and have helped to shape societies. Indeed, I would not bother to write this book if I thought individual voices were unimportant. My main objection is the tendency in America to think we can solve structural problems through independent individual acts. My objection is to the notion that we have made a sufficient contribution to the solution of global warming by putting an Earth Day sticker on our parents' minivan, or by riding our bikes or taking public transportation, while automakers continue to succeed in delaying legislation to limit auto emissions or our presidents weaken or refuse to participate in global environmental treaties.

Another version of the individual protest web site as panacea derives from the much older impulse behind pamphleteering or even what some call pirate radio. As we discussed earlier, in his book *The Brass Check,* Upton Sinclair discussed the corruption of the U.S. press by big business in the early 1900s. In that book, Sinclair critiqued the call to a "return to the custom of the eighteenth century, printing and circulating large numbers of leaflets, pamphlets and books."[12] Sinclair noted that this was the primary method of operation of socialists and that it clearly did not work; besides, he argued: "Is it not obvious that society cannot continue indefinitely to get its news by this wasteful method? One large section of the community organized to circulate lies, and another large section of the community organized to refute the lies? We might as well send a million men out into the desert to dig holes, and then send another million to fill up the holes."[13]

Sinclair's desert analogy is compelling, but even he recognized the value of promoting the competition between "truths." In the earliest editions of *The Brass Check* he promoted a National Press and collected pledges for a number of years to establish one. Whether from lack of support or his commitment to his main love—writing books—Sinclair abandoned the effort.[14] Our republic is, as I have argued, in fact designed with the idea that it is best for there to be factions competing against each other in an open deliberation of public policy. The challenge we had in Sinclair's time, as we have in our own, is that one large section of the community is organized to dig holes, but no other comparatively large sections of the community are organized to fill them. The socialists, no matter how successful they were in the so-called Progressive Era, could not in the long run compete effectively against the organized power of the trusts. Not because their ideas were weak, but because the trusts gained control of the public arena through their control of the mass circulation newspapers and the Associated Press. The socialists were merely, as Sinclair puts it, "conveying some small portion of the truth to some small portions of the population."[15] So at least a part of the solution must be to restore some measure of political equality in the place where the public deliberates.

Another reform suggested by Sinclair was establishing laws intended to promote a fair press by regulating press conduct, such as requiring journalists to publish corrections in their newspapers in places equal in prominence to places the mistakes were published or curbing the monopoly power of the Associated Press (AP). A few commentators have argued that Sinclair's critiques, along with all the other critiques of the press during that period, in fact led to journalism standards, if not government laws, which corrected the abuses of which he complained.[16] Moreover, the power of the AP monopoly, as I have written, was severely curtailed by the government's application of antitrust legislation. But as Murrow's experience shows us, journalistic standards do not suffice to counteract the structural problems of the American system. While the great residual language left us by Justice Hugo Black resounds today and is clearly fitted to the political philosophy of Madison,[17] it is difficult to see that curbing the AP has resulted in less media monopoly.

Sinclair also suggested municipally owned communications might be part of the solution, and he provided the heroic example of the Municipal Press in Los Angeles, which for a brief year served as a counter-point to Hearst and other papers in the city. Sinclair tells the story through Frank E. Wolfe, the paper's editor:

> The "Municipal News"? There's a rich story buried there. It was established by an initiative ordinance, and had an ample appropriation. It was launched in the stream with engines going full steam ahead. Its success was instantaneous. Free distribution; immense circulation; choked with high-class, high-rate advertising; well edited, and it was clean and immensely popular.
>
> Otis [a competing newspaper publisher] said: "Every dollar that damned socialistic thing gets is a dollar out of the 'Times' till." Every publisher in the city re-echoed, and the fight was on. . . . Six times a day they whined, barked, yelped and snapped at the heels of the "Municipal News." New were more lies poured out from the mouths of these mothers of falsehood. . . . Advertisers were cajoled, browbeaten and blackmailed, until nearly all left the paper. [However, the *Municipal News*] was weak and ineffective editorially, for the policy was to print a newspaper. We did not indulge in a clothes-line quarrel—did not fight back.
>
> The "News" died under the axe one year from its birth. They used the initiative to kill it.[18]

Do you hear echoes of the battle in the Tri-Cities? A municipally run communications operation takes place in the context of a brutal global business environment. In the absence of a willingness to expend substantial resources to fight in the arena now dominated by ruthless businessmen, municipal operations don't stand a chance. Finding a way of "cutting the tiger's claws," as Sinclair put it (corporate press being the tiger), is a part of the solution. After that we must find a way to put armed citizens in the arena with the tiger.

One power, Sinclair suggested, which might compete with the corporate press, was big labor. So he advocated a union of newspaper workers.[19] Big labor, as we have seen, has not been effective in competing against big capital. Robert McChesney has documented the defeat of labor by the trusts over the control of radio in the 1930s.[20] Moreover, Sinclair who identified labor with socialism and the left would scarcely recognize the labor power as described by C. Wright Mills, a power that is comparatively atrophied, if not as corrupt, today.

If Sinclair focused heavily on the distortions in a press controlled by the trusts, at least he was not corrupted by the modern notions that either more capitalist bullies competing with each other or "new media" will solve the problem. The real problem with Sinclair's proposals is that they focus on the problems of press distortions rather than on the needs of democracy. Indeed, this is what is wrong with the analysis of too many media reformers. They have a clear sense of the problem, but they are looking at the symptoms rather than the cause, and thus they provide cough drops when the patient clearly requires stronger medicine.

Walter Lippmann, who took issue with Sinclair's characterization of his brethren in the newspaper business, was nonetheless shocked with the rest of the nation about the "quiz show" and payola scandals of the late 1950s.

> There has been, in fact, an enormous conspiracy to deceive the public in order to sell profitable advertising to the sponsors. It involves not merely this individual or that, but the industry as a whole. . . .
>
> The size of the fraud is a bitter reflection on the moral condition of our society. But it is also sure proof that there is something radically wrong with the fundamental national policy under which television operates. The principle of that policy is that for all practical purposes television shall be operated wholly for private profit. There is no competition in television except among competitors trying to sell the attention of their audiences for profit. As a result, while television is supposed to be "free," it has in fact become the creature, the servant, and indeed the prostitute, of merchandising.
>
> Quite evidently, this is an evil which cannot be remedied by a regulating commission or by some form of government or self-constituted censorship. The alternative, which is practiced in one form or another in almost every other civilized country, is competition—competition not for private profit but for public service. The best line for us to take is, I am convinced, to devise a way by which one network can be run as a public service with its criterion not what will be most popular but what is good.[21]

Lippmann wrote this seven years before the creation of the public broadcasting system. But I am certain that had he a chance to listen to the sponsor declarations on noncommercial radio and television, and the programming offered during the endless pledge weeks, he would not recognize this as what he had in mind. In his searing indictment of public broadcasting in the United States, James Ledbetter ends with a series of recommendations, a few of which I will repeat.

1. "What is desperately needed is a renewed commitment to finding a funding plan that makes sense."
2. "The CPB must be liberated from direct presidential control."
3. "Democratize the local boards."[22]

The only thing I would add to Ledbetter's list is that public broadcasting should be charged with airing controversial political speech and providing full and detailed coverage of local, state, and federal government activity. Democratic debate should be at the center of what public broadcasting should do.[23] But the core of Ledbetter's proposals I support wholeheartedly. As he hints, the multichannel broadcasting model made more possible by digital television suggests that much more content can be provided by public broadcasters than is currently available.

Communication Policy for Democracy

If our republican form of government is perishing because communications—the infrastructure of that republic—is under the yoke of international corporations, how, at last, do we save it?

First we must throw off our despair regarding the possibilities of a representative form of government. Our present commercial oligarchy is not a viable substitution. We must restore the pillars of our republic: freedom to participate in governing the community, political equality, and the recognition that factions will form, but must be balanced against other competing interests. Fundamental to this restoration is a fully funded mechanism to guarantee that all Americans have an equal opportunity to participate in political debate.

How do we get there? We must build a confrontational movement to reclaim our democracy, a movement committed to active and sustained protest against the present order. But we must do it while reaching out to all of those who care about democracy. Between 1998 and 2000, I helped to

were not doing a better job. Our work was not simply "educating" local leaders or persuading them about the importance of our ideas, it was to understand what they knew, to embrace their core concerns, and to find a legitimate way to connect their goals to our own.

3. Connect with groups that have already organized the community. There is a classic scene in many westerns, most notably *High Noon*, where the local sheriff is about to do battle with gunmen riding into town. Even though he does not belong to the congregation, he goes to the local church to ask for help. Media reformers must do the same thing—go to the people where they are already gathered. Our means of reaching local communities was through existing national organizations. We reached out to groups that had large constituencies and articulated our message by identifying how our goals fit their core interests. Unlike the sheriff in *High Noon*, those organizations, such as the National Council of Churches and the American Academy of Pediatrics, actively worked to help us and to connect us to their local chapters. Once again, as Alinsky wrote, "the organizer recognizes that each person or bloc has a hierarchy of values."[26] To that end we were able to recruit the National Organization for Women (NOW), the League of United Latin American Citizens (LULAC), and the National Association for the Advancement of Colored People (NAACP) because we adopted their concerns about the media images of women and minorities. We were able to engage the National Association of the Deaf and a dozen other disability rights groups because we embraced their concern about using technology to make media accessible to the sight- and hearing-impaired. We were able to engage the U.S. Catholic Conference because we heard and could respond to their concerns about the loss of air-time occupied by mainstream religious organizations to so-called televangelists willing to pay for program time with the results of their aggressive call for viewer donations. Our task was to craft a goal that would address all these needs and more. That goal became: to make local broadcasters more accountable to all the members of the community of license. Our reasoning was that if local broadcasters were truly accountable to the local public, and not just the local advertiser or the distant parent company or stockholder, then women and minorities and the disabled and religious leaders and others would be in a position to exert greater influence over the actions of those broadcasters.

4. The strategy must have an inside and an outside game. For media reform this means we needed to understand and embrace the necessity of operating both in and outside Washington. As Mike Pertschuk wrote in *The People Rising,* his book on the Bork campaign, "A Washington-centered

campaign on a contested national issue, cut off from a national constituency, was like a head with no body: all brains, no brawn. A grassroots campaign with no Washington base for intelligence gathering and strategic coordination was like a headless body; all brawn and heart, no brain."[27] Grassroots organizations, even those specifically concerned about media, would not have access to the intelligence or the levers of power in Washington where local broadcast obligations are decided.

A key part of our early strategy was to influence the Gore Commission. While we anticipated they would not arrive at recommendations as strong as we would like, we wanted to push them to address some of our concerns. After this we wanted to push the White House to transmit the Gore Commission Report to the FCC and emphasize those aspects of the report we favored. The next step was to get the FCC to initiate an inquiry into the public interest obligations of broadcasters and to follow that up with proposed rules. The final piece was to make certain we had allies in Congress who would support our actions at the FCC, or at least remain noncommittal and open to their constituents when the NAB went to them to block or threaten to block whatever action the FCC would take. Our grassroots activity in the states of Senators Hollings and McCain and Representatives Pelosi (San Francisco) and Maloney (New York) was vital to these efforts. My familiarity with the FCC and the White House, Ralph Neas's expertise on the ebb and flow of Congress, and our steering committee representatives from NOW, the NAACP, and especially former Senator Howard Metzenbaum, chair of the board of the Consumer Federation of America, informed our timing and allowed us to counter the professional lobbying of the NAB.

With as much expertise as we could bring to the inside game, representatives and policy makers from Ed Markey of Massachusetts to Susan Ness of the FCC wanted to know whether we had real people behind us, or whether we were just a paper coalition. We addressed this by bringing locally based organizers and a representative group of supporters to Washington to speak at the FCC and before the legislators who represented them, and we worked to bring legislators and FCC administrators to our supporters in the field.

5. Don't wait for events to unfold on their own. Pressure, pressure, pressure. We understood that we could not simply wait for the Gore Commission to issue its report and hope that the FCC would take it up. If we wanted events to work in a direction that would benefit us, we knew we needed to push. We were looking to advance our objectives, so a purely defensive posture would not work. We needed to apply pressure and to direct that pressure not at the government, but through the government at our true

opposition—the broadcasters. Alinsky again: "The major premise for tactics is the development of operations that will maintain a constant pressure upon the opposition."[28] Our goal was then to encourage all the different groups to adopt a common theme: "Broadcasters got millions of dollars worth of public property for free, the public should get something back in return." This message resonated extremely well with the public, and each group could emphasize something different, such as service to the disabled, or public service announcements, or programs for children, as long as they added public accountability. The goal was for broadcasters to feel the pressure from many quarters.

We were also prepared to accept a certain amount of dissonance within the coalition, and to stay alert to the opportunities that dissonance might create, in order to generate pressure. Alinsky wrote, "The tactic itself comes out of the free flow of action and reaction, and requires on the part of the organizer an easy acceptance of apparent disorganization."[29] We also learned this lesson from the alphabet soup of groups that is called the civil rights movement. Despite the romanticization that Dr. King alone led a group of people to establish voting rights and equal access to education and public accommodations, there were very real tensions and disagreements between the Southern Christian Leadership Conference, the NAACP, the Student Non-Violent Coordinating Committee, and others. All of these groups and individuals like Malcolm X and Thurgood Marshall played important roles in creating pressure on the infrastructure of apartheid in the United States. We embraced the different approaches to media reform, understanding that it generated pressure, pressure, and more pressure on the broadcasters.

6. Communication is a priority. Again drawing from Alinksy, we understood that "one can lack any of the qualities of an organizer—with one exception—and still be effective and successful. That exception is the art of communication."[30] The art of communication is much more than mere public relations or media relations. It is not just a matter of getting media to cover the campaign. That is, undoubtedly, a part of it, but it is also about getting the sort of attention you want, so that the public and your opposition see you and your issues the way you want to be seen. This is called framing. But framing must be strategic. That is, framing must look toward the core long-term goals, not just the short-term rush of publicity.

Too many of today's media reformers are content to discuss the arcane and fragmentary language of open platforms, broadband access, competitive local exchange carriers, and unbundled network elements (or worse,

UNEs and CLECs) and enjoy the clubby notices in equally arcane magazines read by corporate lawyers. Part of the challenge is to communicate more clearly with the public about the core issues of communications policy.

In addition, the art of communication must incorporate internal communication. When asked how he was able to keep the large and unwieldy coalition against Bork together, Ralph Neas, then executive director of the Leadership Conference, said, "Communicate, communicate, communicate. That's the only way to hold the coalition together."[31] Toward that end we had regular coalition meetings, held regular meetings among our organizers and lobbyists, sent out e-mail updates on the campaign, and hired reporters to cover our activity around the nation. We also made "the art of communication" a central part of our work. As Pertschuk wrote, "Though many of the most sophisticated lobbyists have known it for years, there will no longer be any doubt that media strategy must be an integral part of a campaign at all stages, and that it cannot be divorced or subordinated to the issues research, the lobbying, the grassroots organizing, or any other aspect of the campaign."[32]

7. Research is key. We took not only message and public opinion research seriously, we took seriously our obligation to research the activity of our opposition. As Pertschuk wrote, "The coalition's research and analytic efforts [give] intellectual legitimacy and weight to their campaign. By establishing a role as authoritative information resource to [Congress] and the media, the coalition gain[s] access, credibility, and standing."[33] Our research entailed not only public opinion polling, but academic papers presenting economic and social analysis, legal research and analysis, and grassroots research involving the inspection of dozens of television stations' public files. This work not only impressed legislators, the media, and the FCC, it energized and strengthened our coalition partners and supporters. When speaking to reporters or testifying, our members talked not only about what they thought but what they experienced directly.

8. Establish a broad base of funding and never stop raising money. This is perhaps where we were weakest. Despite the million and a half dollars we were able to raise from the Open Society Institute (OSI), and the additional half-million combined from the MacArthur, List, and the Ford foundations, we were never able to raise the funds we needed to hold on to staff or accomplish some of our most important goals. The donation of my time and the time of many of the people and organizations that joined us, was simply not enough. We were far more optimistic than we had any right to be about raising substantial funds from foundations other than OSI, and

276 · RECLAIMING OUR REPUBLIC

OSI was simply, and understandably, unwilling to bear the burden alone. While List put in an extraordinary amount of money as compared to the size of its budget, no other foundation really supported our work. Frankly, we relied on mainstream foundations, such as Ford and Rockefeller and Carnegie, and they simply didn't come through. We didn't devote enough attention to generating additional revenue through public fundraising campaigns. Alinsky is right that people are a source of power, but without adequate funds organizing people effectively cannot be accomplished.

9. Find allies in power. Finally, and where we were perhaps strongest, it's good to have an ally in a position of real power among policy makers. If civil rights leaders such as King had the Kennedys and Johnson, and the anti-Bork campaign had Ted Kennedy, our main ally was Bill Kennard. We met early on with Commissioner Gloria Tristani, and right out of the gate she said, "Where have you people been? You don't need to convince me, convince the chairman, he can move this." Chairman Kennard expressed reservations about our ability to organize the people we needed (so did Commissioner Ness), but he and his Chief Counsel Kathryn Brown gave us time and attention, meeting with members of the steering group in and outside Washington. And ultimately Kennard embraced and promoted the key goals of our campaign. He kept every promise he made to us, and once he was on board we were assured of winning important advances to make local broadcasters more accountable to the local communities they were licensed to serve.

Then the Supreme Court stopped the vote count in Florida and handed the White House to George Bush and the FCC to the right wing.

If there is a tenth lesson, it is a hard lesson that my friend Jack Willis always sought to reinforce. Real change occurs in the long haul. When it comes it will not look like change at all because it has been so gradual. Pushing is essential. Pushing today for change today is good, keep it up. But don't lose hope, don't let your fundamental optimism fade because you can't see all the progress you've made. We did not get the vote we wanted at the FCC when Michael Powell was named chairman, but we energized and engaged hundreds of thousands of Americans in a continuing battle many did not even know was taking place. Those citizens continue to speak and to counter the Bush FCC and the international corporations that influence it.

A Small Proposal

What I propose here is only a general outline of a plan, a continuation of the democratic experiment. Like the Constitution, the details of any plan to reform democracy should be subject to intense public debate. It would be inconsistent to argue that our democracy needs the active participation of community groups without proposing firsthand that community groups participate in the formation of any plan to promote our common interest in their engagement. All Americans, even corporate interests, should participate in this debate, but if it is to succeed it will require a dedicated few to keep it alive and moving toward resolution and action. This debate is the first step of the plan. Restoring the government's responsibility to ensure that all Americans have the ability to participate in the public debate should be the subject of a national conversation. Presidential candidates, in fact, anyone running for local, state, or federal office, any jurist seeking appointment to the bench, should be pushed to declare where they stand on this issue.

Here are some specific important steps:

1. End the federal subsidy of commercial media, particularly cable and broadcast television. As discussed earlier, federal protection of the cable industry by its preemption of the contract negotiations of local communities amounts to a federal subsidy of the national cable television industry. In the absence of this subsidy, local communities would be in a position to negotiate services, customer charges, and public access fees from those cable operations using public property to provide cable service to homes in the local communities. The current arrangement clearly puts the prerogatives of commerce before establishing a place of democratic deliberation. Local representatives should be able to negotiate fair fees, and if they cannot, the local citizens can vote them out of office.

The rationale of the broadcast public trustee is completely bankrupt. Local radio and television broadcasters do not consider themselves public trustees. The public does not consider them trustees. The FCC holds broadcasters to no trustee obligation of responsibility commensurate to their power over either the local debate or the national debate. There is no enforced obligation that might be balanced against the local broadcasters' responsibility to their stockholders or private owners to operate a profitable business. Broadcasters should pay for the great privilege of a federally protected license to operate a business by using the publicly owned spectrum. Just as coal miners or cattle grazers or anyone else who uses the public property has to pay for the privilege, broadcasters should pay.

Federal cable "must carry" obligations should apply only to public broadcasters.

In addition, the current allowable deduction on advertising should be progressively limited. For example, advertising expenses below $5,000 should be fully deductible, expenses between $5,000 and $15,000 should be deductible up to 75 percent, and so on. The additional revenue realized from this limitation and spectrum fees should be earmarked to support citizen communication.

2. The Corporation for Public Broadcasting (CPB) must be reformed along democratic lines and funded at a substantial level. The CPB board should be elected, eight members representing eight regions of the country (New England, Mid-Atlantic, Southeast, Midwest, Plains States, Southwest, Mountain States, and the Pacific Coast) and the chairman appointed by the president, with the advice and consent of the Senate. This body should appoint an executive director, responsible for submitting a budget and funding both national and regional production and distribution operations. The leadership of local public broadcasters should be determined in an equally democratic manner.

Federal and regional broadcast operations and local stations should be funded at levels commensurate with or above those spending levels at which commercial operations are funded. This funding should come from license fees charged to commercial broadcasters. Funding should not come from congressional appropriations. Sponsorship should be prohibited at all public broadcasters.

Local public broadcasters and regional and national communications operations should be required to encourage and broadcast diverse views and programs. These programs should include coverage of all local, state, and federal government meetings, as well as daily news and public issues programming. In addition, educational programs for children and adults, and diverse, independent personal and cultural expression should be encouraged. Local radio and television public broadcasters should be required to work closely with local libraries, community centers, cable public access operations, public schools (K through college), and governments to train and educate citizens on how to use and interpret media. Public broadcasters should be required to ascertain local community interests on a quarterly basis.

Spectrum allocations should be established that create clear preferences for public broadcasters ensuring that regional, local, and neighborhood communities are well served.

3. The FCC should be fully funded with regulatory fees from broadcast, cable, satellite, and telecommunications companies. The FCC should be staffed at regional offices, matching those CPB regions, at levels sufficient to monitor and enforce communication regulation. Clear federal regulations over commercial broadcast and cable programs regarding political advertising and commentary, educational programs for children, the number of

commercials, ratings and information about programs before they are broadcast, and the accessibility of services to the disabled should be established and widely promoted.

4. Universal service support provided by all commercial telecommunications providers (whether they are classified as information services or not) to fund access to advanced telecommunications services should be expanded to include all nonprofit organizations, including higher-level academic and vocational schools, community centers, and 501(c)(3) organizations unaffiliated with either business or government. Municipal ownership, if not operation, of all telecommunications services should be encouraged to compete with commercial providers, with a focus on providing a wide variety of e-government services, especially public safety, legal, and health care services.

5. Postal subsidies should be fully restored to small independent nonprofit presses. Postal subsidies should be reduced for commercial and business press operations. The postal service should be returned to congressional control with the central mission of ensuring that all Americans have access to the post.

6. Public secondary schools should be required to include civics and media literacy as part of their core curriculum. Testing on civic, media, and computer literacy should be required and national standards set. No student should be allowed to graduate who cannot explain the structure of U.S. government and how local, state, and federal representative or appointed officials come to be in office and decide public policy.

* * *

The goal of these proposals is to return communications to a central place in our government, providing full access to citizens and establishing democratic mechanisms of oversight. Imagine the possibilities for civic debate if such a system were in place. The current wrangling over what to do about the future security of the social security system might be informed by the American Association of Retired Persons (AARP) working in conjunction with community senior centers. Working through the national and mid-Atlantic CPB, AARP, and a local senior service center could produce reports, or mini-documentaries, or even mini-dramas examining certain proposals on strengthening social security and the potential human impact of these proposals. Full-length interviews derived from these programs could be made accessible in text or video form on the Internet. The documentaries could be followed by town hall meetings conducted in communities across the country and broadcast around the nation. Experts might be asked to attempt to meld the different approaches together and then present them to the public. Where common ground cannot be found, debates could be held, and designated citizens could vote on which proposal seems best. All programs and Internet activity would be available in all languages spoken in the broadcast area and made accessible to the disabled. All of these programs and the related Internet activity could be promoted across all media platforms, including commercial and print media. Now imagine political candidates talking about social security in front of citizens exposed to such programming.

None of these ideas are new. Barber points to many examples of media being used to spur civic discussion, most notably a project sponsored by the federal government (through the National Science Foundation) and developed by New York University to use the cable system in Reading, Pennsylvania, to establish an interactive communications network for senior citizens, featuring public meetings on interactive cable. The results were increased political participation.[34] The Benton Foundation created an exciting project called Debate America, pulling together local leaders and providing them the opportunity to conduct moderated debates supported by substantial background information on the Internet. Successful deliberations of public policy occurred in Pittsburgh and Seattle; unfortunately a weak foundation community failed to support this effort. Imagine this effort being supported by the CPB.

Many years ago, Norman Lear produced a public affairs program for local television called "The Baxters." A typically squabbling Lear family (think: a younger, more middle-class version of Archie Bunker's family) would confront, but not resolve, issues as diverse as marital rape and nuclear power. I, and hundreds of other talk show hosts and producers across the country, would conduct a discussion program following the drama. The discussion was usually held with a studio audience, or with a group of local "experts," and then edited into a half-hour program. Occasionally the program was followed by live town meetings; several of my "The Baxters" programs in Toledo, Ohio, featured not only live studio audiences (with elected representatives present), but audiences gathered in local malls, and people who called in questions, demonstrating the power of engaging and informative public discussion.

Again, let me stress that the goal should be to equalize democratic deliberation. The goal is not to punish commercial telecommunications or broadcast operations. The goal is only to allow citizens and community groups the same ability as major corporations or government to communicate their messages and concerns *across* those electronic media platforms that have become our new public sphere. The above proposal to support an independent public broadcasting system could also support the work of direct service groups by allowing them to produce and distribute over public broadcast and cable access operations educational programs and public service announcements. For example, instead of a senior center limiting educational sessions on exercise or nutrition or new pharmaceutical products to the few people able to attend classes, these classes could be recorded and provided on demand through web casts. Teen centers might be able to produce programs on drug abuse or the dangers of unprotected sex that could be used by counselors in local schools or community centers and accessed via the Internet.

Community groups could also be encouraged to use their new communications capability in partnership with others, to strengthen community across narrow interests. For example senior centers and teen centers might work together to address the problems of elderly shut-ins or teens who might benefit from mentoring programs with seniors, perhaps via wireless communications systems over a local public broadcasting station's datacasting service. Indeed teens might be able to use broadband communications systems to communicate voice, picture, and data regularly to seniors about the conditions of the local schools and why their support is necessary for a school bond initiative. Perhaps most important, if community groups come to develop close working relationships with local public broadcasters, both broadcaster and association become partners helping to bind a strong community through the preservation and promotion of a true public square. The exciting merging technologies of computer and television provide a chance to restore civic associations to a prominent place in our civil system, but only if they have the funds to participate effectively.

The media tools are available to create a true public square across communications platforms and technologies. An electronic commons is possible, open to government, corporate interests, and community associations, closed to no one on the grounds that they cannot afford to participate effectively in the public debate. What is missing is the political will.

Conclusion

I have tried to show that access to information and opportunity for voice are instrumental to democratic deliberation and that our republic was designed to balance a complex set of factions, including conflicting economic systems, citizen associations, and governments, to protect and advance political equality among citizens. A core element of this balancing act was to put the responsibility for citizen deliberation in the hands of the federal government, the only body where all those factions could be balanced against each other. I have argued that the deep appreciation for the importance of, and public support for, communications was lost on Jacksonian Democrats. This resulted in the abandonment of the national telegraph to private commercial interests, and that the resultant advantage to the northern business interests was exacerbated in the Gilded Age by ruthless capitalists. Neither the early Progressive Era, New Deal, nor the Great Society reforms have corrected the damage done in this period to the structure of our republic. Indeed, the control passed from what Lincoln called capital to national trusts, to international conglomerations that have tightened their control over public discourse through new communications technologies. I have argued that our democracy would be improved if we would create policies to restore the deliberating citizen to the center of our republic.

If I have been hard on private industry, it is not because I do not appreciate the great benefits that faction brings to society. I believe that we can have, indeed that we need, a largely unrestricted commercial media. What I argue here is that what we most need is a vital and competitive alternative, driven by neither business interests nor government. We have the former. We do not have the latter. Our democracy suffers as a result. Indeed, if it is the farce Madison feared, it can hardly be called a democracy.

The values of equal citizen deliberation are deeply rooted in our insistence about what it means to be American. If we fail to live in the republic of our hopes, it is not because we have stopped hoping.

Amartya Sen is a Nobel-winning economist barely heard above the clamor of more popular economists who believe in markets as if on a holy war. In a recent series of essays on *Development as Freedom,* Sen argues for the importance of democracy, and for the need to continually find ways to make it work well . . . including encouraging the participation of "organized opposition groups." Among the freedoms he cites as necessary to development, even development in the United States, is "the liberty of acting as citizens who matter and whose voices count, rather than living as well-fed, well-clothed, and well-entertained vassals."[35]

If we do not put our new communications technologies to the purpose of revitalizing our democracy, the fault lies not in our machines. The American experiment in democracy requires our engagement in restoring our republic and the obligation to restore the founders' commitment to the equal communications capacity of all our citizens.

Notes

Introduction

1. Remarks by FCC Chairman William E. Kennard, *What Does $70 Billion Buy You Anyway?—Rethinking Public Interest Requirements at the Dawn of the Digital Age,* October 5, 2000, at http://ftp.fcc.gov/Speeches/Kennard/2000/spwek023.html.

2. Notice of Proposed Rule Making, *In the Matter of Standardized and Enhanced Disclosure Requirements for Television Broadcast Licensee Public Interest Obligations,* MM Docket No. 00–168, adopted September 14, 2000, Federal Communications Commission at www.fcc.gov/Bureaus/Mass_Media/Notices/2000/fcc00345.txt.

3. See Mike Snider, "FCC Urged to Make Broadcasters Do Better," *USA Today,* May 3, 1999.

4. Remarks by FCC Chairman William E. Kennard.

5. 47 U.S.C° 336 (a); see also Gigi B. Sohn and Andrew Jay Schwartzman, "Pretty Pictures or Pretty Profits: Issues and Options for the Public Interest and Nonprofit Communities in the Digital Broadcasting Debate, October 1995," at www.benton.org/publibrary/prettypics/working13.html.

6. 47 U.S.C° 336 (a).

7. 47 U.S.C° 336 (d) (emphasis added).

8. People for Better TV Comments, at http://ftp.fcc.gov/cgb/dro/comments/99360/5006314434.txt.

9. *FCC Begins Proceeding to Seek Comment on Public Interest Obligations of Television Broadcasters as They Transition to Digital Transmission Technology,* December 15, 1999, at http://ftp.fcc.gov/Bureaus/Mass_Media/News_Releases/1999/nrmm9030.html.

10. What the Public Knows about HDTV, at www.roper.com/news/content/news96.htm.

11. See Joel Brinkley, *Defining Vision: How Broadcasters Lured the Government into Inciting a Revolution in Television* (New York: Harcourt Brace & Co., 1997) for the story of the development of digital television.

12. See People for Better TV Comments, particularly the attached filing by the Consumer Federation of America.

13. Report to Congress on the Public Interest Obligations of Television Broadcasters as They Transition to Digital Television at www.fcc.gov/Speeches/Kennard/Statements/2001/stwek106.doc.

14. Gal Beckerman, "Tripping Up Big Media," *Columbia Journalism Review*, November–December 2003, at www.cjr.org/issues/2003/6/media-beckerman.asp.

15. Joyce Appleby, Lynn Hunt, and Margaret Jacob, "The Future of History," in *Pragmatism: A Reader,* ed. Louis Menand (New York: Vintage Books, 1997), p. 466.

16. See especially Statement of Commissioner Michael J. Copps, dissenting Re: 2002 Biennial Regulatory Review—Review of the Commission's Broadcast Ownership Rules and Other Rules Adopted Pursuant to Section 202 of the Telecommunications Act of 1996 at http://hraunfoss.fcc.gov/edocs_public/attachmatch/DOC-235047A9.doc.

Chapter 1. The Challenge of American Democracy

Note to Epigraph: Gaillard Hunt, ed., *The Writings of James Madison,* vol. IX: *1819–1836* (New York: G. P. Putnam's Sons, 1910), p. 103. James Madison wrote this much-repeated quotation in a letter to a W. T. Barry on August 4, 1822. The letter was in response to a "Circular" Barry had sent him on the appropriations the Kentucky legislature made in support of a state system of education. Given the context, it is likely that when Madison mentioned "popular information" here he was referring to the sort of information students were likely to receive at school, as distinct from the information citizens would exchange in the press or town halls. Still, the quote has taken on a much larger life and meaning, not unlike the famous quote from the Declaration of Independence "all men are created equal." It is this larger sense of popular information that I refer to throughout this book. With all apologies to Madison scholars, my reading of Madison suggests he would not mind the liberties others and I have taken with this quote.

1. As with the major title, I borrow the word *experiment* from Madison. "I can see no danger in submitting to practice an experiment which seems to be founded on the best theoretic principles," Madison declared in defending the new Constitution before the Virginia Ratifying Convention. See also Hunt, *The Writings of James Madison,* vol. V, p. 197; also cited in Neal Riemer, *The Democratic Experiment: American Political Theory* (Princeton: Van Nostrand, 1967), p. 14. Madison also refers to "the experiment of an extended republic" in No. 14 of *The Federalist Papers* (New York: Mentor, 1961), p. 104. Unlike Madison, I do not insist upon a distinction between a republic and a democracy. I take a modern democracy to be representative, and thus a state Madison would likely consider to be a republic.

2. One of the best of these is E. J. Dionne Jr., *Why Americans Hate Politics* (New York: Simon & Schuster, 1991).

3. See Craig Calhoun, ed., *Habermas and the Public Sphere* (Cambridge, Mass.: MIT Press, 1992); and Jürgen Habermas, *The Structural Transformation of the Public Sphere: An Inquiry into a Category of Bourgeois Society,* trans. Thomas Burger (Cambridge, Mass.: MIT Press, 1989). Even the otherwise hardheaded Michael Schudson finds it necessary to tie his analysis of American civic life into the tortured framework of this German intellectual.

4. See Michel Foucault, *The Archaeology of Knowledge* (New York: Pantheon, 1972); and Samantha Ashenden and David Owen, *Foucault Contra Habermas* (London: Sage, 1999). Do Europeans spend as much time wrestling with Richard Rorty and Cornel West?

5. Habermas's public sphere is slightly different. His tends to refer to "the critical reasoning of private persons on political issues." See Habermas, *Structural Transformation,* pp. 27–31, quote from p. 29. While I would wish for critical reasoning, I would settle for a reasonably informed discussion. Not to put too fine a point on it, much of what Habermas writes about abstractly, I hope to write about concretely in historical context. For example, Habermas writes: "When the laws of the market governing the sphere of commodity exchange and of social labor also pervaded the sphere reserved for private people as a public, rational-critical debate had a tendency to be replaced by consumption, and the web of public communication unraveled into acts of individuated reception, however uniform in mode" (p. 161). And that is the translation. Perhaps the original German is not so passive and gives us a better clue about who or what forces directed economic laws to dominate the political realm. Still, this point is central to the story I mean to tell, and in a fashion I hope the reader will find more accessible. Habermas's public sphere is a useful model, but it is, I think, more restrictive than the model I have in mind.

6. James W. Carey, *Communication as Culture: Essays on Media and Society* (Boston: Unwin Hyman, 1989).

7. See Cass Sunstein, *Democracy and the Problem of Free Speech* (New York: The Free Press, 1995), pp. xvi–xviii. Compare especially the Habermas quote in the above note and Sunstein's discussion of the problem of political discourse vis-à-vis consumer sovereignty at pp. 71–72.

8. Ibid., pp. xvi–xvii, citing James Madison, "Report of 1800," January 7, 1800, from David Mattern, ed., *Papers of James Madison,* vol. 17 (Charlottesville: University Press of Virginia, 1991), pp. 346, 344, 341.

9. Paul Starr, *The Creation of the Media* (New York: Basic Books, 2004).

10. Michael J. Sandel, *Democracy's Discontent: America in Search of a Public Philosophy* (Cambridge, Mass.: Belknap Press/Harvard University Press, 1996).

11. Stephen L. Carter, *Civility: Manners, Morals, and the Etiquette of Democracy* (New York: Basic Books, 1998).

12. William J. Bennett, *Moral Compass: Stories for a Life's Journey* (New York: Simon & Schuster, 1995). Bennett's observations may be a bit devalued since the revelations about his gambling.

13. Robert D. Putnam, *Bowling Alone: The Collapse and Revival of American Community* (New York: Simon & Schuster, 2000).

14. Michael Schudson, *The Good Citizen: A History of American Civic Life* (Cambridge, Mass.: Harvard University Press, 1998). While agreeing with much of what Schudson argues, I am discomforted by the fact that he seems resigned to the present status quo. This resignation is particularly apparent in his notion of "monitorial citizens." His invitation to "picture parents watching small children at the community pool" fills me with dread. I see too many distracted parents, too many parents too busy to do anything but drop their children off at the pool. Distracted and absent "parents" are not entirely able to keep "an eye on the scene" of even well-behaved children, much less contested rights. To borrow his metaphor, I like the idea of a lifeguard on duty, though the involved parent is ideal. I am not certain disengaged, uninformed, or badly informed "monitorial citizens" can even see the scene.

Schudson applauds the heroics of Rosa Parks and Martin Luther King, but then warps their efforts into a "rights-based" grievance not essentially different than a demand for a welfare check. I am unconvinced that King or the countless, nameless others who sacrificed themselves in the civil rights movement were animated by such a crabbed dream. King reminded America of its higher ideals of liberty and equality and called upon all of us to rise up, to join together to make those noble ideals real. King and Chavez and Friedan and so many other Americans were insisting upon the deeply rooted American ideal of equal treatment before the law, of freedom to participate in governance. They had the temerity, the "audacity" as King would say, to believe, to insist that they *were* the sovereign people referred to by the Constitution and the Declaration of Independence. Even though they knew the founders thought otherwise two hundred years ago.

Schudson acknowledges our clear failure to stem an increase in inequality, to provide health care and a range of other "rights" similar industrial communities take for granted, but he fails to suggest how mere monitoring can address these failures. I think King and the other leaders of the wide range of moments to improve America in the 1950s and 1960s would urge us to stop monitoring and get involved in creating concrete solutions. Schudson's sunny redefinition of the modern citizen as a monitor of rights fails to wrestle with the problem of how the monitor is informed.

15. Ibid., p. 313.

16. Henry Milner, *Civic Literacy* (Hanover: Tufts University Press, 2002) details the studies examining the political ignorance of U.S. citizens and provides an exceptional comparative analysis of other democracies where citizens seem to have a better grasp of their government. Thanks to Nolan Bowie for recommending Milner.

17. William Greider, *Who Will Tell the People? The Betrayal of American Democracy* (New York: Simon & Schuster, 1992).

18. Ibid., p. 424.

19. Garry Wills, *A Necessary Evil: A History of American Distrust of Government* (New York: Simon & Schuster, 1999).

20. I use the term *founders* as a shorthand for those men who gathered in Philadelphia in 1787 to write the Constitution, but I also include John Adams, Thomas Jefferson, John Marshall, Thomas Paine, Benjamin Rush, and others who strongly influenced the debate at the time of the drafting of the Constitution and helped set in motion the laws that would shape the early operation of the newborn republic.

21. Cass R. Sunstein, *Designing Democracy: What Constitutions Do* (New York: Oxford University Press, 2001).

22. Richard Reeves, *American Journey: Traveling with Tocqueville in Search of Democracy in America* (New York: Simon & Schuster, 1982), p. 244.

23. As documented in Edwin Burrows and Mike Wallace's tome on the history of New York, *Gotham,* while the petitions of aristocrat merchants to the British government for repeal of the Stamp Act were ignored, others from different classes met in taverns and coffee houses, posted notices for meetings, and gathered in public commons to share information and exhort each other to boycotts of British goods. Often looked down upon as a common mob, these different classes ranged from the middle-class privateers (government-sanctioned pirates who plundered the ships of enemy nations), artisans, apprentices, and laborers who made up the Sons of Liberty, to the more destitute poor, including tenant farmers and slaves. These associations of the working class and the poor demanded far more radical remedies than those pursued by the merchant/aristocrats of early New York.—remedies that led eventually to revolution and the nation's founding. Edwin G. Burrows and Mike Wallace, *Gotham: A History of New York City to 1898* (New York: Oxford University Press, 1999), p. 191.

24. Harold A. Innis, *Empire & Communications* (Victoria, British Columbia: Press Porcépic, 1986).

25. Carey, *Communication as Culture: Essays on Media and Society,* p. 206.

26. Putnam argues that it is not simply television that encourages a decline in community activity; it is television entertainment programs. Television news and public affairs, on the other hand, encourage civic engagement. Putnam, *Bowling Alone,* pp. 220–46.

27. "Americans now cite it [the First Amendment] not to begin discussion of the public interest, but as a reason to *close* it." Newton N. Minow and Craig L. Lamay, *Abandoned in the Wasteland: Children, Television, and the First Amendment* (New York: Hill & Wang, 1995), p. 107.

28. Harold A. Innis, *Bias of Communications* (Toronto: University of Toronto Press, 1964), p. 139.

29. Ithiel de Sola Pool, *Technologies of Freedom: On Free Speech in an Electronic Age* (Cambridge, Mass.: Harvard University Press, 1983).

30. Howard Zinn, *A People's History of the United States, 1492–Present* (New York: HarperCollins, 1999).

31. Sandel, *Democracy's Discontent*, pp. 79–81.

32. Sunstein, *Democracy and the Problem of Free Speech*, pp. 1–16.

Chapter 2. The Role of Communications in the Democratic Experiment

Note to Epigraph: Alexander Hamilton et al., *The Federalist Papers*, "No. 1" (New York: Mentor, 1961), p. 33.

1. Bernard Bailyn, *The Ideological Origins of the American Revolution* (Cambridge, Mass.: Belknap Press/Harvard University Press, 1967)

2. To be clear, my emphasis on the founders is not at all to suggest that the work of the delegates in the hot summer of 1787 was perfect. Along with a long line of others I think the Declaration of Independence embodies a superior set of principles, and both the first set of amendments (which we call the Bill of Rights) and the Civil War amendments were a substantial improvement of the Constitution as drafted by the founders. The point is only to understand the mechanisms created by the men who set up our democratic system and, more precisely, to understand their decisions regarding communications as central to democracy.

3. John Milton, *Areopagitica: Freedom of the Press* (New York: Bandanna Books, 1990).

4. John Locke, *Second Treatise of Civil Government* (New York: Prometheus, 1986); see also H. Nelson and D. Teeter, *Law of Mass Communications* (New York: Foundation Press, 1973).

5. As Cass Sunstein notes in *Democracy and the Problem of Free Speech* (New York: The Free Press, 1995), p. xii, "read in the light of history" the term *abridgement* is not as clear as it may seem regarding the prohibitions imposed on the federal government.

6. A. J. Liebling, *The Wayward Pressman* (Garden City, N.Y.: Doubleday & Co., 1947).

7. Roger Wilkins, *Jefferson's Pillow* (Boston: Beacon, 2001).

8. Bailyn, *Ideological Origins*, p. 27.

9. Jean-Jacques Rousseau, *The Social Contract and The First and Second Discourses* (New Haven: Yale University Press, 2002), p. 123.

10. Ibid., p. 136.

11. Bailyn, *Ideological Origins*, p. 27.

12. Connor Cruise O'Brien, "Rousseau, Robespierre, Burke, Jefferson, and the French Revolution," in Rousseau, *The Social Contract*, p. 306.

13. *Federalist Papers*, see especially Hamilton's contribution "No. 9," pp. 73–76, and Madison's "No. 47," pp. 301–3.

14. Albert O. Hirschman, *The Passions and the Interests* (Princeton: Princeton University Press, 1977), pp. 20–27.

15. *Federalist Papers*, p. 72.

16. Ibid., p. 77.

17. Ibid., p. 79.

18. Paul Finkelman, "James Madison and the Bill of Rights: A Reluctant Paternity," *Supreme Court Review* (1990).

19. Jules Witcover, *Party of the People: A History of the Democrats* (New York: Random House, 2003), p. 5. Though many commentators consider the National Republicans and the Federalists to be the first parties, led by Jefferson and Hamilton, respectively, my readings suggest a much more complex and shifting situation. First of all, the word *Democrat* was often used as an epithet by Federalists to hurl at the Jeffersonian Republicans. It was not until the day of Jackson that the term *Democrat* was embraced. Second, while Jefferson provided both intellectual and financial assistance to establishing an opposing party to Hamilton, his nemesis in the Washington cabinet, it was Madison who did much of the heavy lifting, particularly in pulling the querulous members of Congress into line.

20. John Zvesper, "The Madisonian Systems," *Western Political Quarterly* 37 (1984): 236–55.

21. See especially Ralph Louis Ketcham, *James Madison: A Biography*, reprint (Charlottesville: University Press of Virginia, 1990); and Jack N. Rakove, *James Madison and the Creation of the American Republic* (New York: Longman, 2002).

22. Samuel Kernell, ed., *James Madison: The Theory and Practice of Republican Government* (Stanford, Calif.: Stanford University Press, 2003).

23. Lance Banning, *The Sacred Fire of Liberty: James Madison and the Founding of the Federal Republic* (Ithaca: Cornell University Press, 1995), pp. 200–201.

24. Richard R. John, *Spreading the News: The American Postal System from Franklin to Morse* (Cambridge, Mass.: Harvard University Press, 1995), pp. 62–63.

25. Sunstein, *Democracy and the Problem of Free Speech*, pp. 18–23.

26. Banning, *The Sacred Fire of Liberty*, p. 227, note 115.

27. Richard R. John and Christopher J. Young, "Rites of Passage, Postal Petitioning as a Tool of Governance in the Age of Federalism," in *The House and Senate in the 1790s: Petitioning, Lobbying, and Institutional Development*, ed. Kenneth R. Bowling and Donald R. Kennon (Athens: Ohio University Press, 2002), pp. 127–28.

28. John, *Spreading the News*, p. 30.

29. Gouverneur Morris also prepared the final draft of the Constitution.

30. John, *Spreading the News*, p. 26.

31. Ibid., p. 27.

32. Ibid., pp. 27–28.

33. John, "Rites of Passage," p. 129.

34. John, *Spreading the News*, p. 25.

35. Ibid., p. 60.

36. James Madison, "Public Opinion," in *James Madison, Writings*, ed. Jack N. Rakove (New York: The Library of America, 1999), pp. 500–501; see also John, *Spreading the News*, pp. 60–61.

37. James Madison, "January 9, 1792," in Congress, *The Papers of James Madison*, ed. Robert A. Rutland et al. (Charlottesville: University Press of Virginia, 1984), vol. 14, p. 186.

38. John, *Spreading the News*, pp. 37–39.

39. Ibid., pp. 47–48, citing Hamilton to Washington, January 31, 1795, in Harold C. Syrett, ed., *Papers of Alexander Hamilton* (New York: Columbia University Press, 1961–87), vol. 18, p. 239.

40. John, *Spreading the News*, p. 131.

41. Ibid., p. 110.

42. Ibid., p. 51.

43. Theda Skocpol, "The Tocqueville Problem," *Social Science History* (Winter 1997).

44. John, *Spreading the News*, pp. 1–24.

45. Ibid., p. 37.

46. Alexis de Tocqueville, *Democracy in America*, vol. 1 (New York: Vintage, 1990), p. 183. Ithiel de Sola Pool's surprise that Tocqueville did not dwell on the First Amendment seems odd when one looks at the pages Tocqueville devotes to liberty of the press and association and religion—covering the ground of the First Amendment fairly thoroughly. See Ithiel de Sola Pool, *Technologies of Freedom* (Cambridge, Mass.: Harvard University Press, 1983), p. 4. Tocqueville viewed liberty of the press not merely as a legal structure, but as essential to democracy and deeply embedded in American normative values.

47. John, *Spreading the News*, p. 42.

48. Tocqueville, *Democracy in America*, vol. 2, p. 112.

49. Benjamin R. Barber, *A Passion for Democracy*, (Princeton: Princeton University Press, 1998), p. 47.

50. Tocqueville, *Democracy in America*, vol. 1, p. 70.

51. Ibid., p. 405 note.

52. John, *Spreading the News*, pp. 4–5.

53. Ibid., pp. 3–5.

54. Ibid., p. 79.

55. Wayne E. Fuller, *The American Mail: Enlarger of the Common Life* (Chicago: University of Chicago Press, 1972), p. 332.

56. John, *Spreading the News*, p. 297, note 93.

57. Ibid., p. 48.

58. Kevin Phillips, *Wealth and Democracy: A Political History of the American Rich* (New York: Broadway, 2002).

59. Charles Austin Beard, *An Economic Interpretation of the Constitution of the United States* (New York: Macmillan, 1952).

60. Hirschman, *The Passions and the Interests*, p. 60.

61. Burrows and Wallace, *Gotham*, pp. 219–21.

62. Hirschman, *The Passions and the Interests*, p. 59.

63. Adam Smith, *The Wealth of Nations* (London: Penguin Classics, 1986), p. 80. See also Amartya Sen, *Development as Freedom* (New York: Knopf, 1999), pp. 123, 255 for an excellent discussion of Smith on private commercial interests.

64. Tocqueville, *Democracy in America,* vol. 2, p. 311.

65. Merrill D. Peterson, ed., *Thomas Jefferson Writings,* "Letter to John Norvell, Washington, June 14, 1807" (New York: The Library of America, 1984), p. 1176.

66. Jean M. Yarbrough, *American Virtues: Thomas Jefferson on the Character of a Free People* (Lawrence: University Press of Kansas, 1998), pp. 55–101.

67. It is important to note that private delivery services carried letters within cities, and between large urban centers such as Boston and Philadelphia. See Irving Fang, *A History of Mass Communications* (Boston: Focal, 1997), p. 30. See also *United States v. Bromley*, 12 Howard 88, 13 L. Ed. 905 (1851).

68. John, *Spreading the News,* pp. 39–40.

69. Ibid., pp. 7–8.

70. Ibid., p. 62.

Chapter 3. The Break: The Telegraph from Jackson to Hayes (1830–1876)

Note to Epigraph: Wayne E. Fuller, *The American Mail: Enlarger of the Common Life* (Chicago: University of Chicago Press, 1972), pp. 173–74.

1. Richard Hofstadter, *The American Political Tradition and the Men Who Made It* (New York: Vintage Books, 1974), pp. 62–63.

2. A. J. Beitzinger, *A History of American Political Thought* (New York: Dodd, Mead, 1972), p. 319.

3. Brian Winston, *Media Technology and Society, A History: From the Telegraph to the Internet* (New York: Routledge, 1998), pp. 19–26.

4. I take the term *public philosophy* from Michael Sandel, which he describes as "the political theory implicit in our practice, the assumptions about citizenship and freedom that inform our public life." Michael Sandel, *Democracy's Discontent: America in Search of a Public Philosophy* (Cambridge, Mass.: Belknap Press/Harvard University Press, 1996), p. 4.

5. Richard E. Ellis, *The Union at Risk: Jacksonian Democracy, States' Rights, and the Nullification Crisis* (New York: Oxford University Press, 1987), p. 187.

6. Ronald P. Formisano, "Federalists and Republicans: Parties, Yes—Systems, No," in *The Evolution of American Electoral Systems,* ed. Paul Kleppner et al. (Westport, Conn.: Greenwood, 1981), pp. 33–76.

7. "Introduction," *United States Magazine and Democratic Review,* October 1837, reprinted in Joseph L. Blau, ed., *Social Theories of Jacksonian Democracy* (Indianapolis: Bobbs-Merrill, 1954), pp. 26–28.

8. Sandel, *Democracy's Discontent,* p. 157.

9. James D. Richardson, ed., *A Compilation of the Messages and Papers of the Presidents*, vol. II (New York: Bureau of National Literature, 1911), p. 590; see also Hofstadter, *The American Political Tradition*, pp 77–78.

10. Register of Debates, 21st Cong., 2nd sess., December 17, 1830, pp. 368–69.

11. Michael Schudson, *The Power of News* (Cambridge, Mass.: Harvard University Press, 1995), p. 43.

12. Richard John, *Spreading the News: The American Postal System from Franklin to Morse* (Cambridge, Mass.: Harvard University Press, 1995), pp. 206–56.

13. Ibid., p. 3.

14. Ibid., p. 51.

15. Ibid., p. 242.

16. Ibid., p. 248.

17. Ibid., p. 249.

18. Sandel, *Democracy's Discontent*, pp. 156–60.

19. For a full treatment of this period, see Ellis, *The Union at Risk*, especially pp. 63–80.

20. Sandel, *Democracy's Discontent*, p. 163.

21. Ibid., p. 161.

22. John, *Spreading the News*, p. 87.

23. Menahem Blondheim, *News over the Wires: The Telegraph and the Flow of Public Information in America, 1844–1897* (Cambridge, Mass.: Harvard University Press, 1994), pp. 34–36.

24. Gerald Cullinan, *The United States Postal Service* (New York: Praeger Publishers, 1973), pp. 68–69.

25. Fuller, *The American Mail*, p. 120.

26. Ibid., p. 174.

27. John, *Spreading the News*, p. 88.

28. Paul Starr, *The Creation of the Media: Political Origins of Modern Communications* (New York: Basic Books, 2004), pp. 163–65.

29. Ibid., p. 65.

30. 9 Stat. 587–88.

31. 9 Stat. 590.

32. Sandel, *Democracy's Discontent*, p. 158.

33. Ibid., p. 159.

34. Richardson, *Compilation*, p. 590.

35. "Pacific Telegraph Act of 1860," 36 Cong., 1 sess., Chapter 137, June 16, 1860.

36. Richard R. John, "Recasting the Information Infrastructure for the Industrial Age," in *A Nation Transformed by Information: How Information Has Shaped the United States from Colonial Times to the Present*, ed. Alfred D. Chandler and James W. Cortada (New York: Oxford University Press, 2000), p. 75.

37. Richard B. Du Boff, "Business Demand and the Development of the Telegraph in the United States, 1844–1860," *Business History Review* 54 (Winter 1980): 469–71.

38. Amy Friedlander, *Natural Monopoly and Universal Service: Telephones and Telegraphs in the U.S. Communications Infrastructure, 1837–1940* (Reston, Va.: Corporation for National Research Initiatives, 1995), pp. 15–16; see also Gerald W. Brock, *The Telecommunications Industry: The Dynamics of Market Structure* (Cambridge, Mass.: Harvard University Press, 1981), pp. 80–83.

39. Brock, *The Telecommunications Industry*, pp. 82–83.

40. Friedlander, *Natural Monopoly and Universal Service*, pp. 16–17.

41. *Walden & Other Writings of Henry David Thoreau* (New York: Modern Library Edition, 1937), p. 47.

42. John, *Spreading the News*, p. 39.

43. Alexis de Tocqueville, *Democracy in America*, vol. 1 (New York: Vintage Classics, 1990), p. 185.

44. Ibid., p. 186.

45. The General News Association of the City of New York was the official name of the New York Associated Press from 1856 to 1866. I use the terms Associated Press or AP to refer to the various incarnations of this organization.

46. Edwin G. Burrows and Mike Wallace, *Gotham: A History of New York City to 1898* (New York: Oxford University Press, 1999), pp. 676–79; see also Blondheim, *News over the Wires*, pp. 49–50.

47. Ithiel de Sola Pool, *Technologies of Freedom* (Cambridge, Mass.: Belknap Press/Harvard University Press, 1983), pp. 93–95.

48. Erik Barnouw, *A Tower in Babel: A History of Broadcasting in the United States, Volume I—to 1933* (New York: Oxford University Press, 1966), p. 254.

49. The Telegraph Act of 1866, July 24, 1866 (chap. 230, 14 Stat. at L. 221); see also *Western Union Tel. Co. v. City of Richmond*, 224 U.S. 160 (1912).

50. John, "Recasting the Information Infrastructure," p. 78.

51. A. Edward Evenson, *The Telephone Patent Conspiracy of 1876: The Elisha Gray–Alexander Bell Controversy and Its Many Players* (Jefferson, N.C: McFarland, 2001), pp. 19–21.

52. Ibid., pp. 20–21.

53. John, "Recasting the Information Infrastructure," p. 83.

54. Gardiner G. Hubbard, "The Proposed Changes in the Telegraph System," *North American Review* 117, issue 240 (July 1873). This document is made available on-line through the Making of America project, which makes accessible through digital technology a significant body of primary sources. The Library of Congress, Cornell University, and the University of Michigan are collaborators on this project. The *North American Review* can be found at http://memory.loc.gov/ammem/ndlpcoop/moahtml/title/nora.html.

55. Alvin F. Harlow, *Old Wires and New Wires* (New York: D. Appleton-Century, 1936), p. 336.

56. Blondheim, *News over the Wires*, pp. 177–84.

57. Ibid., p. 184.

Chapter 4. The Telephone and the Trusts (1876–1900)

Note to Epigraph: Henry Adams, *The Education of Henry Adams* (Boston: Houghton Mifflin, 1918), p. 254.

1. Abraham Lincoln, *Speeches and Writings 1859–1865,* "Address to the Wisconsin State Agricultural Society, Milwaukee, Wisconsin, September 30, 1859" (New York: Library of America, 1989), p. 197.

2. Ronald Takaki, *Iron Cages: Race and Culture in 19th-Century America,* rev. ed. (New York: Oxford University Press, 2000), pp. 5–15.

3. Full quote is "We may congratulate ourselves that this cruel war is nearing its end. It has cost a vast amount of treasure and blood. . . . It has indeed been a trying hour for the Republic; but I see in the near future a crisis approaching that unnerves me and causes me to tremble for the safety of my country. As a result of the war, corporations have been enthroned and an era of corruption in high places will follow, and the money power of the country will endeavor to prolong its reign by working upon the prejudices of the people until all wealth is aggregated in a few hands and the Republic is destroyed. I feel at this moment more anxiety for the safety of my country than ever before, even in the midst of war. God grant that my suspicions may prove groundless." The passage appears in a letter from Lincoln to (Col.) William F. Elkins, November 21, 1864. See Emanuel Hertz, *Abraham Lincoln: A New Portrait,* vol. 2 (New York: Horace Liveright Inc., 1931), p. 954; see also Archer H. Shaw, *The Lincoln Encyclopedia* (New York: Macmillan, 1950), p. 40. Acknowledgments to Rick Crawford, What Lincoln Foresaw: Corporations Being "Enthroned" After the Civil War and Re-Writing the Laws Defining Their Existence at www.ratical.com/corporations/Lincoln.html, visited on July 21, 2002.

4. Lincoln, "Annual Message to Congress, December 3, 1861," p. 296.

5. United States Summary, Table 4, Population: 1790 to 1990, United States Urban and Rural, see www.census.gov/population/censusdata/popctr.pdf, visited on July 21, 2002.

6. Richard R. John, "Recasting the Information Infrastructure for the Industrial Age," in *A Nation Transformed by Information: How Information Has Shaped the United States from Colonial Times to the Present,* ed. Alfred D. Chandler and James W. Cortada (New York: Oxford University Press, 2000), p. 81.

7. Richard Burket Kielbowicz, "Origins of the Second-Class Mail Category and the Business of Policymaking, 1863–1879," *Journalism Monographs* 96 (1986); see also Mail Classification Act of 1879, 20 Stat. 358, 43 Stat. 1067, 39 U.S.C. 221, 39 U.S.C.A. 221; and *Hannegan v. Esquire,* 327 U.S. 146 (1946).

8. Kevin Phillips, *Wealth and Democracy: A Political History of the American Rich* (New York: Broadway Books, 2002), p. 235.

9. Michael Schudson, *The Good Citizen: A History of Civic Life* (Cambridge, Mass.: Harvard University Press, 1998), p. 145.

10. Mark Twain and Charles Dudley Warner, *The Gilded Age: A Tale of Today* (New York: Penguin Books, 2001).

11. Samuel Clemens, *Mark Twain Speaking,* ed. Paul Fatout (Iowa City: University of Iowa Press, 1976), pp. 74–76 ("After Dinner Speech," Meeting of Americans, London, England, July 4, 1873).

12. Schudson, *The Good Citizen,* pp. 146–60.

13. Michael Sandel, *Democracy's Discontent: America in Search of a Public Philosophy* (Cambridge, Mass.: Belknap Press/Harvard University Press, 1996), p. 186.

14. Robert Wiebe, *The Search for Order, 1877–1920* (New York: Hill and Wang, 1967), p. 66.

15. See A. Edward Evenson, *The Telephone Patent Conspiracy of 1876: The Elisha Gray–Alexander Bell Controversy and Its Many Players* (Jefferson, N.C: McFarland, 2000) for a view of this dispute which takes Gray's side; see also Brian Winston, *Media Technology and Society: A History: From the Telegraph to the Internet* (New York: Routledge, 1998), pp. 54–57.

16. Thomas Jefferson, *Writings,* "Letter to Isaac McPherson, August 13, 1813" (New York: Library of America, 1984), pp. 1291–92.

17. Lawrence Lessig, *The Future of Ideas: The Fate of the Commons in a Connected World* (New York: Random House, 2001), pp. 202–7.

18. Amy Friedlander, *Natural Monopoly and Universal Service: Telephones and Telegraphs in the U.S. Communications Infrastructure, 1837–1940* (Reston, Va.: Corporation for National Research Initiatives, 1995), pp. 68–72.

19. Susan E. McMaster, *The Telecommunications Industry* (Westport, Conn.: Greenwood Press, 2002), pp. 28–31.

20. Kenneth Lipartito, *The Bell System and Regional Business: The Telephone in the South, 1877–1920* (Baltimore: Johns Hopkins University Press, 1989), pp. 190–96.

21. Maury Klein, *The Life and Legend of Jay Gould* (Baltimore: Johns Hopkins University Press, 1986), pp. 197–205, 277–82.

22. See especially *Pensacola Telegraph Company v. Western Union Telegraph Company,* 96 U.S. 1 (1877) (Florida statute favoring locally incorporated telegraph company was a violation of the interstate commerce clause).

23. Phillips, *Wealth and Democracy,* p. 43.

24. Walter Lippmann, *The Good Society* (New York: Grosset & Dunlap, 1943), p. 185.

25. Ibid., pp. 184–92, disputing John Stuart Mill's assertion in *Principles of Political Economy* that laissez-faire "should be the general practice."

26. Ibid., pp. 182–84.

27. Richard Hofstadter, *Social Darwinism in American Thought* (Boston: Beacon Press, 1966), pp. 31–32. While Hofstadter has come under increased criticism for his overly simplified presentation of social Darwinism, Mike Hawkins adds important qualifications but does not explode Hofstadter's essential description of Spencer's complex and badly conceived set of theories and the reaction to them. See Mike Hawkins, *Social Darwinism in European and American Thought, 1860–1945: Nature as Model and Nature as Threat* (Cambridge: Cambridge University Press, 1997). For a contrasting interpretation of social Darwinism, see Robert Bannister, *Social Darwinism:*

Science and Myth in Anglo-American Social Thought (Philadelphia: Temple University Press, 1979).

28. A. J. Beitzinger, *A History of American Political Thought* (New York: Dodd, Mead, 1972), pp. 398–99; see also Louis Menand, *The Metaphysical Club: A Story of Ideas in America* (New York: Farrar, Straus & Giroux, 2001), p. 422.

29. Beitzinger, *A History of American Political Thought*, pp. 405–6.

30. Phillips, *Wealth and Democracy*, p. 332.

31. Beitzinger, *A History of American Political Thought*, p. 406.

32. Andrew Carnegie, "The Gospel of Wealth," in *The Andrew Carnegie Reader, 1835–1919*, ed. Joseph Frazier Wall (Pittsburgh: University of Pittsburgh Press, 1992), pp. 129–54 (originally published as "Wealth" in the *North American Review*, June 1889).

33. Ida M. Tarbell, *The History of the Standard Oil Company* (New York: Norton, 1969) reprinted (New York: McClure, Phillips, 1904). This book can also be found at www.history.rochester.edu/fuels/tarbell/MAIN.HTM*.

34. See generally, George David Smith, *The Anatomy of a Business Strategy: Bell, Western Electric, and the Origins of the American Telephone Industry* (Baltimore: Johns Hopkins University Press, 1985).

35. Phillips, *Wealth and Democracy*, p. 236.

36. *Lochner v. New York*, 198 U.S. 45 (1905).

37. The Sherman Anti-Trust Act of July 2, 1890, 26 Stat. at L. 209, chap 647, U.S. Comp. Stat. 1901, p. 3200.

38. See William J. Baer and David A. Balto, "The Politics of Federal Antitrust Enforcement," *Harvard Journal of Law & Public Policy* 23, issue 1 (Fall 1999): 113; and see *Loewe v. Lawlor*, 208 U.S. 274 (1908).

39. Grover Cleveland, "First Inaugural Address, March 4, 1885," in *A Compilation of the Messages and Papers of the Presidents*, vol. VIII, ed. James D. Richardson (New York: Bureau of National Literature, 1911), pp. 299–303.

40. Stephen Skowronek, *Building a New American State* (Cambridge: Cambridge University Press, 1982), p. 77.

41. Howard Zinn, *A People's History of the United States* (New York: Harper-Collins, 1999), p. 259.

42. William J. Bryan, *The First Battle: A Story of the Campaign of 1896* (Port Washington, N.Y.: Kennikat Press, 1971), pp. 199–206; see also Paolo Enrico Coletta, *William Jennings Bryan*, vol. I: *1860–1908* (Lincoln: University of Nebraska Press, 1964), pp. 139–47.

43. Gil Troy, "Money and Politics: The Oldest Connection," *The Wilson Quarterly* (Summer 1997): 14; and see Edwin G. Burrows and Mike Wallace, *Gotham: A History of New York City to 1898* (New York: Oxford University Press, 1999), p. 1001.

44. George N. Gordon, *The Communications Revolution: A History of Mass Media in the United States* (New York: Hastings House, 1977), p. 65.

45. Adams, *The Education of Henry Adams*, pp. 500–501.

46. John Milton Cooper Jr., *Pivotal Decades: The United States, 1900–1920* (New York: Norton, 1990), p. 11; see also Edmund Morris, *The Rise of Theodore Roosevelt* (New York: The Modern Library, 2001), p. 729.

Chapter 5. From Roosevelt to Roosevelt: Wireless and Radio (1900–1934)

Note to Epigraph: Theodore Roosevelt, Keynote of the Opening State Fair Address "We Must Raise Others While We Are Being Benefited," *Minneapolis Tribune*, September 3, 1901.

1. Charles A. Conant, "The Economic Basis of Imperialism," *North American Review* 167, issue 502 (September 1898): 326–41. This document is made available on-line through the Making of America project, which makes accessible through digital technology a significant body of primary sources. The Library of Congress, Cornell University, and the University of Michigan are collaborators on this project. The *North American Review* can be found at http://memory.loc.gov/ammem/ndlpcoop/moahtml/title/nora.html.

2. W. Joseph Campbell, *Yellow Journalism: Puncturing the Myths, Defining the Legacies* (Westport, Conn.: Praeger, 2001), pp. 71–95; see also "Not likely sent: The Remington-Hearst 'telegrams,'" W. Joseph Campbell, at http://academic2.american.edu/wjc/wjc3/wjc3.html from *Journalism and Mass Communication Quarterly* (Summer 2000). Campbell argues that "the press, including Hearst's Journal, did not possess [the power] of propelling the country into a war that it did not want." Campbell misses the point. Many people in the country wanted war because they were persuaded by the distortions of Hearst, Pulitzer, and all the papers relying upon their dispatches carried by the Associated Press. The story about the telegraph exchange so well disputed by Campbell is useful because it demonstrates the power of media, even histories, and the dangers of distortion.

3. The details for this section come from a variety of sources, especially David Nasaw, *The Chief: The Life of William Randolph Hearst* (Boston: Houghton Mifflin, 2000); John Offner, *An Unwanted War: The Diplomacy of the United States and Spain over Cuba 1895–1898* (Chapel Hill: University of North Carolina Press, 1992); Rodger Streitmatter, *Mightier than the Sword: How the News Media Have Shaped American History* (Boulder, Colo.: Westview Press, 1997), pp. 68–84; W. A. Swanberg, *Pulitzer* (New York: Scribners, 1967).

4. Critics from Mark Twain to the Harvard philosopher William James publicly and repeatedly expressed their horror at the U.S. brutality in the Philippines. See Howard Zinn, *A People's History of the United States* (New York: HarperCollins, 1999), pp. 312–20; see also Mark Twain, "To the Person Sitting in Darkness," in *Mark Twain on the Damned Human Race*, ed. Janet Smith (New York: Hill and Wang, 1962), pp. 3–21.

5. Michael Schudson, *The Power of News* (Cambridge, Mass.: Harvard University Press, 1995), pp. 197–200. Pulitzer began publishing a comic strip entitled "The

Yellow Kid" in early 1896. Hearst hired the creator of that strip to move the "Yellow Kid" to his paper. Their competition in a race to serve the common man and the new sensational style they shared was thus labeled *yellow journalism*.

6. Richard Hofstadter, *The American Political Tradition* (New York: Vintage, 1974), p. 270.

7. Edmund Morris, *The Rise of Theodore Roosevelt* (New York: The Modern Library, 2001), p. 568.

8. Ibid., pp. 568–69.

9. Ibid., pp. 592–93.

10. C. Wright Mills, *The Power Elite* (New York: Oxford University Press, 2000), pp. 171–224.

11. Bernard Bailyn, *The Ideological Origins of the American Revolution* (Cambridge, Mass.: Belknap Press/Harvard University Press, 1967), p. 114.

12. Gary Hart, *Restoration of the Republic: The Jeffersonian Ideal in 21st Century America* (New York: Oxford University Press, 2002), p. 151.

13. Ibid., p. 207.

14. Capt. Linwood S. Howeth USN, *History of Communications-Electronics in the United States Navy,* Bureau of Ships and Office of Naval History (Washington, D.C.: U.S. Government Printing Office, 1963), p. 13.

15. Susan J. Douglas, *Inventing American Broadcasting, 1899–1922* (Baltimore: Johns Hopkins University Press, 1987), pp. 102–31; and Erik Barnouw, *A Tower in Babel* (New York: Oxford University Press, 1966), pp. 14–18.

16. Hofstadter, *The American Political Tradition,* p. 281.

17. Ibid., p. 282.

18. Morris, *The Rise of Theodore Roosevelt,* pp. 731–45.

19. George N. Gordon, *The Communications Revolution: A History of Mass Media in the United States* (New York: Hastings House, 1977), p. 99.

20. Theodore Roosevelt, State papers as governor and president, 1899–1909 (*The Works of Theodore Roosevelt*), Memorial Edition, Vol. 71 (New York: Charles Scribner and Sons, 1925), pp. 97–105.

21. Michael Sandel, *Democracy's Discontent: America in Search of a Public Philosophy* (Cambridge, Mass.: Belknap Press/Harvard University Press, 1996), p. 217.

22. David Mark Chalmers, *The Muckrake Years* (New York: D. Van Nostrand, 1974), pp. 60–61.

23. Matthew Schneirov, *The Dream of a New Social Order: Popular Magazines in America, 1893–1914* (New York: Columbia University Press, 1994), pp. 5–6.

24. Chalmers, *The Muckrake Years,* pp. 80–81, excerpt from S. S. McClure Editorial, *McClure's* (January 1903): 336.

25. S. S. McClure, *My Autobiography* (New York: Frederick Stokes, 1914), pp. 244–45.

26. Arthur and Lila Weinberg, eds., *The Muckrakers* (Chicago: University of Illinois Press, 2001)

27. Schneirov, *The Dream of a New Social Order,* pp. 253–55; see also Upton Sinclair, *The Brass Check: A Study of American Journalism* (Urbana: University of Illinois Press, 2003), p. 239.

28. Willa Cather, *The Autobiography of S. S. McClure* (Lincoln: University of Nebraska Press, 1997).

29. Sinclair, *The Brass Check,* p. 241.

30. Theodore Roosevelt, *An Autobiography* (New York: Macmillan, 1919), p. 592. "In my own judgment the most important service that I rendered to peace was the voyage of the battle fleet around the world."

31. Stuart Ewen, *PR! A Social History of Spin* (New York: Basic Books, 1996), p. 87.

32. Robert W. Garnet, *The Telephone Enterprise: The Evolution of the Bell System's Horizontal Structure, 1876–1909* (Baltimore: Johns Hopkins University Press, 1985), p. 128.

33. Milton L. Mueller, *Universal Service: Competition, Interconnection, and Monopoly in the Making of the American Telephone System* (Cambridge, Mass.: MIT Press, 1997), pp. 4–10. Mueller argues convincingly that AT&T created and promoted a distorted history of the concept of universal service to persuade policy makers in the 1970s and 1980s to allow it to continue as a national monopoly. Universal service did not mean expansive service for all Americans, it did not mean rural service, it did not mean the use of cross-subsidies to provide lower-cost service to residential customers. "One Policy, One System, Universal Service" was meant to convince the government and the public that one system could provide local and long-distance service, and one system deserved their support—AT&T. Ibid., pp. 92–164. Richard John adds that the "civic rationale for communications policy" brought about in the Post Office Department "best explains the origins of universal service as a business strategy at AT&T." Richard John, "Theodore N. Vail and the Civic Origins of Universal Service," *Business and Economic History* 28 (Winter 1999): 74–79 (quote on p. 75).

34. Roland Marchand, *Creating the Corporate Soul: The Rise of Public Relations and Corporate Imagery in American Big Business* (Berkeley: University of California Press, 1998), pp. 48–87.

35. Friedlander, *Natural Monopoly and Universal Service,* p. 76; and Ewen, *PR!* pp. 85–101.

36. John Milton Cooper Jr., *Pivotal Decades: The United States, 1900–1920* (New York: Norton, 1990), p. 175.

37. Ibid., p. 177.

38. Woodrow Wilson, *The New Freedom,* ed. William E. Leuchtenburg (Englewood Cliffs, N.J.: Prentice-Hall, 1961), p. 121.

39. Hofstadter, *The American Political Tradition,* p. 332.

40. Woodrow Wilson, *The New Freedom: A Call for the Emancipation of the Generous Energies of a People* (New York: Doubleday, Page & Co., 1913), p. 57.

41. Ibid.

42. Cooper, *Pivotal Decades,* p. 180.

43. Wilson, *The New Freedom,* p. 207.

44. Woodrow Wilson, "First Inaugural Address, March 4, 1913," in *Inaugural Addresses of the Presidents of the United States* (Washington, D.C.: U.S. Government Printing Office, 1989), p. 227.

45. Gerald W. Brock, *The Telecommunications Industry: The Dynamics of Market Structure* (Cambridge, Mass.: Harvard University Press, 1981), p. 156.

46. Michael K. Kellogg, John Thorne, and Peter W. Huber, eds., *Federal Telecommunications Law* (Boston: Little, Brown, 1992), pp. 16–17.

47. Barnouw, *A Tower in Babel,* p. 31.

48. Douglas, *Inventing American Broadcasting,* pp. 216–39.

49. After Congress ratified the first international radio treaty in 1912, 37 Stat. 1565, it enacted the Radio-Communications Act of August 13, 1912, to fulfill obligations under that treaty. 37 Stat. 302, 47 U.S.C.A. 51 et seq.

50. Pub. Law No. 264, August 13, 1912, 62d Congress.

51. Barnouw, *A Tower in Babel,* p. 32.

52. Cooper, *Pivotal Decades,* p. 228.

53. Ibid., p. 264.

54. Ibid., p. 266.

55. Barnouw, *A Tower in Babel,* pp. 47–48.

56. Ibid., pp. 50–51.

57. Ibid., p. 53.

58. Ibid., p. 55.

59. Ibid., pp. 57–73.

60. Zinn, *A People's History of the United States,* p. 345.

61. Alan M. Dershowitz, Shouting "Fire!" *The Atlantic Monthly,* January 1989 at www.theatlantic.com/issues/89jan/dershowitz.htm.

62. Zinn, *A People's History of the United States,* p. 366.

63. T. H. Watkins, *The Great Depression: America in the 1930's* (Boston: Back Bay Books, 1993), p. 46.

64. Noobar R. Danielian, *AT&T: The Story of Industrial Conquest* (New York: Vanguard Press, 1939), p. 252.

65. Adam D. Thierer, "Unnatural Monopoly: Critical Moments in the Development of the Bell System Monopoly," *The Cato Journal* 14, no. 2 (Fall 1994), at www.cato.org/pubs/journal/cjv14n2-6.html.

66. Guy H. Loeb, "The Communications Act Policy Toward Competition: A Failure to Communicate," *Duke Law Journal* (1978): 14.

67. Willis-Graham Act of 1921, ch. 20, 42 Stat. 27 (repealed by the Communications Act of 1934, ch. 652, 48 Stat. 1064, 1102).

68. Friedlander, *Natural Monopoly and Universal Service,* pp. 76–77.

69. Michigan Public Utilities Commission, Citizens Telephone Co. of Grand Rapids. Public Utility Regulations 1921 E: 308, 315 and 1921: 315.

70. Warren G. Lavey, "The Public Policies That Changed the Telephone Industry into Regulated Monopolies: Lessons from around 1915," *Federal Communications Law Journal* 39 (1987): 184–85; see also Kellogg et al., *Federal Telecommunications Law,* p. 3.

71. Barnouw, *A Tower in Babel,* p. 70.

72. Ibid., p. 91.

73. Arthur Schlesinger Jr., *The Crisis of the Old Order* (Boston: Houghton Mifflin, 1957), p. 67.

74. Barnouw, *A Tower in Babel,* p. 94; see also Herbert Hoover, *Memoirs,* vol. 2: *The Cabinet and the Presidency, 1920–1933* (New York: Macmillan, 1951–52), p. 140.

75. Barnouw, *A Tower in Babel,* p. 120.

76. Ibid., 122.

77. Ibid., p. 172.

78. Ibid., p. 174.

79. *United States v. Zenith Radio Corporation,* 12 F.2d 614 (D.C. N. D. Ill. 1926) Cf. *Hoover v. Intercity Radio Co.,* 52 App. D.C. 339, 286 F. 1003 (1923) (secretary had no power to deny licenses, but was empowered to assign frequencies)

80. Public Law No. 632, February 23, 1927, 69th Congress.

81. Irwin Krasnow, *The "Public Interest" Standard: The Elusive Search for the Holy Grail,* Briefing Paper Prepared for the Advisory Committee on Public Interest Obligations of Digital Television Broadcasters, October 22, 1997 (www.ntia.doc .gov/pubintadvcom/octmtg/Krasnow.htm#N_8_).

82. Hofstadter, *The American Political Tradition,* p. 384.

83. Schaeffer Radio Co. (FRC 1930), quoted in John W. Willis, The Federal Radio Commission and the Public Service Responsibility of Broadcast Licensees, 11 FED. COM. B.J. 5, 14 (1950).

84. Barnouw, *A Tower in Babel,* p. 209.

85. Robert McChesney, *Telecommunications, Mass Media and Democracy: The Battle for the Control of U.S. Broadcasting, 1928–1935* (New York: Oxford University Press, 1994), p. 20.

86. Ibid., p. 19.

87. General Order 40 as interpreted by the commission in a number of decisions forced labor and religious broadcasters from the air. The rationale was that labor-owned stations would likely present biased coverage of industrial issues (*Chicago Fed'n of Labor v. Federal Radio Comm'n,* 3 Fed. Radio Comm'n Ann. Rep. 36 [1929]) and that the operation of WCBD, which aired only the services and philosophies of Zion Temple, was not in the public interest (*Great Lakes Broadcasting Co.* 3 Fed. Radio Comm'n Ann. Rep. 32 [1929]).

88. McChesney, *Telecommunications, Mass Media and Democracy,* p. 27.

89. Barnouw, *A Tower in Babel,* p. 219.

90. John Kenneth Galbraith, *The Great Crash, 1929* (Boston: Houghton Mifflin, 1972), p. 2.

91. McChesney, *Telecommunications, Mass Media and Democracy*, p. 124.

92. Ibid., p. 127.

93. Ibid., p. 150.

94. Ibid., p. 125.

95. Ibid., pp. 201–8.

96. John Brooks, *Telephone: The First Hundred Years* (New York: Harper & Row, 1975), p. 196.

97. David Kennedy, *Freedom from Fear: The American People in Depression and War, 1929–1945* (New York: Oxford University Press, 1999), p. 229.

98. William E. Leuchtenburg, *Franklin D. Roosevelt and the New Deal, 1932–1940* (New York: Harper & Row, 1963), p. 165.

99. Ibid., p. 149.

100. Erik Barnouw, *The Golden Web: A History of Broadcasting in the United States, Volume II—1933–1953* (New York: Oxford University Press, 1968), p. 170, cites Roosevelt's one-line note to Fly in December 1940: "Will you let me know when you propose to have a hearing on newspaper ownership of radio stations."

101. *Second Report & Order*, 50 FCC 2d 1046, 1075 (1975), recon. 53 FCC 2d 589 (1975), *aff'd sub nom. FCC v. National Citizens Comm. for Broadcasting*, 436 U.S. 775 (1978).

102. *Report on Chain Broadcasting*, FCC Docket No. 5060, May 1941, 91–92.

103. Barnouw, *The Golden Web*, pp. 178–82.

104. *National Broadcasting Co., Inc. v. United States*, 319 U.S. 190 (1943).

105. Barnouw, *The Golden Web*, pp. 226–27.

106. *Charting the Digital Broadcasting Future*, President's Advisory Committee on the Public Interest Obligations of Digital Television Broadcasters, at www.benton.org/PIAC/report.html.

107. Barnouw, *The Golden Web*, p. 234.

108. Ibid., p. 243.

109. 26 U.S.C. Section 1071 (repealed 1995); *see also* S. Rep. No. 78–627, at 53 (1943).

110. George Haas, Memo on Tax Revision Studies, September 1937, Division of Tax Research, Treasury Department at www.tax.org/THP/Civilization/Documents/Surveys/hst23734/23734–1.htm.

111. Barnouw, *The Golden Web*, p. 166; see also Erik Barnouw, *The Sponsor: Notes on a Modern Potentate* (New York: Oxford University Press, 1978), pp. 37–41.

112. Barnouw, *The Golden Web*, pp. 155–58.

Chapter 6. From Truman to Eisenhower: The Birth of Television (1935–1959)

Note to Epigraph: C. Wright Mills, *The Power Elite* (New York: Oxford University Press, 2000), p. 267.

1. Susan J. Douglas, *Inventing American Broadcasting, 1899–1922* (Baltimore: Johns Hopkins University Press, 1987), see especially pp. 240–90.

2. See Noam Chomsky, *The Chomsky Reader* (New York: Pantheon, 1987), pp. 207–19.

3. Philippa Strum, ed., *Brandeis on Democracy* (Lawrence: University Press of Kansas, 1995), pp. 74–154.

4. The Public Works Agency provided support for rural electrification projects until that work was taken over by the Rural Electrification Agency (REA) in 1935. In 1949 the REA was given the authority to provide low-interest loans to rural cooperatives to develop telephone services.

5. Eric Foner, *Who Owns History? Rethinking the Past in a Changing World* (New York: Hill and Wang, 2002), pp. 114–16.

6. See generally Howard Zinn, *A People's History of the United States, 1492-Present* (New York: Harpers, 1999).

7. See especially Michael Goldfield, "The Color of Politics in the United States: White Supremacy as the Main Explanation for the Peculiarities of American Politics from Colonial Times to the Present," in *The Bounds of Race: Perspectives on Hegemony and Resistance*, ed. Dominick LaCapra (Ithaca: Cornell University Press, 1991).

8. As quoted in George M. Fredrickson, *Racism: A Short History* (Princeton: Princeton University Press, 2002), p. 42.

9. Ibid., p. 170.

10. Pauline Maier, *American Scripture: Making the Declaration of Independence* (New York: Knopf, 1997), pp. 146–47.

11. Joseph Ellis, *Founding Brothers: The Revolutionary Generation* (New York: Vintage, 2002), pp. 108–19.

12. *Dred Scott v. Sandford*, 19 How. 393 (1857).

13. William Lee Miller, *Lincoln's Virtues: An Ethical Biography* (New York: Knopf, 2002), p. 370.

14. Richard R. John, *Spreading the News: The American Postal System from Franklin to Morse* (Cambridge, Mass.: Harvard University Press, 1995), pp. 257–59.

15. Ibid., pp. 260–75.

16. John Hope Franklin and Alfred A. Moss Jr., *From Slavery to Freedom: A History of Negro Americans*, 6th ed. (New York: Knopf, 1988), p. 152.

17. Fredrickson, *Racism*, p. 99.

18. Mary Frances Berry, *My Face Is Black Is True: Callie House and the Struggle for Ex-Slave Reparations* (New York: Knopf, 2005).

19. See generally, Ronald Takaki, *Iron Cages: Race and Culture in 19th Century America*, rev. ed. (New York: Oxford University Press, 2000).

20. John M. Coward, *The Newspaper Indian: Native American Identity in the Press, 1820–1890* (Urbana: University of Illinois Press, 1999), p. 17.

21. Take up the White Man's burden—
    send forth the best ye breed—Go, bind your sons to exile
    To serve your captives' need; To wait, in heavy harness,

On fluttered folk and wild—Your new-caught sullen peoples,
Half devil and half child.

Rudyard Kipling, "The White Man's Burden, the United States and the Philippine Islands," *McClure's Magazine* 12 (February 1899); see also Geoffrey Wheatcroft, "A White Man's Burden, Rudyard Kipling's Pathos and Prescience," *Harper's* (September 2002): 81, an essay on Kipling and a review of David Gilmour's *The Long Recessional: The Imperial Life of Rudyard Kipling*. Regarding the view of Asian immigrants, see Takaki, *Iron Cages,* p. 246.

22. Edmund Morris, *Theodore Rex* (New York: Modern Libraries, 2002), pp. 52–56.

23. Franklin and Moss, *From Slavery to Freedom,* pp. 278–81; see also Maurine H. Beasley, "The Muckrakers and Lynching: A Case Study in Racism," *Journalism History* 8 (Autumn–Winter 1982): 86–91.

24. Ibid., pp. 292–93.

25. Foner, *Who Owns History?* p. 202.

26. Franklin and Moss, *From Slavery to Freedom,* pp. 378–79.

27. See Jesse B. Blayton, at www.radiohof.org/pioneer/jessebblayton.html. I have been told that Blayton, as a bank president in Atlanta, was able to purchase the station only because he operated behind the scenes through a white broker.

28. Fredrickson, *Racism,* pp. 100–102.

29. Ibid., p. 129.

30. W. E. B. Du Bois, *Selected Writings of W.E.B. Du Bois,* ed. Walter Wilson (New York: Mentor, 1970), p. 172.

31. Franklin and Moss, *From Slavery to Freedom,* pp. 386–89.

32. Nadine Cohodas, *Strom Thurmond and the Politics of Southern Change* (New York: Simon & Schuster, 1993), p. 177. In 2003 it would come to light that Thurmond fathered a child with an adolescent black housekeeper working for his parents while he was in his twenties.

33. Harry S. Truman, *Memoirs: Years of Trial and Hope,* vol. 2 (New York: Doubleday, 1956), pp. 175–76.

34. *In the Matter of Allocation of Frequencies to the Various Classes of Non-Governmental Services in the Radio Spectrum from 10 Kilocycles to 30,000,000 Kilocycles* (Docket No. 6651) at www.fcc.gov/fcc-bin/assemble?docno=450627.

35. Erik Barnouw, *The Golden Web: A History of Broadcasting in the United States, Volume II—1933–1953* (New York: Oxford University Press, 1968), pp. 285–86.

36. Ibid., p. 293.

37. Ibid., p. 294.

38. James Day, *The Vanishing Vision: The Inside Story of Public Television* (Berkeley: University of California Press, 1995), pp. 24–25.

39. *Sixth Report and Order,* 941 FCC 148, 158 (14 April 1952), in Frank J. Kahn, ed., *Documents of American Broadcasting,* 3rd ed. (Englewood Cliffs, N.J: Prentice Hall, 1978), pp. 236–45.

40. Erik Barnouw, *The Image Empire: A History of Broadcasting in the United States from 1953* (New York: Oxford University Press, 1970), p. 73.

41. See *In the Matter of Editorializing by Broadcast Licensees,* Docket No. 8516, 13 F.C.C. 1246 (1949).

42. *Associated Press v. United States,* 326 U.S. 1, 20 (1945).

43. See *In the Matter of Editorializing by Broadcast Licensees,* Docket No. 8516, 13 F.C.C. 1246 (1949).

44. Sec. 315, 1934 Communications Act.

45. See *The Handling of Public Issues Under the Fairness Doctrine and the Public Interest Standards of the Communications Act,* 49 FCC 2nd 1, 6 n. 6 (1974).

46. *Editorializing* at 1270.

47. Fred W. Friendly, *Due to Circumstances Beyond Our Control . . .* (New York: Random House, 1967), pp. 3–22.

48. Alexander Kendrick, *Prime Time: The Life of Edward R. Murrow* (New York: Avon, 1970), p. 421.

49. Friendly, *Due to Circumstances,* p. 75.

50. Ibid., p. 76.

51. Kendrick, *Prime Time,* pp. 459–65.

52. Barnouw, *The Golden Web,* pp. 298–300.

53. Steve Neal, *Harry and Ike: The Partnership That Remade the Postwar World* (New York: Scribner, 2001), p. 250.

54. Earl Muzo, *Richard Nixon: A Political and Personal Portrait* (New York: Harper Bros., 1959), p. 108.

55. For an excellent discussion of the intraparty conflict and the corruption charges, see Sean J. Savage, *Truman and the Democratic Party* (Lexington: University Press of Kentucky, 1997), pp. 184–91.

56. Walter Lippmann, "The Eisenhower Mission," January 5, 1954, in *The Essential Lippmann: A Political Philosophy for Liberal Democracy,* ed. Clinton Rossiter and James Lare (New York: Vintage, 1965), p. 502.

57. Stanley K. Schultz, "Eisenhower and Kennedy," see http://us.history.wisc .edu/hist102/lectures/lecture25.html.

58. Richard F. Weingroff, "Federal-Aid Highway Act of 1956: Creating the Interstate System," see www.tfhrc.gov/pubrds/summer96/p96su10.htm.

59. Barnouw, *The Image Empire,* p. 126; see also "'Headless Fourth Branch' Denounced by FCC Prober," Harvard Law Record—April 3, 1958 at www.law.harvard .edu/studorgs/forum/Schwartz.html.

60. Wiley Branton, quoted from a speech given at the Smithsonian Institution in 1988, part of the radio series *Afro-Americans and the Evolution of a Living Constitution,* Joint Center for Political Studies and Radio America, 1989.

61. W. E. B. Du Bois, "Negroes and the Crisis of Capitalism in the United States," *Monthly Review* 4 (April 1958): 478–85; also quoted in David Levering Lewis, *W.E.B.*

Du Bois, The Fight for Equality and The American Century, 1919–1963 (New York: Henry Holt, 2000), p. 570.

Chapter 7. Kennedy, Johnson, and Satellites (1960–1968)

Note to Epigraph: John Dewey, *The Public and Its Problems* (Athens, Ohio: Swallow, 1927), pp. 141–42.

1. For an engaging report of the U.S. reaction to the Soviet launch of *Sputnik*, see Paul Dickson, *Sputnik: The Shock of the Century* (New York: Penguin Putnam, 2003); many of the details here and following regarding the development of communications satellites rely on David Joseph Whalen, *The Origins of Satellite Communications: 1945–1965* (Washington, D.C.: Smithsonian Institution Press, 2002).

2. The National Aeronautics and Space Act of 1958, Pub. L. No. 85–568.

3. Dwight D. Eisenhower, "Farewell Address to the Nation, January 17, 1961," in *Public Papers of the Presidents of the United States* (Washington, D.C.: U.S. Government Printing Office, 1961), no. 421, p. 1038.

4. John F. Kennedy, "Inaugural Address, January 20, 1961," in *Public Papers of the Presidents of the United States* (Washington, D.C.: U.S. Government Printing Office, 1962), no. 1, pp. 1–13.

5. John F. Kennedy, "Special Address to Congress on Urgent National Needs, May 25, 1961," in *Public Papers of the Presidents of the United States* (Washington, D.C.: U.S. Government Printing Office, 1962), no. 205, pp. 403–4.

6. Whalen, *The Origins of Satellite Communications*, pp. 70–100.

7. Communications Satellite Act of 1962, 47 USC 701.

8. Whalen, *The Origins of Satellite Communications*, pp. 119–27, 140–41.

9. Newton Minow and Craig L. LaMay, *Abandoned in the Wasteland: Children, Television and the First Amendment* (New York: Hill and Wang, 1995), "Address to the National Association of Broadcasters, May 9, 1961," pp. 185–96.

10. A number of the popular television quiz shows were revealed by congressional investigations to have provided answers to certain contestants beforehand, most notoriously college professor Charles Van Doren, who became famous for his participation in the quiz show "Twenty-One." See Erik Barnouw, *The Image Empire: A History of Broadcasting in the United States from 1953* (New York: Oxford University Press, 1970), pp. 122–25. Congressional investigations revealed that popular radio disk-jockeys had accepted bribes from record companies to play their records.

11. *En banc Programming Inquiry,* 44 FCC 2303 (1960).

12. Newton Minow, "Introduction," published in *How Vast the Wasteland Now?* (New York: Columbia University and Gannett Foundation Media Center, 1991).

13. Kennedy, "Televised Address on the Emergency in Alabama," June 11, 1963," in *Public Papers of the Presidents of the United States* (Washington, D.C.: U.S. Government Printing Office, 1962), no. 237, pp. 468–71.

14. Barnouw, *The Image Empire*, pp. 210–11.

15. Martin Luther King Jr., *Why We Can't Wait* (New York: Harper & Row, 1963), p. 88.

16. Kay Mills, *Changing Channels: The Civil Rights Case That Transformed Television* (Jackson: University Press of Mississippi, 2004).

17. *Office of Communication of the United Church of Christ v. F.C.C.*, 359 F.2d 994 (1966).

18. *Office of Communication of the United Church of Christ v. F.C.C.* 425 F.2d 543 (D.C. Cir. 1969).

19. *Red Lion Broadcasting v. FCC*, 127 U.S. App. D.C. 129, 381 F.2d 908 (1967). 395 U.S. 367, 373.

20. *RTNDA v. FCC*, 400 F.2d 1002 (1968).

21. *Red Lion Broadcasting v. FCC*, 395 U.S. 367, 390 (1969).

22. Primer on Ascertainment of Community Problems by Broadcast Applicants, Part I, Sections IV-A and IV-B of FCC Forms, Report and Order, 27 FCC 2d 650, 651 (1971).

23. Nondiscrimination in the Employment Policies and Practices of Broadcast Licensees, Report and Order, 60 FCC 2d 226, 229–30 (1976).

24. National Defense Education Act of 1958, 20 USC 401 et seq.

25. Barnouw, *The Image Empire*, pp. 5, 67–68.

26. James Day, *Vanishing Vision: The Inside Story of Public Television* (Berkeley: University of California Press, 1995).

27. James Ledbetter, *Made Possible By . . . : The Death of Public Broadcasting in the United States* (New York: Verso, 1997).

28. Lyndon B. Johnson, "Health and Education Message to Congress, Feb. 28, 1967," in *Public Papers of the Presidents of the United States* (Washington, D.C.: U.S. Government Printing Office, 1968), no. 77, pp. 250–51.

29. "Public Television: A Program for Action," New York: Carnegie Corporation of New York, January 26, 1967; see also "Carnegie Commission on Educational Television, Summary, 1967" in Public Broadcasting PolicyBase at www.current.org/pbpb/carnegie/CarnegieISummary.html.

30. My mentor at the University of Michigan's WUOM, Ed G. Burrows, spearheaded the successful campaign to include educational radio in the bill, and so CPT became CPB. See Edwin G. Burrows Papers at www.lib.umd.edu/NPBA/papers/burrows.html.

31. Ledbetter, *Made Possible By . . .*, pp. 25–26; see also Public Broadcasting Act, 47 U.S.C. 396.

32. Johnson, "Remarks Upon Signing the Public Broadcasting Act of 1967, November 7, 1967," in *Public Papers of the Presidents of the United States* (Washington, D.C.: U.S. Government Printing Office, 1968), no. 474, pp. 995–98.

33. Day, *Vanishing Vision*, p. 122.

34. Bruce J. Schulman, *Lyndon B. Johnson and American Liberalism: A Brief Biography with Documents* (Boston: Bedford, 1995), p. 97.

35. Dewey, *The Public and Its Problems,* p. 98.

36. Schulman, *Lyndon B. Johnson,* p. 98.

37. Chon A. Noriega, *Shot in America: Television, the State, and the Rise of Chicano Cinema* (Minneapolis: University of Minnesota Press, 2000), pp. 81–82.

38. *Report of the National Advisory Commission on Civil Disorders* ("Kerner Commission Report") (Washington, D.C.: U.S. Government Printing Office, 1968).

39. Ibid., p. 296.

40. Ibid.

41. Stanley Karnouw, *Vietnam, A History—The First Complete Account of Vietnam at War* (New York: Viking, 1983).

42. Barnouw, *The Image Empire,* p. 287.

43. Herbert Gans, *Deciding What's News* (Evanston: Northwestern University Press, 2004), p. 292. In the late 1960s and through the 1970s news media in general seemed to present a more critical eye on at least the executive and legislative branches of the federal government as compared to earlier periods. However, as Gans demonstrates, dominant news sources regularly conveyed a rather myopic middle-class white establishment bias not only in their decisions about what to cover, but in how it was covered and who got to participate in the coverage as reporter or source.

44. Schulman, *Lyndon B. Johnson,* p. 101.

Chapter 8. From Nixon to Reagan: Backlash and Cable (1968–1991)

Note to Epigraph: President Ronald Reagan, "State of the Union Address to Congress, January 25, 1988," in *Public Papers of the Presidents of the United States* (Washington, D.C.: U.S. Government Printing Office, 1990), pp. 84–90, quote on p. 87.

1. Michael Harrington, *The Other America: Poverty in the United States* (New York: Macmillan, 1970).

2. Isabel V. Sawhill, "Poverty in the U.S.: Why Is It So Persistent?" *Journal of Economic Literature* 26 (September 1988): 1073–1119.

3. David Zucchino, *The Myth of the Welfare Queen* (New York: Touchstone, 1997), pp. 64–65.

4. Sawhill, "Poverty in the U.S."

5. Bruce J. Schulman, *The Seventies: The Great Shift in American Culture, Society, and Politics* (Cambridge, Mass.: Da Capo Press, 2002), p. 27.

6. Waldemar A. Nielsen, *Golden Donors* (New York: Transaction Press, 2002), p. 27.

7. Bernard D. Reams, *Tax Reform 1969: A Legislative History of the Tax Reform Act of 1969, with Related Amendments* (Buffalo, N.Y.: W. S. Hein, 1991) (see also Public Law 91–172).

8. James Ledbetter, *Made Possible By . . . : The Death of Public Broadcasting in the United States* (New York: Verso, 1997), p. 60; see also James Day, *Vanishing Vision: The Inside Story of Public Television* (Berkeley: University of California Press, 1995), p. 213.

9. Day, *Vanishing Vision*, p. 176.

10. Ibid., pp. 214–15.

11. Ibid., p. 221.

12. Ibid., p. 217.

13. Ledbetter, *Made Possible By . . .* , p. 76.

14. Day, *Vanishing Vision*, p. 228.

15. Ibid., p. 229; see also Ledbetter, *Made Possible By . . .* , p. 77.

16. Day, *Vanishing Vision*, p. 234.

17. Ledbetter, *Made Possible By . . .* , pp. 170–176; see also Willard D. Rowland Jr., "Public Service Broadcasting in the United States: Its Mandate, Institutions, and Conflicts," pp. 174–75.

18. Wayne E. Fuller, *The American Mail: Enlarger of the Common Life* (Chicago: University of Chicago Press, 1971), pp. 331–42.

19. Ibid., quote on p. 338.

20. See Fuller generally; see also "History of the U.S. Postal Service," at www.usps.com/history/history/his3.htm#, and Reorganization, Exec. Order No. 11570, Nov. 24, 1970, 35 F.R. 18183, as amended by Ex. Ord. No. 12107, Dec. 28, 1978, 44 F.R. 1055.

21. John Anner, "Fighting to Save the Distribution of Independent Magazines," Independent Press Association at www.indypress.org/indynews/postal_brief.html.

22. Ralph Nader and Commercial Alert, Letter to Postmaster General William J. Henderson, United States Postal Service, February 27, 2001, at http://lists.essential .org/pipermail/commercial-alert/2001/000068.html.

23. In the 1987 Oliver Stone film *Wall Street* Michael Douglas portrays an attractive and ruthless Wall Street inside trader speaking to a group of stockholders of a company he wants to take over and break up and sell off for a greater profit. His character is named Gordon Gekko.

24. *MCI v. FCC*, 561 F.2d 365 (D.D.C. 1977), cert. denied, 434 U.S. 1041 (1978); and see *MCI v. FCC*, 580 F.2d 590 (D.D.C. 1978), cert. denied, 439 U.S. 980 (1978).

25. *United States v. AT&T*, 552 F. Supp. 131 (D.D.C. 1982) (Modification of Final Judgment) aff'd sub nom., *Maryland v. United States*, 460 U.S. 1001 (1983)(mem.); see also Elizabeth A. Nowicki, "Competition in the Local Telecommunications: Legislate or Litigate," *Harvard Journal of Law and Technology* 9, no. 2 (Summer 1996): 354; also at http://jolt.law.harvard.edu/articles/pdf/v09/09HarvJLTech353.pdf.

26. Megan Mullen, *The Rise of Cable Programming in the United States: Revolution or Evolution?* (Austin: University of Texas Press, 2003), pp. 107–8.

27. Ibid., p. 36; see also Cable Industry Timeline at www.cablecenter.org/history/timeline.

28. Mullen, *The Rise of Cable Programming*, pp. 38–43.

29. *First Report and Order*, 38 F. C. C. 683 (1964).

30. *United States v. Southwestern Cable Corporation*, 392 U.S. 157 (1968).

31. Cable Television Report and Order, 36 FCC 2d 143 (1972).

32. *United States v. Midwest Video Corp.*, 441 F.2d 1322 (8th Cir., 1971) (FCC's local origination rules rejected but FCC authority over cable affirmed); *United States v. Midwest Video Corp.*, 406 U.S. 649 (1979).

33. *Home Box Office v. FCC*, 567 F.2d (D.C. Cir., 1977) cert. denied, 434 U.S. 329 (1978).

34. Mullen, *The Rise of Cable Programming*, pp. 113–14.

35. Ibid., pp. 142–43.

36. Ibid., p. 122; see also Michael Freeman, *ESPN: The Uncensored History* (New York: Taylor, 2002), pp. 76–86.

37. Nicholas Johnson, "CATV Promise or Peril," *Saturday Review*, November 11, 1967, pp. 87–88.

38. William H. Dutton, Jay G. Blumler, and Kenneth L. Kraemer, eds., *Wired Cities: Shaping the Future of Communications* (Boston: G. K. Hall, 1987), p. 5.

39. Gilbert Gillespie, *Public Access Cable Television in the United States and Canada* (New York: Praeger, 1975), pp. 35–36.

40. Ralph Engelman, "Origins of Public Access Cable Television, 1966–1972" (Columbia, S.C.: Journalism Monographs, 1990), no. 123, October, p. 32. (The fee required aroused local community protest and was later dropped.)

41. *Public Access Channels: The New York Experience, A Report for The Fund for the City of New York by the Center for the Analysis of Public Issues* (New York: New York City, 1972), p. 4; see also Gillespie, *Public Access Cable Television*, p. 36; and Engelman, "Origins of Public Access Cable Television," p. 32.

42. See also Bill Olson, "The History of Public Access Television" at www.geocities .com/iconostar/history-public-access-TV.html.

43. *Report and Order* in Docket No. 20363, 54 F. C. C. 2d 207 (1975).

44. *Report and Order* in Docket No. 20508, 59 F. C. C. 2d 294 (1976).

45. *FCC v. Midwest Video Corp.*, 440 U.S. 689 (1979), pp. 708–9.

46. Ken Freed, "When Cable Went Qubist" at www.media-visions.com/itv-qube.html.

47. Ibid.; see also Carol Davidge, "America's Talk-Back Television Experiment: QUBE," in *Wired Cities*, pp. 75–101.

48. Robert Pepper, "Competitive Realities in the Telecommunications Web," in *Wired Cities*, p. 69.

49. Freed, "When Cable Went Qubist."

50. Ibid.

51. Mullen, *The Rise of Cable Programming*, pp. 123–25; see also Stephen Frantzich and John Sullivan, *The C-span Revolution* (Norman: University of Oklahoma Press, 1996); and "About C-SPAN," at www.c-span.org/about/company/.

52. Jerry Landay, "Murdoch, Malone and Monopoly," *Christian Science Monitor*, January 31, 1997; note, however, that after a savvy campaign by C-SPAN founder Brian Lamb, and howls of protest from loyal and influential viewers, TCI reversed its position—at least temporarily. Patricia Aufderheide, "C-SPAN's Fight for Respect," *Columbia Journalism Review* (July–August 1997): 13.

53. Brian Lamb, "Debunking the Myths: Speech," The National Press Club, January 6, 1997, at www.c-span.org/about/company/debunk.asp?code=DEBUNK2.

54. Pub. L. No. 98–549, Section 2, 98 Stat. 2780 (1984) (codified at 47 U.S.C. Sections 521–559).

55. M. I. Meyerson, "The Cable Communications Policy Act of 1984: A Balancing Act on the Coaxial Wires," 19 GA. L. Rev. 543, 545 (1985)(citing 130 Cong. Rec. H10,435 (daily ed. Oct. 1, 1984) (statement of Rep. Wirth).

56. 47 U.S.C. Sec. 531.

57. Mark Herring, "The FCC and Five Years of the Cable Communications Policy Act of 1984: Tuning Out the Consumer?" *University of Richmond Law Review* 24 (Fall 1989): 151–70.

58. Patricia Aufderheide, "Cable Television and the Public Interest," *Journal of Communication* (Winter 1992): 52–65.

59. Mark S. Fowler and Daniel L. Brenner, "A Marketplace Approach to Broadcast Regulation," *Texas Law Review* 60 (1981): 207, 209–10.

60. Caroline E. Mayer, "FCC Chief Fears: Fowler Sees Threat in Regulation," *Washington Post*, February 6, 1983, p. K6.

61. *Revision of Applications for Renewals of License of Commercial and Non Commercial AM, FM and Television Licensees,* 49 RR 2d 740 (1981). One of the primary rationales for postcard renewal was the burden placed on broadcasters in defending against citizen petitions to deny their broadcast license. Even though citizen groups had almost no chance of having a license denied, the process of renewal forced negotiations with community groups, settlements requiring both program expenses and community relations personnel, and the expenditure of hundreds of hours of staff time and legal bills rising into six figures. Joseph A. Grundfest, *Citizen Participation in Broadcast Licensing before the FCC* (Santa Monica, Calif.: Rand, 1976), p. 63.

62. See Erwin G. Krasnow, "Briefing Paper Prepared for the Advisory Committee on Public Interest Obligations of Digital Television Broadcasters, October 22, 1997," at www.ntia.doc.gov/pubintadvcom/octmtg/Krasnow.htm#N_44_.

63. Reed Hundt and Karen Kornbluh, "Renewing the Deal Between Broadcasters and the Public: Requiring Clear Rules for Children's Educational Television," *Harvard Journal of Law and Technology* 9, no. 1 (Winter 1996): 11–21 at http://jolt.law .harvard.edu/articles/pdf/v09/09HarvJLTech011.pdf; see also Newton Minow, *Abandoned in the Wasteland,* (New York: Hill and Wang, 1995), pp. 17–57 generally for a discussion of children and television and for a discussion of the battle over children's programming, and D. Walsh, *Selling Out America's Children: How America Puts Profits Before Values and What Parents Can Do* (Minneapolis: Fairview Press, 1995).

64. *Revision of Programming and Commercialization Policies, Ascertainment Requirements, and Program Log Requirements for Commercial Television Stations,* 98 FCC 2d 1076, 1116 (1984), 49 Fed. Reg. 33,588 (1984).

65. Robert W. Crandall, "Telecommunications Policy in the Reagan Era, Regulation," The Cato Institute, www.cato.org/pubs/regulation/regv12n3/regi2n3-crandall.html.

66. Charles Ferris was a Democratic Party insider who served as chief counsel to U.S. Senate majority leader Mike Mansfield from 1963 to 1977, and then as general counsel to House Speaker Thomas P. O'Neill Jr. in 1977. He was appointed to the FCC by President Carter in 1979.

67. See *In re Deregulation of Radio, Memorandum Opinion and Order,* 87 F.C.C.2d 797 (1981); *In re Deregulation of Radio, Report and Order,* 84 F.C.C.2d 968 (1980).

68. Crandall, "Telecommunications Policy."

69. *UCC v. FCC,* 359 F.2d 994 (1966).

70. Mark Hertsgaard, *On Bended Knee: The Press and the Reagan Presidency* (New York: Farrar Straus Giroux, 1988).

71. Eric Alterman, *What Liberal Media? The Truth About Bias and the News* (New York: Basic Books, 2003); see also R. Delgado and J. Stefancic, *No Mercy: How Conservative Think Tanks and Foundations Changed America's Social Agenda* (Philadelphia: Temple University Press, 1996); see also *Buying a Movement,* People for the American Way, 1996.

Chapter 9. The Internet: Communications Policy in the Clinton Era (1992–2000)

1. For a general report of the Reagan years, see Haynes Bonner Johnson, *Sleepwalking Through History: America in the Reagan Years* (New York: W. W. Norton & Company, 1991).

2. I worked very briefly both on the Clinton Transition Team in 1992 and in the Clinton White House for a few months in 1993. Like many others I was extraordinarily impressed with Clinton's intelligence and his kindness, and like many others I was extraordinarily disappointed by his policies on welfare and by his affair with Monica Lewinsky. I recommend Peter Edelman, *Searching for America's Heart: RFK and the Renewal of Hope* (New York: Houghton Mifflin, 2000).

3. Joe Conason and Gene Lyons, *The Hunting of the President: The Ten-Year Campaign to Destroy Bill and Hillary Clinton* (New York: Thomas Dunne Books, 2001); see also Joe Conason, *Fools for Scandal: How the Media Invented Whitewater* (New York: Franklin Square Press, 1996).

4. Senator Larry Pressler, *Telecom Reform: It Ain't Over 'Til It's Over,* Roll Call, March 11, 1996.

5. White House, Office of the Press Secretary, *Remarks by President Bill Clinton at Signing of Telecommunications Act of 1996,* February 9, 1996.

6. There is a large body of literature on "deregulation"; see especially Stephen Breyer, *Regulation and Its Reform* (Cambridge, Mass.: Harvard University Press, 1982); Martha Derthick and Paul J. Quirk, *The Politics of Deregulation* (Washington, D.C.: The Brookings Institution Press, 1985); Marc Allen Eisner, Jeff Worsham, and Evan J. Ringquist, *Contemporary Regulatory Policy* (Boulder, Colo.: Rienner, 2000); Richard A. Harris and Sidney M. Milkis, *The Politics of Regulatory Change: A Tale of Two Agencies* (New York: Oxford University Press, 1989); James Q. Wilson, *The Pol-*

itics of Regulation (New York: Basic Books, 1980). I lean toward what is referred to as a "contingency" framework and accept the negotiations between different industry segments and the public interest and consumer interest groups as more reflective of the result of regulation, rather than the notion that the "industry" always gets what it wants. My main point is that core economic benefits provided to industry have not, by and large, been subject to debate because of the exercise of political power by citizen-consumers. The dismantling of AT&T and the defeat of broadcaster prerogatives over the cable industry represent the victory of one segment of the corporate faction over another segment. While there are legitimate disputes regarding the degree of power segments of the industry wield over either Congress or the administrative agencies that oversee them, there is no persuasive argument presented that the public, represented by associations, exercises a true countervailing force.

7. Much of the information for this section was based on Katie Hafner and Matthew Lyon, *Where Wizards Stay Up Late: The Origins of the Internet* (New York: Simon & Schuster, 1998); and Janet Abbate, *Inventing the Internet* (Cambridge, Mass.: MIT Press, 2000); see also Mary Bellis, "The History of Computers" at http://inventors.about.com/library/blcoindex.htm?PM=ss12_inventors.

8. David Mindell, *Between Human and Machine: Feedback, Control, and Computing Before Cybernetics* (Baltimore: Johns Hopkins University Press, 2002).

9. Abbate, *Inventing the Internet*, pp. 8–17.

10. Ibid., pp. 17–41.

11. Mary Bellis, Inventors of the Modern Computer: The First Hobby and Home Computers: Scelbi, Mark-8, Altair, IBM 5100 at http://inventors.about.com/library/weekly/aa120198.htm.

12. IBM—History at www-1.ibm.com/ibm/history/exhibits/pc/pc_1.html; and Apple-History at www.apple-history.com/frames/?

13. Public Law 99–383.

14. Richard F. Weingroff, "Federal-Aid Highway Act of 1956: Creating the Interstate System, U.S. Department of Transportation—Federal Highway Administration" at www.fhwa.dot.gov/infrastructure/rw96f.htm.

15. Charles Lewis et al., *The Buying of the President* (New York: Avon Books, 1996), pp. 61–65.

16. Former Labor Secretary Robert Reich eloquently warns us of the disconnection from local or national concerns felt by leaders of global conglomerates, and he takes pains to point to the international nature of the major communications companies. Robert Reich, *The Work of Nations: Preparing Ourselves for 21st Century Capitalism* (New York: Knopf, 1991), see pp. 120–21 especially.

17. Lewis et al., *The Buying of the President*, pp. 116–17.

18. Ken Auletta, "Pay Per Views," *The New Yorker*, June 5, 1995, pp. 5–56.

19. Common Cause, "Your Master's Voice," *Wired*, August 1997, p. 45.

20. I have heard Charles say this at more than a few public meetings. He also uses this line in the documentary, *Free Speech for Sale*, a Bill Moyers Special (Princeton: Films for the Humanities & Sciences, 1999).

21. Senator Robert Dole, Congressional Record, Auctioning the Telecommunications Spectrum, February 1, 1996, p. S685.

22. See especially Tom Shales, "Fat Cat Broadcast Bonanza," *Washington Post*, June 13, 1995.

23. See *Free Speech for Sale*, and Dean Alger, *Megamedia: How Giant Corporations Dominate Mass Media, Distort Competition, and Endanger Democracy* (Lanham: Rowman & Littlefield, 1998), p. 109.

24. According to a Roper poll published in May 1998, chances are that you watched a television program at home this week, like the vast majority of Americans (93 percent). About two-thirds watched cable, less than a quarter of Americans watched premium cable, and about 15 percent went online. In its annual report on media use, Roper cited television as the first choice of most Americans for entertainment and the most trusted source for news. Sixty-nine percent of Americans cite television as the most trusted source compared to newspapers (37 percent), radio (14 percent), magazines (5 percent), and the Internet (2 percent). See www.roper.com/news/content/news10.htm; see also www.tvb.org/tvfacts/tvbasics/index.html.

25. *An Open Message to the Nation's Broadcasters*, The Benton Foundation, 1996, www.benton.org/Policy/TV/message.html.

26. Much of the attention of the Telecommunications Act of 1996 was focused on the clearly unconstitutional Communications Decency Act. That section is available as part of the Telecommunications Act of 1996 at ftp://ftp.loc.gov/pub/thomas/c104/s652.enr.txt; see also David L. Sobel, The Constitutionality of the Communications Decency Act: Censorship on the Internet, 1 J. TECH. L. & POL'Y 2, http://journal.law.ufl.edu/techlaw/1/sobel.html (1996).

27. Cable rates outpaced the inflation rate in 1996 by a factor of 2 to 1, according to the Labor Department. M. Perez-Rivas, "Cable Rates Not a Hit in Montgomery," *Washington Post*, May 22, 1997, p. A1.

28. P. Phillips, *Censored 1997* (New York: Seven Stories Press, 1997), p. 99 (see M. Lowenthal article *Censoring the Telecom Debate*); see also Mark Crispin Miller, "Free the Media," *The Nation*, June 3, 1996; and *Prospects for Employment in Competitive Local Telephone Markets: A Labor Perspective*, Communications Workers of America, March 1997.

29. Kenneth Auletta, *Three Blind Mice: How the TV Networks Lost Their Way* (New York: Random House, 1991), pp. 32-33.

30. Esther Dyson et al., *Cyberspace and the American Dream, Future Insight*, August 1994.

31. Alvin Toffler, *The Third Wave* (New York: Bantam Books, 1981), p. 392.

32. Neil Postman, *Informing Ourselves to Death*, speech before the German Informatics Society, October 11, 1990, at http://www.eff.org/pub/Net_culture ... informing_ourselves_to_death.paper; see also Neil Postman, *Technopoly: The Surrender of Culture to Technology* (New York: Vintage Books, 1993), pp. 3-20.

33. Postman, *Technopoly,* pp. 9–11.

34. "The Exasperating, Empowering E-Rate," the American Library Association, March 1999, at www.ala.org/ala/alonline/inetlibrarian/1999columns/march1999exa sperating.htm om/e-rate_news.html.

35. Percent of U.S. Persons Using the Internet Outside the Home by Selected Places by U.S., Rural, Urban, Central City Areas 1998, at www.ntia.doc.gov/ntiahome/fttn99/InternetUse_II/Chart-II-15.html.

36. *Local & Long Distance Telephone Companies Give Record Soft Money During Final Months of Telecommunications Overhaul,* Common Cause, February 9, 1996, at http://216.147.192.101/publications/296com.htm; see also *Channeling Influence, The Broadcast Lobby and the 70-Billion Dollar Free Ride,* Common Cause, at http://216.147.192.101/publications/040297_rpt3.htm.

37. Alger, *Megamedia,* pp. 109–11.

38. *The Telecommunications Act of 1996,* Federal Communications Commission, at www.fcc.gov/telecom.html.

39. Peter S. Goodman, "A Hot Sector Burns Out," *The Washington Post,* February 28, 2001, at www.washtech.com/news/telecom/7919–1.html; see also James K. Glassman, "Death of Telecom Competition," *Washington Times,* December 27, 2000, at www.aei.org/ra/raglas001227.htm.

40. V. Cerf and B. Kahn, Al Gore's support of the Internet, Declan McCullagh's Politech at www.politechbot.com/p-01394.html.

41. "And it seems as though our vice president who invented the Internet is at it again [light laughter]. You know, this morning, Gore caught in another exaggeration. Today Gore claims he was the guy who let the dogs out [music playing]; who let the dogs out? who let the dogs out?" Tonight Show w/Jay Leno, October 26, 2000, at www.cmpa.com/comedy/demjokes_1Page4.html.

42. "The Laugh Is on Gore," *Wired News* at www.wired.com/news/print/0,1294,18655,00.html.

43. Richard Wiggins, "Al Gore and the Creation of the Internet," First Monday, at www.firstmonday.dk/issues/issue5_10/wiggins/#w5.

44. *Office of Communication of United Church of Christ v. F.C.C.,* 359 F.2d 994 (1966).

45. See *TV 9, Inc. v. FCC,* 161 U.S. App. D.C. 349, 357, n.28, 495 F. 2d 929, 937, n.28 (1973), cert. denied, 419 U.S. 986 (1974); see also 1 U.S. Commission on Civil Rights, Federal Civil Rights Enforcement Effort 1974, p. 49 (Nov. 1974).

46. See *Newhouse Broadcasting Corp.,* 37 Rad. Reg. 2d 141, decided April 21, 1976.

47. Statement of Policy on Minority Ownership of Broadcasting Facilities 68 FCC 2d 979 1978.

48. FCC Minority Ownership Task Force, Report on Minority Ownership in Broadcasting (1978).

49. *Metro Broadcasting, Inc. v. FCC,* 497 U.S. 547 (1990).

50. Ibid.

51. See "FCC Freezes Comparative Proceedings in Response to Court Integration Ruling," *Communications Daily*, February 28, 1994, p. 3.

52. *Adarand Constructors, Inc. v. Pena*, 515 U.S. 200 (1995).

53. *Lutheran Church-Missouri Synod v. FCC*, 141 F. 3d 344 (1998).

54. Robert Entman and Andrew Rojecki, *The Black Image in the White Mind* (Chicago: University of Chicago Press, 2000), pp. 113–14.

55. See Mark Robichaux, "A Cable Empire That Was Built on a Tax Break," *Wall Street Journal*, January 12, 1995, p. B1.

56. To amend the Internal Revenue Code of 1986 to permanently extend the deduction for the health insurance costs of self-employed individuals, to repeal the provision permitting nonrecognition of gain on sales and exchanges effectuating policies of the Federal Communications Commission, and for other purposes. Public Law No: 104–7.

57. See "Minority Commercial Broadcast Ownership in the United States," a Report of the Minority Telecommunications Development Program, National Telecommunications and Information Administration, U.S. Department of Commerce, at www.ntia.doc.gov/reports/97minority/.

58. Patricia Aufderheide, "Cable Television and the Public Interest," *Journal of Communication* (Winter 1992): 52–65.

59. "Halt Called for TCI–AT&T Merger Until TCI Non-Compliance and Civil Rights Record Examined, TCI's Record of Poor Performance," The Civil Rights Forum on Communications Policy, at www2.ctcnet.org/lists/members98/0842.htm.

60. In 2000 Johnson sold BET to Viacom, hearing complaints from some of the same people who criticized BET's content; see Dwayne Wickham, "Profit not all that drives BET content," *USA Today*, November 27, 2000, at www.usatoday.com/news/opinion/columnists/wickham/wick167.htm.

61. Douglas S. Massey and Nancy A. Denton, *American Apartheid: Segregation and the Making of the Underclass* (Cambridge, Mass.: Harvard University Press, 1993).

62. Stuart Elliott, "Blacks Prefer TV Fare with Black Casts, But Tastes of Blacks and Whites Are Converging, Study Says," *New York Times*, April 21, 2003. The headline oddly emphasizes black as distinct from white preferences, and the tenor of the article sugarcoats the great differences in viewing habits, but the numbers in the article as reported above tell a less comfortable story. See also Lisa de Moraes, The TV Column, *Washington Post*, April 17, 2003.

63. Report of the National Advisory Commission on Civil Disorders ("Kerner Commission Report"), March 1, 1968, U.S. Government Printing Office, Washington, D.C.

64. Richard Morin, "Misperceptions Cloud Whites' View of Blacks," *Washington Post*, July 11, 2001, p. 1.

65. See Massey and Denton, *American Apartheid*; see also E. J. Bienenstock, P. Bonacich, and M. Oliver, "The Effect of Network Density and Homogeneity on Attitude Polarization," *Social Networks* 12 (1990): 153–72.

66. Franklin D. Gilliam Jr., Shanto Iyengar, et al., "Crime in Black and White: The Scary World of Local News," *Harvard International Journal of Press/Politics* 1 (1996): 6–23; see also Gilliam and Iyengar, "Prime Suspects: The Influence of Local Television News on the Viewing Public," *American Journal of Political Science* 44, no. 3 (July 2000): 560–73; and Franklin Gilliam, "Moral Literacy: Virtue and the Renewal of Civil Society," National Funding Collaborative on Violence Prevention, at www.peacebeyondviolence.org/res_mono_gil_hero.html.

67. Entman and Rojecki, *The Black Image*, p. 81.

68. Radio Television News Directors Association, 2000 Women and Minorities Survey, at www.rtnda.org/research/womin.html.

69. Av Westin, "The Color of Ratings," *Brill's Content*, April 2001, 83–84.

70. Entman and Rojecki, *The Black Image*, p. 87.

71. "Who's On the News? Study shows network news sources skew white, male & elite," Fairness and Accuracy in Reporting, www.fair.org/press-releases/power-sources-release.html.

72. See Gilliam and Iyengar, "Prime Suspects."

73. Cornel West, *Race Matters* (New York: Vintage Books, 1993), p. 27 (italicized in the original).

74. Bill Gates, *The Road Ahead*, 2nd rev. ed. (New York: Penguin Books, 1996), p. 307.

75. "Americans in the Information Age: Falling Through the Net," NTIA at www.ntia.doc.gov/ntiahome/digitaldivide/.

76. "A Nation Online: How Americans Are Expanding Their Use of the Internet," NTIA at www.ntia.doc.gov/ntiahome/dn/index.html.

77. See "Harris Interactive Survey Shows Internet's Growth as Primary Source of News and Information in Weeks Following September 11 Attacks" at www.harrisinteractive.com/news/allnewsbydate.asp?NewsID=%20371.

78. See "The Internet and Campaign 2002" at www.pewinternet.org/reports/reports.asp?Report=82&Section=ReportLevel1&Field=Level1ID&ID=360.

79. See Melanet at www.melanet.com/.

80. See Robert Putnam, *Bowling Alone: The Collapse and Revival of American Community* (New York: Simon & Schuster, 2000), pp. 177–79; and Cass Sunstein, *republic.com* (Princeton: Princeton University Press, 2002).

81. "Less Access to Less Information By and About the U.S. Government," ALA, 1996; also at www.ala.org/washoff/lessaccess.html.

82. E-Government Act of 2002, at www.ala.org/Content/NavigationMenu/Our_Association/Offices/ALA_Washington/Issues2/Government_Information/Details_on_the_E-Government_Act.htm.

83. "ALEC-backed Attacks on E-Gov't Move in States," OMB Watch, at www.ombwatch.org/article/articleview/1490/1/83/.

84. Ibid.

85. "A Post-September 11 Attack on Right-to-Know," at www.ombwatch.org/article/articleview/212/1/1/.

86. William Greider, *Who Will Tell the People? The Betrayal of American Democracy* (New York: Simon & Schuster, 1992), p. 424, note 2.

87. Herbert Schiller, *Information Inequality* (New York: Routledge, 1996), p. xi.

88. Pew Internet Project, Digital Town Hall: "How local officials use the Internet and the civic benefits they cite from dealing with constituents online," October 2, 2002, at www.pewinternet.org/reports/toc.asp?Report=74.

89. I served with Senator Paul Simon on the board of the Benton Foundation. Any American grown cynical about either politicians or journalists should have met Paul. See also J. J. Johnson, "Real American Campaign Finance Reform, Serious Solution to Soft Money—and Soft Senators," Sierra Times, February 24, 2002, at www.sierratimes.com/02/02/24/jjjohnson.htm.

90. Richard Davis, *The Web of Politics: The Internet's Impact on the American Political System* (New York: Oxford University Press, 1999), p. 72.

91. John Dewey, *Freedom and Culture* (New York: Prometheus Books, 1939), p. 102.

Chapter 10. The End of History

Note to Epigraph: Walter Lippmann, *The Good Society* (New York: Grosset & Dunlap, 1943), p. 372.

1. Hanna Arendt, *On Revolution* (New York: Peter Smith, 1977), p. 218, note 2.

2. Michael Sandel, *Democracy's Discontent* (Cambridge, Mass.: Belknap Press/Harvard University Press, 1996), p. 290.

3. Ibid., p. 285.

4. See Mark Lloyd, "The Digital Divide and Equal Access to Justice," *Comm/Ent* 24, no. 4 (Summer 2002) for a full treatment of the problem of unequal access to justice.

5. See generally Charles Lindblom, *Politics and Markets* (New York: Basic Books, 1977). Lindblom refers to the U.S. system as a "polyarchy."

6. Robert D. Putnam, *Bowling Alone: The Collapse and Revival of American Community* (New York: Simon & Schuster, 2000), pp. 50–53.

7. Ibid., p. 343.

8. Both Common Cause (www.commoncause.org/) and the Center for Public Integrity (www.publicintegrity.org/dtaweb/home.asp) have extensive reports on corporate contributions to both major American political parties.

9. See especially James Carey, *Communication as Culture: Essays on Media and Society* (Winchester, Mass.: Unwin Hyman, 1989), p. 75; and Michael Schudson, *The Power of News* (Cambridge, Mass.: Harvard University Press, 1995), pp. 205–7. Carey calls Lippmann's book *Public Opinion* "the founding book in American media studies."

10. Walter Lippmann, *The Essential Lippmann: A Political Philosophy for Liberal Democracy,* ed. Clinton Rossiter and James Lare (New York: Vintage Books, 1965), p. 95.

11. Ibid., p. 107.

12. William James, "Talks to Teachers on Psychology: and to Students on Some of Life's Ideals," in *The Moral Philosophy of William James*, ed. John K. Roth (New York: Crowell/Apollo, 1969), p. 215.

13. Lippmann, *The Essential Lippmann*, p. 152.

14. Ibid., p. 114.

15. Putnam, *Bowling Alone*, p. 46.

16. Ibid., pp. 283–84.

17. Ibid., pp. 247–76.

18. Ibid., pp. 367–401.

19. Ibid., pp. 376–77.

20. Ibid., pp. 216–46.

21. Henry Milner, *Civic Literacy: How Informed Citizens Make Democracy Work* (Hanover, Mass.: Tufts, 2002), pp. 1–2.

22. Ibid., p. 98.

23. Ibid., pp. 95–97.

24. Erik Barnouw, *A Tower in Babel* (New York: Oxford University Press, 1966), p. 280.

25. History of the BBC at www.bbc.co.uk/thenandnow/history/1920s-1.shtml; see also Asa Briggs, *History of Broadcasting in the United Kingdom* (Oxford: Oxford University Press, 1985); and Tom O'Malley, *Closedown? The BBC and Government Broadcasting Policy 1979–92* (London: Pluto Press, 1994).

26. BBC License Fees at www.bbc.co.uk/info/licencefee/.

27. Association of Public Television Stations, Frequently Asked Questions at www.apts.org/html/faq/faq.html. Note also James Ledbetter, *Made Possible By . . .* (New York: Verso, 1997), p. 4; and Milner, *Civil Literacy*, p. 96.

28. For an interesting discussion of these issues, see Valeria Camporesi, *Mass Culture and National Traditions: The B.B.C. and American Broadcasting, 1922–1954* (Florence: European Press Academic Publishing, 2002).

29. Newsnight Thursday, February 6, 2003, Transcript of Blair's Iraq interview at http://news.bbc.co.uk/2/hi/programmes/newsnight/2732979.stm.

30. NBC News, www.nbc.com/nbc/NBC_News/.

31. President's first postwar interview with NBC's Tom Brokaw at www.msnbc.com/news/905108.asp.

32. Paul Krugman, "The China Syndrome," *New York Times*, May 13, 2003; see also Krugman's *New York Times* articles "Standard Operating Procedure," June 3, 2003, and "Who's Accountable," June 10, 2003.

33. Prime Minister Tony Blair, a leader of the moderate-left Labour Party in Britain, has joined with the Tories on the right and the ultra-right-wing Rupert Murdoch in attacking the BBC given its criticism of his determination to take his country into war in Iraq. The battle between the BCC and Blair led to a government inquiry into the suicide of Dr. David Kelly, the government scientific advisor who leaked information to the BBC that Blair's administration "sexed up" intelligence

reports on the danger of Saddam Hussein. The inquiry resulted in a highly critical report of the BBC and increased pressures to end the television tax that supports it. The "Hutton Inquiry" was highly contested, but led to the resignation of top BBC officials. Even if the report by Lord Hutton was right in its critique of a specific report by a BBC reporter, this does not suggest that the BBC fares poorly when compared to either British or American commercial counterparts. Indeed, the fact of a rigorous government inquiry into the reports of a powerful broadcaster is a good indication about the importance of a truly independent source of information. The BBC should be subject to public debate. So should CBS, NBC, ABC, and Fox. See Nicholas Fraser, "To BBC or Not to BBC," *Harper's Magazine,* May 2004, pp. 55–64.

34. Joe Conason, Salon quoted in Howard Kurtz, "Media Notes: Dissing the Democrats," *Washington Post,* June 16, 2003, at www.washingtonpost.com/ac2/wp-dyn/A4075–2003Jun17?language=printer. "The White House can't fool all the people all of the time, but with the help of the mainstream media the administration has deceived a lot of people about issues of global importance. A national survey reported in Knight-Ridder newspapers says that one-third of the American public 'believes U.S. forces found weapons of mass destruction in Iraq'—which means they also believed the false (and universally quoted) statement to that effect the president made two weeks ago on Polish television. The political science professors who analyzed that survey for the University of Maryland are wondering why a substantial minority would think they have seen proof that doesn't yet exist.

"Theories aside, the most suggestive fact found by the mid-May poll is that respondents who supported the war are more likely than others to believe that weapons of mass destruction have already been discovered. They won't let the facts disturb their opinions. Weak, credulous media coverage of administration claims also serves to confuse the citizenry.

"That explains why pollsters find strikingly different results in Britain, where the press treats the Blair government with the skepticism it has earned on this issue. Nearly 60 percent of the British public suspects that their own government and ours 'exaggerated the threat of Iraq's weapons of mass destruction,' while a third said the Iraq war has diminished their trust in the prime minister."

35. Milner, *Civic Literacy,* pp. 66–104.

36. Ibid., pp. 111–14.

Chapter 11. A Few Lessons

Note to Epigraph: FCC Chairman Michael Powell Launches "Localism in Broadcasting" Initiative, August 20, 2003, at http://hraunfoss.fcc.gov/edocs_public/attachmatch/DOC-238057A1.doc.

1. In the Matter of 2002 Biennial Regulatory Review—Review of the Commission's Broadcast Ownership Rules and Other Rules Adopted Pursuant to Section 202 of the Telecommunications Act of 1996, Report and Order Notice of Proposed

Rulemaking, Adopted June 2, 2003, at http://hraunfoss.fcc.gov/edocs_public/attachmatch/FCC-03–127A1.doc.

2. Robert MacMillan, "Editorials Weigh In on FCC's Media Ownership Vote," *Washington Post*, June 2, 2003.

3. Stephen Labaton, "Senate Begins Process to Reverse New F.C.C. Rules on Media," *New York Times*, June 20, 2003; Stephen Labaton, "F.C.C. Media Rule Blocked in House in a 400-to-21 Vote," *New York Times*, July 24, 2003. President Bush vowed to veto any bill that blocked the revised media ownership rules, and a legislature controlled by Republicans compromised on the most controversial of the new rules, allowing the television ownership cap to be 39 percent of the national audience instead of the FCC limit of 45 percent. The other FCC rules were left untouched. See Sheryl Gay Stolberg, "Media Ownership Deal Reached, Clearing Way for Big Spending Bill," *New York Times*, November 25, 2003.

4. FCC Commissioner Michael Copps Criticizes Willingness to Let Media Consolidation Continue, August 20, 2003, at http://hraunfoss.fcc.gov/edocs_public/attachmatch/DOC-238079A1.doc.

5. Ben H. Bagdikian, *The Media Monopoly*, 6th ed. (Boston: Beacon Press: 2000), p. 177.

6. Frank M. Bryan, *Real Democracy: The New England Town Meeting and How It Works* (Chicago: University of Chicago Press, 2004). Bryan provides an important and vivid accounting of the New England town meeting, but fails to tell us how the citizens who participate in either the best or worst of these get their information. He focuses on how they exercise their voice and vote, but not on how they might organize or learn about issues.

7. Cambridge, Mass., Census 2000: Data & Analysis, at www.ci.cambridge.ma.us/CDD/data/census2000.html.

8. 2002 Cambridge Town Gown Annual Report Data, at www.ci.cambridge.ma.us/CDD/data/educ/towngown2002.html.

9. Cambridge Land Use Summary, at www.ci.cambridge.ma.us/CDD/data/landuse/landuse.html.

10. Comparison of Education Attainment Persons 25 or Older: 1990, at www.ci.cambridge.ma.us/CDD/data/educ/educcomp.html.

11. Candi Carter, "The Top 10 Cambridge Newsmakers of 2002," *Cambridge Chronicle*, December 23, 2002, at www.townonline.com/cambridge/news/local_regional/cam_feacctop12232002.htm.

12. U.S. Labor Department, Monthly Local Area Data Files for 2002, at www.detma.org/lmi/laus/monthly/laus0201.txt.

13. U.S. Census Bureau, SF3 Summary Profile (includes educational status, residence in 1995, nativity, language spoken at home, ancestry, employment status, income, and various housing data, including rents, among others), at www.ci.cambridge.ma.us/CDD/data/demo/2000_sf3profile.pdf.

14. Cambridge Household, Family & Per Capita Income by Census Tract: 1989–1999, at www.ci.cambridge.ma.us/CDD/data/income/income_x_ct_1990to 2000.html.

15. Robert D. Putnam, *Bowling Alone: The Collapse and Revival of American Community* (New York: Simon & Schuster, 2000), pp. 18–19. "The core idea of social capital theory is that social networks have value. Just as a screwdriver (physical capital) or a college education (human capital) can increase productivity (both individual and collective), so too social contacts affect the productivity of individuals and groups.... Social capital refers to connections among individuals—social networks and the norms of reciprocity and trustworthiness that arise from them."

16. Ibid., pp. 216–46.

17. Ibid., pp. 166–80.

18. See The MIT Community Lab, Local Media at http://web.mit.edu/cms.881/www/resources/home.htm.

19. Jovonne Bickerstaff, Report on Community Lab Survey, September 8, 2003.

20. Social capital may have negative consequences, referred to by Xavier de Souza Briggs as bonding, where strong in-group preferences and out-group prejudices are developed, or it may make interacting with diverse groups easier by creating bridges to link them. See Putnam, *Bowling Alone*, pp. 21–24.

21. Letter from Mr. Robert Healy, Cambridge City Manager, to AT&T and Comcast, denying the transfer request of local cable franchisee Mediaone, June 27, 2002.

22. Issued on March 17, 2003; put forward by Councillors Decker, Maher, and Galluccio.

23. See James Horwood, Municipal Provision of Telecommunications: Power Line, Fiber to the Home and Other Developments, Spiegel & McDiarmid, October 28, 2003.

24. *Final Report of the Special Commission Established (Under Section 238 of Chapter 184 of the Acts of 2002) for the Purpose of Making an Investigation and Study Relative to the Adequacy and Effectiveness of Existing Licensing and Regulations of the Cable Television Operation by Municipalities and the Commonwealth*, received by the Joint Committee on Government Regulations, December 30, 2003, p. 19, FTN 2.

25. See Sharon Eisner Gillette, *Berkshire Connect: A Case Study of Demand Aggregation*, MIT Program on Internet & Telecommunications Convergence, November 2001, at http://itc.mit.edu/itel/docs/2001/Berkshire_Connect.pdf; see also www.bconnect.org/index.htm.

26. See *City of Abilene v. FCC*, 164 F.3d 49 (DC.Cir. 1999).

27. See Andrew Michael Cohill and Andrea Lee Kavanaugh, eds., *Community Networks: Lessons from Blacksburg, Virginia* (Boston: Artech House, 1997), pp. 15–28; Blacksburg Facts & Figures at www.blacksburg.gov/economic_development/community_profile.php; and Blacksburg Electronic Village at www.bev.net/.

28. See Charles Cleveland, "Big Jim," at www.lib.niu.edu/ipo/ii7510295.html; also Chris Serb, "Chicago Politics," at www.frommers.com/destinations/chicago/

0006020050.html, and conversations with Marjorie Nicholson, November 2, 2002, and Gordon Quinn, December 12, 2002.

29. Ibid., and files provided by Gordon Quinn and Barbara Popovic.

30. Popovic files.

31. Conversation with Barbara Popovic on January 13, 2003.

32. Popovic files and Mary Stamatel, notes from August 12, 2002.

33. Popovic files and Mary Stamatel notes from August 14, 2002.

34. Popovic files, *Chicago Tribune*, February 19, 1999.

35. Popovic files, CAN TV Connection, Winter 2003.

36. CAN TV Connection, Fall 2002.

37. Popovic files, CJ Research.

38. Popovic files.

39. See *City of Abilene v. FCC*, 164 F.3d 49 (DC Cir. 1999)(FCC reasonably determined that Section 253 of the Communications Act does not compel a state to authorize municipal provision of telecommunications services).

40. The details from this paragraph are excerpted from a variety of publications: "History of Pierce County, WA" by William Pierce Bonney, "Tacoma Beginnings" by Winnefred L. Olsen, "Tacoma 1869–1969," by Charles F. A. Mann, ed., "The Tacoma Public Utilities Story," by John S. Ott and Dick Malloy, Tacoma Public Utilities, 1993. See also www.wa.gov/esd/lmea/labrmrkt/eco/piereco.htm.

41. Ibid.; in addition, see Murray C. Morgan, *Puget's Sound: A Narrative of Early Tacoma and the Southern Sound* (Seattle: University of Washington Press, 1979), and www.tpl.lib.wa.us/v2/NWRoom/MORGAN/Olmstead.htm.

42. Ibid.

43. Ibid.

44. The Tacoma Public Utilities Story, John S. Ott and Dick Malloy, Tacoma Public Utilities, 1993.

45. Conversation with Diane Lachel, Government and Community Relations Manager, Click!Network—Tacoma Power, December 6, 2002.

46. Ibid.

47. Ibid.; see also Project History at www.click-network.com/news/history_m.htm.

48. Ibid.

49. Ibid.; see also Hengyuen Yan, "City of Tacoma: Breaking Up Monopoly, Opening Up Competition," *Economic Daily*, China.

50. Ibid.; see also Click Network at www.click-network.com/news/other.htm.

51. See, for example, Joseph L. Bast, "Municipally Owned Broadband Networks: A Critical Evaluation," The Heartland Institute (November 2002); Jeffrey A. Eisenach, "Does Government Belong in the Telecom Business?" The Progress & Freedom Foundation (January 2001); Kent Lasserman and Randolph J. May, "A Survey of Government-Provided Telecommunications: Disturbing Growth Trend Continues Unabated," Progress & Freedom Foundation (October 2003); David G. Tuerck

324 · NOTES TO PAGE 256

et al., "Cashing In on Cable: Warning Flags for Local Government," The Beacon Hill Institute at Suffolk University (October 2001). The reports by all of these industry-sponsored advocates tend to quote each other. They operate as a strange sort of echo chamber in which opposing views are drowned out or ignored. In the absence of steady and reliable foundation support, there is no effective counter to the dominance of their views on the pages of the *New York Times*, the *Washington Post*, or the *Wall Street Journal.*

52. Jube Shiver Jr., "Tired of Slow Speeds, Some Cities Build Their Own Net, Cable Firms," *Los Angeles Times*, January 11, 2004.

53. Paul Guppy, "When Government Enters the Telecom Market: An Assessment of Tacoma's Click! Network," Progress & Freedom Foundation (February 2002).

54. See Diane Lachal's statement on the Tri-City Broadband website, "Broadband Failures" at Fiber for Our Future, Tri-City Broadband, available at www.tricities-broadband.com/failures.htm.; confirmed over the telephone in conversation with Diane Lachal on January 13, 2004.

55. Peter Behr, "Papers Show That Enron Manipulated Calif. Crisis," *Washington Post*, May 7, 2002, p A1; for another interesting report on this see, Enron "manipulated energy crisis," BBC News, Tuesday, May 7, 2002, at http://news.bbc.co.uk/1/hi/business/1972574.stm.

56. Paul Somners and Deena Heg, "Spreading the Wealth: Building a Tech Economy in Small and Medium-Sized Regions," The Brookings Institution Center on Urban and Metropolitan Policy (October 2003). Available at www.brookings .edu/es/urban /publications/200310_Sommers.pdf.

57. At least seven states explicitly bar municipalities or public power utilities from providing telecommunications services. These states include Arkansas, Missouri, Nebraska, Nevada, Tennessee, Texas, and Virginia. Ark. Code Ann.° 23_17_409(b)(1) states governmental entities are prohibited from providing "basic local exchange service.". Missouri statute R. S. Mo.° 392.410(7) prohibits political subdivisions of Missouri from providing telecommunications services and facilities, except services for the political subdivision's own use, services for emergency, educational and medical purposes, and "Internet-type" services. This law was affirmed by the Supreme Court in *Nixon v. Missouri Municipal League* (541 U.S. 125 [2004] 299 F.3d 949, *reversed*). Decided March 24, 2004, the Telecommunications Act of 1996 does not protect municipalities from state regulations barring them from providing telecommunications service. Nebraska Rev. Stat.° 86_2301 et seq. prohibits governmental entities from providing telecommunications services but allows them to lease dark fiber under certain conditions. Nevada Rev. Stat.° 268.086(1)(a) bans all cities with populations of 25,000 or more from providing telecommunications services. Under Nev. Rev. Stat.° 268.086(1)(b) a city can "purchase or construct facilities for providing telecommunications that intersect with public rights-of-way, if the governing body: (1) conducts a study to evaluate the costs and benefits associated with purchasing or constructing the facility; and (2) determines from the

results of the study that the purchase or construction is in the interests of the general public." Tennessee Code Ann.° 7_52_601 and° 7_52_406 allows public power utilities to provide cable service, two-way video transmission, video programming, Internet services, or any other like system or service, but prohibits them from providing paging and security services. Texas Util. Code° 54.202 prohibits its municipalities and municipal electric utilities from providing telecommunications services either directly or indirectly through a private telecommunications provider. The FCC declined to preempt this prohibition in its Texas Order, and the D.C. Circuit upheld this decision in *City of Abilene, Texas v. FCC*, 164 F.3d 49 (D.C. Cir. 1999). Subsequently, the Texas legislature amended the prohibition, Tex. Util. Code° 54.2025, to clarify that municipalities and some municipal electric systems may lease excess dark fiber on a nondiscriminatory, nonpreferential basis; and Virginia (Code Ann.° 15.2_1500(B) prohibits localities from providing telecommunications services or facilities, but it allows them to lease dark fiber under certain onerous conditions. This provision was declared unconstitutional under the Supremacy Clause of the United States Constitution and Section 253(a) of the Telecommunications Act in *City of Bristol, Virginia v. Earley*, 145 F.Supp.2d (W.D. Va. 2001), appeal pending sub nom, *Virginia Beales v. City of Bristol*, Nos. 01_17041(L) and 01_1800 (4th Cir.). Several other states have enacted laws that do not expressly prohibit public power utilities from providing telecommunications services but discourage entry by imposing special burdens on potential governmental providers. Florida Stat. Ch. XII,° 166.047 imposes various extraordinary accounting and tax burdens. Minnesota Stat.° 237.19 requires municipalities to obtain a super-majority of 65 percent of municipal electors before becoming telecommunications providers. Utah Code Annotated° 10_18_201 et seq. imposes burdensome procedural and accounting requirements on municipal telecommunications providers.

58. Conversation with Diane Lachel, December 13, 2002.

59. Tri-Cities Broadband Feasibility Study and Frequently Asked Questions at www.geneva.il.us/bb/faqold.htm; see also Joseph L. Bast, Municipally Owned Broadband Networks: A Critical Evaluation, Heartland Study, at www.heartland.org/pdf/10687.pdf.

60. Karl Bode, *Municipal Vote Fails: Illinois citizens reject broadband plan*, DSL Reports at www.dslreports.com/shownews/27259.

61. Fiber for Our Future continues to provide information countering the distortions by industry think tanks; see "Broadband Failures."

Chapter 12. Reclaiming Our Republic

1. Henry Milner, *Civic Literacy: How Informed Citizens Make Democracy Work* (Hanover, Mass.: Tufts University Press, 2002), p. 28.

2. Gary Hart, *Restoration of the Republic: The Jeffersonian Ideal in 21st-Century America* (New York: Oxford University Press, 2002), p. 69.

3. Robert Putnam, *Bowling Alone: The Collapse and Revival of American Community* (New York: Simon & Schuster, 2000), pp. 48–64.

4. Michael J. Sandel, *Democracy's Discontent: America in Search of a Public Philosophy* (Cambridge, Mass.: Belknap Press/Harvard University Press, 1996), p. 324.

5. Hart, *Restoration of the Republic,* p. 133.

6. Sandel, *Democracy's Discontent,* p. 343. Sandel also quotes from one of my favorite Dickens' novels, *Bleak House,* that author's description of Mrs. Jellyby, a character who neglects her own children while focusing on the plight of Africans. She had "a curious habit of seeming to look a long way off. As if . . . [she] could see nothing nearer than Africa."

7. Hart, *Restoration of the Republic,* p. 180.

8. A variety of surveys over the years have noted results similar to the one reported by Rocky Mountain Media Watch in 1998, that "news about health, government and the economy each average almost 10 per cent of the news," while crime stories are dominant in the news, comprising 26.9 percent and natural disasters and fires comprise a little over 12 percent. See 1998 National Survey: Local TV News in America, March 11, 1998, Not in the Public Interest at www.bigmedia.org/texts5.html. Studies by the Project for Excellence in Journalism confirm this trend; see Local TV News Project—2001 at www.journalism.org/resources/research/reports/localTV/2001/look.asp.

9. Eric Alterman, *What Liberal Media? The Truth About Bias and the News* (New York: Basic Books, 2003). Alterman gets the better of the argument about bias, and takes apart conservative critics.

10. Bill Kovach and Tom Rosenstiel, *Warp Speed: America in the Age of the Mixed Media Culture* (New York: Century Foundation Press, 1999).

11. See generally Mark Hertsgaard, *On Bended Knee: The Press and the Reagan Presidency* (New York: Farrar Straus & Giroux, 1988).

12. Upton Sinclair, *The Brass Check: A Study of American Journalism* (Urbana: University of Illinois Press, 2003), p. 403.

13. Ibid., p. 404.

14. Ibid., p. 440; see also the excellent Introduction by Robert McChesney and Ben Scott, p. xxv.

15. Ibid., p. 404.

16. See ibid., McChesney and Scott, p. xii.

17. "It would be strange indeed however if the grave concern for freedom of the press which prompted adoption of the First Amendment should be read as a command that the government was without power to protect that freedom. The First Amendment, far from providing an argument against application of the Sherman Act, here provides powerful reasons to the contrary. That Amendment rests on the assumption that the widest possible dissemination of information from diverse and antagonistic sources is essential to the welfare of the public, that a free press is a condition of a free society." *Associated Press v. United States,* 326 U.S. 1, 20 (1945).

18. Sinclair, *The Brass Check*, pp. 408–409.

19. Ibid., p. 401.

20. See especially Robert W. McChesney, *Telecommunications, Mass Media, and Democracy: The Battle for the Control of U.S. Broadcasting, 1928–1935* (New York: Oxford University Press, 1995).

21. Walter Lippmann, *The Essential Lippmann: A Political Philosophy for Liberal Democracy,* ed. Clinton Rossiter and James Lare (New York: Vintage Books, 1965), "Television and Press," Today and Tomorrow, March 3, 1960, pp. 412–13.

22. James Ledbetter, *Made Possible By . . .* (New York: Verso, 1997) pp. 224–230.

23. Even though U.S. public broadcasting has a severely limited voice in the U.S. public sphere, it provides a stark alternative to commercial broadcasting and a hint of what is possible if it is ever fully funded. A poll conducted by the Program on International Policy (PIPA) at the University of Maryland and Knowledge Networks in October 2003 found that those Americans who primarily listen to NPR or watch PBS were significantly less likely (23 percent) to hold the misperceptions that weapons of mass destruction were found in Iraq and that Saddam Hussein was involved in the 9/11 attacks than viewers who relied on commercial media. Eighty percent of Fox viewers, 71 percent of CBS viewers, 61 percent of ABC viewers, 55 percent of NBC and CNN viewers, and 47 percent of those who relied primarily on print sources were likely to hold these misperceptions. See Misperceptions, the Media and the Iraq War at http://65.109.167.118/pipa/pdf/oct03/IraqMedia_Oct03 _rpt.pdf.

24. Saul D. Alinsky, *Rules for Radicals: A Pragmatic Primer for Realistic Radicals* (New York: Vintage, 1972), p. 113. Perhaps the most famous quote of Alinsky is: "Power has always derived from two main sources, money and people," note on 127.

25. Ibid., p. 105, emphasis in the original.

26. Ibid., p. 76.

27. Michael Pertschuk and Wendy Schaetzel, *The People Rising: The Campaign Against the Bork Nomination* (New York: Thunder's Mouth Press, 1989), p. 280.

28. Alinsky, *Rules for Radicals,* p. 129.

29. Ibid., p. 165.

30. Ibid., p. 81.

31. Pertschuk and Schaetzel, *The People Rising,* p. 53.

32. Ibid., p. 284.

33. Ibid., p. 253.

34. Benjamin Barber, *A Passion for Democracy* (Princeton: Princeton University Press, 1998), p. 243.

35. Amartya K. Sen, *Development as Freedom* (New York: Oxford University Press, 2001), pp. 287–88.

Index

MARK LLOYD is a senior fellow at the Center for American Progress, where he writes and conducts research on media and telecommunications policy. An award-winning former broadcast reporter and producer, and a communications attorney, he has also taught at the Massachusetts Institute of Technology and at Georgetown University.

THE HISTORY OF COMMUNICATION

Selling Free Enterprise: The Business Assault on Labor and Liberalism, 1945–60—
Elizabeth A. Fones-Wolf

Last Rights: Revisiting *Four Theories of the Press*—*Edited by John C. Nerone*

"We Called Each Other Comrade": Charles H. Kerr & Company, Radical
Publishers—*Allen Ruff*

WCFL, Chicago's Voice of Labor, 1926–78—*Nathan Godfried*

Taking the Risk Out of Democracy: Corporate Propaganda versus Freedom and
Liberty—*Alex Carey; edited by Andrew Lohrey*

Media, Market, and Democracy in China: Between the Party Line and the Bottom
Line—*Yuezhi Zhao*

Print Culture in a Diverse America—*Edited by James P. Danky and
Wayne A. Wiegand*

The Newspaper Indian: Native American Identity in the Press, 1820–90—
John M. Coward

E. W. Scripps and the Business of Newspapers—*Gerald J. Baldasty*

Picturing the Past: Media, History, and Photography—*Edited by Bonnie Brennen
and Hanno Hardt*

Rich Media, Poor Democracy: Communication Politics in Dubious Times—
Robert W. McChesney

Silencing the Opposition: Antinuclear Movements and the Media in the
Cold War—*Andrew Rojecki*

Citizen Critics: Literary Public Spheres—*Rosa A. Eberly*

Communities of Journalism: A History of American Newspapers and
Their Readers—*David Paul Nord*

From Yahweh to Yahoo! The Religious Roots of the Secular Press—
Doug Underwood

The Struggle for Control of Global Communication: The Formative Century—
Jill Hills

Fanatics and Fire-eaters: Newspapers and the Coming of the Civil War—
Lorman A. Ratner and Dwight L. Teeter Jr.

Media Power in Central America—*Rick Rockwell and Noreene Janus*

The Consumer Trap: Big Business Marketing in American Life—*Michael Dawson*

How Free Can the Press Be?—*Randall P. Bezanson*

Cultural Politics and the Mass Media: Alaska Native Voices—*Patrick J. Daley and
Beverly A. James*

Journalism in the Movies—*Matthew C. Ehrlich*

Democracy, Inc.: The Press and Law in the Corporate Rationalization of the
Public Sphere—*David S. Allen*

Investigated Reporting: Television Muckraking and Regulation—*Chad Raphael*
Women Making News: Gender and the Women's Periodical Press in Britain—
   Michelle Tusan
Advertising on Trial: Consumer Activism and Corporate Public Relations in the
   1930s—*Inger Stole*
Speech Rights in America: The First Amendment, Democracy, and the Media—
   Laura Stein
Freedom from Advertising: E. W. Scripps's Chicago Experiment—
   Duane C. S. Stoltzfus
Waves of Opposition: The Struggle for Democratic Radio, 1933–58—
   Elizabeth Fones-Wolf
Prologue to a Farce: Communication and Democracy in America—*Mark Lloyd*

The University of Illinois Press
is a founding member of the
Association of American University Presses.

Composed in 10.5/13 Minion
with Meta display
by BookComp, Inc.
Manufactured by Thomson-Shore, Inc.

University of Illinois Press
1325 South Oak Street
Champaign, IL 61820-6903
www.press.uillinois.edu